# Hasidism, Haskalah, Zionism

JEWISH CULTURE AND CONTEXTS

Published in association with the Herbert D. Katz Center
for Advanced Judaic Studies of the University of
Pennsylvania

*Series Editors:*

Beth Berkowitz

Shaul Magid

Francesca Trivellato

Steven Weitzman

A complete list of books in the series
is available from the publisher.

# HASIDISM, HASKALAH, ZIONISM

## Chapters in Literary Politics

Hannan Hever

**PENN**

UNIVERSITY OF PENNSYLVANIA PRESS

PHILADELPHIA

Originally published in Hebrew as *Hasidut, Haskalah, Zionut: Perakim be-Politikah sifrutit* by Bar-Ilan University Press 2021

English translation copyright © 2023 University of Pennsylvania Press

All rights reserved. Except for brief quotations used for purposes of review or scholarly citation, none of this book may be reproduced in any form by any means without written permission from the publisher.

Published by
University of Pennsylvania Press
Philadelphia, Pennsylvania 19104-4112
www.upenn.edu/pennpress

Printed in the United States of America on acid-free paper
10 9 8 7 6 5 4 3 2 1

Hardcover ISBN: 978-1-5128-2507-7
eBook ISBN: 978-1-5128-2508-4

A catalogue record for this book is available from the Library of Congress.

# Contents

| | |
|---|---|
| Introduction | 1 |
| Chapter 1. Rabbi Nahman of Bratslav's Journey to the Land of Israel | 8 |
| Chapter 2. Isaac Erter's Anti-Hasidic Satires and the Watchman for the House of Israel | 52 |
| Chapter 3. Isaac Erter's Anti-Hasidic Satire "Hasidut ve-Hokhmah" | 98 |
| Chapter 4. The Politics of the Hasidic Story in the Russian Empire | 143 |
| Chapter 5. The Politics of *Sefer Hasidim* by Micha Yosef Berdichevsky | 166 |
| Appendix. Isaac Erter, "The Plan of the Watchman" | 191 |
| Notes | 193 |
| Index | 235 |
| Acknowledgments | 249 |

# Introduction

At the heart of this book lies the premise that the political reading of hasidic, maskilic, and Modern Hebrew literary texts allows us to transcend the hermeneutic, national, and particularly the Zionist framework or paradigm within which Hebrew literature is generally read and studied. The discussion of hasidic literature, its maskilic adversaries, and modernist successors presented here is post-national and interpretive, locating the text beyond the nation. This kind of critical reading allows us to understand the deep processes of national Hebrew culture in ways that are much harder to identify and analyze when the reader or interpreter is rooted in the phenomenon itself and thus fails to maintain a critical distance from the texts under examination.

Hasidic literature was heard and written in the context of the institutions of the hasidic movement—a Jewish, religious movement, founded, according to tradition, by Rabbi Israel ben Eliezer Shem-Tov, better known as the Ba'al Shem-Tov or Besht, in the mid-eighteenth century. Hasidism split into various streams, organized around courts, which existed as hierarchical institutions headed by a *tzadik*, who would deliver sermons and recount hasidic tales to a community of *hasidim* or followers.

The deep political conflict that developed between the literature of the *maskilim* (exponents of the Haskalah or Jewish Enlightenment) and the hasidic tale may be characterized as a clash between two different Jewish, political approaches to the Jewish Question. In contrast to the political struggle of the maskilim for civil equality, the political actions of the hasidim often aimed to develop mechanisms of greater insularity, as a bulwark against attempts to acculturate them by the Russian and Austro-Hungarian Empires and subsequently by the maskilim.

From the perspective of the maskilim, who sought civil equality for the Jews, Hasidism was a Jewish movement that undermined the chances of achieving civil emancipation for all Jews. The fact that the maskilim represented a considerably smaller proportion of the Jewish population than the hasidim further hindered their efforts to obtain civil equality without radically setting themselves apart from their coreligionists.

Contrary to the maskilim, who set out to fundamentally change the lifestyle and consciousness of the Jews of Eastern Europe, the hasidim in both the Russian Empire and the Austro-Hungarian Empire developed a defensive approach, which can be termed a "politics of survival." The hasidic politics of survival stressed the fundamental difference between the maskilic aspiration to play an equal role in the imagined rationality of imperial public space, under the sovereignty of czar and emperor, and the closed, irrational space of the hasidic court, under the rule of the charismatic tzadik.

To better understand the relationship between maskilic and hasidic literature, we must consider the fact that, in the eyes of the maskilim, the obstacles that the hasidim placed before the realization of their political project essentially stemmed from what they (the maskilim) viewed as the inferior culture of the hasidim—a culture that provoked, in the maskilim, political feelings of anger and shame. This politicized sense of anger and shame may explain maskilic literature's extensive use of satire, the barbs of which were inevitably aimed at the hasidim.

The studies on the hasidic tale, its reworkings in modernist Hebrew literature, and the anti-hasidic literature of the Haskalah included in the present volume examine the historical and political action of the literary text, employing a materialist critical method. The principles of the political reading of the literary texts addressed in the chapters that follow may be illustrated by means of a discussion of the story "The Besht's Prayer Produces Rain," published in a seminal collection of hasidic tales in 1815:

> There was also an occurrence [tale] when there was no rain. The gentiles took out their idols and carried them around the village, according to their custom, but it did not rain. Once the Besht said to the tax collector: "Send for the Jews in the surrounding area to come here for a minyan [the quorum of ten Jewish adult men required for holding liturgical services]." And he proclaimed a fast. The Besht himself prayed before the ark, and the Jews prolonged the prayer. One gentile asked: "Why did you remain at prayer so long today? And why was there a great cry among you?" The tax collector said that the truth is that they prayed for rain—and the gentile mocked him sharply, saying, "We went around with our idols

and it did not help. What help will you bring with your prayers?" The tax collector told the words of the gentile to the Besht, who said to him, "Tell the gentile that it will rain today." And so it did.[1]

The structure and language of this hasidic story create an effect of truth, drawing both upon the sanctity of the Hebrew language in which they are written and upon the theological rhetoric that convinces the reader of the veracity of the magical causes of the phenomena it describes. Indeed, its materially successful conclusion ("And so it did") is supported by the story's narrative form, which creates a "rhetoric of truth," based on a teleological structure that renders belief in the validity of the magical act necessary.

The political aspect of the story may follow from the anticipated reaction of the maskilic reader who challenges the validity of the magical act and therefore sees the connection between the rainfall and the magical prayer as little more than a coincidence. The maskil's expected negative response is to the rhetoric of the narrative, that is, to the literary form that links the tzadik's prayer, as cause, to the rainfall, as effect. This response constitutes a political act, with the power to deny the political authority of the tzadik as a true intermediary between his followers and God. The maskil's political reading clashes with the story's political role in shaping its hasidic readers into a collective with a shared belief in the sovereignty of the tzadik.

Maskilic satire, which engaged in the denigration of the hasidim, was developed as a genre in sharp and uncompromising conflict with the literary genre of hasidic hagiography. It was, in effect, a mirror image that created a symmetrical polarity between exalting hagiography and disparaging satire, with the two opposing genres generally sharing a common object: the hasidic tzadik and his flock. This mirrored polarity also emerges from Jonatan Meir's characterization of the satires and parodies of the Haskalah, "the purpose of which was to lift the veil of holiness and hasidic enchantment by means of parody, which imitates in order to uproot the hagiography from within."[2]

The mirror image that appears so clearly on the surface of the literary texts, however, belies a far more complex relationship between the genres. At the root of the relationship between the hagiographic hasidic tale and maskilic satire we also find attempts to dull the contrast between universal, rationalistic enlightenment, and the particularistic attachment to categories of difference such as gender, nationality, ethnicity, and class that existed between Hasidism and the Haskalah. This softening of the contours of identity is reflected in the absence of an unequivocal polarity between the genre of the hasidic tale and the way hasidim and Hasidism are treated in maskilic literature. The fact that the literary conflict occurred within the boundaries of Jewish space—all the more so when it occurred in Hebrew, the Holy Tongue—meant that, in practice, it played out through categories such as sovereignty, citizenship, theology, the body, desire, suffering, and violence.

The undermining of the boundary, the ostensible dichotomy between universal, rationalistic enlightenment and particularistic hasidic irrationality, may be described by means of what Michel Foucault called the "blackmail of enlightenment"—that is, the demanding use that enlightenment makes of its rational authority in order to impose a clear and binary distinction between joining and opposing it. In contrast to the schematic description of the polarity between rational enlightenment and irrational particularism, Foucault pointed to the fact that enlightenment is rooted in a range of particularistic political, economic, social, institutional, physical, and cultural events. Foucault gave expression to the undermining of the ostensible dichotomy between universal and ahistorical reason and historical particularism in his treatment of the well-known text in which Immanuel Kant defined enlightenment as the mature and autonomous courage of rational subjects to use their minds to express eternal, universal truth. Foucault rejected the autonomy of ahistorical critical rationalism, viewing it as contingent on the subject's material, physical, and historical conditions.[3]

Following Foucault, we may read the conflict between Hasidism and the Haskalah as one that occurs within a concrete historical context and therefore reflects a wide range of nonbinary power relations. An example of the undermining of the ostensible dichotomy between Hasidism and Haskalah can be found in Isaac Erter's anti-hasidic satire "Hasidut ve-hokhmah" (Hasidism and Wisdom), discussed in chapter 3. This undermining of the dichotomy is rooted in the shaping of the image of the satirist as flesh and blood, object of the political struggle between Hasidism and Wisdom. The satirical speaker in "Hasidut ve-hokhmah" is a rational maskil who aims his arrows at the allegorical figure of Hasidism, the contemptible seductions and falsehoods of which he seeks to expose. Erter's speaker is the Watchman for the House of Israel, whose rational, Olympic gaze is that of an omniscient narrator, outside and above the materiality of those subject to his authority. Erter's *ha-Tzofeh le-Veit Yisra'el* (Watchman for the House of Israel) first appeared in the essay "Tekhunat ha-Tzofeh" (The Plan of the Watchman), published posthumously as the introduction to his book of satires, edited by his friend Meïr Letteris. The designation comes from the book of Ezekiel, in which it is conferred by God, who charges the prophet with the task of guiding the Jewish people at the time of the Babylonian exile. Erter's Watchman has played a central political role in the history of Hebrew literature, as a modern-day prophet who guides the Jewish people in the path of righteousness.

The satire appears to be about a figure whose relationship with reality is unidirectional and whose words are based on a rational perspective. The literary situation that actually unfolds in Erter's satire, however, is quite different. A materialist reading of the Watchman's rational gaze reveals that he himself exists as the human and therefore physical-material object of the gaze that is returned to him. Opposite the domineering reason of the Watchman's penetrating gaze, the object of that gaze may cast its own gaze upon him and make its voice heard.

As the object of Hasidism's unbridled desire, the satirist—who fearlessly defends himself against its onslaught—is presented as a sensual subject struggling against his own desires. The battle the satirist wages against his desires thus makes his supposedly rational, all-seeing but unseen gaze, which is transparent and spiritual, a part of the stormy and material arena in which he and Hasidism are shaped as active, flesh-and-blood figures. The Watchman does not only gaze but is also gazed upon. He does not only look with disgust upon desire-ridden Hasidism but is himself the object of her desire.

The struggle between the two allegorical figures, Hasidism and Wisdom, each of which makes considerable rhetorical efforts to draw the satirical speaker to his side, is, in effect, a struggle between two perspectives, counterposed as if they were flesh-and-blood bodies that share a common Jewish identity. The struggle between satirical rationality and allegorical Hasidism is realized in Erter's satire not as an abstract struggle between ideas but as a struggle between living, concrete symbols. Both sides—Hasidism, which is the object of the satirist's criticism, and Wisdom, to which he lends his support—act within a single, shared situation, which combines rationality, sensuality, and desire. Rather than present the ostensible dichotomous symmetry between Wisdom (a positive figure, representing the Haskalah) and Hasidism, Erter's maskilic satire gives the two sides a common poetic, political foundation. An expression of the rejection of this dichotomous symmetry—which appears to exist between Hasidism and Haskalah in Erter's maskilic satire—can be found in the author's personal, autobiographical introduction to the work, in which he tells the story of the rational, spiritual development of a flesh-and-blood maskil.

The literary commonality between Hasidism and Haskalah is given clear expression in Jospeh Perl's anti-hasidic parodies *Megaleh Temirin* (The Revealer of Secrets; 1819) and *Bohen Tzadik* (Investigating a Righteous Man; 1838). Parody creates satirical tension, entailing scathing criticism, based on the gap between parodic language and the object of its imitation. At the same time, we cannot ignore the fact that while it constitutes this essential difference, it also creates a common political, linguistic space, which makes it the arena of bitter political struggle, the rules of which are also common to both camps.

On the literary consequences of the shared and contrasting actions of hasidic and maskilic literature, Shmuel Werses correctly observed:

> The literature of the Haskalah indirectly attests to the powerful attraction that Hasidism held, even sweeping up a part of the maskilic camp itself. And indeed Hasidism acted on *maskilic* literature, albeit unintentionally, as a fortifying and consolidating factor. It imbued literary satire and parody with great vitality, and rendered the Haskalah movement more prepared and effective. In other words, the slogans and consciousness of the Haskalah were clarified and refined through its polemic descriptions of Hasidism and, what is more, the existence and success of the hasidic movement at times animated the goals of the Haskalah.[4]

The first chapter of the present book discusses the political structure of the hasidic novella about Rabbi Nahman of Bratslav's journey to the Land of Israel, which was written by his disciple and secretary, Rabbi Nathan Sternhartz. This journey narrative performs an extraordinary political act, in the context of the struggle between Hasidism and the Haskalah. By approaching the story as a sea voyage, we are able to gain a better understanding of its political role as formulating and thus shaping the status of the Land of Israel in hasidic theology. Rabbi Nahman's journey to the Land of Israel and back to Eastern Europe is described as a series of milestones that embody the internal tensions of his teachings on the subject of hasidic survival in the diaspora, as well as his attitude to the imperial age and the ideas of civil emancipation to which it gave rise.

Introduction

The second chapter is dedicated to Isaac Erter's satire "Moznei Mishkal" (Scales), in which the Galician maskil takes aim at Rabbi Jacob Meshullam Orenstein, chief rabbi of Lvov. Erter wrote the satire as an act of revenge against Orenstein, for having taken away his livelihood and forced him to move to Brody. The discussion of the mechanisms employed in this satire focuses on the way in which they draw upon the material object of a halakhic work, the tearing of which challenges Rabbi Orenstein's authority. The dubious originality of the rabbi's book is expressed by means of its allegorical weighing, and involves the constitution of the Watchman for the House of Israel, who exerts his violent sovereignty.

The third chapter, discussed above, addresses the literary mechanisms of the satire "Hasidut ve-Hokhmah," by means of which Isaac Erter recruited the figure of the Watchman for the House of Israel to attack Hasidism. The fourth chapter includes a reading of a story by Jacob Kaidaner—a hasidic writer, a member of the Habad-Lubavitch sect—that affords some insight into the dynamic of relations between the hasidim and the Russian imperial authorities. At the heart of the chapter lies a discussion of the political ramifications of the writing of a hasidic tale in the political and cultural field of the Russian Empire. Through this analysis of Kaidaner's story we discover its political role in shaping the tactics whereby Hasidism, as a religioethnic movement, forged a path for itself in the field of imperial power and internal colonialism. The fifth chapter looks at the ways in which the modernist Hebrew writer Micha Yosef Berdichevsky, in his *Sefer Hasidim* (Book of Hasidim; 1900), reworked hasidic tales and thought. In these reworkings of hasidic texts, Berdichevsky employed the mechanisms of neoromantic poetics, thereby nationalizing the nonnational hasidic text and turning it into a significant political tool for the constitution of Zionist literature.

Chapter 1

# Rabbi Nahman of Bratslav's Journey to the Land of Israel

I

On 18 Iyyar 5558/4 May 1798, Rabbi Nahman of Bratslav left his home in the town of Medvedevka and set out for the Land of Israel, in the company of someone referred to as "one of his people with whom to travel together," in *Šivḥei ha-Ran* (Praising Rabbi Nachman),[1] the book written by R. Nathan Sternhartz of Nemirov, R. Nahman's disciple and secretary, who went to great lengths to record his master's teachings and renowned tales. The "man" in question was probably R. Nahman's disciple R. Simeon,[2] who told the story to R. Nathan, who, in turn, wrote it down in the travel narrative genre known as *itineraria*.[3] R. Nathan's voice as the narrating authority is already apparent in the story's title: "Seder ha-Nesi'ah šelo le-'Ereṣ Yiśra'el" (Chronicle of His Journey to the Land of Israel), which refers to R. Nahman in the third person. R. Nahman and R. Simeon traveled by coach to Nikolayev and from there, on a barge transporting wheat, down the Dnieper to Odesa. R. Nahman preferred this route to the longer and more dangerous journey to the port of Galati (Galats). From Odesa, they sailed to Istanbul, and from there to Jaffa—where the authorities refused to allow R. Nahman to disembark, because they suspected him of being a French spy. The captain therefore proceeded to Haifa, where, on the eve of Rosh Hashanah 5559/10 September 1798, R. Nahman and his companion went ashore.

There are two versions of the story of the journey. The present chapter deals only with the first version, "Seder ha-Nesi'ah šelo le-'Ereṣ Yiśra'el," as our focus is the political dynamic and action that followed its initial publication. This version was included in the first edition of R. Nahman of Bratslav's *Sippurei ma'asiyot* (*Tales*; 1815) and, subsequently, in *Šivḥei ha-Ran*—from the very first edition, *Magid śiḥot* (*Preacher's Conversations*), published in Zhovkva (Zolkva) in 1850. The passages quoted here from "Seder ha-Nesi'ah šelo le-'Ereṣ Yiśra'el," based on the 2008 edition, follow the first version. The second version of the story of R. Nahman's journey to the Land of Israel is entitled "Nesi'ato le-'Ereṣ Yiśra'el" ("His Journey to the Land of Israel") and first appeared in the first volume of *Ḥayyei Moharan* (*R. Nachman's Biography*), published in 1874. Both versions were written after R. Nahman's death, in 1810: "Seder ha-Nesi'ah šelo le-'Ereṣ Yiśra'el" between 1810 and 1815; and the second version after 1822.[4]

The hierarchy of importance between journey and destination created by the narrative demands further inquiry into the place of the Land of Israel in hasidic theology in general, and the political context in which this particular text was written—including the struggle between Hasidism and the Haskalah (Jewish Enlightenment). This inquiry pays attention to the efforts of Hasidism to survive in the diaspora, hasidic attitudes toward the Age of Imperialism and the emancipatory ideas to which it gave rise, as well as their influence on hasidic theology, and as compared to the maskilic conception of emancipation. The journey offers a number of indications regarding each of these topics, which I try to develop and describe in the present chapter.

At first glance, R. Nahman's journey appears to have been entirely within the tradition of hasidic journeys to the Land of Israel—beginning with that of the Ba'al Shem Tov's brother-in-law, R. Gershon of Kuty (Kitov), who migrated to the Land of Israel in 1747. Prior to that, we know of a failed attempt by the Ba'al Shem Tov himself to do so. As recounted by R. Nathan of Nemirov, however, R. Nahman's journey was shrouded in mystery. The story begins: "Before he traveled to the land of Israel he was in Kamenets, and his journey to Kamenets was a great wonder, for he suddenly left his home, and said he had a way before him to travel; and he left his home, taking the road to Medzhybizh, and said that he himself did not yet know where he was going."[5] The decision to go is taken suddenly, to the point that "when his wife learned of it, she sent her daughter to him to ask him how he could leave them, who would support them? He replied: 'You will go to your father-in-law's; your elder sister—someone will take her into his home as a *niyonke* (nursemaid); your younger sister—someone will take her into his home out of compassion; and your mother will be a cook; and all that is in my house—I will sell everything to defray the costs of the journey."[6] R. Nahman did not yield to his family's anxiety over the journey, although "when the members of his household heard, they all burst into tears, and wept for days, yet he took no pity on them,"[7] and he said: "I wish to go immediately, no matter what, even without money."[8]

He "travels secretly, as merchants do," that is, concealing his identity, and later experiences expulsion, violence, and shunning. Those who knew of his journey "offered interpretations," "but all were mistaken—even those who praised [him] did not understand his intentions at all; and even those who knew a little because he himself had given them some intimation, nevertheless they did not fully know his intention."[9] "Know this," R. Nahman tells them, "that I will certainly not reveal the true intention of my journey to the Land of Israel, for my heart has not [even] revealed it to my mouth."[10]

Furthermore, there were the dangers of the journey itself, for "at that time was the French war."[11] Napoleon, in the wake of his Italian campaigns (1796)—by means of which he began, through violence, to bring the ideals of the French Revolution to Europe—invaded Egypt (1798), engaging in naval battles in the eastern Mediterranean. This fact impeded R. Nahman's journey, inasmuch as the Jewish community of Istanbul forbade Jews to travel to the Land of Israel. The Jews of Istanbul were already committed to pay for the released Jewish captives and did not want to take responsibility for further travelers at such a dangerous time.[12] R. Nahman responded by expressing his willingness to assume the risk entailed by a sea journey to the Land of Israel, for the exalted purpose of bringing about a dramatic change in his religious personality—even suggesting to his companion, R. Simeon, that he turn back without him. R. Simeon refused, and together they embarked on the perilous journey. The fact that Napoleon constituted the greatest threat illustrates the imperial context in which R. Nathan wrote his account of the journey.

Dangers continued to plague R. Nahman, even during his time in the Land of Israel itself. Shortly before the end of R. Nahman's stay, Napoleon wrested control of most of the country from the Ottoman Turks. Having seized Haifa, he set out for Acre and, on 20 March 1799, laid siege to the city, ultimately failing to take it. The city was still under bombardment from Napoleon's artillery when R. Nahman set sail from its port, only six months after his arrival. R. Simeon had managed to secure passage for them on a ship leaving Acre, which, in all the confusion, turned out to be a Turkish warship, and they came under French fire during the course of the voyage. The story presents all the powers fighting for control of the Middle East—the Turks and the English on one side, and Napoleon on the other—as clear enemies of R. Nahman and the Jews. Nor did the Arab and Mamluk rulers of Palestine, which was a district of Syria at the time, spare the Jews: those suspected by the governor of Acre, al-Jazzar, of spying for the French were put to death.

Thus, as R. Nahman and his companion fled Acre under a barrage of artillery, they experienced hostility from all sides: bombarded by Napoleon and destined to be sold into slavery by the Turkish captain,[13] from whom they hid in terror, with no food throughout the voyage save the coffee smuggled to them by the ship's cook:

> And in the morning, soldiers of the *brand vakh* (coast guard) came aboard the ship. And our Rabbi, of blessed memory, with his aforementioned companion, still wished to go and fall at the captain's feet, to plead with him to return them to shore. In the meantime, however, the *ankers* (anchors) had been weighed and they fled in fear, wherever the wind took them, because the war had suddenly flared up and was very loud. And on the ship they heard a very great din of *hormates* (cannons) and *bombes* (bombs) and other such sounds of war, which could be heard at a great distance.[14]

During the course of the voyage, the ship ran into a terrible storm, and R. Nahman and R. Simeon were very afraid. The ship took on a great deal of water, and all of its cargo was thrown overboard. It was on the verge of sinking, and the two men, who feared leaving the cabin in which they had hidden, climbed onto the furniture in order to keep from drowning. Their chances of survival were very slim, and they feared that even if they were to survive, they would be sold into slavery.[15] The difficulties of their return journey did not end there, however, and after a month of danger and trepidation, the ship reached Rhodes, where the local Jews ransomed them from the captain, and their rabbis were honored to host R. Nahman, grandson of the daughter of Ba'al Shem Tov. From there they traveled to Istanbul and, after many difficulties caused by the fact that their passports had not been stamped, set sail for Galati. On the voyage to Galati they encountered another storm. From Galati they traveled to Jassy, finally reaching home in June 1799.

2

While in Istanbul, as he awaited passage to the Land of Eretz-Israel, R. Nahman placed himself in a heterogeneous situation, in which his identity assumed a fluid and contradictory form. There, as he waited, R. Nahman concealed his identity and, in order to avoid being recognized, constantly changed identities: "For in Istanbul, he engaged in all manner of *qaṭnut* (lit. "smallness"): going barefoot, without a belt and without a hat, wearing only the lining of some garment he had. And he would go about the market like a child, running and laughing, and would play war games, as children do, calling one side France and the other side by another name. And they would make war, employing real military strategy. And he engaged a great deal in matters of *qaṭnut* there, in Istanbul."[16] The state of *qaṭnut* in Hasidism is one in which the tzadik (Hasidic Rabbi) emotionally releases himself from *devequt* (communion with God) and bonds with the common people in order to raise them up to him, to the devequt that characterizes his state of *gadlut* (lit. "greatness"). In the state of qaṭnut, "when he acts as a simple man, the *tzadik* is able to engage with his hasidim and to fulfill his responsibilities *toward* his community, functioning as its religious and social fulcrum."[17] It would seem, however, that that the purpose of R. Nahman's masquerading and concealment in Istanbul was to exploit the liminal situation in which he found himself,[18] in order to ensure the opposite—that his actions would not have a leadership effect on the Jewish collective. In Victor Turner's terms, the circumstances were those of "communitas"—the unbounded spontaneous relations of solidarity engendered by the pilgrimage process, which call social rules into question and create a universality beyond particular identities.[19] We are also struck by the parodic simulation of the Napoleonic Wars, which thoroughly undermines any attempt to relate seriously to questions of leadership and sovereignty. In other words, the war games and concealment were meant to prevent the creation of a proto-national subject that would have inevitably transcended the immediate individual presence of R. Nahman and his companion. As we will see, however, there is in fact no contradiction between the qaṭnut, that is, the tzadik's involvement in his community, and his masquerading and concealment from the hasidic community, because, in R. Nahman's case, it is a dialectic process, whereby the more he engages in qatnut the greater he will become in his gadlut.[20]

Qatnut is the point of departure for a dialectic process that begins with the tzadik's connection to the community of his own hasidim, which is a social format destined to be raised up through the tzadik's actions. The hasidic social format may be characterized by contrasting it to the "imagined national community" defined by Benedict Anderson as a community in which members do not know each other face to face. The hasidic community is, in fact, founded on the construction of an intimate collective, a face-to-face community.[21]

In this case, both types of community—the national and the hasidic—are rooted in shared Jewish race, religion, and ethnicity. The fundamental difference between them is that the imagined national community, by means of abstraction, surmounts the anonymity of the bearers of those particular identities. The national abstraction renders transcendent distinct identities of ethnicity, race, and religion that exist in contrast to the hasidic community, which is defined by a tangible, direct, interpersonal contact that creates an unimagined community that is different from an imagined national identity.

A complex version of hasidic community developed, for example, around the court of Habad-Lubavitch, which expanded the hasidic mechanism of collectivization, while maintaining the principle of face-to-face community, by means of concrete intermediaries, as "the deep significance that the hasidim ascribed to personal contact with the rabbi, and the difficulties involved in making pilgrimage, gave rise to a new phenomenon: the chance returnee—a pilgrim who would describe before the members of his community what he had heard and seen at the [rabbi's] court at the time of his pilgrimage."[22]

Hasidism, from its inception and for many years thereafter, distanced itself from national or proto-national narratives written in Hebrew and in Yiddish. Instead, the social structure within which the hasidic tale was told and composed was far removed from national social structure. "Hasidism was essentially an oral culture. The organization and conduct of hasidic life was largely a matter of oral tradition. This tradition was passed on from father to son and veteran to novice. Spreading of the doctrines was done through personal encounter and face-to-face teaching. The oral *derashah* (homily) served an important social purpose in binding the group together; it was not initially viewed as a spiritual legacy to be carefully recorded."[23] The oral basis of the hasidic text, which also resulted in disdain for the editing and printing of hasidic works,[24] establishes its audience as a community with a limited number of members.

Hassidism also adopted the principle of pneumatic leadership, opposed to rabbinic leadership.[25] The popular telling of the hasidic tale is,[26] therefore, constitutive of a limited mystic community,[27] which Martin Buber called the hasidic congregation (*'edah*), in which the tzadik serves as an intermediary between the community and God.[28] Among the hasidim of Bratslav, this was termed a *kibbutz*, the Rosh Hashanah (Jewish holiday of the first day of the year) gathering whose members all knew each other personally. The cohesion of the congregation is thus based on what the Ba'al Shem Tov called "my ḥavurah [company],"[29] by virtue of which the tzadik is able to mediate between the congregation and the Jewish people as a whole.[30] The charismatic tzadik's hasidim are bound to him and to one another by mystical affinity,[31] sometimes having recourse to a "letter of binding" (*mikhtav qišur*) or note, by means of which the hasid connects with the tzadik at the hasidic court, in keeping with its specific rules and practices.[32] The tzadik is merely an intermediary and God's representative in a theocratic regime in which the sovereign is God.

It is this structure that leads to Ada Rapoport-Albert's assertion that the decentralization and division of the hasidic movement into separate congregations occurred during the Ba'al Shem Tov's lifetime and not, as previously claimed, only after the death of his successor, Dov Ber—the "Maggid"—of Mezhirech.[33] As Rivka Dvir-Goldberg notes, the internal politics of the various hasidic courts are at times the essence of the hasidic tale, which lacks national significance.[34] In addition, the fact that, as a rule, the protagonist of such tales must be a concrete tzadik[35] runs counter to the imagined abstraction of national community that creates shared, future-oriented national time, in which Anderson locates the development of the novel genre. R. Nahman's hasidic identity, which is apparent from the very beginning of the story of his journey, goes much further, as the story not only lacks a national focus but also avoids collective expressions of any kind—even those pertaining to the intimate hasidic community itself: "And all of his travels were simple, as simple people travel, without any grandeur or celebrity. Although he was already renowned in the world at that time, he greatly admonished those who traveled with him to take care lest they reveal [his presence] anywhere he travels; and nowhere he traveled did they know of his presence, for he traveled secretly as merchants do."[36] The salient feature of masquerading is that it is an attempt to avoid the other's gaze. In the public domain, the gaze of the other has the power to fix the identity of the object it observes. Like any pilgrim, R. Nahman saw his journey to the Land of Israel as a lever to dramatic self-change. He therefore insisted on avoiding any gaze that might be directed at him and fix his identity, thus affording it the kind of stability that would have made it a part of Jewish collective identity. From his perspective, and in the political context of the late eighteenth and early nineteenth centuries, such an eventuality might have led—against his will—to the establishment of an imagined national community with shared values.

R. Nahman greatly feared that the narrative of his pilgrimage, intended to effect secret personal change in his individual identity, would consolidate it as a stable component of collective identity. He was therefore adamant in his desire to avoid becoming the object of any external gaze that would have made him a fixed part of the public domain—a public domain in which the Land of Israel played a collective role that R. Nahman refused to accept. The narrator thus begins by noting the "simplicity" with which R. Nahman traveled, as opposed to celebrity, thereby highlighting the great importance of the public dimension in the process of change. In demanding that his companions not reveal his whereabouts, he sought to preclude the possibility of being gazed upon, as "nowhere he traveled did they know of his presence."[37] The contradiction between his being in a place and simultaneously not being there may be reconciled if the part of his identity determined by those who observe him is reduced to an anonymous existence, detached from those observers. The image of R. Nahman's traveling "secretly as merchants do" further strengthens the idea of avoidance of the other's gaze, which fixes its object as one possessing a specific identity. Merchants, or rather the money that is the instrument of their actions, famously "does not not smell," that is to say that it is abstract, lacking specific characteristics. The value of money is quantitative, not qualitative, and it is therefore easily and simply exchanged. So too the lack of specificity of an identity that is not established by those who observe and identify it.

One of the stages in the series of reversals effected by R. Nahman occurred when he arrived in Istanbul and conducted himself in a manner that ran completely counter to expectations for a hasidic leader en route to the Land of Israel. His ambivalence toward the Land of Israel—repulsion as well as attraction—stems, to R. Nahman's mind, from its holiness. Holiness is separation, and the holiness of the Land of Israel is a matter of physical separation. In the Torah portion of *Qedošim* ("You shall be holy"),[38] the concept of holiness is rooted in the prohibitions against illicit sexuality and the separation from sinners, in constituting the holiness of the people of Israel. Moreover, toward the end of the portion, it is stated explicitly that this separation is the basis for God's choosing the Israelites and settling them in the Land of Israel: "And I said to you, it is you who will take hold of their soil, and as for Me, I shall give it to you to take hold of it, a land flowing with milk and honey. I am the Lord your God Who set you apart from all the peoples."[39]

Despite this explicit sanctification of the Land of Israel—clearly distinguished from the lack of holiness that lies outside its boundaries—the hasidic story of R. Nahman's journey proposes a sanctifying approach to the diaspora. Such sanctification is apparent in the story's opening passage, which tells of R. Nahman's mysterious journey to Kamenets-Podolsk in the spring of 1798, even before he had decided to go to the Land of Israel. Kamenets-Podolsk was well known as the scene of the great disputation between the Frankists and rabbis, in 1757, and as the Frankist stronghold. It is very possible, as Hillel Zeitlin suggests, that R. Nahman encountered the Frankists, even if only on a symbolic level, as there were probably no Frankists left in Kamenets by that time.[40] In order to return them to Judaism, as a means of neutralizing the radical messianism that had led to their departure from the Jewish people, R. Nahman performed a hasidic tikun (restoration) and purification rite there, by reciting a blessing and having a drink, apparently in homes formerly inhabited by Frankists.[41] In so doing, R. Nahman marked the restoration of holiness to Kamenets, in the diaspora, as a necessary stage in his ascent to the Land of Israel. The fact that the holiness of Kamenets appears as a necessary condition for a journey to the Land of Israel shifts emphasis toward the diaspora, thereby diminishing the messianic implications of his journey there, in terms of conquest and national settlement in the land.

R. Nahman's reaction to the possibility that he might be sold into slavery by the captain of the Turkish ship on which he had fled Acre under French artillery fire also attests to the religious rather than proto-national significance of his visit to the Land of Israel. He asserted that even if he were to be sold into slavery and would thus be unable to fulfill the precepts, he "had grasped the worship of the patriarchs, which they had practiced prior to the giving of the Torah, for they observed all the precepts although they did not do so in a literal fashion,"[42] and this assertion can be understood as a spiritual rather than a practical possibility that had opened up to him in the wake of his visit to the Land of Israel. In light of this spiritual realization of the Torah, "Nahman's journey . . . [may be] seen as an attempt to gain access to those areas of the Torah that apply in the land alone, so that afterwards he might include them in his 'spiritual observanc' of the *miẓwot* [Jewish commandments],"[43] outside the land.

R. Nathan Sternhartz writes that he heard from R. Nahman that he wished to go to the Land of Israel in order to attain what he called "supernal wisdom" (*ḥokhmah 'ila'ah*), achieving "total transcendence of self."[44] And indeed, R. Nahman went to the Land of Israel for reasons that did not place collective, Jewish, messianic existence in the Holy Land at the center. He kept his reasons secret, and we know only what his biographer, R. Nathan, speculated: first, that he desired to visit the grave of his grandfather, R. Nahman of Horodenka; and that he sought religious illumination that could be achieved only by journeying to the Holy Land.

3

R. Nathan Sternhartz's decision to write the story of R. Nahman of Bratslav's journey to the Land of Israel was a religious one. The masquerading and games played by R. Nahman in Istanbul were, in effect, an *ars poetica* allegory of the telling of a hasidic story, which is a religious act that embodies the kabbalistic concept of qaṭnut (lit. "smallness"), explained above as the weakening of hasidic devequt so that the tzadik's actions and words might reach the masses.[45] The implication is that hasidic propaganda, to be successful, must be wrapped in a captivating tale.[46] Although the hasidic tale is holy in itself, and fulfills a theurgic function—that is to say that its very telling is an act of tikun of the divine, it intended to disguise the power and importance of the tzadik, that his teaching might be accepted and that it might cause those who hear it to repent.[47] In other words, the dissemination of hasidic propaganda assumes the outward form of a story, embodying the dual status of the tzadik, as one who is both transcendent and descends to the lower worlds, to the masses.[48] The story's intended audience is thus not limited to the hasidic community. The purpose of its telling is that the miraculous events it describes might also be accepted by the "maskilim" and "mitnagdim"—the bitter enemies of Hasidism from the very beginning: the mitnagdim because they saw Hasidism as a deviation from the path of the Torah; and the maskilim because they considered the hasidim "rebels against the light" (*mordei 'or*), full of superstition and strange practices.

Chapter 1

This multifaceted political approach provides a crucial key for the interpretation of the journey narrative, in which R. Nahman's behavior is self-contradictory—self-contradiction that may be understood in terms of dual discourse: intended both for the believer and for the heretic. In this way, we may explain his paradoxical position, during the storm, that ceasing to pray will bring salvation; as well as the paradox with which he began his journey—first setting out for Kamenets-Podolsk. There is a kind of paradox in the act of pilgrimage itself, which is a liminal phenomenon, existing outside systems of social relations such as community and family.[49] As such, it locates the a pilgrim like R. Nahman in what Michel Foucault termed a "heterotopia," that is, "a sort of counter-arrangement, of effectively realized utopia, in which all the real arrangements . . . are at one and the same time represented, challenged and overturned."[50] Within the framework of the story of R. Nahman's journey, his identity appears, at times, to be that of a hasidic tzadik and, at times, that of a clown or an ordinary man. Nevertheless, from the moment he arrives in the Land of Israel to his attack of melancholy—another element in his series of reversals—he acts as a tzadik in every way.

From the fact that R. Nahman was, above all, a hasidic tzadik, it may be assumed that the story was intended primarily for the hasidic community—a collective with whom the narrator shares insights and feelings of wonder, and to whom he ascribes such feelings. Thus, in the story's opening passage, the narrator refers to the great wonder with which the news of R. Nahman's journey to Kamenets was met[51]—presumably by the narrator (created by R. Nathan) and the hasidic collective.

Yet, specifically for this intimate readership—first and foremost the collective of the hasidim of Bratslav—R. Nathan bases his story upon a secret. He presents his readers with a riddle that blatantly places the story of R. Nahman's journey beyond their grasp. The enigma of R. Nahman's journey to the Land of Israel may reach its climax when "immediately after Rosh Hashanah, one day after his arrival, it was the wish of our rabbi, of blessed memory, to return home straight away, and he did not want to travel anywhere, neither to Safed nor to Tiberias."[52] Although persuaded to remain for a time, "after Simhat Torah, he said to his companion, 'Thank God, I have effected what I wished to effect, in the best and most fitting manner possible. Nevertheless, I had intended to tarry here for love of the Land of Israel, but now I wish to travel to our home, to the diaspora. Therefore, go and hire a ship to Istanbul.'"[53]

Moreover, faithful to its title, "Seder ha-Nesi'ah šelo le-'Ereṣ Yiśra'el" the story devotes forty-four pages to detailed accounts of the journey there and back, which it sums up with the words: "Thus far we have recounted only a tiny fraction, like a drop in the sea, of the immense travails and adventures, the tremendous dangers, terrible hardships, and great fears that our rabbi of blessed memory suffered on the journey to the Land of Israel, there and back."[54] This is followed by only twenty pages on "the understanding he attained in the Land of Israel," which "cannot be explained or recounted at all; never before has such a thing been heard or seen, that one born of woman should attain such understanding by means of the climate of the Land of Israel; and it cannot be spoken of or recounted."[55] In other words, the journey itself, there and back—which took place mostly at sea and is marked by nautical metaphors—is the essence of the story, rather than the destination: the Land of Israel.

Although the text is silent where the knowledge that R. Nahman "attained in the Land of Israel" is concerned, it would appear from the story's composition that any attempt to explain the role of the secret as justification for the structure and motivation of the narrative of R. Nahman's journey must focus, first and foremost, on the sea, as the locus constituting the central obstacle in the narrative of both the outbound and the return journey. Indeed, a significant part of the journey narrative is marked by representations of the sea and its fixed metonymies: terms associated with ships and sailing. The first detailed description of the sea itself in the story appears in the account of the voyage from Istanbul to the Jaffa shore:

> And when they sailed the sea, there was a very very great storm, called (a very great *apirtine*), and the ship was in great peril, "They go up to the heavens, come down to the depths etc.," and none thought they would be spared from death, and all cried to God. And one night was like Yom Kippur (day of atonement) itself, with everyone crying and confessing their sins and seeking atonement for their souls, reciting *seliḥot* and other prayers and supplications; and our rabbi of blessed memory sat in silence. A number of people began to ask him why he is silent at such a time of calamity, but he did not reply. The wife of the rabbi of the community of Khotyn, however, who was a learned woman and had wept and cried out all night, also began to say such things, [asking] why he is silent. And he seemed to curse her and said to her: "If only you too would fall

silent, it would be best for you; and by this you will be tested—if you fall silent, the sea too will fall silent." And so it was. They ceased their cries and fell silent, and as soon as day broke, "He turns the storm into silence, and its waves are stilled, and they rejoice etc."[56]

The sea, one of the forces of nature and part of God's creation, is an obstacle on R. Nahman's journey to the Land of Israel. As a hasidic tale, the text is laden with theological meaning. In this sense, the story of R. Nahman's pilgrimage is entirely devoid of theophany (divine revelation in a holy place)[57] in relation to the territory of the Land of Israel. Not only does he fail to visit Jerusalem, the ultimate place for theophany in pilgrimage stories of all religions that consider it holy,[58] but the place where he actually does experience theophany—the only such place in the entire story of his journey—is on the sea.

As opposed to the schematic descriptions of nature, including the sea, typical of the *Sippurei ma'asiyyot*, which contrast with representations of the sea in maskilic literature, the story of R. Nahman's journey, which is very precise in its concrete descriptions of the sea,[59] is also filled with allusions to biblical verses, by means of which R. Nathan represents the forces of nature. The fact that the text representing the sea is so rich and vivid is only reinforced by the use of verses from Scripture. Thus, the description of the storm, "They go up to the heavens, come down to the depths,"[60] is taken from Psalm 107:26: "They go up to the heavens, come down to the depths, their life-breath in hardship grows faint," which refers to the punishment of the wicked, whose "life-breath" will ebb away; that is, they will be mortally stricken. The conclusion of the passage, "He turns the storm into silence, and its waves are stilled, and they rejoice," is taken from the same psalm: "He turns the storm into silence, and its waves are stilled, and they rejoice that these have grown quiet, and He leads them to their bourn."[61] It is thus revealed that the entire passage is based on Psalm 107, which refers to the sins of Israel, for which they will be punished by God, who will also ultimately deliver them:

> 11 For they rebelled against God's sayings, the Most High's counsel they despised.
> 12 And He brought their heart low in troubles. They stumbled with none to help.
> 13 And they cried to the Lord from their straits, from their distress He rescued them.

14 He brought them out from the dark and death's shadow and their bonds He sundered.

15 Let them acclaim to the Lord His kindness and His wonders to humankind.

And the seafarers ("those who go down to the sea") are destined to feel God's wrath but also to be delivered by Him:

23 Those who go down to the sea in ships, who do tasks in the mighty waters,

24 it is they who have seen the deeds of the Lord, and His wonders in the deep.

25 He speaks and raises the stormwind and it makes the waves loom high.

26 They go up to the heavens, come down to the depths, their lifebreath in hardship grows faint.

27 They reel and sway like a drunkard, all their wisdom is swallowed up.

28 And they cry to the Lord from their straits from their distress He brings them out.

29 He turns the storm into silence, and its waves are stilled,

30 And they rejoice that these have grown quiet, and He leads them to their bourn.

31 Let them acclaim to the Lord His kindness and His wonders to humankind.

The encounter with the sea en route to the Land of Israel is thus an encounter with sinners, whom God strikes and terrifies to death but ultimately saves. R. Nahman too is a sinner,[62] who sees in the journey, as is often the case in pilgrimage stories, an act of penance.[63] It is he who is stricken, in effect punished by the power of God, but it is also he who saves the passengers of the ship by the power of God, when he rebukes the wife of the rabbi of Khotyn and even curses her, demanding that she be silent: "If you fall silent, the sea too will fall silent."[64] What he was, in fact, asking the passengers to do was to stop praying to God—in keeping with the view attributed to him in *Sefer ha-Middot*, s.v. *tzadik*, 66: "Sometimes, prayer does not help except at the appropriate time, and when one stops praying, the Holy One, blessed be He, carries out His will and desire."[65] In the present case, it was God's will to save the seafarers—the assertion in Psalm 107:28, "And they cry to the Lord from their straits from their distress He brings them out" notwithstanding. The demand that the sinners be silent in the face of the storm can be understood in light of *Liqquṭei Moharan*, I, 38, which opens with the verse "Pharaoh's chariots and his force He pitched into the sea."[66] In this passage, R. Nahman explains:

> And this stormwind is a great accuser, from which all accusations and trials arise. And it is "after the words" [i.e., after or below the sefirah of *Malkhut*—a sefirah being a realm symbolizing divine power—associated with "speech," which is the lowest level of holiness], for it imbibes speech, when it finds an opening to imbibe holiness. This is [the meaning of]: "at the opening sin crouches"[67] (as it searches for an opening to imbibe holiness), and it is written: "Guard the openings of your mouth etc."[68] (alluding to the fact that man must guard his speech, in order to deny the *qelippot*—a kabbalistic term referring to the forces of evil or spiritual waste—an opening through which to imbibe from the sefirah of Malkhut).

Hasidim recite Psalm 107, on which the description above of the storm at sea is based, during the afternoon service on the Sabbath eve, and the psalm is the subject of a well-known hasidic commentary known as the "Commentary on *Hodu*," attributed to the Ba'al Shem Tov.[69] In the commentary, first published in a booklet in 1885, it is asserted, in a kabbalistic vein, that the descent of the tzadik is a struggle with sin, while "those who go down to the sea" in Psalm 107 refers to the souls that descend from on high to the qelippot that represent sin, in order to raise up and deliver the souls trapped there.[70]

A vigorous expression of the theological density of sea representations in the teachings of R. Nahman, upon which R. Nathan would appear to have drawn, can be found in *Liqquṭei Moharan*. For example, in a homily on the words of Rav Safra in the Talmud, regarding a sea voyage, and the fish that he and his fellow travelers had observed[71]—which R. Nahman compares to proselytes—one of whom raises his head up out of the water and says: "I am the lightest of the creatures in the sea." The word *yam* (sea) is interpreted by R. Nachman as follows: "I am the lightest of the creatures in the sea, that is I am above all of the worlds. *Yam* [spelled *yod-mem*], that is: the *mem* is four worlds, and the *yod* is wisdom that expands to all of the worlds, as it is written 'in wisdom You made them all.'"[72] The four worlds in the *mem* are emanation (*aṣilut*), creation (*beri'ah*), formation (*yeṣirah*), and making (*'asiyah*). First was created the world of emanation, from which descended (in a process called *hištalšelut*) the world of creation, from which the world of formation, from which the world of making, from which the material world. *Yod*, the first letter of the tetragrammaton, the sefirah of *Hokhmah* ("wisdom"), which is the first sefirah, the light of which expands to all of the ten sefirot that constitute the universe. "And as the lightest thing floats to the top, so the soul, which is the good, is above all of the worlds, intimated by the word *yam*. For all of the worlds were created for the sake of the souls of Israel; hence the souls of Israel are on a higher level than all of the worlds."[73]

In *Liqquṭei Moharan* (lesson 73), there is a homily on Isaiah 43 that R. Nahman delivered upon his return from the Land of Israel.[74] The text in Isaiah reads as follows: "1 But now, thus says the Lord who created you, O Jacob, and He who formed you, O Israel: Fear not, for I have redeemed you, I have called you by your name, you are Mine; 2 When you pass through the water, I will be with you, and through the rivers, they shall not sweep over you; when you walk through the fire, you will not be burned, the flames will not consume you." And R. Nahman explains: "This is the meaning of the verse: 'When you pass through the water'–'pass through' (*ta'avor*) in the sense of revelation, as it is written (Exodus 12), 'And the Lord shall pass through to strike Egypt,' which Onkelos renders 'And the Lord shall reveal Himself...'; and 'water' (*mayim*) signifies 'Torah' (*Bava Kamma* 17). The meaning is that when you wish to have the hidden part of the Torah revealed to you, 'I will be with you,' that is, you will see that you will make the vessel called 'I.'"[75] R. Nahman's homily heightens the problem of divine revelation and concealment, rendering it dynamic. He seeks to highlight the active role of the tzadik in the constant process of creation and revelation and, to that end, offers an interpretation of the words "pass through" (*ta'avor*) and "water" (*mayim*), in Isaiah 43:2. He explains "pass through" (*ta'avor*), citing Targum Onkelos on Exodus 12:23, in which the verb *ve-'avar* is translated "shall reveal Himself" (*ve-'itgele*). The real innovation in R. Nahman's homily, however, lies in his understanding of "water" as Torah, based on a Talmudic interpretation of the words "Ho, all who are thirsty, come for water," in Isaiah 55:1, as "none other than Torah." "When you pass through the water" is thus explained "when you pass through Torah,"[76] that is to say, if you dare to give prominence to the outer shell of the Torah through prayer and also secretly probe the depths of the Torah or of God, that is, engage in its homiletic interpretation (*deraš*), "I will be with you."[77]

R. Nachman's "I" is thus dedicated to the service of God through his mystical union with the divine, as he passes through the sea of the Torah—the text, which is compared to the sea—never ceasing to record his teachings, as he sails upon it. Moreover, R. Nahman saw mystical significance in every journey he undertook,[78] including, of course, those by sea. Thus, for example, in R. Nahman's allegorical tale, "The King and the Emperor," the sea is a divine force that must be contended with on a religious plane by the tzadik, who lies at the heart of hasidic endeavor, as one who embodies the power of God on earth and constantly ascends and descends.

Thus, not only is the obstacle of the sea in the story not a negative element, it paradoxically provides the opportunity to demonstrate God's power and His intimate relationship with the tzadik. This position is openly declared by R. Nahman when, prior to Passover, he echoes the words of Moses as he led the Israelites across the Red Sea.[79] The sea—contrary to its role in the national narrative, as a "conduit" from the diaspora to the Land of Israel,[80] that must be skipped over and suppressed—appears in the teachings of R. Nachman as an independent, theological stage devoid of national significance. The crossing of the sea is, here, an end in itself, and not merely a means to reach the Holy Land. This highlights just how distant Bratslavian narrative is from any collective, Jewish, proto-national utopian vision, for which the sea is merely an obstacle that stands between the immigrants and the land in which they wish to settle.[81] Indeed, in a homily that R. Nahman delivered to his followers on the eve of Passover 5558 (1798), he offered an interpretation of Psalm 77:20, "and Your path in the mighty waters, and Your footsteps left no traces," without making any reference to his upcoming journey to the Land of Israel.[82] In so doing, he gave preeminence to the sea itself, viewing not merely as a means by which to reach the Land of Israel. As Arthur Green remarks, "It is the voyage rather than the destination that seems to occupy Nahman's thoughts."[83]

4

In nineteenth-century European literature, the sea is portrayed as a modernist site, and embarking upon it in great ships symbolized the modern spirit. Crossing the sea in modern vessels was seen as a testimony to the human spirit and an ability to overcome the forces of nature through technology, for example longitudinal navigation made possible in 1759,[84] and a clear expression of modernity and the rise of capitalism. Representations of the sea in these works of literature reflect a high point in the fulfillment of the enlightened rationalistic aspiration to nature by means of the spirit of modern humanity.

This aspiration to modernity had been embraced by the maskilim, and R. Nathan Sternhartz—known for his sharp criticism and attacks against them[85]—wrote the story of R. Nahman's journey to the Land of Israel in an anti-maskilic vein. R. Nathan portrayed R. Nahman's sea, shrouded in mystery and imbued with religious motifs, in contrast to the sea of the maskilim—viewed as a force of nature that could be mastered through human ingenuity and the seafaring skills to which it had given rise.

R. Nathan Sternhartz, the hassid, presents his readers with an alternative to the maskilic sea narrative, when he writes the story of R. Nahman's journey in opposition to the manner in which the sea and the other forces of nature were portrayed by the maskilim. The maskilim, who saw nature as a field for scientific research, the fruits of which they wished to convey to their readers—as in the case of Joseph Perl's calendar, for example[86]—read Psalm 107 in a literal fashion,[87] presenting the storms and obstacles overcome at sea as sublime testimony to modern man's ability to master the forces of nature. The hasidim, on the other hand, as noted by Ken Frieden and Nancy Sinkoff, allegorized Psalm 107, in which the sea is a central theme, ascribing kabbalistic meaning to the seafarers' "going up" and "coming down," while highlighting the wondrous and the miraculous.[88]

This literary confrontation also had a theo-political dimension, as R. Nathan, in *Liqqutei Halakhot*, attacked the social approach taken by the maskilim, who viewed the Torah as an instrument of social organization, proposing a hasidic-kabbalistic political theology in its place. According to this political theology, the Torah is the basis for the theocracy of the hasidic community, in a way that extends well beyond the organization of social life, providing Jews with a means to divine understanding and spiritual renewal.[89]

Such a representation of the sea as a heterotopic site, comprising contradictory elements, already appears in R. Nahman's well-known tale "The King and the Emperor," which he probably recounted in the autumn and winter of 5567 (1806–7).[90] The series of voyages undertaken by the emperor's daughter, who had vowed to wed the king's son and broken her vow—leading to further attempted betrothals, which she violently thwarted—are all sea voyages. It is the sea to which she escapes in order to contend there with the impasses she encounters on land, and it is also where she finds her victims. The sea is, simultaneously, both the most tranquil and the most violent of places. The sea in the story of R. Nahman's journey is the way to reach the Land of Israel, but it is also the greatest obstacle to doing so. Every shore that is reached is also a starting point, resulting in escape back to the open sea, and vice versa. The violence and aggression that mark the passage between sea and land are imbued with considerable sexual tension on the part of the emperor's daughter, as well as gender dynamics, as she disguises herself as a man. All of this attests to the way in which the royal allegory in "The King and the Emperor" also finds expression in the political representation of the sea in the story of R. Nahman's journey.

As we know, the Haskalah was not a secular movement. It is therefore important to stress that its presentation of humanity's ability to master nature in no way detracted from its sense of wonder at God's creation. In fact, many maskilic texts sought to demonstrate that there is no contradiction between enlightenment and Judaism.[91] In order to contrast fear of God and what they considered to be superstition, the maskilim even encouraged wonder at God's works, by means of a kind of "natural theology," that is, a theological discourse in which the divine is examined in the light of natural reason but without contradicting revelation.[92]

The attitude of the maskilim to the scientific achievements that enable human beings to control forces of nature such as the stormy sea may be characterized as "physico-theology," which is a form of "natural theology" that strives to afford religious meaning to the successes of the scientific revolution and develops theological apologetics on the basis of physical discoveries.[93] This approach is evident, for example, in the works of Mordechai Schnaber Levison, who discovered in the writings of Carl Linnaeus, father of scientific taxonomy, "a genuine resource for demonstrating the critical priestly role of the naturalist in confirming God's existence and continual involvement in his creation."[94]

Ken Frieden demonstrated that travel narratives were an area of debate between Hasidism and the Haskalah, citing the works of the maskil Mendel Lefin, written in response to hasidic tales,[95] as well as the general hasidic tendency against modern science and medicine, which led to skepticism toward the mystical worldview.[96] In 1810, R. Nathan Sternhartz, a frequent critic of the Haskalah, took part, together with R. Nahman, in a confrontation that was also an ambivalent dialogue (to the point of making it necessary to pray with the maskilic "sinners")[97] between R. Nahman and the maskilim of Uman, with whom R. Nahman had forged ties,[98] which concerned, inter alia, the "maskilic heresy." R. Nathan, who criticized the maskilim for their pursuit of "secular wisdom" and exclusive study of the Bible (while ignoring postbiblical literature—an approach he called "Karaism," considering it a substitute for religious belief, leading to assimilation), derided the maskilic interest in the natural sciences in general, singling out the maskilic text *Masaʿ ba-ʿArav*, by Samuel Aaron Romanelli, which includes a sea voyage.[99]

Within the framework of the confrontation between hasidic and maskilic texts, the story of R. Nahman's journey contends with maskilic sea-travel literature. It seems that the main texts that R. Nathan, the writer of "Seder ha-Nesiʿah šelo le-ʾEreṣ Yiśraʾel," fabricated indirectly according to R. Nahman's reading list, were two translations of a book on the discovery of America, originally written in German by Joachim Heinrich Campe, a leading eighteenth-century German writer of didactic literature for children.[100] Campe adapted Daniel Defoe's *Robinson Crusoe*, turning it into a universalist and Enlightenment text, extolling altruism and hard work, and filled it with useful scientific information. The resulting work was particularly suited to the literary purposes of the maskilim who, between 1784 and 1825, produced a number of adaptions of Campe's version (*Robinson der Jüngere*), in Hebrew, Yiddish, and German printed in Hebrew characters. Nevertheless, it seems that the specific translation that R. Nathan had before him was *Meṣiʾat ha-ʾareṣ ha-ḥadašah* (Discovering the New Land),[101] translated into Hebrew and adapted by Moses Mendelssohn-Frankfurt (different from the philosopher Moses Mendelssohn) from the book *Die Entdeckung von Amerika*, which had been adapted in turn by Campe (1781) from William Robinson's *The History of America* (1777), as well as stories from other sources.[102] The translation of Mendelssohn-Frankfurt's adaptation into Hebrew is founded on the biblical story of the Flood and the biblical "Song of the Sea," and includes a glossary of nautical and geographical terms from the Bible. In 1823, the maskil Mendel Lefin published his Hebrew translation (translated from the original Dutch into French, from French into German, and from German into Hebrew) of Willem IJsbrantsz Bontekoe's nautical journal, under the title *ʾOniyyah soʿarah*.

In juxtaposing the maskilic text with the chaos of the sea, the boundaries of the subject of the text are redrawn, fashioned in the spirit of the Enlightenment and its *Bildung* model. Such is the case of *ʾIggerot Mešullam ben ʾUriyyah ha-ʾEštamoʿi*—a maskilic text by Isaac Euchel, published anonymously in *ha-Me'asef* in 1789—which R. Nathan may have had in front of him. The sea journey represented in this text reflects the liminal situation of European Jews, in transition from insular Jewish society to the world of German, European values.[103] The encounter, at sea, with members of other peoples and faiths, leads the subject to doubt his own identity: "And none among us knew who I was or of what people";[104] and to prepare for its refashioning.

In contrast to this maskilic model, in which the subject is constituted as one formed and educated through the encounter with the sea, R. Nathan describes an entirely different process. Thus, already in Istanbul, in anticipation of the upcoming sea journey, R. Nahman places himself in a situation in which his identity is fluid and contradictory. This is one stage in a frenetic and twist-filled adventure story, over the course of which R. Nahman's identity drifts and is shaped, without assuming any stable form. Aboard the storm-tossed ship, he appears, for a moment, to consolidate his religious identity as the tzadik R. Nahman of Bratslav (an identity he concealed on land). When the wife of the Rabbi of Khotyn addresses him as such, however, he rejects that identity, choosing rather to constitute himself in contrast to the widow and the other passengers, distinguishing himself from her by means of the curses he hurls at her.

In the spirit of Christian pilgrimage, which viewed the hardships of land and sea travel as an instrument for salvation,[105] R. Nahman is portrayed as experiencing his encounter with the stormy and frightening sea as a necessary stage in the consolidation of his identity as one who strives to encounter the Land of Israel. The story of his journey is not presented as a teleological narrative, with the goal of settling in the Land of Israel, or even, in the manner of pilgrimage tales, as shaping its "sacred geography";[106] witness the meandering and fluid way in which R. Nahman's identity is constructed. Rather than systematically constructing a modern identity, as in the European Bildung—based on overcoming a crisis, leading to the creation of a mature identity fit to take part in and contribute to the construction of the proto-national subject, the story disrupts every constitutive structure of strong and stable individual identity capable of participating in the development of the imagined proto-national community.

What the hasidic and maskilic texts have in common is that they both relate to events that take place on a ship—a clear expression of the confrontation between modern technology and tempestuous nature; and that both are narratives of personality crisis (the great crisis of modernity), provoked by an encounter with the stormy sea, after which a new personality is formed. What sets R. Nahman's story apart from the maskilic text is that the character experiencing the crisis is a true tzadik (as opposed to the rational, enlightened man of the maskilic text, who overcomes nature). Furthermore, contrary to the maskilic text, which is a Bildung text based on a realistic dialectic continuum of cause and effect, leading to emergence from the crisis, the solution to the crisis in the hasidic text is religious and miraculous, based, as noted above, on a paradoxical approach to the role of prayer, explained in *Sefer ha-Middot* (in a passage on the essence of the tzadik): "When one stops praying, the Holy One, blessed be He, carries out His will and desire."

R. Nathan thus presents a model that simultaneously resembles and is the opposite of the maskilic model, while the central conflict between R. Nathan's text and the Hebrew translation of Campe's work concerns fear of the sea. Both in the maskilic narrative and in the hasidic text, confrontation with the sea is a mechanism that places the subject in grave danger, and in overcoming it the subject is constituted and shaped. In *Meṣi'at ha-'areṣ ha-ḥadašah* (*Die Entdeckung von Amerika*, The Discovery of America), the translator approaches this fear and its mastery by means of "natural theology" that combines knowledge and science with faith in the Jewish God, while characterizing the sages of the Talmud and the Midrash as men "who loved and resorted to all manner of knowledge."[107] In the story of R. Nahman's journey, on the other hand, the fear of the sea is not scientific at all, and he succeeds in overcoming it and gaining mastery over it by means of theurgic actions.

The scientific attitude to the sea also appears in a Yiddish version of Campe's *Entdeckung von Amerika*, translated by the Central European modernist and forest merchant, the maskil Haim (Haikl) Hurwitz (1749–1822),[108] which the latter titled *Tsofnas paneyekh*, alluding to its scientific and enlightened nature (like the name given by Pharaoh to Joseph, Zaphenath-paneah [*Ṣofnat pa'aneaḥ*, "he who explains hidden things," Rashi ad hoc] for his wisdom and administrative ability). Although the book was published in Berdichev in 1817, after R. Nathan had already completed the first version of the story of R. Nahman's journey to the Land of Israel, a connection between the two texts may be postulated, as Haikl Hurwitz was on friendly terms with R. Nahman, when he lived in Uman, as was his son, Hirsch Baer Hurwitz (1785–1857). The latter immigrated to England in 1825, converted to Christianity, and became a professor of Oriental languages at the University of Cambridge. In 1810, however, while still in Uman, he produced a further translation of Campe's *Entdeckung von Amerika* into Hebrew, subsequently lost.[109] Both father and son had a close intellectual relationship with R. Nahman, to whom they would read from contemporary German literature—the works of Schiller (1759–1802), for example.

R. Nahman and R. Nathan also had close ties to other Hebrew maskilim in Uman at the time of R. Nahman's arrival there in 1810, following the fire that destroyed his home in Bratslav, and during the period in which he lived in the home of the maskil Nahman-Nathan Rapoport there.[110] In Uman, R. Nahman sought to act for the tikun of the maskilim, by means of what he termed the "descent of tzadik" to the forces of impurity in order to raise them up.[111] Another factor was certainly R. Nahman's ambivalent attitude to the pursuit of science and secular knowledge, which he considered a sacred heresy, and which he characterized in paradoxical Lurianic terms of divine withdrawal (*ṣimṣum*), which creates a space devoid of God's but which originates from God.[112] Uman thus appears to have been a place in which there was direct contact between maskilim and R. Nahman and his followers, not least where travel narratives were concerned.[113] We may therefore presume that R. Nathan was exposed to the translation of Campe's *Entdeckung von Amerika* even before it was published, drawing upon it when he wrote the first version of R. Nahman's journey, which presents both a "Judaized" version of Campe's text and an explicit discussion of God's power.[114]

In *Meṣi'at ha-'areṣ ha-ḥadašah*, translated by Mendelssohn-Frankfurt, the fear that grips those aboard the ship en route to America elicits a professional, scientific response from Columbus—as befits one who longed to from the Portuguese, who "alone of all the peoples, knew the sea routes to distant lands. And their wise men arose and took counsel, saying, 'Let us seek and explore, for we may find a way to cross the sea from the shores of our own land southward, to the southern limit of Africa. And from there we will turn and pass beyond Africa to the east until we reach the land of East India.'"[115] Columbus considers the discovery of America a rational scientific achievement or, in the words of the author of an anonymous review of the book, published in *ha-Me'asef*, something "which no one before [Columbus] knew, from the day that man was placed upon the earth: one of the greatest wonders ever performed in the history of the world by scientific inquiry and the exertion of the human mind to discover the unknown."[116] As Moses Mendelssohn-Frankfurt wrote in his translation: "And what man other than

Columbus would not have been terrified to sail the seas in [such boats] to the ends of the earth? But he did not fear or tremble, and he gathered all foodstuffs that he and the ninety men that were to set sail with him would require over the course of a year"; Mendelssohn-Frankfurt also highlights Columbus's skill as an experienced seaman: "And he swiftly took the lead stone on the sounding line and cast it into the sea, to see whether the waters had abated."[117] So too Isaac Euchel, although he expresses awe at the greatness of the sea, praising God's creation and even describing the storm at sea with the words "And God cast a stormwind over the sea, and we were unable to reach land."[118] This description, although rooted in "natural theology," lacks the element of revelation experienced by R. Nahman, who is in intimate revelational contact with God, even when the storm dies down and throughout the journey.

The story of R. Nahman's journey is at odds with the Haskalah in its linguistic choices as well. R. Nathan, who frequently criticized and even defamed the Haskalah, strove in his story to oppose the maskilic attempt—particularly in the biblical style of its poetry and narrative—to reconstitute the independent political existence of the Jewish people in biblical times. Thus, the very linguistic choices in this hasidic tale posed a direct challenge to the Haskalah. Contrary to the purist biblicisms of maskilic Hebrew, presented as a classical, universal language,[119] the language of hasidic tales in general and R. Nathan's account of R. Nahman's journey to the Land of Israel in particular is "Yiddishized Hebrew," in which many prepositions and expressions are, in fact, loan translations (calques) from Yiddish. This resulted in a mixed Yiddish-Hebrew language that openly challenged the biblical linguistic purism of maskilic Hebrew.

Although the story of R. Nahman's journey, as written by R. Nathan, was a remonstrance against the Haskalah at a time of bitter struggle between the two movements, it is also evident from the story that R. Nahman was greatly attracted by the Haskalah, as he found a particular allure in scientific heresy that coincided with his admiration of nature and its effect on religious feeling.[120] This ambivalence is apparent in the dual nature of R. Nahman's words concerning the sea, during the voyage to the Land of Israel, as a radical religious trial between irrational expectation of divine salvation and rational recognition of the limits of human efforts: "For thus should each and every one cry out to the Lord, blessed be He, and lift his heart to Him, blessed be He, as if he were at sea, [his life] hanging by a thread, the stormwind raging to the heavens so that he does not know what to do and barely has pause to cry out, but in truth he has no counsel or escape but to lift his eyes and heart to the Lord, blessed be He."[121]

Indeed, although he rejected the Haskalah, R. Nahman acted as a maskil, in his rational approach to planning his route to the Land of Israel. Such was the nature of the rational, practical considerations that led R. Nahman to choose, as noted above, to travel with R. Simeon by coach to Nikolayev and from there, on a barge transporting wheat, down the Dnieper to Odesa—a shorter and less dangerous route than the one generally preferred by Jewish travelers, via Galati.[122] From the beginning of the story *in medias res*, however, it is clear that the opposite is also true, and R. Nahman's journey was not guided by any kind of planning based on rational, maskilic logic. At the very outset, the author describes the great "wonder" with which his journey began, and the guidance he received from Heaven. R. Nathan's ambivalence to the maskilic representation of the sea may thus be understood as an extension of R. Nahman's attitude to modern innovation and the Haskalah that came in its wake. Yehuda Liebes put it as follows: "The novelty of R. Nahman should thus be understood in the spirit of these paradoxical words. It is a path that is simultaneously both 'very old' and 'entirely new.' In practical terms, this meant complete and total adherence to the ancient faith and the traditional, religious way of life within the modern world—the very same world that, to R. Nahman's mind, expresses complete rejection of faith and religion."[123] Maintaining such a position requires a particularly active consciousness, and indeed Green defined R. Nahman's faith as "not merely a passive matter of giving assent to the truth of tradition or Scripture, it is rather the highly active means man uses to fight off those challenges and inner demons that seek constantly to overpower him."[124] In other words, since R. Nahman's approach to the rationalism of the Haskalah was paradoxical, a kind of irrationality that is rational on a higher order,[125] his approach to the sea was irrational and based on faith, but its success was the result of the rational use of the ship's resources to overcome the dangers of the sea. For example, he is saved from drowning thanks to the pumps employed on the Turkish warship he had boarded at Acre.

In political terms, the Jewish maskilic narrative joined the European colonialist narrative of mastering the sea in order to expand imperial dominion over distant regions. The maskilic text describes overcoming all of the obstacles at sea in order to reach America and thereby accomplish the enlightened, rational task at the heart of the European colonial project: conquering "uncivilized" parts of the world and bringing "Western" culture to them. The hasidic text, on the other hand, took an anti-colonialist position, rejecting the maskilic espousal of the European Enlightenment and Europe's enlightened rulers.[126] This Enlightenment, which provided the basis for European imperialism, may also be observed in *Meṣi'at ha-'areṣ ha-ḥadašah*, in its description of the settlement of "Europeans in the new land."[127]

It is in this context that a clash occurs between R. Nathan's narrative "Seder ha-Nesi'ah šelo le-'Ereṣ Yiśra'el" and the maskilic text, with regard to the colonial "other." Maskilic literature severely criticized the brutality with which Spain and Portugal treated the inhabitants of the lands they conquered and. And indeed, in *Meṣi'at ha-'areṣ ha-ḥadašah*, translated by Moses Mendelssohn-Frankfurt, there is harsh criticism of the European treatment of the natives of the Americas,[128] describing their suffering at the hands of Columbus and his men,[129] while showing sympathy for their "innocence" and their "savage nobility"[130]—even to the point of expressing opposition to colonialism.[131] Haikl Hurwitz also showed sympathy for the indigenous peoples and denounced the Spanish, whom he considered barbarians.[132] To this we may add Campe's admiration for the "noble savage," which marked his criticism of Europe's sins,[133] although this did not bring him to reject colonialism.[134]

Maskilic literature did not question the colonial project itself, choosing to limit its criticism to the fact that the conquest of America and other territories should be done in an enlightened fashion.[135] The maskilim empathized with the victims of colonialism but ultimately embraced the colonial narrative and supported it, even using the subject of the conquered "other" to constitute their own Judeo-Christian identity, by contrast.[136]

Yet when R. Nathan addresses colonialism in his book, he follows R. Nahman's ambivalent path, rooted in rationalistic denial of the rationalistic possibility of unbroken thought or, as Joseph Weiss wrote: "While optimistic rationalism was winning the hearts and minds of members of the European and Jewish Enlightenment, such rationalism was already in flames in the mind of a man whose intellect was said to 'burn with fire.' R. Nahman was an extreme rationalist, whose extreme rationalism actually turned on itself."[137] R. Nathan, who adopted R. Nahman's ambivalent attitude (the irrationalism in his rationalism) toward scientific research,[138] also embraced the Haskalah's ambivalent approach to colonialist enlightenment, as reflected in *Meṣi'at ha-'areṣ ha-ḥadašah*. Although R. Nahman did not support colonialism, his approach to the native "other," like that of the Haskalah, was indeed extremely undecided.

When R. Nahman was in Haifa, he met a young "Ishmaelite," whom he liked very much. At one point, as their friendship developed, the Ishmaelite attacked him with a weapon and challenged him to a duel. The Ishmaelite subsequently changed his mind and declared his affection for R. Nahman. R. Nathan quotes R. Nahman, who "suffered more from the Ishmaelite's love than from his hatred and anger. And it was heard from his holy mouth that there was, in this matter that he had with the Ishmaelite, great danger, and I believe I heard from his holy mouth that this Ishmaelite was Satan (*ha-samekh mem*) himself."[139] The position that R. Nathan presents here is fundamentally anti-colonialist: the land is not empty, nor is it inhabited by natives who should be ignored or wiped out. Therefore (unlike the future position of Zionism), it does not foster a new nativism that erases the local past. R. Nathan's position avoids colonialist objectification of the conquered (for good or bad) and, in place of colonialist representation, focuses on theological fear of Satan—not without an element of homoerotic passion, reflected in the torments of love and hatred—and defuses implications of violence. Thus, in effect, R. Nathan reveals that the colonialist narrative of conquering uninhabited new territory is an invention, a myth, and that even when the conquerors recognize that the territory is inhabited, it is, in their opinion, by inferior, exotic and alluring natives.

## 5

At the beginning of the story, when R. Nahman and his companion reach Kamenets-Podolsk, some 450 kilometers from his home in Medvedevka, R. Nathan recounts: "Before he traveled to the land of Israel he was in Kamenets, and his journey to Kamenets was a great wonder, for he suddenly left his home, and said he had a way before him to travel; and he left his home, taking the road to Medzhybizh [the town and burial place of the Ba'al Shem Tov], and said that he himself did not yet know where he was going. And he went to Medzhybizh, and in Medzhybizh it was made known to him from Heaven that he must go to Kamenets, and he went to Kamenets."[140] The story goes on to tell how, at that time (the late eighteenth century), Jews were not allowed to reside in Kamenets, and those who visited it were required to leave the city every evening. "And he [R. Nahman], of blessed memory, stayed there, alone, in the city, and instructed that man [his companion] to enter the city on the following day, and he would find him there."[141]

R. Nahman himself spent the night in the city, but "not a soul knows what he did there."[142] The secret of his activities there that night is apparently related to the assertion that "after our rabbi, of blessed memory, slept there, from that time forward permission was given to the people [i.e., the Jews] of Kamenets to dwell within the city."[143] By means of his secret activities, R. Nahman succeeded in bringing about a change in the prevailing relations between Jews and non-Jews in the empire, effectively affording the Jews rights they had been denied. On the one hand, he acted in the spirit of the Haskalah, which strove to obtain equal rights for the Jews of the Russian Empire. On the other hand, the solution he offered the Jews constituted an alternative to the one offered by the maskilim. R. Nahman's success in obtaining this particular right for the Jews was the fruit not of a rational, egalitarian, and enlightened aspiration to full civil rights but of a deep secret that remained a deep secret even after R. Nahman's success came to light. The story of R. Nahman's journey expresses ambivalent opposition to the Haskalah, while offering the hasidic narrative as an alternative.

R. Nahman shared the goals of the Haskalah with regard to improving the conditions of the Jews within the empire, but by founding his own political path to obtaining such improvement. This is precisely the pattern of irrational rationality in the context of which the secret is, for all intents and purposes, a political weapon, employed in the political arena of the Russian Empire.

The most striking imperial element in the story of R. Nahman's journey, however, is undoubtedly the figure of Napoleon Bonaparte. The rise of Napoleon on the world stage had far-reaching significance for the Jews of Europe in general and of Western Europe in particular. At the time of his Palestine campaign in 1799, French newspapers published thoughts regarding the possible benefits the campaign could afford to all Jews, and in April 1799 the organ of the French government, *Le Moniteur*, published a report, "which according to the journal had been dispatched from Istanbul on 17 April 1799, stating that Napoleon Bonaparte had issued a proclamation from Palestine to the Jews, in which he promised their imminent return to their land. According to the report, a 'great number' of Asian and African Jews had flocked to join Bonaparte's forces. It seems that rumors were also spread in Germany, by word of mouth and in writing, regarding such intentions on Napoleon's part."[144]

The rumor that Napoleon had called upon the Jews to gather under his flag and reestablish their state in the Land of Israel would seem to have won many ardent supporters. We may assume, however, that R. Nahman, from his nonnational stance, did not welcome the proclamation. Napoleon and his fleet had fought against the English and the Turks with the intention of seizing control of Palestine, and R. Nahman, during his flight from the Land of Israel, was caught in the middle of Napoleon's failed siege of Acre. Contrary to the maskilim, who viewed Napoleon as the savior of the Jewish people and sang his praises, R. Nahman saw him as yet another of the forces of evil in the world. He thus shared the indifference and rejection of Napoleon that prevailed among Orthodox Jews in Eastern Europe.[145] Although R. Nahman considered him a king,[146] he also believed that Napoleon's many victories, despite not being of royal lineage, could be attributed to the fact that his soul had been switched with that of another, inferior soul, as in his tale "The King's Son and the Servant's Son Who Were Switched." This tale is one more example of the fact that Hasidism was not proto-national, nor of course was it a precursor to Zionism, and viewed life in the diaspora as preferable to life in the Land of Israel. Although the Land of Israel is central to hasidic theology, settlement and the establishment of a Jewish polity founded on political theology are relegated to the Messianic Age, thereby precluding their current realization.

The attitude of R. Shneur Zalman of Liadi to Napoleonic imperialism was one of suspicion and opposition. He feared that Napoleon's conquests would have a devastating effect on hasidic communities, and predicted and prayed for Bonaparte's downfall.[147] The Napoleonic Wars created considerable ferment among Jews in general and hasidim in particular. Contrary to R. Shneur Zalman, some saw Napoleon's campaigns as the war of Gog and Magog that heralds the coming of the Messiah (as described by Martin Buber in his novel about Hasidism, *Gog and Magog*, in circulation at that time). Hasidic support for Napoleon was thus the result of theological considerations: not support for Napoleonic imperialism, but the messianic hope that from this evil might stem the good of redemption.

As for the makilim, the modern state was only prepared to recognize the individuality of Jews as citizens, according to the eighteenth-century Enlightenment principle that they were "men like any other men," without historical, ethnic, or religious heritage.[148] The maskilic attitude to Napoleon was generally positive and ultimately accepted his position regarding the Jews of France, inspired by the universal principles of the French Revolution and encapsulated in comte de Clermont-Tonnerre's famous declaration before the National Assembly, in December 1789: "The Jews should be denied everything as a nation but granted everything as individuals."[149] In other words, what was demanded of the Jews of France was the absolute loyalty entailed by the individual citizenship they were promised, without affording them any collective rights. This demand stood in sharp contrast to hasidic opposition to any denial of Jewish collectivity. Their opposition was founded on a profound awareness of the irreconcilable contradiction in the presence of Jews, as members of the Jewish collective, in the Christian public sphere—something to which the maskilim aspired.

The opposition expressed in the story of R. Nahman's journey to the Land of Israel concerns both powers and their violent presence in the Mediterranean: opposition to Napoleonic imperialism, certainly, but also to the actions of the Turks, who were the target of Napoleon's offensive. On top of this we find England and its soldiers,[150] who also fought against Napoleon in the Holy Land, and the Russian Empire, which had annexed the Polish Jews who, after the partition of Poland, found themselves living in the empire's Pale of Settlement.

R. Nahman adopts a neutral stance in the conflict between the powers, opposing imperialism not by taking sides but by objecting to it in general, including a terrible fear of the tyranny of empires contending with one another for control over land and sea. To R. Nahman's mind, all of these powers oppressed Jews everywhere. He thus adopted a policy—common to Hasidism in general—geared toward the survival of an ethnic and religious group living under Russian rule. It is worth reiterating that, contrary to the Haskalah, Hasidism had no interest in emancipation, and when emancipation failed the Jews, Hasidism rejected the pull of assimilation and a long time later also rejected the auto-emancipatory project of Zionism.

According to the radical position taken by the French Revolution and Napoleon, the Jews were required to define themselves in keeping with the ethnic and religious blindness of the modern state, which strove to separate the political from the religious. In so doing, Napoleon's regime and the regimes under his sway presented the Jews with the momentous challenge of citizenship in a modern state.

6

The story of R. Nahman's journey also reveals his positions, as well as his actions, in the realm of internal hasidic politics. The great danger to his journey stemmed from the fact that he had chosen to make his pilgrimage at a time of great crisis in relations between the hasidim of the Land of Israel and those of Eastern Europe. Contrary to other currents in late eighteenth-century Hasidism, R. Nahman left no successor and, to this day, remains the first and last hasidic rabbi (*'admor*) of Bratslav. In other hasidic groups, there were often battles of succession, as well as struggles between different groups. Indeed, at the very time that R. Nahman made his journey to the Land of Israel, R. Abraham of Kalisk, one of the greatest disciples of the Maggid of Mezhirech, clashed with R. Shneur Zalman of Liadi, regarding hasidic leadership and the control of funds sent to the Land of Israel to support the hasidic community there.

R. Abraham of Kalisk departed for the Land of Israel together with R. Menahem Mendel of Vitebsk in 1777, settling first in Safed and then in Tiberias. Although he had designated R. Shneur Zalman as leader of the hasidic movement in Eastern Europe, his intention had been to continue leading the movement from the Holy Land, with R. Shneur Zalman continuing to follow the path of hasidic leadership as he (R. Menahem Mendel) saw it—particularly with regard to the question of revealing the secrets of the Kabbalah and the dissemination of R. Shneur Zalman's *Sefer ha-tanya'*. It would seem that at the heart of the conflict lay fears that the funds collected from hasidim in the diaspora for the benefit of those in the Land of Israel would not reach their destination or would not be distributed in accordance with R. Abraham's wishes.[151]

Indeed, already in Istanbul R. Nahman was suspected of having set out for the Land of Israel in order to sow political dissent among the hasidim there, ostensibly on the diaspora side of the conflict, and perhaps even to follow in the footsteps of R. Elazar of Disna, a supporter of R. Shneur Zalman who had acted in the Land of Israel against R. Abraham of Kalisk.[152] Thus, in Istanbul, two emissaries from the Holy Land suspected him of being an enemy of the hasidim of Tiberias: "And they were convinced, with regard to our rabbi, of blessed memory, that he was traveling from the *kordan* [representative of the Austrian emperor] to dispute with the renowned man of piety (*ḥasid*), the holy lamp (*buṣina' qadiša'*), our teacher R. Abraham of Kalisk, of blessed memory, and with his companions. And they were so convinced of this error that they had weighty proof of it, according to their error, and it seemed to them as if he [R. Nahman], of blessed memory, had been sent by many to dispute with him [R. Abraham]."[153] This is a clear example of the storyteller's attitude to internal hasidic politics in particular, and to politics in general. The story seeks to present R. Nahman as one who is beyond and perhaps even above the conflict, whose only intention is to bring peace between the factions.[154] This is done in order to clear R. Nahman of any suspicion whatsoever of involvement in the conflict between R. Abraham of Kalisk and R. Shneur Zalman of Liadi. And indeed, upon his arrival in the Land of Israel, R. Nahman met with R. Abraham of Kalisk, who is described as having shown him great respect, although R. Nahman refused to utter words of Torah before one whom he considered greater than himself, and praised R. Abraham's own teachings.[155]

R. Nahman's neutral approach to politics in the case of the internal dispute between the hasidic leaders of the Land of Israel and those in Eastern Europe (R. Abraham Kalisker versus R. Shneur Zalman of Liadi) led him to adopt a policy of systematic avoidance of any involvement in the conflict, playing games with his identity when questioned by the emissaries from the Land of Israel. Each time they asked his name, he gave a different answer, and so too with regard to the suggestion that he was the son of the tzadik of Komarno. Since political conflict requires stable identities, without which clear political positions cannot develop, we may assume that R. Nahman chose to present shifting, unstable identities in order to avoid become embroiled in the conflict:

> And they went to him [R. Nahman], of blessed memory, in order to inquire who he is, from what place and what family, but he would reveal nothing. And they spoke to him cleverly, trying to inquire in a number of ways, in order to extricate something from him and thereby understand from him who he was. And he answered cleverly and they were unable to understand a thing. And he confused them greatly and deceived them and twisted their minds—to the point that they were unable to fathom him at all or to understand anything whatsoever from him, and each time he seemed to be someone else. For example, when they asked him if he was a *kohen*, he replied, "Yes." The following day, they asked him whether he was a *yiśra'el*, and he replied, "Yes." They asked him: "Yesterday you said you were a *kohen* [Jewish priest], and now you say that you are a *yiśra'el*?" And he replied: "*Kohen* represents the quality of loving kindness and *yiśra'el* another quality and, thank God, I possess both this quality and the other."[156]

The ruse that R. Nahman uses to avoid political conflict is unsuccessful, however. He is repeatedly accused of fanning the flames of controversy in the matter of R. Abraham of Kalisk: "And they said to him: 'One can see in you that you are certainly one of the disputers, but you do not wish to reveal yourself.' And they began to despise him utterly, and they humiliated him in various ways and cursed him intensely and without end for days. And most of the humiliations were on the part of one of these two men."[157] Avoidance of areas of internal Jewish discord is also evident in the story's positive portrayals of Sephardic Jews as staying out of the disputes between Ashkenazim, willing to help all, without bias. It is Sephardic Jews who rescue R. Nahman from the ship that had brought him to the Land of Israel. When the ship reached Jaffa, the "Ishmaelites" (that is, the local Arabs) denied him entry, "because they looked at his dress and countenance, with long sidelocks as is the custom in our land, and [the fact] that he did not know their language and so forth, and concluded that he must be a French spy. Coaxing and pleading were to no avail, and our rabbi, of blessed memory, remained aboard the ship."[158] The ship's captain decided to remain at anchor for a few days, "but the ship could not stay there because the waves threatened to capsize it, and no counsel or stratagem could stop it. And it was a great wonder in the eyes of the captain, who asked why and wherefore it was so."[159] At this point, it is important to mention that according to Rabbi Ha-Cohen Maymon's guess, the Sephardic Jew Yom Tov Algazi ("the Great Sage from Jerusalem"), an emissary of the rabbis of the Land of Israel, joined R. Nahman on his voyage from Istanbul to the Land of Israel.[160] As a local resident, Algazi solved the problem, explaining to the captain why he had to leave and persuading him to sail to Haifa, where R. Nahman was able to disembark. Sternhartz notes, in his text, that Sephardic rabbis persuaded the captain, using an argument rooted in Scripture.

The Sephardic rabbis replied that they had been told of a tradition that this was the place in which the prophet Jonah, son of Amittai, had been cast (into the sea during the storm],[161] and the ship could not remain there that night and had to leave. And they departed from there and, on the eve of *Zekhor berit* (a *piyyuṭ* recited, inter alia, the day before Rosh Hashanah), arrived at the holy city of Haifa and stood near Mount Carmel in front of Elijah's cave.[162]

### 7

R. Nahman's rational irrationality toward the Haskalah was not merely an ambivalent clash with the Jewish Enlightenment but also entailed a theological-hasidic proposal regarding the fate of the Jewish people in the transition from the eighteenth to the nineteenth century. The political and theological status of the Land of Israel was, first and foremost, a function of R. Nahman's political messianism. The messianic question is, in effect, the way in which the story of R. Nahman's journey deals with the standing of the Land of Israel as a sublime destination, the Jewish convergence upon which will bring redemption.

Following Mendel Piekarz's identification of 1806 as the year in which R. Nahman's self-identity as the Messiah was established[163] and Zvi Mark's deciphering and publication of R. Nahman's *Scroll of Secrets* (Megillat setarim),[164] there is no doubt that R. Nahman saw himself as the Messiah who would redeem the Jewish people and the entire world. Nor is there any doubt that that is how his close followers, including R. Nathan Sternhartz, author of the journey story, saw him as well. In light of this perception of R. Nahman as the Messiah, R. Nathan's account of his journey clearly stands out, in terms of genre, as an alternative to the stories of pilgrimage to the Land of Israel as a holy place. From a literary perspective, it can be described as a "shift from place-centred to person-centred sacredness ... [that] does not always rest upon a secular, political model; [but] in some cases ... is a matter of independent transformation *within* the religious domain *itself*, albeit one that may be stimulated by other processes outside the cults."[165]

R. Nahman's messianism does not coincide with the total avoidance of messianic or national teleology in Hasidism, which, in the view of Gershom Scholem, the leading scholar of Jewish mysticism, embraced a kind of neutralized messianism.[166] It is also incompatible, however, with the view of Ben Zion Dinur, who found copious evidence of messianism in hasidic thought.[167]

Scholem believed that Hasidism had shifted away from ideas of national redemption, whereby history is seen as a product of human action—including the use of messianic power for the immediate achievement of national, political goals.[168] It is not the messianism of R. Nahman that scholars cite when characterizing hasidic messianism as future oriented, with no demand for its immediate realization—for fear of "hastening the End."[169] Nevertheless, Simon Dubnow's observation regarding the messianism of the Ba'al Shem Tov's Epistle—of which he wrote that "the national element is insignificant ... compared to the religious element"—may equally be applied to the messianism of R. Nahman.[170] And indeed, R. Nahman's messianism did not run counter to the messianism of the hasidic *'aliyot* (migrations) to the Land of Israel beginning in the eighteenth century, the interests of which lay not in establishing a unique and exclusive center in the Holy Land, in a proto-Zionist spirit, but in creating a Jewish center like any other—an idea that would have been in keeping with Dubnow's Autonomist views.

The attitude of R. Nahman's messianism to the Land of Israel is far from simple. For example, it corresponds to neither of the typical types of messianism, restorative and utopian-apocalyptic: it does not entail the rebuilding of the Temple in Jerusalem—a city that R. Nahman did not visit on his journey to the Land of Israel; nor does it long for the realization of an apocalypse and, as noted above, unlike other hasidic groups, does not view the Napoleonic campaigns as the messianic war of Gog and Magog. This runs counter to Zionist interpretations of the story of R. Nahman's journey[171] and is reinforced by Jonatan Meir's criticism of Zvi Mark's interpretation of the "Scroll of Secrets," as an expression of "political Zionism," whereby when the Messiah reaches the Land of Israel, the ingathering of the exiles will occur, "and then he will be the king of Israel."[172] Meir argues that the reference in the "Scroll" is not to a messianism of physical expansion but to one of spiritual expansion alone.[173]

The fact that R. Nahman's sea voyage lies at the center of R. Nathan's narrative establishes the Land of Israel as a secondary destination. R. Nahman's messianism does not propose a restoration of the Land of Israel and the Kingdom of Israel to their ancient glory as the story's supreme goal, as R. Nahman's journey is not an act of 'aliyah (the immigration of Jews from the diaspora to the geographical Land of Israel) but one of pilgrimage. In other words, it is a journey with spiritual and religious goals to be achieved specifically upon the pilgrim's return to his community and home in Europe, to which he brings the spiritual experience he acquired during the course of the journey.

The structure of the story seeks, at all costs, to leave the spatial aspect of the Land of Israel obscure. In this sense, the narrative of R. Nahman's journey is based on a paradox. On the one hand, it is geared entirely toward the Land of Israel; on the other hand, it avoids and even denies readers knowledge of the land's significance. On the one hand, it is descriptive—that is, a narrative exposition of information regarding a journey to the Land of Israel; on the other hand, it strives to provide as little information as possible regarding the land itself.

The story of R. Nahman's journey to the Land of Israel fulfilled no national function. As noted, contrary to Benedict Anderson's "imagined national community,"[174] members of which do not know each other face to face and almost certainly never will, the community of hasidic audiences and readership is not an imagined but rather a face-to-face community, lacking the necessary imagination for national abstraction. The Ba'al Shem Tov did not seek to impart devequt to each and every Jew; rather, his intended audience "consisted of a narrow band of associates—the group to which scholarship gives the label 'the Besht's circle.'"[175] Even the Besht's commitment to the Jewish people as a whole, found primarily in the Epistle sent to his brother-in-law, R. Gershon of Kuty,[176] which is devoid of national messianic aspirations,[177] was ultimately rooted in the limited community of his own, close associates,[178] in the context of which the letter was sent from one specific individual to another. The aspiration to interpersonal contact led, as noted, to the creation of the role of intermediaries, who sustained such contacts despite the many obstacles that stood in their way. Immanuel Etkes thus wrote, regarding the possibility of the existence of shared and imagined national time, "*The Besht had no plan!* He did not work toward any sort of final date or event of a revolutionary cast,"[179] thereby defining the nonnational foundation of the hasidic project.

Contrary to Zionist interpretations of the story of R. Nahman's journey—as a Jewish story of 'aliyah for the purpose of permanent settlement in national territory—the redemptive role assigned to the sea precludes any kind of national narrative, and presents the Land of Israel as a symbolic, secret place, even brief physical contact with which suffices to complete the narrative. Thus, throughout his stay in the Holy Land, R. Nahman wishes only to return to Europe. He has no desire to visit the city of Tiberias and does so only at the urging of his followers. In brief, when R. Nahman reaches the Land of Israel, he immediately wants to return to Medvedevka, eschewing even the remotest possibility of any involvement in a national project to settle in the Land of Israel.[180]

## 8

R. Nahman's entire journey was an act of self-sacrifice (*mesirut nefeš*), of intentionally incurring risk with the primary goal of overcoming *meni'ot*—spiritual obstacles.[181] Green termed this a "rite de passage," following Turner, who identified the phases of this rite as follows: separation from home and community of origin (R. Nahman leaves the women of his household with no economic support); the journey to the sacred place; the time spent there, as in a liminal place; return home and reaggregation with the community.[182] R. Nahman claimed that the journey to the Land of Israel had effected a dramatic change in him and, in *Ḥayyei Moharan*, is quoted as having said "that he is ashamed of all of the teachings and insights he had attained before having been to the Land of Israel, and considered them worthless."[183] He therefore instructed his disciples not to record his teachings from before his journey.[184] R. Nahman's constant purpose in gaining acceptance in the society he had left behind—to which end he examined his faith in God and sought to transcend his bodily self[185]—was not for the sake of establishing a bond between the Jewish people, or even the adherents of Hasidism, and the Land of Israel, based on settlement there in the wake of his journey. Rather, it was for the sake of establishing himself, paradoxically, as a spiritual leader without successor or dynasty and, therefore, unencumbered by the temporal-historical axis of the connection between the collective and the physical territory. So too with regard to his self-debasement in Istanbul, intended, as he explained, to enable him not to die there and to reach the Land of Israel as a way of overcoming the meniʿot of his journey, that is, to deal with the sins of the tzadik in the vein of "descent for the sake of ascent," the Sabbatean, messianic sting of this hasidic dialectic having been removed.[186]

Since pilgrimage is not meant to create a stable bond between pilgrims and the territory they visit, which is, in fact, a liminal place, the secret of the Land of Israel in the story of R. Nahman's journey is textual rather than territorial. As a result of this textual secrecy, the physical territory of the Land of Israel cannot be embodied in representations that imbue the journey with national meaning. Indeed, R. Nahman writes texts throughout the journey, and *'Ereṣ Yiśra'el* (the Land of Israel) appears in the story as a single, indivisible expression. Text as text, however, enjoys a more profound and fundamental status in the journey story. The text, the expression "'Ereṣ Yiśra'el," is, in effect, an alternative to the actual territory to which R. Nahman was traveling. For this reason he sought to prevent the teachings he had revealed before his journey from being recorded, that is, realized in material text, for only after his journey to the Land of Israel could they serve as an alternative to the material territory. The fact that the story of R. Nahman's journey cannot be interpreted as one of national messianism or the proto-nationalism of Jewish bonds to, and aspirations to exist within, the territory of the Land of Israel, establishes the very textual act as a spiritual alternative that clings to the materiality of the text as a replacement for the materiality of the soil of 'Ereṣ Yiśra'el. Ora Limor described the Jerusalem of Christian pilgrimage as a "textually-sacred place, because its sanctity is a direct function of sacred text."[187] In a similar vein, R. Nahman's pilgrimage to the Holy Land may be termed a "textual pilgrimage," the essence of which is not the journey to the sacred site, but the physical verification of the "sacred scriptures,"[188] which R. Nathan himself creates. R. Nathan, who tells the story of R. Nahman's journey to the Land of Israel as an anti-maskilic tale, uses the expression "'Ereṣ Yiśra'el," in his *Liqquṭei Halakhot*, not to refer to a physical place but as a literal marker of holiness that is antipodal to exile from holiness ("diaspora and distance from the Land of Israel"), which is where the heretical maskilim reside.[189]

The text of the journey story serves as a ritual substitute for the concrete space of the Land of Israel. Through the construction of "liturgical time," the ritual representation of the land/text supplants the collective and progressive dimension of time,[190] with cyclical, ritual time neutralizing the linear and messianic violence inherent in the act of pilgrimage. This neutralization is based on the textual holiness of the journey story itself—similar to R. Nahman's auto-messianic text, the "Scroll of Secrets," in relation to which R. Nahman himself said that its importance lay in its very existence as a story, that is, as a textual event.[191]

The textuality of R. Nahman's journey to the Land of Israel may be defined using Jacques Rancière's description of the travel narrative as a process of identification, through spatialization, with the "flesh" of the physical space and the body of the traveler. The journey of the apostles from Jerusalem to Tiberias in Galilee (on instructions from the angel of the resurrection, who guided them to a place where Jesus had already preceded them) renders the text of the Gospel true "out of itself," as it shapes the mapping of "there" (Tiberias) and "here" (Jerusalem), "making flesh with words and sense with flesh." "The living word the traveller meets is written in the very flesh of things, in the very framing of natural scenery. It is written 'here' [the place in the diaspora where R. Nathan writes the journey story] but it is only visible on condition that a traveller goes 'there' [to the Land of Israel] and relates the coincidence of its *ecceity* with the discovery of a new land."[192]

The story of R. Nahman's journey is also part of a tradition, beginning in the seventeenth century, of Hebrew and Yiddish travelogues to the Land of Israel, the diasporic nature of which Shlomo Berger described as a textual substitute for physical visits to the Land of Israel.[193] And indeed, in *Liqquṭei Moharan tinyana'*, lesson 78, R. Nahman notes the textual reality of the Land of Israel, which preceded the giving of the Torah:

> Even before the Torah was received, certainly then as well, the Torah already existed, because the Torah is eternal. At that time, however, before the giving of the Torah, the Torah was hidden, for all of the Torah is included in the Ten Commandments . . . and all was created by ten utterances, in which the Torah was hidden before the giving of the Torah. And the *tzadik*, when he withdraws from Torah and is like a simple man, receives vitality of the kind that existed before the giving of the Torah. And this is the way of the Land of Israel mentioned earlier, for the *tzadik* vitalizes himself when he is in a state of simplicity from there, because the essence of the power of holiness of the Land of Israel is by means of "The power of His deeds He told His people, to give them the nations' estate" (Psalms 111:6). . . . Thus, the ten utterances—clothed in the way of the land, that is the settlement of the world, for through them [the ten utterances] the world was created—are the way to the Land of Israel, for through the ten utterances the Land of Israel may be conquered, so it appears to me. And this is the meaning of the way of the land, that is that it is a way and a path to the Land, that is the Land of Israel."[194]

R. Nahman thus refers to virtual, nonpolitical, and nonviolent conquest of the Land of Israel as text. Ada Rapoport-Albert cites this teaching in the course of her discussion of the connection between this view of the qaṭnut of the tzadik and R. Nahman's theological discussion regarding observance (or nonobservance) of the precepts associated with the Land of Israel during his journey. In this context R. Nahman noted: "The true *tzadik* vitalizes himself at the very time that he is a simple man, so it appears to me from the way of the journey to the Land of Israel," citing Babylonian Talmud, *Menaḥot* 99: "Violation of the Torah is its fulfillment."[195]

> The connection between R. Nahman's concept of *pešiṭut* [simplicity], expounded in 5570 [1809/10]—that is the connection between the experience of fulfilling the precepts of the Torah when in a state of simplicity, even or specifically by violating them, as they were be-

fore the giving of the Torah—and his real and presumed experiences of *qaṭnut* during his journey to the Land of Israel in 5558–5559 [1798–1799] . . . is intimated in teaching 78 itself. There is no doubt that the theoretical formulation of the concept of *pešiṭut*, as established by R. Nahman prior to his death, may be traced back to the events of his journey to the Land of Israel, some twelve years earlier, and the great and new insights he gained through these events. R. Nahman intimates as much in his interpretation of "good manners" (*derekh 'ereṣ*)—which, according to the Midrash [*Leviticus Rabbah, Ṣav* 9], preceded the giving of the Torah by twenty-six generations, and according to which the inhabitants of the world conducted themselves at that time, when the Torah was hidden from them—as "the way to the Land of Israel" (*derekh le-'Ereṣ Yiśra'el*). [In other words, "the way to the Land of Israel"], that is, the conquest of the Land of Israel by the Israelites from the peoples of Canaan—which, in itself, occurred only many generations after the creation of the world—was, nevertheless, planned and already existed in potential if not in reality, at the time of creation.[196]

Indeed, from the very beginning of the journey story, the text appears as a goal to which R. Nahman aspires. It is thus recounted, with regard to his journey to Kamenets, that "some said he went in order to find the writings of the Baʿal Shem Tov that he had sealed up in stone, which some say are in Kamenets."[197] According to R. Nathan, however, "He, of blessed memory, laughed at this, and said that he had not journeyed there for this purpose at all, because he has no need of it. And he said that had he wanted those writings, they would have been brought to his house, but he has no need of them whatsoever."[198] The story refers, of course, to the writings of R. Adam that the Baʿal Shem Tov hid inside a stone, as recounted in *Šivḥei ha-Bešt*.[199] R. Nahman's categorical denial of the idea that he had gone to Kamenets in order to obtain writings that the Besht had hidden there may be understood as an allusion to the fact that R. Nahman had writings of his own and therefore had no need of those of the Besht (and had he needed them, they would have been brought to him).

The journey to the physical Land of Israel appears, from the very outset, as a text written by R. Nahman—echoes of which may be discerned in the reconstruction undertaken by R. Nathan, in writing the story of the journey. In fact, when R. Nahman and his companion boarded the barge at

Nikolayev ("and there was there a ship for wheat, and he sailed on that ship via Odesa"),[200] R. Nahman turned to his companion, "and he commanded the man who was with him to buy a lot of paper and ink, and as soon as they were aboard the ship, he began to write [words of] Torah. And he warned the man not to look at all upon what is written, and compelled him to give him his word, and then he believed him and gave him the key to the chest."[201]

In the story of R. Nahman's journey to the Land of Israel, this fundamental principle of holy text as an alternative to holy soil is developed to the point that "The *Land of Israel* is no longer the name for a particular local [*sic*], but rather signifies a qualitative status of sanctity which embraces the world at large."[202] In other words, this view is unlike that expressed in Leviticus, whereby the people of Israel inherited the Land of Israel by virtue of their status as a chosen people, that are set apart and therefore holy. Rather, the sanctity of the people of Israel is not always and necessarily intertwined with the sanctity of the territory of the Land of Israel. The sanctity of the land is distinct from that of the people chosen by God to rule over it and exists even without it. In a well-known remark on the relation between the Land of Israel and Canaan, R. Nathan quoted R. Nahman as follows: "And our rabbi, of blessed memory, said: One who knows why the Land of Israel was first in the hands of Canaan and only then did it come to the hands of Israel knows why he first went to Kamenets and only then to the Land of Israel."[203] This quote from R. Nahman begins as direct speech, and then shifts to indirect speech, replacing the first-person voice of R. Nahman with that of R. Nathan, relating to R. Nahman in the third person: "Why he first went." This mixed quotation, in which the words of R. Nahman intermingle with those of R. Nathan strengthens the interpretation of the editors of the 2008 edition of *Šivḥei ha-Ran* that, for the sake of clarity, this part of the journey story borrows from R. Nathan's words in *Liqquṭei Halakhot* (*Yoreh deʿah, Hilkhot milah* 3):

> And therefore, if the Lord, blessed be He, had given the Land of Israel to [the people of] Israel immediately, at the time of the creation of the world, and it had never been in the possession of the nations from the beginning, and the sanctity of the Land of Israel had been revealed immediately, then as soon as Israel had sinned, heaven forbid, the Land would have spewed them out, and its holiness would have disappeared, never to be revealed again. It was

therefore necessary for "the husk to come before the fruit," that the Land of Israel be given to Canaan for so many years. And in truth, even then, when the Land of Israel was in the hands of Canaan, even then the Land of Israel was holy, as it is now, because the sanctity of the Land of Israel is everlasting.[204]

In other words, the sanctity of the Land of Israel is independent and unrelated to Jewish control of it. It thus follows that the parallel drawn between the Canaanite possession of the Land of Israel and the journey to Kamenets before the journey to the Land of Israel effectively portrays the conquest of the Land of Israel as a simulation, the material basis of which, in fact, lies in the territory of the diaspora.

The basic connection between Jewish nationalism and the territory that it seeks to control (to "inherit") does not derive from the holiness of the land, which exists independently and may exist before (and thus after as well) the Land of Israel becomes a territory, as defined by modern nationalism. Thus, an even greater gap is revealed between R. Nahman's hasidic teachings and nationalism, highlighting the fact that attempts to appropriate R. Nahman's teachings for modern, territorial Jewish nationalism, that is, Zionism, are without basis. Thus, efforts to see R. Nahman as a modern, on the one hand—even one who may be counted among the greatest modernists, like Kafka and Borges—and his definition as a premodern, on the other, fail to understand the complexity of his approach. Contrary to this narrative of enlightenment that binds together the premodern and the modern, as stages along the same continuum, R. Nahman's dual and contradictory attitude to the Haskalah and modernity, which displays, at one and the same time, both enchantment and opposition, clearly demonstrates that it lies entirely beyond such categories of Enlightenment narrative.

The journey's narrative of reversals is not a linear one. In order to achieve the greatness of the tzadik, that is the realization of the ideal of devequt required of him as he approaches the Land of Israel, which possesses the quality of greatness, R. Nahman must first attain qatnut,[205] reflected in his behavior in Istanbul.[206] Although the Land of Israel is the final destination, at which the tzadik completes his mission, R. Nahman did not go to Jerusalem, which should have been the climax of the pilgrimage, and is even defined as such by R. Nahman himself.[207] As one who would often say of himself, "Wherever I go, I am going to the Land of Israel," R. Nahman casts aspersions on the teleology of the journey to the concrete Land of Israel, which was, for him, not a journey to the territory of the Land of Israel, defined in space, within the framework of sacred geography, but rather a concept, a text, that is the locution "Ereṣ Yiśra'el." As a narrative based on the rejection of maskilic values of change and progress,[208] R. Nahman's narrative is not enlightened, linear, progressive, or teleological, much less national. It is, rather, a narrative of pilgrimage, in which the Land of Israel is the object of the pilgrim's desire—to visit, but no less so to leave in order to bring its sanctity to a place where it is needed more, that is, of course, the diaspora. And indeed, contrary to Ben Zion Dinur's redemptive-Zionist interpretation of the hasidic 'aliyyot, Israel Halpern maintained that "the path to redemption, according to the 'Maggid' [of Mezhirech, disciple of the Ba'al Shem Tov], is to raise up the sparks of holiness (that fell during the breaking [of the vessels]) *by means of exile/diaspora*."[209] In light of this, it is worth noting R. Nahman's diasporic view of tikun, expressed in the story of his journey to the Land of Israel in his assertion that "one who knows why the Land of Israel was first in the hands of Canaan and only then did it come to the hands of Israel knows why he first went to Kamenets and only then to the Land of Israel."[210]

In hasidic thought, rooted in the Kabbalah, the Land of Israel is a symbol that enables one to pass from the land in this world to the spiritual, supernal land, and represents the last sefirah, that of Malkhut ("kingdom").[211] The fact of God's immanence throughout the cosmos weakens the importance of the Land of Israel as a preferred place for the divine presence and extends the experience of the Land of Israel beyond its physical borders.[212] Although the spiritual vitality that flows from the Jewish people is contingent upon the land, the tzadik—as R. Elimelekh of Lizhensk wrote—enjoys vitality everywhere, inasmuch as it is not a spiritual experience but an energetic quality by means of which the tzadik replaces the axis mundi. Such replacement, however, is not permanent, as the tzadik does not fulfill a national role.[213] Thus, according to Moshe Idel, even if the geographical Land of Israel is not completely neutralized as an immediate and messianic solution, it remains in the realm of a spiritual experience, with which even minimal contact is sufficient.[214]

For R. Nahman, the Land of Israel is certainly a physical place, but because the tzadik is equivalent to the Land of Israel and, therefore, everything he sets his eyes upon becomes the Land of Israel, it is thus transformed into a means for the discovery of spirituality beyond its physical territory and the extension of its holiness to the diaspora. The Land of Israel, which

R. Nahman identifies with the sefirah of *Keter* ("crown") rather than Malkhut,[215] is spiritual energy and, as such, is capable of breaking out of its territorial boundaries. As energy, it also lacks national significance, which would have required a direct bond to the territory of the Land of Israel itself.[216]

According to R. Nahman's "Scroll of Secrets," neither sovereignty nor kingdom (malkhut) will be the most important elements of the Messianic Era but rather the presence of the messiah as a tzadik and a holy man;[217] and since mere contact with the Land of Israel will raise the vital energy of the tzadik, he may, like R. Nahman, depart from it almost as soon as he has arrived there.

Chapter 2

# Isaac Erter's Anti-Hasidic Satires and the Watchman for the House of Israel

I

In the early nineteenth century, a maskil Isaac Erter (born Koniuszek, 1791; died Brody, 1851) wrote a short essay entitled "Tekhunat ha-Tzofeh" (The Plan of the Watchman).[1] In this essay, penned before his departure for Budapest in 1825 to study medicine, Erter began to develop the figure of the Watchman for the House of Israel (*ha-Tzofeh le-Veit Yisra'el*), central to the history of modern Hebrew literature from the early nineteenth century to the present.

The expression "watchman for the House of Israel" comes from the third chapter of the book of Ezekiel, in which the prophet recounts the words of guidance that God spoke to him as he sat in the exile of Tel Aviv on the river Chebar: "Son of man, I have made you a watchman for the House of Israel; therefore hear a word from My mouth, and give them warning from Me."[2] The task of serving as Watchman for the House of Israel, as explained to Ezekiel, consists of warning the people lest God punish them for their sins. The mission is then divided into two separate categories: warning the wicked sinner and warning the righteous sinner. Should the prophet fail to warn either, he is told, he will bear responsibility for their deaths. Should his warning to the wicked go unheeded, however, he will still have saved his own soul;[3] and should the righteous heed his warning and repent, he will have saved the life of the one he has warned as well as his own soul.[4]

The fact that warning in and of itself is construed in Ezekiel's prophecy as a moral act lends moral-political significance to the maskilic writer's satire, as an act of admonition. The Watchman, who serves as the narrator in Erter's satires, is charged with the task of guiding and, more important, warning the people—apparently including local rabbis and hasidic *tzadikim*. The satirical, literary act thus becomes a moral one, which also assumes political significance in the context of the power struggle between Hasidism and the rabbinate, on the one hand, and the Haskalah, on the other.

The Watchman's position in relation to the people does not simply entail the rational enactment of Foucault's panoptic gaze.[5] It also implies location within the power dynamic determined by a situation in which the Watchman gazes at the people, supervising them and exercising control over them.[6] Foucault invoked the structure of the Panopticon, conceived by the utilitarian philosopher and Erter's contemporary Jeremy Bentham, as a space in which the supervision of prisoners might be carried out while realizing the old Enlightenment project of linking reason and illumination. The Panopticon's mechanism of total supervision serves the goal of social control in the name of enlightenment, excluding irrationality while allowing nothing to escape its gaze. Furthermore, the gaze of the Panopticon, like that of Erter's Watchman, is the hegemonic gaze of sovereign power, which observes individuals and normalizes them as members of society by using a potential punishment for any deviation on the part of the observed objects from the moral norms it dictates. The total "sovereign power of the empirical gaze" thus acts on "the stable and opaque surface of the body," that is, the *matter* that is observed.[7]

Solomon Judah Leib Rapoport's claim (contrary to the view of Jacob Samuel Bick) that the Haskalah concerns itself with the fate of the entire Jewish people may help to clarify the position of the Watchman for the House of Israel, symbol of the sovereign power of the Jewish Enlightenment. In constituting himself as representative and guide of all Jews, it is ultimately the Watchman who styles the Jews as the "House of Israel." Thus, by means of potential or actual violence intended to mold the behavior of the collective, the Watchman enjoys the status of a ruling sovereign. As Simon Halkin aptly put it, "The satirical element in [Joseph] Perl and Erter's stories signifies the writer's (or narrator's, in this case) *profound interest—not in the Jewish individual* whose flaws he condemns, *but in Jewish society* the flaws of which he condemns."[8]

This sense of collectivity affords the Watchman the legitimacy to act as a national sovereign, whose harsh criticism of Hasidism and the rabbinate reveals his maskilic, colonial fantasy of representing all the Jews of the diaspora.

The integrity of this national collectivity, however, was both threatened and shaped by these internal rifts in the Galician Erter's texts, within its Jewry.[9] What is more, it is a rather tenuous and ambivalent kind of collectivity, as the satirical Watchman, who purports to be both prophet and sovereign, offers no indication of the specific goals or paths along which he hopes to lead the nation.

In the wake of the French Revolution, which linked sovereignty and nationalism, Erter's Watchman constitutes himself as a sovereign with a national, civilizing mission or Bildung—to rectify and revolutionize the life and character of diaspora Jews as they progress toward nationalism.[10] In other words, Erter's approach is an expression of Western European colonialism and Orientalism (originating in Berlin), which acts as an arm of the Enlightenment (in imparting the "pure German language," for example), especially in relation to the hasidim, whom he viewed as backward easterners.

It is by the very act of representation that the Watchman constitutes the materiality of the nation. Erter's use of lampoonery (satire aimed at a specific, real-life figure) evokes in his readers a sense of continuity between their own lives and the act of literary representation, which, for them, assumes the force of material reality. Erter, in turn, uses the narrative to design the body of the sovereign, whose biopolitical power over the people is the product of his gaze, as the omniscient narrator of that text. The gaze, in turn, enables the constitution of an imagined national community (as defined by Benedict Anderson)—not as an abstract analogy of a nation but as a materialistic representation created by the discourse within its social space.[11]

The fact that Erter's Watchman, that is, the Hebrew satirist's fictional character,[12] ascribes divine revelation to himself, by association with Ezekiel,[13] lends greater authority to his sovereignty. He becomes—like the sovereign described by Carl Schmitt, as analogous to God. Following Schmitt, we can define the Watchman as a political and theological authority, which is being constructed by a state of emergency.[14] Indeed, the political and materialistic situation of Eastern European Jewry could be described as a state of emergency. The Watchman's actions performed not only in the name of God, whose worldly representative he is, but divine in and of Jews. By the same association with the visions of Ezekiel, the Watchman appears not only as a sovereign but also as a messiah bearing a message for his people.[15]

Erter's satire is thus a theological act with far-reaching political-messianic ramifications. Even at this relatively early stage in modern Jewish history, Erter attempted, through his writing, to establish a Jewish sovereign. A sovereign, explained Schmitt, is also one who by proclaiming a state of emergency in which a state may and indeed must respond with violence to violence used against it by those it has marked as aberrant, that is to say its internal and external enemies.[16] The ongoing antisemitism and persecution suffered by the Jews of Eastern Europe defined Jews as aberrant and enemies of the state. The maskilic Jewish response to this was a desire for some form of Jewish sovereignty, including the struggle for emancipation, which was essentially a struggle for Jewish participation in the sovereignty of the European state.

The solution advocated by Erter and a majority of maskilic writers was the constitution of a Jewish subject for whom citizenship, acquired through emancipation, would afford a degree of participation in European state sovereignty. The sovereignty he envisioned was of an abstract, universal nature that would create a bond between individuals—to form a collective, independent of consanguinity and ethnicity, thereby affording legitimacy to the sovereign power, that is, to the control of the collective by means of the threat of potential violence. Ultimately, however, even the collective itself is a construct founded on violence—a fact that it seeks to conceal and deny.

From the very beginning, the Haskalah movement sought the support and collaboration of European governments in its efforts to change Jewish society. Although Isaac Baer Levinsohn, in *Te'udah be-Yisra'el* (Testimony in Israel), equated Haskalah with Enlightenment (*Aufklärung*), Simon Halkin identified two distinct and sharply contrasting facets of the Haskalah: the universal "heavenly Haskalah" that resembled the Enlightenment; and the Haskalah that was "wholly a practical plan for the actual transformation of Jewish life" in Europe.[17] Furthermore, the Schmittian sovereignty that Erter represented by means of the Watchman for the House of Israel was of an illiberal nationalist variety, anticipated by a nascent nationalism among the Jewish intellectuals of the Galician Haskalah, who were loyal to the absolutist Habsburg regime.[18] Indeed, Erter's Schmittian-theological political stance rested largely on the internalization of his political position as just such a Galician maskil, who not only considered himself a loyal subject of Habsburg absolutism but also distanced himself from the secular republicanism of the French Revolution.

The Jewish intellectual movement that Halkin describes suffered from the same weakness that Foucault identified in the Enlightenment in general—the ostensible dichotomy between universal and ahistorical reason and historical particularism.[19] Halkin's distinction between the universal and particular aspects of the Haskalah falls apart, because, according to Foucault, all universalism entails both cognitive reflection and actual practices, which cannot be viewed as distinct categories. In Erter's satire, we are struck by the fact that the Watchman is a satirist, circumscribing his absolute commitment to the universal values of the Enlightenment, in lieu of which he nurtures romantic and nationalist ideals. What Foucault seeks to refute in fact is Kant's cognitive condition: the subject's autonomy of reason and the universality of reason. "Reason," claimed Foucault, "created a new dominatory power," in which "the modern model of rationality goes hand in hand with a new kind of systematic oppression."[20]

A critical description of constructing Erter's Watchman that does not presume, a priori, the abstract necessity of the satirist's commitment to his moral mission—by focusing rather on the material means of its construction—locates the construct of the Watchman's supervising gaze within a specific historical field of power. Drawing upon Foucault's hegemony of sight,[21] we discover how, within this particular field of power, the Watchman explicitly proclaims the Jewish state of emergency of his time, while lamenting the absence of a Jewish sovereign who might control the chaos that mandates such a proclamation: "The Kingdom of Israel toppled as it failed to heed the voice of its seers; their realm was lost, Jacob ceased to have a ruler and a king. Countless hardships and centuries of adversity have not yet expiated the sin of the House of Israel and its rebellion in flouting the word of the Lord's prophets. Now the soul of the people is broken under the guilt it has incurred, and with a crushed heart it repents its former trespasses, but the celestial windows will open no more, and the apertures of heaven are forever sealed."[22] Erter, like other Galician maskilim, developed literary practices that distinguished between the sovereignty constituted by the maskilic text, and the ideal model of sovereignty established by the Peace of Westphalia in 1648 and articulated in the works of Thomas Hobbes, Jean Bodin, Carl Schmitt, and others. The features of Westphalian sovereignty are supremacy, perpetuity, decisionism (adherence to the law that permits states of exception or emergency), absoluteness and completeness (sovereignty cannot be partial), nontransferability (at the cost of annulling itself), and specified jurisdiction (territorial rule).[23] Long before the literature of the Hebrew national revival ever considered the possibility of a Jewish nation state (in the writings of M. J. Berdichevsky, for example), it reacted to currents that had begun to question certainties of identity, ideology, violence, capital, and political and religious allegiances, as well as the aspiration to a nation-state sovereignty blind to theology, race, and gender. It is thus safe to say that the subject envisioned in Galician Hebrew literature of the early nineteenth century was not the autonomous subject of a sovereign nation-state but rather the subject of a "weak" sovereignty susceptible to infiltration by external and internal forces, resulting in a contradictory and heterogeneous range of sovereignties.[24] This political stance stemmed from the combined realization that exile is "the framework within which self-determination is shaped amid tension between one's own self-image and the self-image one perceives in the eyes of the other—the gentile," and that there is no fundamental contradiction between "exile" and "sovereignty."[25]

The integration of Isaac Erter's Jewish text into the broader context of European history through the historicization of Jewish intellectual discourse within European discourse is indeed an important juncture in the development of modern Jewish national politics. The prevailing tendency among scholars of maskilic literature is to view this body of work as a precursor to Jewish nationalism or even an early stage of Zionism. I would suggest here, however, that not every expression of nationalism need be understood as a stage in a teleological journey toward the realization of Jewish sovereignty (generally reduced to Zionism). Zionist historiography has long asserted that Jewish nationalism began intensively in the 1880s, when pogroms in Russia proved that there was no hope for Jewish emancipation, as antisemitism had become rife even in liberal circles, leaving no hope for European Jews but auto-emancipation (in Leo Pinsker's *Auto-Emancipation*, 1882). In reality, however, signs of modern Jewish nationalism appeared in Hebrew literature as early as the beginning of the nineteenth century. A parallel Zionist claim, on the other hand, projects the Zionist narrative back in time, along a continuum beginning in the seventeenth century or even earlier. Particularly relevant in this context is Etienne Balibar's observation that the rise of nationalism need not be ascribed to a continuous narrative of national development.[26] Instead, Balibar suggests that we seek nationalist "moments" in time, not necessarily connected to one another. The moment constituted by Isaac Erter in the early nineteenth century, with the publication of his first satire, "Moznei Mishkal" (Scales; 1823), in *Bikurei ha-Itim* (First Fruits of the Epochs), may thus be seen as a proto-nationalist moment, which found conscious expression in the motto poem with which the editor, Shalom HaCohen, opened the first issue of *Bikurei ha-Itim*:

> Garden of Hebrews! Saplings of amusement were sown in you,
> At a time when your skies dropped teaching like rain.
> The time has passed, your footsteps have left no trace,
> You are abandoned, covered in thorns.
> You will again be renewed, your seeds sown,
> Now all the first fruits of your times (*bikurei itekha*) will ripen.[27]

Erter's early nineteenth-century nationalism should not, however, be construed as a harbinger of Jewish nation-state sovereignty. The Watchman's "weak" sovereignty is reflected in his theological ambivalence, since the Schmittian analogy between the sovereign and God is, at once, both present and absent. While he evokes the biblical model of the prophet, Erter's Watchman also essentially affirms the opposite, complicating matters considerably. He draws upon Ezekiel's divine, prophetic gaze yet cites the rabbinic view that prophecy ceased with the destruction of the Temple:[28] "I am neither seer nor a prophet, but a watchman for you, House of Israel."[29] To call Erter a deist and a "secular prophet,"[30] however, would be to ignore his deep connection to Judaism as a historical revelation-based religion and his firm commitment to the legacy of Moses Mendelssohn, father of the Haskalah. Although Mendelssohn, the rationalist, did in fact believe in the moral equivalence of all religions, he was by no means a deist. While he found justification for the tolerance of different faiths in "natural religion," he considered the Sinaitic revelation the foundation of historical, legislative (as opposed to metaphysical) Judaism and regarded the precepts of the Torah as based on reason.[31] The Galician Haskalah was imbued with Mendelssohn's spirit long before the middle of the nineteenth century,[32] when it took a Hegelian direction, under the influence of Nachman Krochmal.

Further considering the fact that Erter received a religious education and wrote and edited religious texts,[33] a veritable contradiction arises, whereby the gazing, sovereign Watchman simultaneously affirms and denies the theological basis of his own existence, rejecting divine revelation while remaining faithful to it. Erter presents his Watchman as a sovereign, unique in his time, a writer of rare theological and political ability. It is, in fact, to the moral decline of society and its inability to recognize divine revelation to which the Watchman attributes his failure to constitute himself as sovereign, expressing contempt for Jewish people's books and writings:

Nevertheless there are many seers among the people, who say that the windows of the firmament are closed but transparent,[34] and through them we see the visions of heaven. These people are powerless to do anything, but possess an arm like God's, to create sons of God and angels of the Lord. With a movement of the lips they create an angel and with a stirring of the tongue a seraph. The heart of the Lord is like flowing water in their hands, spun at their pleasure. By the work of their hands they give life, and bring death by the breath of their lips. Were it not for them, the Lord God would not establish His dominion on earth. They remove government from His shoulder and for perpetual delight place a consort, wife and concubine, at His right. Such misleading and destructive words the seers speak and even write in books, and the people of the sons of Israel—a people accustomed to hearing the voice of prophets since ancient times—listen and heed with open ears.[35]

Erter's revelation is not that of a traditional seer but of a modern prophet acting within a theologically significant dream that simulates revelation. It is a revelation tainted by secularism, leading Erter's narrator to define himself as follows: "I am a watchman for you, House of Israel. God has never appeared to me eye to eye, but His image is before me when I behold the world and its fullness, the laws and cycles of its hosts. When my eyes rove over the face of this earth, when I gaze upon the array of order and change that the Creator established at the time of creation, then does my heart contemplate the loving-kindness, greatness, goodness, and wisdom of God. Then my hand stretches to the inkwell and my heart's longing emerges in the fruit of my pen, to rouse even the ear of my people with these teachings."[36] Erter offers an overtly maskilic description of the revelation that moved him to engage in literary pursuits. It is an alternative revelation,[37] deistically inferred from nature but also, perhaps primarily, from the author's observation of God's loving-kindness in the world. It is not an unequivocal, conscious revelation but one that occurs in the Watchman's dreams.[38] He is thus able to level theological criticism at the books he addresses, unimpeded by any aura of holiness they may enjoy in the waking world—charging them with plagiarism (a violation of the commandment "You shall not steal") or using them as a metonymy for Hasidism and contesting the study of Kabbalah.

While revelation may no longer be possible in the manifest, familiar world, and as I show later, sleep provides the Watchman with the opportunity to weigh books on the scales of reason—an integral part of theological judgment. The books are thus deprived of their aura of holiness, in the name of reason and religion, that is to say the book fetish is supplanted by another fetish. This is the theological explanation for Erter's use of dreams in his satires. The fact that the revelation occurs in a dream affords the dream, including the ritual of weighing the books, the status of a maskilic alternative to divine revelation. It is not the revelation of the biblical prophets but the fact that its recipient identifies himself with Ezekiel, as the Watchman for the House of Israel, that renders it a rationalist, theological alternative to biblical revelation—as if to say that revelation itself, from a rationalist perspective, is nothing more than a dream. Erter thus declares that he is not a prophet, but this in no way implies that his judgments do not derive their authority from revelation. On the contrary, the revelation provided by the dream and the weighing of the books allows him to determine the "truth" of the "people of the book" by means of its own books, while rejecting those that are false.

Indeed, it is this alternative revelation that affords the Watchman his rational, supervising gaze. In the spirit of Mendelssohn, Erter's revelation does not conflict with intellectual truth but in fact reinforces it. Upon awaking from his dream-revelation, the Watchman (the narrator of "Moznei Mishkal") draws his rational conclusions from it,[39] as they pertain to waking reality, and thus concludes his satire: "The eyes of my flesh opened and the eyes of my spirit shut. The visions had passed and, as sleep departed from me, the scenes of the night fled and left, and my spirit was agitated; my soul was pained for the disappearance of the golden scales, the balance of justice and law to adjudicate good and evil, falsehood and righteousness. But this I took to heart and was comforted: God has given mankind intellectual scales, the balance of knowledge and reason, whereby a man might level his foot's path, weigh his thoughts, and grasp the measure of his every step."[40]

2

Although completed in 1820,[41] Erter's first satire, "Moznei Mishkal,"[42] was published only in 1823, after his appointment as a teacher of Hebrew and German language and superintendent of studies at the *Realschule* in Brody.[43]

The satire appeared in the journal *Bikurei ha-Itim*, published in Vienna from 1820 to 1831. As its name suggests, the journal was a harbinger of the Galician Haskalah, also known as the "Galician School."[44] The founder and first editor of *Bikurei ha-Itim* was the Hebrew poet and playwright Shalom HaCohen.[45]

Following publication of "Moznei Mishkal," Erter enjoyed considerable fame among maskilim throughout Eastern Europe,[46] becoming an important figure in the Galician Haskalah, on close terms with its leading lights—men such as Joseph Perl, Shneur Sachs, Meïr (Max) Halevi Letteris, Jacob Samuel Bick, Solomon Judah Leib Rapoport, and Judah Leib Mieses (1798–1831), author of the radically anti-hasidic tract *Kin'at ha-Emet* (Zeal for the Truth; 1828). Erter was greatly influenced by Mieses and, as a physician, attended him on his deathbed during the cholera epidemic that swept through Galicia in 1831.[47]

At the center of "Moznei Mishkal" stands the book, as a tangible object—an object crucial to the task of developing a modern Hebrew literary culture, undertaken in 1755, with the publication of the Hebrew journal *Kohelet Musar* in Berlin.[48] The significance of books for the "people of the book" cannot be overstated. It thus comes as no surprise that they lay at the heart of the bitter struggle between Hasidism and the Haskalah. Both movements were keenly aware of the fact that if they wished to have any significant public, political impact, they would have to publish books.[49] From the perspective of the maskilim, this book-centered struggle would indeed bear fruit, bringing about real change. A key figure in this respect was Joseph Perl, who sought to subvert the sacred literature, proposing a universal approach to these works that "he hoped would lead to the complete eradication of Hasidism."[50] Ironically, hasidic texts rooted in magic, mysticism, and popular beliefs owed their success to the technology of printing, which was, for the maskilim, a symbol of intellectual elitism, rationalism, modernization, and humanism.[51] The book as a printed object played a central role in the dramatic developments spurred by the Haskalah—toward a tolerant, humanistic culture, aspiring to perfection. The modern book was presented as an alternative to the religious book, and served the Haskalah as a weapon in its battle against clerical and conservative forces.[52] This phenomenon within European Jewish society was almost certainly influenced by the widespread use of printing as a political tool in the culture of pamphlets and satires that flourished in the Habsburg Empire after the lifting of censorship under Joseph II.[53] With the restoration of censorship following the Napoleonic

Wars, the imperial authorities banned hasidic, kabbalistic, and Yiddish works.[54]

This struggle between the modern book and the religious book lies at the heart of Erter's biting, maskilic satire, aimed at the rabbinate and Hasidism. The narrator describes a dream, in which weights are placed in the pans of golden scales. At a certain point, the weights are replaced by books: "Whenever I placed a book on the scale, an outstretched hand appeared to tear it to pieces, removing all matters exploited or stolen, anything the author had plundered from the books of his fellows to use in his own without noting its source. From this treatment, countless weighty tomes emerged transformed into meager booklets, gaunt and shrunken."[55] The material book is the explicit target of Erter's satire and serves as a metonymy for books' authors, whom he attacks as plagiarists. Erter's satire judges plagiarists according to radical, utopian standards of originality. Simon Halkin follows Schiller in defining satire as "an inner rebellion in the writer's heart, against a known contradiction and a familiar dissonance; against the contrast between human ideals and transient reality."[56] Erter's use of the scales implies that the books are judged by rational, universal parameters, yet the final verdict is delivered by the brutal mechanism of the tearing hand.

Erter probably took the idea of making the book the object of his satire from Perl's *Megaleh Temirin* (The Revealer of Secrets)—the leading anti-Hassidic satirical work of the Haskalah period, which tells the story of hasidim in pursuit of a maskilic German *Buch* (as opposed to the rabbinical, Hebrew *sefer*) that agitates against them and maligns them. For both satirists, the struggle is against a book branded as false and fake—although in Perl's case it is a hasidic struggle against a maskilic book, while Erter portrays a maskilic offensive against rabbinical and hasidic books. Nevertheless, Erter closely followed in Perl's footsteps, surpassing him in the severity of his attack. In his scathing parody of hasidic literature, Perl sought to demolish its content. Erter's satire takes this a step further, actually destroying the books themselves.

The intervening hand allows the narrator in Erter's text to successfully conduct the judicial process, carefully placing weights and counterweights on the scales. The entire incident, however, including the process of rational judgment, occurs in a dream—presented as a form of superior consciousness and (as in the biblical story of Joseph) a source of true knowledge founded on prophetic authority. The satirist thus uses the scales to offer a rational-intellectual evaluation of something that lacks a definite,[57] rationally quantifiable value in the real world. In so doing, the author seeks to quantify abstract human values, measuring wisdom against wealth, mortal existence against the hereafter, extravagance against temperance.[58]

The dream is a device that can be used in satire to proffer a utopian ideal, repudiating the present in the name of a better future. The function of the dream in Erter's satire, however, is a little more complicated. One would expect devotion to an ideal future to produce a dream in which such a vision has already been realized—in stark contrast to the deplorable present.

It looks like an interesting point to compare the authority of Erter's dream to the authority of his revelation. Indeed, the fact that Erter's vision of moral judgment takes place in a dream actually weakens his critique. In fact, and in contrast to Erter's revelation, the implication of the entire episode is that true moral judgment can be realized only in a dream and never in the real world—not even hypothetically. Erter's satire is further weakened by the limited nature of his struggle against hasidim and *mitnagdim* (who shared the Haskalah's opposition to Hasidism, albeit for different reasons),[59] inasmuch as he did not take a thoroughly secular position rejecting the Jewish religion altogether.[60]

Erter's own religious commitment limited his attacks to what he, as a maskil, perceived to be negative expressions of the Jewish faith—above all Hasidism, of which he wrote that "the weight of the books produced by these kabbalists and 'true scholars' is equal to that of the books of the prophets of deceitful minds, who sell lies at a dear price and bequeath evil and foolishness to the people, only to fill their own pockets with gold and their bellies with delicacies."[61] Thus Erter, like most maskilim, established himself as a kind of representative of the Habsburg Empire in a context of intense "internal colonialism."[62] Erter himself, recruited by the Austrian government in the war on cholera and other contagious epidemics,[63] presented the targets of his attacks as colonials, subject to the onslaughts of maskilic colonialism—thereby sowing the seeds of early Jewish nationalism.[64]

Such proto-nationalism made its debut even before the writings of Moses Hess, who saw in the international Jewish response to the Damascus Affair of 1840 the birth of Jewish nationalism. In other words, contrary to the prevailing historiographical view, modern Jewish nationalism did not arise in opposition and as an alternative to the Haskalah. Rather, it was the political and especially the sovereign practices of the Haskalah that evolved into a hesitant, heterogeneous form of nationalism,[65] lacking a clear, teleological narrative to constitute and guide it.

Erter's satire acts as a rational quantifying mechanism employed by the maskilic author—nowhere to greater effect than when the brutal treatment reserved for books guilty of plagiarism results in the complete elimination of the spiritual content of the texts they contain. The satirist treats the books merely as physical matter, lumps of paper, reducing their spiritual value and significance to the moral question of their originality. This is the work's satirical climax, but the concept is presaged earlier, when spiritual and moral content is placed on the scales and translated into quantifiable values, by weight:

> In this great multitude [of books] I saw the works of great and renowned men, who led the people in the paths of righteousness and justice and, with the pillar of fire of their intellects, walked before [the people], to light up the night for them. And [I saw] the works of evildoers and deceivers, who led the members of their generation down twisted paths, and with the pillar of cloud of their foolishness darkened the noonday sun for them. And I weighed the books on the scales, book against book, booklet against booklet, but what I saw I will keep to myself, lest I arouse the ire of authors who are still alive, by exposing the shame of their booklets in public. Furthermore I will say that often, a small book the size of man's hand was too heavy to carry, while a thick volume, a cubit long, weighed no more than dust by comparison.[66]

The weighing of the books is thus a rationalist-satirical act, exposing (through quantification) what lies behind their dignified, physical exteriors. On the basis of this knowledge of the shameful truth, Erter the satirist accuses some of the books' authors of fraud and deception, although he is careful not to reveal their names. Erter's narrator ascribes this decision to his fear of the disgraced authors' wrath. One author, however, is clearly identified, his book singled out for its sheer physical size:

> And as I continued to weigh and measure, delighting in what I beheld, I placed an immense volume on the scale that was nearly as big as I was. And behold, its copiousness grew slender—the hand tearing out page after page, distributing them among the books of other authors. All that remained on the scale was the book's cover and introduction. I read the inscription on its title page and dis-

covered it to be the work of a man raised on high for the redemption of Jacob (*yeshu'ot Ya'akov*) in a preeminent Jewish city, the book of a man who holds a rabbinical position, previously held by great lawmakers and men of renown, from whose mouths Torah came forth to the entire community of the sons of Israel.[67]

The allusion is clearly to *Yeshu'ot Ya'akov* (Zhovka, 1809), which is indeed a large book (23 × 37 × 4 centimeters).[68] The treatise, a commentary on the *Shulhan Arukh* (code of Jewish law), was written by Jacob Meshullam Orenstein (1774–1839), a leading Galician rabbi and expert on Jewish law, who served as the chief rabbi of Lvov from 1805 to 1839. Orenstein, often referred to as "the *Yeshu'ot Ya'akov*," after the name of his book, is also known in Jewish historiography as "the Galician inquisitor," a fierce opponent of the Haskalah and religious reform.[69]

In 1819 a group of zealots, probably sent by Orenstein,[70] posted a notice on the doorway of Lvov's main synagogue,[71] excommunicating the maskilim Solomon Judah Leib Rapoport, Binyamin Zvi Natkes, Judah Leib Pastor, and Isaac Erter (collectively referred to as "the Four Fathers of Damage," a play on the taxonomy of the agents of damage in the Talmudic tractate *Bava Kamma*). Orenstein was later forced to lift the ban in a humiliating ceremony, by order of the government.[72] Thus, the maskilim—acting in the spirit of Moses Mendelssohn's opposition to the practice of excommunication,[73] and with the backing of the state—managed to defeat the rabbis in the internal Jewish struggle for control of the Jewish public sphere in Habsburg Galicia. The lampooning genre allowed Erter to portray Orenstein, with whom he had a personal score to settle, in a polarized, one-dimensional fashion, ignoring the fact that "Orenstein's attitude to moderate Haskalah was clearly far more complex, and his characterization as a fanatic seems somewhat exaggerated."[74]

Rapoport, Mieses, Natkes, and Elijah Bardach later testified against Orenstein in a case involving the collection of funds for Palestine. The maskilim had joined forces against him due to his ties to Hasidism (the existence and extent of which are debatable), primarily through his son Mordecai Zeev, who was himself a hasid, and because they had initially counted on his support in the battle against the movement.[75] They had hoped that Orenstein would prove an ally because his tenure as rabbi of Lvov witnessed not only the growing influence of the Berlin Haskalah and the promotion of the maskilic ideal in Galicia but also the increasing popularity of

Hasidism, which established new centers throughout the region—thanks, in part, to the policy of religious tolerance pursued by the Austro-Hungarian authorities.[76]

Erter turned his satire into a lampoon, directed at Orenstein personally, as an act of revenge for having excommunicated him—the ban having led to Erter's dismissal from his position as a teacher and his forced move from Lvov (no earlier than 1818) to Brody, where he lived until 1825.[77]

### 3

In the satire "Moznei Mishkal," the narrator (that is, the Watchman) acts both to establish the book as a flawless fetish and as witness to its destruction and de-fetishization. It looks as though both of them represent the messianic dimension of Jewish proto-nationalism. The obvious messianic connection is also the source of Erter's mocking of the messianism entailed in the title of the great tome *Yeshu'ot Ya'akov*—The Redemption of Jacob. One could say that Erter, who refers explicitly to redemption in a "preeminent Jewish city," mocks both Orenstein's presumption to lead the Jews of Lvov to redemption and the nationalist-messianic context of the complaint filed against him with the authorities.[78]

Erter was probably not opposed to the idea, in and of itself, of a redeeming Messiah but merely sought to give biting satirical expression to the fact that Orenstein's pretensions to political leadership were utterly preposterous. According to Erter, the rabbi's flagrant plagiarism attested to his moral failings, effectively barring him from serving as a leader. When the narrator examines the different books he saw in his dream, distinguishing the moral from the immoral, Orenstein's book is given as an example of the latter type, completely fraudulent by virtue of its plagiarism. Moral books, on the other hand, are characterized as those written by political and spiritual leaders, books that speak truth: "In this great multitude [of books] I saw the works of great and renowned men, who led the people in the paths of righteousness and justice and, with the pillar of fire of their intellects, walked before [the people], to light up the night for them." The desirable messianic model (contrary to the one embodied by Orenstein) is one of political leadership, formulated in manifestly maskilic terms of justice and shining intellect.

The messianic potential in Erter's text thus flows directly from the physicality of Orenstein's book, exposed in the satire for its false pretenses. The book as an object can be defined as a fetish, a magical object, a source of information and a commodity set ablaze in times of political turmoil, a tangible materiality that both returns and mirrors our gaze. Henry Sussman, following Gilles Deleuze and Félix Guattari, highlights the "Janus figure" of the book, which simultaneously faces "both its own dismemberment and the orders and totalities that it summons into being."[79] Messianic energy is thus created by the drama of the conflict between the totality of the book and its dismembered parts.

In the satire, the dismembering of the book also implicitly signifies totality—the very possibility of which affirms the possibility of redemption. In this way, the book's dismembered parts convey a messianic message, as an alternative to Orenstein's false messianism. This messianism is a *"weak* Messianic power," created through negotiation with the totality of the human past, that is history, to which the materiality of the book may allude. In his "Theses on the Philosophy of History," Walter Benjamin points out that "there is a secret agreement between past generations and the present one. Our coming was expected on earth. Like every generation that preceded us, we have been endowed with a *weak* Messianic power, a power to which the past has a claim," because "only a redeemed mankind receives the fullness of its past."[80] In other words, Benjamin the Marxist historical materialist is convinced that material history includes a messianic dimension, albeit a weak one, of hope for redemption and happiness.

In "Moznei Mishkal," Erter rejects the local messianism of Lvov, which the figure of Rabbi Orenstein is meant to embody, offering instead a "pan-Galician" Jewish messianism that, with the two large ethnic groups in Galicia in mind (the Ukrainians in the east and the Poles in the west), promotes a Jewish pan-Galicianism along the lines of an imagined national community, in which participants do not know each other face to face but share an imagined collective.[81] It is here that signs of nationalism, a kind of Jewish proto-nationalism, begin to emerge. Although preceded by scattered dreams and isolated declarations (such as Napoleon's declaration of 1799) regarding plans for the foundation of a Jewish state,[82] the proto-nationalism proposed by Erter predates, by two or three decades, the Jewish nationalism that developed in Galicia in the wake of the 1848 European "Spring of Nations."[83]

The difference between Erter's approach to the fetish and release from it and that of Mendelssohn is primarily temporal. For the nonnationalistic Mendelssohn, Judaism was a rational and ahistorical faith—that is, one that does not exist within history or within a progress-oriented process.[84]

Therefore, according to Mendelssohn, release from the vicious cycle of abstraction and objectification does not entail the realization of a utopian Jewish collective moving forward together in shared time toward a common, that is to say national, future. Erter, on the other hand, conveys his political critique through the image of the scale, which functions as an allegory of the rational, quantitative measurement of theological and political values, turning the rational maskil into the final arbiter of the political value of a book, that is, of its author. It is thus the maskil who decides who is worthy and who is unworthy of leading the people. In this sense, the scale also acts as a material yardstick for the establishment of a national literary canon, which plays an important role in the makeup of proto-nationalism.

In Erter's satire, the material book is signified as an object capable, by means of its physical dismemberment, of guiding the people and forging a path through Jewish and European history. Indeed, at the very beginning of the satire, as the narrator describes the pleasure he takes in books, he explicitly characterizes reading them as revealing the history of human thought: "And like the changing of the seasons, so change the thoughts of all ephemeral creatures."[85] This historicity, provided by the very act of reading books, allows Jews to take part in European history. It is a nationalism-signifying moment, at which static Jewish theology receives inspiration from a dynamic, collective, European narrative external to it but which it seeks to join. Furthermore, inasmuch as Judaism is a religion of obligations, while Christianity is a religion of rights,[86] there is reason to believe that a Jewish collective living within Christian space will eventually internalize the Christian discourse of rights and will aspire, if only in the distant future, to the acquisition of collective rights for the Jews—that is, recognition as a nation.

According to Hannah Arendt, European recognition of national minorities arose "when the Protestant principle of freedom of conscience accomplished the suppression of the principle *cuius regio eius religio*."[87] It was Jacob Katz who first pointed out the proto-nationalism of the Eastern European Haskalah, citing the example of the Galician maskil Solomon Judah Leib Rapoport, who, while serving as the rabbi of Prague, met German Jewish religious innovation (influenced by Christianity) with nationalism, which he saw as a new basis for religion.[88] A similar phenomenon occurred in Poland, when "the triumph of the Counter-Reformation Church and the symbiotic relationship between the Church and the beginnings of Polish national consciousness were important ingredients in the development of Polish Catholicism in the eighteenth century."[89]

The theological approach adopted by maskilim such as Nachman Krochmal,[90] and indeed Erter—historicizing the religious concept of "the Jewish people," including its system of religious law, by constituting it as a nation with a common destiny[91]—further contributed to the development of Jewish proto-nationalism. This process is reflected in Erter's satire of the material object of the book, which bears both theological and political significance for early nineteenth-century Jewish Galicia, as a means to the articulation of national identity. The physical brutality of tearing away more and more of Orenstein's book exposes the criminal and material history of its composition. The use that Erter makes of this physical assault against the book as a material object not only posits a moral, textual, and temporal alternative free of plagiarism but also presents the satire itself as such an original work, capable of serving as a source for the development of a national narrative.

To better understand the limitations of the weak nationalist ideology (based on "weak messianism") that Erter develops in his satire, we may compare it to a later story, by the quintessentially nationalist Hebrew writer Micha Joseph Berdichevsky. There are certain similarities between his 1906 story "Parah Adumah" (The Red Heifer)[92] and Erter's "Moznei Mishkal." Berdichevsky's story revolves around a group of butchers in the Eastern European shtetl of Dashia who steal Reuven's cow—a beautiful, perfect, red, Dutch heifer with a queenly demeanor[93]—and slaughter her in a vicious and bloody ritual. The red heifer, which is identified in the traditional Jewish imaginary with an ancient (and future messianic) purification ritual for those defiled by contact with the dead,[94] and which Reuven and the other town folk worship, is in fact a fetish dismembered by the cruel butchers. The fetishistic alternative that Berdichevsky offers in "The Red Cow" is that of the blood that flows "like a great fountain . . . describing a broad arc and shining in the light of the lantern hanging from the ceiling above," while the bloody flesh is greedily devoured by the butchers, in blatant violation of religious law.[95] As in Erter's satire, the alternative fetish—the murdered cow—is both metonymy (the pieces of flesh signifying the whole, living cow) and metaphor (the color of the spilled blood is analogous to the color of the cow's coat). Indeed, it is the fact that Berdichevsky's alternative fetish comes into being through a severe violation of religious law that constitutes it as a modern, national, Jewish subject. The Jewish butcher, creator of the new fetish, is a coarse, cruel, and greedy figure, counterposed to the spiritual, God-fearing Jew. He is somewhat lax in his religious practices and has even been known to sell nonkosher meat as kosher meat, from time to time.[96] The murderous, sinful butcher is the gnostic origin of the theology of the fetish, as Berdichevsky's critical approach to religious law and preference for personal, unmediated religious experience led to his gnostic rejection of a transcendent God in favor of an immanent divinity. In the words of Yotam Hotam: "Berdichevsky's modern gnostic strategy here reaches its peak with the political conclusion—a return to the political framework (of the people in its land) facilitates rediscovery of an 'original' Jewish condition, of an occult, immanent nature, and eradication of the diasporic Jewish condition, victims of *halakhic* law and the burden imposed by the transcendent God."[97]

For Berdichevsky, the butcher is the modern Jew whose cruelty and violence are celebrated as essential for Jewish defense against those who would attack them.[98] As such, the butcher who murders the cow fetish is in fact an extreme version of the hand that tears the pages of plagiarized books in "Moznei Mishkal," written eighty-three years earlier. Contrary to Erter's "weak" sovereignty, however, Berdichevsky constituted the subject of a modern, sovereign, Jewish nation state, that is, Zionism.

What stands out is the inherent contradiction in the satirical discourse that Erter creates by means of the material object. On the one hand, the rabbinical book is a fetish, a material object in a state of reification that, like Marx's fetishized commodity, entails a theological dimension of mystery that gives it independence and thereby conceals the human forces that produced it.[99] The rational quantification of the physical book's theological value deprives it of any historical dimension, just as the value of a commodity is reduced to its exchange value, disregarding the human efforts invested in its production. The destruction of the fetish by tearing it to pieces is thus, in effect, the destruction, or murder, of the biographical author, for whom the book is a metonymy. If the fetish as an object obscures the human individuals and relations that produced it, the destruction of the object as a fetish entails both the murder of the author and the violent exposure of the human component that it had previously concealed. The narrative of the slain messiah who, in his rediscovered humanity, embodies the messianic message, thus becomes reality. The violent exposure of the fetish's messianic dimension may be construed as the de-reification of the rabbinical book, highlighting the temporal and historical aspects of the book's representation, suppressed by reification, in favor of spatial representation.[100]

The contradictory nature of the fetish[101] is manifested here in the clash between space and time, as Erter combines rational, spatial quantification with the temporal dimension entailed in reading a book. As in Joseph Perl's satirical and parodic attack on the "holiness" of hasidic books,[102] Erter uses satirical representation to expose the false holiness of the rabbinical fetish. He does so, however, in the name of an alternative theological temporality that signifies the possibility of national messianism. Erter's narrator can be said to act as one who knows full well that "once the objects cease to be objects of human activity and become independent beings [i.e. subjects], man himself remains devoid of objects and realization."[103] Therefore, in order to enable the book-object to further the ends of an active, historical subject, that is, to bring about the national condition to which he aspires, the author introduces a mysterious invisible hand to act, in his stead, against the fetishistic object, the book, and dismember it. Following Slavoj Žižek we may describe the rabbinical book that is the object of Erter's attack as an ideological fetishistic realization of the sublime. Throughout the dream, Erter attacks the material form of the book as a fetishistic commodity—which, as in Freudian dreamwork, is a material articulation of the signs that produce the fetish[104]—by means of metonymy (for the author, Rabbi Orenstein) and metaphor (the signification of the torn sheets of paper as a representation of plagiarism). The act of tearing the physical book is a tangible act of signification, which creates the material signs of national identity, because breaking the appearance of the sublime object-fetish always entails a continued fascination with it, primarily with its form.[105] This results in its immediate substitution with an alternative sublime—a messianic and possibly national sublime in this case. The alternative offered by Erter is a sublime of fetishistic commodity, which includes a strong element of universal abstraction (similar to Marxist equal exchange value), created by means of the rationality of the scales on which the books are weighed. Rather than undermining the sublime of the rabbinical book, Erter's satire posits the alternative sublime of the golden scales.

To use Žižek's terminology, the national ideology realized by Erter in "Moznei Mishkal" could be called an "invented symptom"—one that may and indeed should be enjoyed. On the other hand, Erter also limits the sensual pleasure of national ideology, by creating a sensual object that plays the predominantly rational role of measuring moral values. In other words, the equality of value (or weight) between the fetish of the book as a commodity and the fetish of the scales weighing it as a commodity does not exhaust the national fascination exerted on the narrator by the materiality of the rabbinical book, attacked for its low value, determined by the materiality of the scale, arbiter of true value. The narrator knows the rational quantitative value of each but in fact knows more than that. He knows the national sublime beyond the abstract value of the exchangeable material.[106]

The weak and partial nationalism developed in Galician Hebrew writing created a hybrid, similar to the materialistic phenomenon described by Ran HaCohen with regard to the Berlin Haskalah and later the Viennese-Galician periodical *Bikurei ha-Itim*: the printing of German-language texts in Hebrew characters. The publication of such German-Hebrew texts undoubtedly constituted a hybrid maskilic presence in the public sphere, and since "script follows religion,"[107] one might say that it was the Jewish religion—common to both maskilim and their opponents—that signified this presence: "In political terms, the use of German in Hebrew characters represented a relinquishing of *sovereignty* over Jewish textual space—embodied in the use of Hebrew or Yiddish, in which Jews enjoyed full independence—in favor of Jewish textual *autonomy*, subject to the external sovereignty of standard German, but still partially independent in the choice of script. In other words, writing German in Hebrew characters enabled the transformation of a part of the Jewish 'literary republic' into a German-Jewish autonomous region within a broader German federation."[108] This is a proto-national solution, which seeks to create a Jewish domain, safe from outsiders and enemies unable to decipher the Hebrew characters.[109] More than offering a conclusive solution to the conflict arising from the Jewish presence within Christian space, it may be described as an exploratory movement, through the articulation (literary, in this case) of a hybrid proto-nationalism. It is the articulation of difference that produces the hybrid and unstable identity signifier located "in between," while rejecting the stable, "original," racial, gender, ethnic, and national identity that ostensibly preceded and gave rise to it.[110] Scholar of nationalism Eric Hobsbawm provides an illuminating example of the articulation of proto-nationalism:

> In his short and brilliant book, *The Balkans*, Mark Mazower describes the difficulties that Greek and Bulgarian patriots encountered a century ago, when they tried to convince the peasants of Ottoman Macedonia that they [the peasants] were either Greek or Bulgarian. The peasants would simply stare at them uncomprehendingly. "Asking each other what my words meant, crossing themselves, they would answer me naïvely, 'Well, we're Christians—what do you mean, *Romaioi* or *Voulgaroi?*'" In fact, even the Greeks didn't define themselves in modern terms, as a single ethno-linguistic

people, but as "Romans," that is subjects of the former (Byzantine) Roman Empire.[111]

The interesting thing about the peasants' response, at what can be seen as a moment of articulation of incipient national consciousness, is that the identity of which they are certain is their religious, Christian identity. As with the principle that "script follows religion" in the case of German texts printed in Hebrew characters, here too religious identity is the default to which the peasants relate when asked to respond to an identity signifier that has yet to form in their consciousness. This moment of semantic movement from the new and virtually unknown to the old and familiar is the moment of proto-nationalism. Like Jacques Derrida's *différance*,[112] proto-nationalism is not signified by the stable signifier of a "transcendental signified" with permanent essence. It does not stem from the dichotomous opposition between the national and the nonnational but stems rather from the movement between them. In the case of Galician maskilim this is the movement between the contradictory aspirations to universal citizenship and to obtaining it without relinquishing their particular identity as Jews.

The proto-nationalism in Erter's satire is embodied in his disruption of linguistic continuity—contrary to the literary Hebrew later introduced by Mendele Moykher-Sforim (Shalom Jacob Abramovitsh),[113] which synthetically and harmoniously created national culture by reducing the distance between language and the objects of its representation ("And where others saw a world blurred by a screen of verses—his eyes saw a clear world without barriers").[114] Hayim Nahman Bialik, the Hebrew national poet, criticizes the Haskalah writers' excessive use of biblical language, accusing them of "standing outside of place and time."[115] He is filled with praise, however, for the "integrity and unity" created by Abramovitsh[116]—in his realistic style and the national, sovereign political role it plays, exercising control over language as if it were a geographical territory: "Mendele does not disdain even the smallest element that the spirit of the people once grasped. If 'uniqueness' and nationality are one and the same, Mendele is the first *national artist* of our literature. . . . He greatly extended the borders [of Hebrew literary language]. He restored all of its estates, subtracted by his maskilic friends, and gave us the *'great and unified Hebrew language.'*"[117] In contrast to this conception of the sovereign political role of Hebrew literary style,[118] Erter's satires offer a limited expression of national sovereignty, lacking the power and decisiveness that Bialik attributes to Abramovitsh's language.

This is also reflected in Erter's use of the dream device in "Moznei Mishkal." Many Haskalah thinkers, Moses Mendelssohn foremost among them, rejected any comparison between the Sinaitic and later revelations in modern Jewish belief. This would appear to be the reason behind Erter's declaration, in "Tekhunat ha-Tzofeh," that he is not a prophet. Yet he does resort to a kind of revelation, in a dream, which allows him to pass moral and rational judgment on rabbinical and hasidic books. Erter's ambivalent attitude to the validity of the dream coincides with Mendelssohn's views on dreams, signs, and symbols, as explained in *Jerusalem*: "Miracles and extraordinary signs are, according to Judaism, no proofs for or against eternal truths of reason. . . . For miracles can only verify testimonies, support authorities, and confirm the credibility of witnesses and those who transmit tradition. But no testimonies and authorities can upset any established truth of reason, or place a doubtful one beyond doubt and suspicion."[119]

4

The political position implied in Erter's attack on Orenstein allows us to read "Moznei Mishkal" and "Tekhunat ha-Tzofeh" in parallel.[120] Erter's non-revelational revelation accurately reflects the ambivalence of the Galician maskil, who wished to live and work in the non-Jewish public sphere, while knowing full well that there was no way to do so as a Jew in a European country.

Central to the maskilic vision of Jewish modernization was the goal of emancipation, which Erter shared,[121] and which, in the wake of Emperor Joseph II's edicts of tolerance, led the Hebrew Haskalah to embrace the political project of reforming the Jewish condition. Naphtali Herz Wessely's *Divrei Shalom ve-Emet* (Words of Peace and Truth), written in response to the emperor's edicts,[122] greatly contributed to the politicization of the Haskalah and, ultimately, to the transformation of Jewish education in Germany.[123] Indeed, the duality of Jewish existence in the Habsburg Empire reflects the ambivalence of the Crown toward the Jews. Despite the ongoing pressures to which the Jews of Galicia were subjected following the province's annexation to Austria (taxation, expulsion, restrictions on marriage, exclusion from certain professions, mandatory conscription, dress regulations, the imposition of German surnames), Emperor Joseph II's rule was, on the whole, marked by enlightened absolutism. The emperor sought to spread the gospel of enlightenment among the Jews—an endeavor in which the maskil Herz Homberg played a central role, actively, even aggressively, pursuing Jewish educational reform, military conscription, and settlement in agricultural colonies.[124] It is important to note that the emperor had no desire to convert the Jews, only to Germanize their lifestyle and outward appearance,[125] including that of the hasidim.[126] In other words, the goal was not conversion but to bring the Jews closer to non-Jewish society and to enable them to take their place in the public sphere.

In 1785, Joseph II promulgated the Galician Patent, which was more liberal than his previous edicts of tolerance, concerning Jews in other parts of the empire. The official purpose of the patent was to eliminate differences between Christian subjects and Galician Jews, who would henceforth enjoy full civil rights. Despite the solemn declarations at the time of its promulgation, this patent, which led to the imposition of civil duties (notably, military conscription) on the Jews, did not include such important matters as the right to work in the civil service or to reside in villages without engaging in agriculture or crafts. Rabbis were later required to keep birth, death, and marriage registries in German, which was the dominant language in the empire. It was hoped that Jewish fluency in German would make it easier for the Crown to govern its Jewish subjects.[127] To that end, every Jewish community was required to maintain its own German school.

Matters worsened after Joseph II's death in 1790 and his succession by Leopold II. The taxes on kosher meat and candles for Jewish religious use were raised; the right to lease land for purposes other than direct cultivation by the leaseholder was withdrawn; the option of providing substitutes for military service was revoked; German schools for Jews were closed and their replacement with Jewish schools forbidden.[128]

Indeed, the achievements of Jewish emancipation were reduced, particularly with the promulgation of the Emancipation Edict by Frederick William III of Prussia in 1812, and were canceled entirely after the Congress of Vienna in 1815. At the time of publication of Erter's "Moznei Mishkal," the goal of Jewish emancipation in Galicia appeared more elusive than before. Nevertheless, the Galician maskilim continued to strive for emancipation within the Austrian Empire, which they considered their homeland.[129] This is clearly articulated in the "Reshimot min ha-Moledet" (Notes from the Homeland) section, included in early issues of *Bikurei ha-Itim*, which features reports on Jewish participation in the modernization of economic and cultural life in the empire. Other examples of Jewish loyalty to the Crown include the publication of a genealogy of the imperial family and a paean to Francis II, emperor of Austria, Hungary, and Bohemia, by Juda Jeitteles.[130] It is also evident in Jeitteles's sharp rejection of Mordecai Manuel Noah's attempt to found a Jewish homeland called Ararat, on Grand Island, New York.[131] Jeitteles's criticism of Noah's plan included a declaration of the Jews' absolute allegiance to the Habsburg Empire, their true homeland and the only place in which he—as a maskil striving to rectify the condition of his people—could envisage their future with great optimism.[132]

The development of the Habsburg Empire—the dominant power in seventeenth- and eighteenth-century Europe—into a modern state was greatly hampered by its ethnic diversity. The Napoleonic Wars shifted its power base from central to east-central Europe, including Galicia, the inhabitants of which were effectively colonial subjects of the empire. The empire's militant Catholicism also meant that it could not be considered religiously neutral.[133] Indeed, none of the European states in which the maskilim dreamed of emancipation were religiously neutral. The public presence of Jews as Jews (as opposed to converts like the maskil Joseph Tarler, who had guided Erter in his path from Hasidism to the Haskalah and introduced him to the work of Moses Mendelssohn),[134] thus posed a significant obstacle to their civil integration. This would later form the basis of Bruno Bauer's famous claim, described by Yoav Peled as follows:

> Judaism, as a religion of precepts rather than belief, is by nature a public religion, and therefore unsuited to life in a free country, in which religion can only be a private matter. . . . He also claimed that the Jews could never be free, even in a constitutional state in which there is a separation between state and religion, like the July Monarchy (1830) in France. As long as religion receives some form of public recognition—if only in the very fact that a particular faith is declared the "majority religion"—religious minorities will, by definition, be oppressed. Only the complete elimination of all religious privileges—which he [Bauer] equated with the elimination of religion itself—could guarantee true freedom and equality for the Jews.[135]

Jewish existence in the European public sphere entailed irresolvable contradictions in all areas of life (the day of rest, for example). The reduction of Jewish religious life to the private sphere, in the Protestant spirit adopted by

Moses Mendelssohn and later reflected in the slogan "Be a man in the streets and a Jew at home,"[136] was an unattainable goal, because certain aspects of Jewish religious identity would inevitably stand out in the European public sphere. In other words, the private Jewish sphere is, to a large extent, public as well. This contradiction would appear to lie at the heart of expressions of Jewish nationalism, created by what Hannah Arendt (in *The Origins of Totalitarianism*) described as the disenfranchisement of national minorities and the concomitant association of the "private" with the interests of capital that dominate the public sphere, emptying it of private content and blurring the distinction between public and private.[137]

Aamir Mufti's book *Enlightenment in the Colony* addresses the crisis of Enlightenment, especially that of enlightened postcolonial secularism, which oppresses minorities, threatened by the enlightened state. Mufti highlights the Jewish Question, that is, hostility toward Jews on the part of their European "host" countries, after having taken clear steps toward Jewish emancipation during the course of the eighteenth century, including: publication of Gotthold Ephraim Lessing's play *Nathan the Wise* (1779), which celebrated values of religious tolerance and rationalism; the debate surrounding Christian Wilhelm von Dohm's *On the Civic Improvement of the Jews* (1781); Joseph II's Edict of Toleration, which granted the Jews civil rights (1782); publication of Mendelssohn's *Jerusalem* (1783), which called for a rethinking of the Enlightenment citizen-subject; publication of the journal *ha-Me'asef* (1773–1811); and the French National Assembly's decree of emancipation (1791).

The European Jew was perceived as the "other within," an immigrant, a postcolonial displaced person—as well as a marker of resistance against Enlightenment secularism, which arose in late eighteenth-century and which Mufti views as a source of a set of narratives subsequently disseminated throughout the world. Mufti explores Jewishness as a challenge to categories of identity and their relation to secularism in the modern state, in which Jewishness exists as a minority seeking decolonization. For the "host" country, Mufti argues, following Marx's essay "On the Jewish Question," the Jew poses a threat, as one who is at once both particular and irrational, as well as universal, abstract, and rootless. The Jew is a hybrid, both Jew and non-Jew, part of the state and external to it. The Jewish Question thus encompasses the unresolved tension between emancipation and assimilation. And so, according to Lessing's *Nathan the Wise*, although the signs of religious and communal affiliation must cease to have a public existence, the contradiction will always remain.[138]

Despite this internal contradiction, the Galician maskilim never sought auto-emancipation, which was the basis for late nineteenth-century Zionism: that is, the establishment of a Jewish nation-state that would provide the oppressed and persecuted Jews of Europe with a political alternative. In other words, modern Jewish nationalism would never have emerged had it not been for the Jewish Question raised in nineteenth-century Europe. Following the French Revolution, the nation-state, unable to sustain "a state within a state," required the emancipation of Jews.[139] Even in the Habsburg Empire, however, which included Galicia and was in fact multinational, attempts were made as early as the late eighteenth century to grant the Jews at least partial, civil emancipation. Ostensibly, the legal and judicial integration of Jews (equality before the law) should not have posed a problem, in light of the long-standing Jewish tradition of respect for the law of the land (*dina de-malkhuta dina*). Nevertheless, the fact that such legal-judicial emancipation required a degree of assimilation for the purpose of social integration created a conflict between Jewish identity and a civil identity that was, for all intents and purposes, a Christian identity.[140]

Awareness of the contradiction between the aspiration to civil emancipation and involvement in the Habsburg state and the desire to continue to live as Jews in the public sphere led the Galician maskilim to create a hybrid national movement. While this movement did entail an element of national self-determination, that is, the creation of a collective entity within history and as a means to the historicization of the Jewish religion, it was nevertheless a loose hybrid, rather than an unequivocal, utopian definition of the subject of a Jewish nation-state. This development was related, inter alia, to the fact that nowhere was the interaction between nation and state as complex and as difficult as in the Habsburg Empire. The state, which maintained a neutral position on ethnic, territorial, and cultural matters, enabled Jews who felt alienated from the traditional Jewish community but nevertheless rejected assimilation to engage in cultural and political life,[141] and to develop diverse forms of national consciousness not limited to the paradigm of the nation-state. Gayatri Spivak argues that it is impossible to make a clear-cut distinction between self-determination and nationalism, regionalism, and nationalism. She also stresses, however, that the concept of sovereignty is neither stable nor dichotomous but negotiable, which is why regionalism can be discontinuous.[142] Thus, in a political situation of "void-filled," heterogeneous sovereignty,[143] nationalism may not be constituted by rigid and dichotomous self-determination but may exist as an ambivalent, uncertain signifier, not defined by a clear, material distinction, such as a specific territory in which the nation dwells, over which it exercises control, and to which it is bound by a theology of holy land.

Isaac Erter lived the contradiction in full, longing for both distinct and indistinct Jewish existence in the European public sphere—an aspiration that was greatly heightened after the 1815 Congress of Vienna. This is the context in which Erter wrote his satires, developing a complex and contradictory political-theological world view. On the one hand, he located his work within the venerable tradition of the prophets of Israel, including a revelation in a dream. On the other hand, he rejected this characterization, limiting the role of the Watchman to that of a modern, rational observer, for whom the dream is, following Plato,[144] a rational tool for the attainment of maskilic truths. The Watchman's position is not a passive one, as the gaze itself is an exertion of power and control. Erter's Watchman should therefore be treated as a sovereign subject, although one who clearly faces a contradiction, which he seeks to resolve (if only temporarily) by means of allegorical satire.

Moreover, the fact that the Watchman constitutes himself as sovereign by means of a political event witnessed in a dream highlights the weakness of his sovereignty and the fact that it is not the sovereignty of a nation-state but of a national minority that does not aspire to territorial control and linguistic exclusivity. The Watchman's gaze at the moment of his constitution as sovereign is obstructed and internal; it is the gaze of a dreamer, who may be seen as one who is not among the living, albeit temporarily, as sleep is likened to death. In Erter's Watchman, Foucault's controlling gaze becomes that of a man dreaming in his sleep, whose ability to exercise control is limited and inward facing. It is not the gaze of a Jew at Jews who exist in the European public sphere but rather a Jewish gaze that controls Jewish interiority and is meant to prepare it for its public existence among non-Jews. The object of the Watchman's gaze is the Jewish private sphere, but unlike Mendelssohn, who makes a clear distinction between the Jewish private sphere and the European public sphere, in which the Jew can exist as an equal citizen with equal rights and duties, Erter follows his dream with a return to consciousness: "The eyes of my flesh opened and the eyes of my spirit shut. The visions had passed and, as sleep departed from me, the scenes of the night fled and left, and my spirit was agitated; my soul was pained for the disappearance of the golden scales, the balance of justice and law." The inward-gazing dream is meant to affirm the existence of advocates of the Haskalah in the European public sphere: "But this I took to heart and was comforted:

God has given mankind intellectual scales, the balance of knowledge and reason, whereby a man might level his foot's path, weigh his thoughts, and grasp the measure of his every step."[145]

Erter's Watchman thus fixes his gaze on those Jews who sought, in vain, to distinguish between their existence in the private sphere of the Jewish home and their existence as Jews in the European public sphere. The Berlin maskilim sought to create a maskilic public sphere (by means of the periodical *ha-Me'asef*, for example) where they could exist, not as secular intellectuals, as Shmuel Feiner suggests,[146] but as Jews in a religiously neutral public sphere, where any remaining contradictions might be resolved through tolerance. The Galician maskilim, on the other hand, appear to have experienced, firsthand, the difficulties entailed in maintaining such a Jewish public sphere within a Christian country. This stands to reason in light of Larry Wolff's assertion, in *The Idea of Galicia*, that there was no more fitting place in the entire Habsburg Empire than Galicia, with its large Jewish population, to serve as "an experimental domain for completely recasting relations between Christians and Jews."[147]

The Galician maskilim also felt the contradiction of Jewish existence within the Christian public sphere. Unlike the Berlin maskilim, however, they were forced to accept it as a possibility with which one might and perhaps should live openly. This was due primarily to the fact that the Galician maskilim had a further element to contend with—the hasidic movement, which was very active and wielded considerable power in Galicia. Hasidism had little if any relevance for the Berlin maskilim, as scant information about the movement had reached them and—with the exception of Aaron Halle-Wolfssohn, author of the play *Kalut Da'at u-Tzvi'ut* (Frivolity and Hypocrisy; 1794), who was well acquainted with Hasidism and presaged the approach of the Galician Haskalah[148]—it was simply not on their political and theoretical agenda.[149] The Galician maskilim, on the other hand, were forced to deal with Hasidism and play by its rules, engaging in a struggle that took shape under the watchful eye of the Habsburg state, which not only revoked the autonomy of the Jewish communities but also actively sought to Germanize the Jews under its control.[150] Hasidism thus turned the Haskalah, which fought against it and was strengthened by it,[151] into a Jewish political entity that laid the foundations for a kind of existence that was both civil and religious, that is to say a national existence.

Following the maskil Jacob Samuel Bick—who was sympathetic to the hasidic movement and stressed that the hasidim, unlike the followers of the would-be Messiah Sabbatai Zevi, had never left the Jewish fold and remained an integral part of the Jewish people[152]—the struggle between Hasidism and the Haskalah should be viewed as an open struggle between two Jewish political entities, which took place within the Christian public sphere, and in which the state had long refrained from interfering. Despite the best efforts of the maskilim, the state did not take sides in the dispute, and when it finally began to persecute the hasidim (referred to as "religious enthusiasts") in the 1820s and 1830s, the victory of Hasidism was already assured.[153] The struggle of the Galician maskilim against the hasidim was conducted as a struggle between Jewish collectives, which clashed while demonstrating their presence in the public sphere of the Habsburg state—for example, by filing complaints and informing on one another to the authorities. The reason for this was "not only because the maskilim, most of whom were young, lacked all political influence, but because the civil authorities in Austria also oversaw matters pertaining to religion. Complaints were a political tool meant to entrench respect for the law and the idea that the state exercises exclusive regulatory control over all areas of civilian life, including religion—an idea that was entirely new and by no means self-evident."[154] The maskilim in Galicia acted in this spirit of the state's involvement in religion, considering it a natural ally in their war against Hasidism. They informed the government of hasidic contempt for and violations of the law, such as sending money out of the empire (to the Holy Land, by means of donations or pilgrimages disguised as emigration in order to avoid paying departure fees), or engaging in *Schwärmerei*, a term employed in Enlightenment discourse to condemn ecstatic religious enthusiasm, exorcism, and recourse to supernatural powers, perceived as violations of the law forbidding actions that promote religious sectarianism.[155]

Unlike Mendelssohn, who objected to the marking of Jews as a separate collective in the non-Jewish public sphere, early nineteenth-century Galician maskilim, including Erter, chose to identify the Jews as a distinct collective within the European state. Unlike the hasidim, who rejected Joseph II's Edict of Toleration—which gave the Jews freedom of movement and livelihood but also imposed compulsory military service and higher taxes, while reducing Jewish autonomy—maskilim like Naphtali Herz Wessely, who wrote his *Divrei Shalom ve-Emet* (1782) in response to the edict, considered it an important change for the better.[156] The response of the Galician maskilim to the edict clearly demonstrated that the only way in which they could mark themselves as a separate ethnic collective was by means of the Jewish religion, in which they saw the faith of a distinct collective within the non-Jewish public sphere. Since the national signified has no primordial existence but is created through the process of signification,[157] the religious signifier "the Jew within the empire" became the national signified.[158]

The fundamental difference between the Haskalah in Galicia and in Berlin may thus be traced to the presence or absence of the hasidim. Indeed, the Galician maskilim, who openly fought against Hasidism by informing on the hasidim and collaborating with the authorities in their persecution, thwarting them, and seeking their "acculturation," acted not merely as citizens but as a Jewish collective present as such within the Christian, European public sphere. The Galician maskilim collaborated with the authorities against their own coreligionists, the hasidim, facilitating and even inviting official interference in the Jewish sphere (by keeping an eye on the district rabbis and the hasidim or, to cite a specific example, favoring government intervention in the case of Orenstein ban of excommunication).[159]

Ultimately, the maskilic struggle against Hasidism was an effort to reform and ameliorate the hasidic presence within the Christian public sphere. Erter's Watchman may thus be understood as an apparatus of colonial domination by the maskilim of the hasidim and the Jewish people as a whole. Indeed, the Watchman for the House of Israel can be seen as an expression of the maskilic aspiration to reform and control the hasidim and Jews in general, which assumed the form of colonial discourse, the objective of which is "to construe the colonized as a population of degenerate types on the basis of racial origin," in order to justify their control, by means of instruction, administration and the dissemination of knowledge.[160] The Galician maskilic struggle against Hasidism was thus an internal Jewish struggle, characterized by abjection and disgust toward those they deemed incorrigible and unrestrainable. By means of this rejection, the maskilim also constituted their own identity, prefiguring modern nationalism.

## 5

Erter's "Moznei Mishkal" is thus a text that allows Galician Jews to take part in European history, by articulating a national discourse in which static Judaism emerges from the contradictions of modern Jewish existence in Europe to join a dynamic, collective, European narrative that is both internal and external to it. The physical act of tearing the book in "Moznei Mishkal" is a symbolic national act that dismembers the fetish of Orenstein's tome and invalidates the rabbinical solution to the contradictions of modern Jewish existence in Galicia, consisting primarily in increasing isolation. Erter does so by physically destroying the book as a commodity, thereby revealing the criminal history of the book's production, dismantling the ostensibly static presumption of holiness of the rabbinical book and replacing it with national messianism. In Marxist terms, this action may be described as eliminating the book from the cycle of production and consumption (writing and reading), critically exposing it as a fetishistic commodity.

For theological reasons, however, as noted above, the belief of Galician maskilim in political emancipation as Jews ran counter to their ambition to integrate into Christian society. In response to this contradiction, a postcolonial hybrid subject developed. Since the maskilic struggle was an internal Jewish struggle, rooted in dissociation from its Jewish enemies, while continuing to identify as Jewish, the Hebrew maskil evolved as a hybrid subject, disrupting the dichotomy between "self" and "other," "inside" and "outside."[161]

The internal Jewish struggle between maskilim and hasidim unfolded before the eyes of the Habsburg state, exhibiting the Jews in the European public sphere and rendering the hybrid maskilic subject visible. Not only did this nationalism lack a definite national subject, based to some degree on a coherent imagined narrative,[162] its presence within the European public sphere shared by Christians and Jews disrupted the sharp dichotomy between them. When Jewish religious existence comes into contact with Christian existence, its religious identity expands, to include new, universal elements, bringing it closer to the model of European national identity—no longer purely religious.

And indeed the Jewish religious subject did constitute itself as a sovereign subject, albeit not as the subject of a nation state but as a hybrid product of the relationship between the colonial (the maskil) and the colonized (the hasid), who share the same faith and religious identity. In other words, the tension between particularism and universalism—an inherent part of the existence of Jews as a minority within the empire—remained, for the Galician maskilim. That is to say, it assumed national characteristics without being "resolved" by what Hannah Arendt described as "the conquest of the state by the nation," when, "in the name of the will of the people the state was forced to recognize only 'nationals' as citizens, to grant full civil and political rights only to those who belonged to the national community by right of origin and fact of birth."[163] Thus, contrary to Aamir Mufti's claim,[164] the mere existence of such hesitant Jewish nationalism does not imply that Zionism was the only solution to the deep conflict created by the Jewish Question.

The fact that Benedict Anderson's theories fail to explain the rhetoric of nationalism—a modernist phenomenon originating from the state (in response to Enlightenment but not in opposition to it) yet rooted in "antimodernist" elements such as religion—demands a complex, dialectical approach.[165] Thus, contrary to Mendelssohn's view of Judaism as atemporal, existing outside history, with no progressive narrative,[166] the proto-nationalism of the Galician maskilim posited a dialectical movement in history. And that is how the Galician maskilim, faced with the challenge of Hasidism, responded to the passage of the Haskalah from Berlin (where the movement began to wane in the 1790s) to the Austrian Empire—including Galicia. One of the agents of this transition was the maskil Mendel Lefin, who settled in Brody and Tarnopol after having spent four years in Berlin, in close contact with Moses Mendelssohn and his circle.[167] The ban issued by Jacob Orenstein, who openly condemned study of Mendelssohn's German translation of the Bible,[168] was clearly an attempt to stop the Berlin Haskalah from making inroads into Galicia.

In Galicia, the most influential of the transitional figures, who spread the Berlin Haskalah throughout Europe, was Herz Homberg (1749–1841), who served as a private tutor in the Mendelssohn household and went on to pursue a successful career in the Austrian Empire, forcefully and provocatively acting to transform Jewish education and promote the Germanization of Jewish culture. Also worth noting is the role played by Vienna's Hebrew publishers, who offered maskilim employment as well as the possibility of publishing their own works. One of the most prominent figures in this context was Shalom HaCohen, who left Berlin after an unsuccessful attempt to revive the journal *ha-Me'asef*, subsequently roaming Europe, from London to Vienna. Upon his arrival in Galicia, he met with an ardent welcome from none other than Isaac Erter (in a letter dated 7 Tevet 5581/12 December 1820): "Your arrival in our midst, sir! Your arrival in our midst from the far reaches of the land of Ashkenaz [Germany] to the lands of our dispersal, is like the arrival of the sun at the end of winter from the chambers of the south to the inhabitants of the north. With the rays of your countenance revive, as it [the sun] does, the face of a desolate land, desolate for eons, to bear delightful fruits to gladden heart and soul."[169] HaCohen worked as a proofreader at the publishing house of Anton Schmid, where he also printed the journal he founded, *Bikurei ha-Itim*—around which Hebrew maskilim coalesced to form a "republic of letters."[170] An interesting aspect of the creation of such a republic, which laid the groundwork for the constitution of an imagined national community, was the development of the literary awareness that a reader may also be a literary critic. Literary criticism proper only appeared later in Galician Hebrew literature—in *Bikurei ha-Itim*, for example.[171] As early as 1821, however, Juda Jeitteles, a regular contributor to *Bikurei ha-Itim*, published a collection of his early works called *Benei ha-Ne'urim* (Children of Youth), in Prague—that is, within the confines of the Habsburg Empire. The book includes a poem entitled "El ha-Mevakrim Bein Tov le-Ra Ohavey ha-Emet ve-ha-Tushiyah" (To the Discerners Between Good and Ill, Lovers of Truth and Wisdom): "Men of truth! Show no partiality in judgment / Love honesty, judge righteously / Spare neither the father nor the sons / Examine thoroughly, seek every breach / Faithfully scrutinize the flaws of the children / Conceal neither the obvious nor the obscure / Note every error, let nothing pass / Pray tell if something is as a closed book / Fire criticism in a crucible, strike the writers with a staff / But in anger remember compassion / For these children all—are the sins of youth."[172] To this we may add the maskilic literary elite's self-awareness, evident in another of Jeitteles's poems, "'Al ha-Medabrim Alay Lemor Sone Hu et Hevrat ha-Adam" (To Those Claiming I Hate the Company of People): "I love company as much as you / But my life is short and I loathe / To spend moments consorting with the ignorant / Therefore I abhor and spurn all society / For it has been my observation / The ignorant nowadays are many."[173]

The Galician maskil Meïr (Max) Halevi Letteris made a significant contribution to the constitution of Jewish proto-national discourse with his "Be'ur Kitvei Kodesh" [Exegesis of Holy Scriptures][174]—an interpretive essay on the second chapter of Psalms, written from a critical, literary perspective, focusing—following Mendelssohn's aesthetic reading of Scripture—on the sublimity of the poetry of the psalm and its rhetorical structure. The essay was published in the Galician journal *ha-Tzfirah* (Zolkva, 1823), founded and edited by Letteris himself. *ha-Tzfirah*—in many ways a Galician successor to *ha-Me'asef*—was short lived, however (lasting only a single issue), due to opposition by the Galician rabbis. The rabbis' ire may have been aroused by the journal's publication of an essay by the radical maskil Judah Leib Mieses (1823), or by Letteris' own Hebrew translation of Lucian's satire "Alexander the False Prophet," about the oracle Alexander of

Abonoteichus[175]—apparently aimed at the figure of the hasidic tzadik. It was primarily Letteris' maskilic militancy that set him (and Galician maskilim in general) apart from the Berlin Haskalah. Letteris went well beyond satire—whether in his appeal to the "gentle reader" or in his explicit attack on the unseemly practices of Galician Jews in general and of the hasidim in particular.[176] It is interesting to note that, alongside the universalist maskilic texts published in *ha-Tzfirah*, Letteris included his unmistakably nationalistic poem "Yonah Homiyah" [Cooing Dove].[177] Similarly, in his preface to *ha-Tzfirah*, Letteris celebrates both the theological importance of Hebrew, as the language of Scripture, and the language's appeal by universal standards—reflecting the German-Hebrew linguistic duality of the Galician maskilim.[178] In "Yonah Homiyah," Letteris also expresses "negation of the diaspora"—a standard that would later be borne by Zionism—as well as the self-accusation of having abandoned God,[179] marking the theological basis of the poem, essential to the articulation of proto-nationalism.[180]

## 6

The fact that the Galician maskilim acted as a proto-national Jewish collective in the European public sphere was thus largely the result of their bitter struggle against Hasidism, in the context of which the maskilim constituted themselves as a collective, literary republic,[181] providing a kind of nursery for the cultivation of national articulations. The resistance they encountered, primarily on the part of the hasidim, strengthened the Galician maskilim[182] and fostered the development of extensive ties between them, mostly around the journal *Bikurei ha-Itim*,[183] to the point that they may be viewed as having constituted an imagined national community. Indeed, it was the fierce battle between Hasidism and the Haskalah, which defined shared Jewish political space in early nineteenth-century Eastern Europe, that gave rise to the first signs of the constitution of a Jewish national subject in Hebrew literature. These two Jewish movements essentially acted as complementary political opposites, with their respective literary works representing diametrically opposing genres, both relating to the same object: the hasidic tale, in which the tzadik is glorified and exalted above ordinary mortals; and maskilic satire, in which the tzadik and his followers are mocked and belittled. What the two enemy camps had in common was that both considered the tzadik and his followers the main target of their literary and political endeavors. In offering two opposing visions of ideal Jewish existence in Eastern Europe, they actually reinforced the commitment and solidarity that characterized Jewish life in early nineteenth-century Eastern Europe. Most important of all, it would seem, neither Isaac Erter nor Joseph Perl before him had any intention of excluding the hasidim from the Jewish people. Rather, they wished to reform their perverse ways and bring them into line with the modern norms that governed the Eastern European public sphere.

The barbs of Erter's satire were aimed at the holiness that the hasidim ascribed to their own texts. The hasidim perceived the material books as magical objects, capable of acting in both the upper and the lower world. Erter, probably inspired by Perl's scathing satire on the holy writings of Rabbi Adam, received by the Ba'al Shem Tov,[184] sought to release the book from the realm of holiness. His attempt to afford the book messianic significance, however, prevents him from completing the task, leaving the holy presence of the book as it was.

Employing satire, Erter attacks the irrational and superstition-filled world of the hasidim, painting their material and spiritual lives in a ridiculous light—by the rationalist, universalist standards of the Haskalah. It is worth noting once again, however, that Erter does so without denigrating the Jewish religion in any way. Ultimately, his attacks are those of a believer, who observes the precepts. In this he resembles most of the maskilim of his and the following generation, who, for all their attempts to reform Jewish life and their rationalist approach to religion, rarely crossed the threshold into deism—that is, the repudiation of divine revelation and belief in "natural religion," which posits the existence of religious elements common to all rational people.[185]

Erter's satire is thus an unusual admixture of genres, the poetic complexity of which has been pointed out in a number of critical reviews. While Samuel David Luzzatto crowned Erter "Ne'im Satirot Yisra'el" (the Sweet Satirist of Israel—a play on the Psalmist's well-known epithet "Ne'im Zemirot Yisra'el," the Sweet Singer of Israel),[186] and Simon Halkin saw in Erter's collection *The Watchman for the House of Israel* "a series of true satires,"[187] it is nonetheless often described as an allegory. The very focus of Erter's satire—the book—is perceived as both an object of satire and an allegorical signifier.[188] As Halkin wrote of "Moznei Mishkal": "The story does not develop through the dream, but rather the dream develops through story, as intended. Since the intention was to weigh real values, the author effectively moves forward using the same staging with which he began, and weighs the various values on the scales in the dream. . . . Even if the narrative framework that describes human qualities were to be taken away, nothing would be lost, because the discussion of qualities of the soul stands on its own, without any framework."[189]

The Watchman for the House of Israel that Erter created appears in the text as one whose satire flows from the basic contradiction in which he lives, as a Jewish intellectual in a Christian country. The Watchman is thus a maskil writer but also a maskil reader, who soothes his spirit with the works of the "ancient poets and bards of times past, whose language I know."[190] The contradiction inherent in Erter's (and the Watchman's) situation in fact fuels his allegorical satire, which—as in Žižek's analysis of antisemitism—chooses the hasidim and the rabbis as objects of a hatred meant to resolve the satirist's own, internal contradiction, through excess, surplus, and literary pleasure.[191] As in any satire, Erter's attack against the rabbis and the hasidim is categorical and unrelenting. Its universalist criterion ignores nuance, portraying the Haskalah as the antithesis of Hasidism and the rabbinate. Erter's satirical use of the fetishization of the rabbinical book represents Orenstein, as well as the authors of hasidic texts, as stereotypes of fraud and cultural backwardness. However, "the fetish or stereotype gives access to an 'identity' which is predicated as much on mastery and pleasure as it is on anxiety and defence, for it is a form of multiple and contradictory belief in its recognition of difference and disavowal of it."[192] In other words, the fetish of the book is a metonymy for the stereotypical hasidic writers and Orenstein, by means of which the maskilic Watchman establishes his supervision and control over them—identifying with them as Jews while recoiling from their vulgar backwardness as Jews (simultaneously recognizing and denying the difference between them). The economy of desire thus allows the Watchman/Erter (from the contradictory perspective of a maskilic Jew in the European sphere) to derive the pleasure of nationalism from the act of representing the stereotype that he opposes. Indeed, the fact that Erter's rationalist satire spills over into ironic exaggeration, into the grotesque—the comical spectacle of the weighing of the books—serves the desire entailed in the articulation of the national sign.[193]

Erter's battle against Hasidism is a battle between coreligionists and, as a proto-national struggle, naturally seeks commonality with its (internal) adversaries. Thus, despite the dichotomous nature of the conflict between the satirist and members of his own people, the allegory he employs acts as an additional, opposing force. Erter's allegory, inasmuch as it is proto-nationalist, may be described as national allegory and, as such, runs counter to the universalizing aspect of his satire. In fact, the contradiction between Jewish religious particularism and the universalism of the modern state—ultimately Christian—parallels the contradiction within Erter's allegorical (particularist) satire (universal), written as a national allegory. Viewing it in Marxist terms, as a fetishized commodity, we may call upon Žižek's analysis (following Jacques Lacan) of Marx as the inventor of the symptom, the fissure, the asymmetry, the imbalance of the bourgeois universalism it undermines. The symptom is "a particular element which subverts its own universal foundation, a species subverting its own genus,"[194] realized in the ideology created by the fetish, through the stupefying ritual of the weighing of the books on golden scales.[195]

This allegorical (particular) subversion of the satirical (universal) lies at the heart of Reuben Brainin's criticism of Erter's satires, as lacking the qualities of European satire.[196] It is this subversion that affords Erter's text its hybridity—between East and West, Judaism and Christianity, the literature of a persecuted minority and that of a sovereign civil society. This subversion is also the subversion of the universality of the utopian ideal,[197] limiting the political aspirations of Erter's utopia (like those envisaged in many other Hebrew maskilic satires) to a weak form of sovereignty, far from the paradigm of the sovereign nation-state. Contrary to the realization of an ideology (a national ideology, for example) that acts as if a particular thing is indeed an embodiment of universal value,[198] the weakness of Erter's national ideology lies in the nature of satire itself, since the laughter and irony that subvert ruling authority and ideology (such as Hasidism or the rabbinate) are often an integral part of the system[199]—that is, the Jewish theological framework common to Erter and his ideological opponents. Both Erter and his opponents know full well that they are lying (stealing others' letters or, like the hasidim in Perl's *Megaleh Temirin*, consciously and cleverly plotting their crimes), effectively taking the position that Žižek calls cynical.[200]

Erter's literature is collectivist—always political and primarily disruptive of the normative territorial order of the nationalism of the nation-state—termed "minor literature" by Deleuze and Guattari.[201] What is unusual about Erter's texts is that they are written in Hebrew, that is to say, contrary to Deleuze and Guattari's definition of minor literature, not in the language of the state. At the same time, however, Erter acted within the European state, with his desire for emancipation standing in sharp contradiction to his desire to preserve Jewish identity. The maskilim were thus caught between the contradictions ascribed to Jews by the Enlightenment with which they identified. On the one hand, Jews were particularist and irrational, their loyalty to the state questionable. On the other hand, they were on the verge of creating a national identity—likely (in the manner of national identities) to be no less creative and constructive than disruptive. The liminal figure of the Jew located Jewish national identity within the surrounding European sphere (albeit as a problematic element), thus necessarily entailing both exclusion and inclusion, marking boundaries and seeking to erase them, but primarily within the self-constitution of the Jew as a member of a national minority and consequently exposed to the dangers of displacement and banishment.[202]

This political hybridity is typical of the poetics of Erter's allegorical satire. The maskilic satirist's primary tool is irony,[203] expressed in "Moznei Mishkal" as it is in Erter's satire "Gilgul Nefesh" (Transmigration of a Soul, 1845), described by Shmuel Werses as "based on the interplay between two different planes—the one flowery and exalted, drawing upon the language of the Bible, and the other the murky, profane reality of the Jewish present."[204] Moshe Pelli described the essential feature of this type of irony as the application of sacred or biblical terminology to fundamentally secular situations. According to Pelli, Erter was the first Modern Hebrew writer to use this method as a literary device to satirical effect.[205] There is, however, no such dichotomy between sacred and secular. Nevertheless, what Pelli fails to demonstrate with regard to language, he finds in Erter's approach to Jewish religion, which Erter, like other maskilim, had no intention of undermining, focusing rather on what he saw as superstition and negative social phenomena.[206]

It is the internal conflict of genre between allegory and satire at the core of "Moznei Mishkal" that enables the literary constitution of Erter's protonational subject. Particularist allegory and universalist satire contradict each other, never creating the "concrete universal" of the national subject. The passage from the fetish of the rabbinical book to the fetish of the golden scales is neither simple nor smooth, as the abstraction of the fetishisized commodity is not maintained throughout the narrative. The history of critical writing on "Moznei Mishkal" reflects this vacillation and the unsuccessful efforts to reconcile the two poles of the contradiction. See, for example, the debate between Joseph Klausner, who stressed the author's successful integration of the work's various components, and Simon Halkin, who emphasized the lack of connection between them. Klausner, saw Erter as a national writer for all intents and purposes, who "gave a tremendous impetus to the rebirth of the nation by reviving its national literature in its new-ancient tongue,"[207] anticipating the Jewish nationalism of the second half of the nineteenth century—reflected in the writing of Eliezer Zweifel and Peretz Smolenskin.[208] Klausner describes the form employed by Erter in his satires as that of "the romantic vision: supernatural apparitions, dreams, and fantasies." On the other hand, Klausner argues that "the content of the satires is realistic: the actions condemned by the satirist, the beliefs and opinions underlying the events, are entirely real, absolutely true." Ostensibly, there is a contradiction between the dream/fantasy of the allegory (the particular allegory of the narrator recounting his dream) and the satire (the universal judgment of the scales), which takes place in the real world. Klausner's harmonizing nationalist approach resolves the contradiction through the implied identification of the allegory with romantic vision (in fact creating a national allegory). He thus concludes that "truth and fantasy coalesce in Erter's satires, making them all the more appealing."[209]

Contrary to Klausner and his nationalizing viewpoint, Halkin did not seek the harmonious resolution of the internal conflicts within Erter's satire. Halkin, who explicitly stated that Erter's work displays only the initial signs of nationalism,[210] rejected Klausner's romantic interpretation, focusing rather on the satire's irreconcilable component parts and hybridity. According to Halkin, "The situation (a dream, a conversation with the dead) is not essential to the narrative itself. It does not interact with the content, but merely provides it with a discursive framework."[211] Halkin thus recognized the postcolonial nature of early nineteenth-century Galician maskilic literature. Unlike Klausner's blatant nationalization, Halkin identified what has been described here as the hybridity of the maskilic literary text that constituted a proto-national moment—apparently in response to the deep contradiction at the root of Jewish civil existence in the multinational Habsburg Empire. This discrepancy between universal citizenship and particular religion comes to the fore whenever the two are present together in the public sphere, they and are accurately reflected in the poetic poles of "Moznei Mishkal": the particularist allegory and universalist satire. The abstraction of the fetish form is not readily exchangeable and therefore fails to conform to the Marxist description of the smooth transition of commodities from seller to buyer, by virtue of its abstract equality of value.

Erter's text openly displays the contradiction between allegory and satire as well as the contradictions internal to each, culminating in the satirical lampooning of Jacob Orenstein, whose ban against the maskilim in Lvov forced Erter to leave the city. The lampoon is, at once, personal and specific, actualizing the text,[212] as well as an allegory for the general struggle conducted by the maskilim. On the one hand, the explicit reference to Orenstein as the target of the satire turns the satirical narrator, the Watchman, from a champion of the universal values of integrity and decency to a proponent of his own particularist revenge. In other words, the satire passes from the universal to the particular. On the other hand, the private allegorical sign created by the dream confession of the biographical Erter, who had personally suffered at Orenstein's hands, represents all the antagonists of the Galician Haskalah. The lampoon is thus the culmination of the literary process that establishes the satire "Moznei Mishkal" as a national allegory, in the sense described by Fredric Jameson, that is, as a literary form in which the private, libidinal story becomes a national-political one.[213] It also embodies the kind of collectivization and politicization by means of which Deleuze and Guattari identified minor literatures—in this case, that of a national, or rather a proto-national, minority. The fact that it is a proto-national narrative may also be observed in the fact that the conflict created by Erter's Watchman (unlike Frantz Fanon's national intellectual) appears to pertain only to the Jewish people. The Watchman is a partisan spokesman, who criticizes only Hasidism and the rabbinate, as a representative of the Haskalah. Moreover, although he claims to be the "Watchman for the [entire] House of Israel," his sovereignty is extremely partial, embracing a specifically rabbinic, religious Jewish identity (reflected, for example, in the fact that *Bikurei ha-Itim* did not support the Reform movement),[214] subordinate to the sovereignty of the Christian state. Through his rational, enlightened gaze, the Watchman creates the effect of unity and continuity between language and vision, criticized by Foucault.[215] At the same time, however, the tearing of the physical book and the satirical irony that disrupts the effect of coherent continuity between language and reality created by mimesis undermine the abstract, universal maskilic utopia of the rational, enlightened gaze, thereby giving rise to the concrete, political effect of proto-nationalism.

7

Printed books and periodicals were essential to the maskilim, who hailed their physical substantiality, as they used them to further their political and educational goals. At the end of the satire "Gilgul Nefesh," in which Erter juxtaposes maskilic (Moses Mendelssohn) and hasidic texts, the author gives voice to this idea:

> And the spirit said to me: All that you have heard, write in a book, print it and disseminate it among the Jews, that one who has acted as I have and taken the path that I have taken may read it and turn back from his evil and foolish ways. The *hasid* will turn back from drinking his spirits and leaving his family to travel to see his rabbi. The cantor will desist from singing drinking songs and raucous tunes, and intone holy melodies in the house of God. The collector of taxes on meat and candles will have mercy on his people and his community. The kabbalist will return to belief in the God of Israel— one God without image or likeness. The undertaker will return to his holy task without being led astray by greed and without desecrating the dead. The zealot for God and his people will cease persecuting all who deviate from his own zealous path, for judgment is the Lord's. The hasidic rabbis will give thanks to God and say to his followers: Leave me, fools, for I am a scoundrel. The physician will turn back from deception and blinding every eye. He will no longer boast of his wisdom, nor will he look meanly upon his colleagues, even in life. The well-born will come to recognize that a man's entire worth lies in his soul within, that a wise heart, good deeds, and successful actions are a man's glory, and that a brutish man is none improved by all of the honor of his fathers' house. He will come to recognize all of these things, cease his arrogance and his disdain for his brothers and his people, and wed his daughter to a good man, though poor or of low birth. And when even one of these things shall come to pass, I will rise up, soar to the heavens, and rest to my destiny at the end of days.[216]

The invention of the printing press is, of course, closely related to the rise of nationalism. The printed book offered the material possibility of conveying the progressive narrative of the nation to large numbers of readers, greatly extending the boundaries of the imagined national community—to become an imagined community of readers and writers that exists only in the minds of readers who have never met each other face to face.[217] In Vienna, the publisher Anton Schmid printed not only maskilic literature, such as the journal

*Bikurei ha-Itim*, but religious works as well.[218] It is clear, however, that he chose to publish maskilic rather than hasidic works—first and foremost, *Shivhei ha-Besht* (In Praise of the Ba'al Shem Tov), published in 1815.

Erter located this messianic possibility of progressive national narrative in the physical object of the book. Although he does denounce Orenstein's book, *Yeshu'ot Ya'akov*, for its false messianism, this merely serves to highlight his own messianic desire, and since Erter believed in the messianic potential of the rabbinical Hebrew book, it was never his intention to reject the rabbinate outright. On the contrary, his was an expression of hope that the rabbinate, through the medium of Rabbinic Hebrew, might offer an element of true messianism. What is more, in the eyes of Erter and maskilim like him, the Hebrew book itself, in its very physicality, constituted a locus in which the territorialization of the Hebrew language was unfolding. The physical book is a material-linguistic object that offers deterritorialization, that is, a material alternative to the territorialization presented by the national soil. Destroying the physical rabbinical book thus creates a Jewish national moment, albeit one that does not lend itself to teleological interpretation as a harbinger of Zionism, as the "territory" it proposes is not that of the Land of Israel.

Isaac Erter assumes responsibility for a dramatic change in the lifestyle of the collective to which he belongs and the religious identity in which he shares. In this, he follows in the footsteps of the deterritorialized political theology of Moses Mendelssohn, who argued that "he who must sojourn outside the land . . . is subject to alien political laws which, unlike those of his own country, are not at the same time a part of the divine service."[219] As long as he is in exile, however, he must "give to Caesar, and give to God too! To each his own, since the unity of interest is now destroyed. And even today, no wiser advice than this can be given to the House of Jacob. Adapt yourselves to the morals and the constitution of the land to which you have been removed; but hold fast to the religion of your fathers too."[220] Unlike Mendelssohn, however—whose deterritorialization led him to distinguish between the private Jewish sphere, in which religious law must be meticulously observed, and the European public sphere, in which precepts "that depend upon the possession of the Land [of Israel]" are irrelevant[221]—Erter sought to blur the distinction between the spheres, and his struggle against Hasidism and the rabbinate became a revolutionary project to change the way of life of the modern Jew within the European public sphere. Erter's was an attempt to bring Jewish nationalism into European history, rooted in the assumption of responsibility for the fate of the Jewish collective in modern European society. Contrary to the prevailing view in Zionist historiography, which identifies nationalism with auto-emancipation, I would suggest that auto-emancipation is by no means a necessary condition for nationalism. Nationalism may exist in the context of a national minority, which obtains or merely seeks to obtain emancipation from the ruling state rather than constituting it itself. Bruno Bauer was thus wrong in his theological assertion, following Hegel, that "since the moral law that governs Judaism is not based on the community's own will but rather imposed from without [by God], it can never . . . produce a true nation, but merely an imaginary one."[222] The flaw in Bauer's argument lies in the binary opposition he creates between a "real nation" and an "imaginary nation," presupposing the complete identity between communal self-will and auto-emancipation. This binary opposition denies the possibility of partial national existence—whether based on negotiation between communal self-will and emancipation external to the community and beyond its control, or especially on the negotiation between divine law and human will that produced the theological-political heterogeneity at the core of modern Jewish nationalism. It is in this vein that the maskilic nationalism that developed under the Habsburg Empire, in Galicia and in Vienna, should be understood.[223]

The fact that the sovereignty of the Watchman for the House of Israel is weak and partial—a far cry from the "Westphalian sovereignty" of the modern nation-state—is readily apparent in the rhetoric of "Moznei Mishkal." First of all, we must remember that the Watchman, the narrator, clearly exercises his political and moral judgment from an ironic standpoint. The Watchman's sarcastic-political voice is imbued with biting irony—a trope that Paul de Man, in "Rhetoric and Temporality," compares to the symbol, a rhetorical mainstay of sovereign national literature. Erter, however, like other Haskalah writers, notably Joseph Perl, chose satire over symbol, as the literary device most suited to the constitution of weak sovereignty.

Although irony may be a way of saying one thing and meaning another, or of blaming by praise and praising by blame,[224] in terms of its approach to historical reality, irony becomes self-conscious as it demonstrates the inability of the ironist (the Watchman, in this case) to be an integral part of actual history.[225] The ironic Watchman possesses an all-seeing and sovereign gaze while remaining imperceptible to others yet also exists as an ordinary person (anyone can operate the Panopticon), a fact within actual history. In other words, the Watchman not only observes but is also observed and is thus the "observed spectator," whose replacement of the "absent spectator" (the king) is, according to Foucault, the basis for humanism.[226]

For example, in the following passage, the Watchman refers to the hasidim ironically as "sages of truth": "The books of these kabbalists and their rabbis are, measure for measure, like the books of the idolaters and their priests. My heart went out when I saw the books of the kabbalists and the sages of truth equal in weight to the books of the prophets of deceitful minds, who sell lies at a dear price and bequeath evil and foolishness to the people, only to fill their own pockets with gold and their bellies with delicacies."[227] The maskilic irony of Erter's Watchman for the House of Israel thus adopts a universalist stance, criticizing Jewish (hasidic and rabbinical) history from without—paradoxically, a fact within Jewish history. It therefore comes as no surprise—since the traditional image of satire as a constant and dichotomous confrontation between absolute good and absolute evil, devoid of nuance or ambivalence, is in fact without basis[228]—that the Hebrew maskilim, who used irony as a tool in their struggle against Hasidism, were themselves, albeit not in a constant and fixed manner, an integral part of the ethno-theological object of their attacks. It is Jewish satire and irony directed at Jews and, as such, is incapable of creating a symbolic, progressive narrative with a clear teleology, the utopian realization of which would lie on the universal plane of Enlightenment morality, well beyond the confines of internal Jewish affairs. The irony of the Watchman's satire functions within Jewish ethnic and theological boundaries, and is thus a far cry from absolute, unequivocal, universal irony. Furthermore, if we consider that it is also, primarily, the irony of the weak maskilic minority, pitting itself against the growing power of Hasidism in Galicia, it becomes clear that it is the irony of a weak and limited Jewish national sovereign.

As early as 1823, Jacob Samuel Bick, in his essay "El Maskilei Benei 'Ami" (To the Maskilim Among My People), published in Meïr (Max) Letteris's journal *ha-Tzfirah*, called upon Galician Jews to pursue agriculture in the diaspora, not in the Land of Israel.[229] More than a decade after the appearance of "Moznei Mishkal," Galician Hebrew literature presented an array of options for territorial Jewish nationalism outside the Land of Israel—Jewish agricultural settlement in the Crimea, for example, promoted by Joseph Perl in *Boḥen Tzadik*.[230] Erter himself, in "Kol Kore li-Vney Yisra'el Toshvei Eretz Galitzyah" (Appeal to the Children of Israel Residing in the Land of Galicia), written in 1848/9, invited Galician Jews, following their emancipation by Emperor Franz Joseph I, to join an association he had helped found, which aimed to settle Jewish laborers as farmers in Galicia (the Galizischer Jüdischer Ackerbau-Verein). In this appeal, Erter relates to the contradiction posed by Jewish existence in the Christian public sphere, suggesting that the association's founder, the esteemed Meir Kalir, might (due to his lofty standing) help to resolve the contradiction, by seeking imperial guarantees for the safety of Jewish farmers working the land on Sundays.[231] Turning the rabbinical Hebrew book into the physical arena of the internecine war between the Haskalah, Hasidism, and the rabbinate would appear to have paved the way for anchoring Galician Hebrew maskilic discourse in territory other than the Land of Israel. Shifting the focus of national discourse from territory to language as printed word created a linguistic space the national territorialization of which could serve as an instrument for the constitution of a modern Jewish national identity in any territory, even outside the Land of Israel.

Chapter 3

# Isaac Erter's Anti-Hasidic Satire "Hasidut ve-Hokhmah"

I

Isaac Erter published his anti-hasidic satire "Hasidut ve-Hokhmah" (Hasidism and Wisdom) in 1836, in the maskilic periodical *Kerem Hemed* (Vineyard of Delight).[1] In it, the Watchman tells his own story, "as one of the children of our people who reside in the land of Poland"[2]—that is, the collective biography of a typical Jewish boy from Poland, probably Galicia (part of Poland before partition). The story includes the boy's marriage at a young age to a girl who died soon after, and was followed by another ("And my relatives laid another in my bosom, in her place"). He is entirely passive and dutifully accepts the woman he is given as a wife. In the spirit of maskilic criticism, no stock is placed in the active emotion of love, and he treats the entire affair as a kind of financial transaction. He has inherited some money from his father and expects his prospects to improve with the dowry he will receive from his new father-in-law. His own money soon runs out, however, and his father-in-law turns out to be a swindler. The manner in which the boy loses his money is emblematic of the economically unproductive lifestyle of European Jews who, as "righteous and decent folk,"[3] borrowed for a living. The explanation the Watchman offers for his desperate financial circumstances and inability to provide for his family exposes him to the full brunt of maskilic disapproval of those who spend their time in study rather than engaging in honest labor: "I had not been accustomed to labor from my youth, to find a hand's living by the work of my fingers, and I dared not turn the soil of the land with a hoe, for it is a shameful thing that my people which resides in the land of Poland should dig her food from the earth's embrace and make sustenance grow in its furrows to satisfy her hunger."[4]

Rather than trying to earn a living, the narrator abandons his family and joins a hasidic community, described in the most offensive and appalling terms, highlighting its utter wretchedness and lack of basic hygienic standards: "I longed to join their community and did so. Like one of their rabbis, I cleansed myself and anointed my feet [passed my water] early in the morning, and the walls of the study hall reeked and rotted, so great was the quantity of water that I emptied on them day after day, inside and out. As I prepared myself for prayer; my sidelocks would drip with water, having washed my flesh clean in a pool of fetid water [the *mikve* or ritual bath]."[5] Suspicious of the sanctimonious dishonesty of the hasidim and their miracles, the narrator begins to search for answers in books, tentatively exploring the Haskalah but venturing no further. It is only after meeting with a true maskil that he embraces its path and joyfully immerses himself in its texts.

The Watchman then falls asleep, and the plot shifts to his dream, in which two allegorical female figures ("unlike any daughter of the earth"),[6] *Hasidut* (Hasidism) and *Hokhmah* (Wisdom), fight over him. The figures are described in sharp contrast to each nother: Hasidut as vulgar and blatantly sexual, and Hokhmah as pure and cultured. The narrator (the Watchman) goes on to describe the "rite of passage" from hasid to maskil as a dramatic struggle between these two female figures, each presenting arguments she believes will attract him to her side.

The Watchman's panoptic gaze allows him to exercise social supervision in the name of Enlightenment universalism. The universality of the Panopticon removes, or rather eliminates, all opposition to the rational efficacy of his supervision, as nothing can withstand the power of his gaze. The gaze of Erter's narrator, the Watchman for the House of Israel, is the hegemonic gaze of sovereignty, supervising all Jews—the hasidim in particular—in order to normalize—through Haskalah—their incongruous and indecorous presence in the public sphere.[7]

In order to constitute himself as sovereign—or rather to render necessary his self-constitution as such—the Watchman must, as Carl Schmitt argues, proclaim a state of emergency. This is precisely what Erter does in his manifesto, "Tekhunat ha-Tzofeh," in which he appoints himself sovereign over the entire Jewish people. In the essay, he does not merely describe the political state of European Jewry but declares it a state of exception: "The kingdom of Israel toppled as it failed to heed the voice of its seers; their realm was lost, Jacob ceased to have a ruler and a king."[8] In the very act of proclaiming a state of emergency, the Jewish precarious condition, according to Schmitt, the proclaiming subject constitutes himself as sovereign.

Setting this mechanism in motion is both effective and just, as the sovereign's authority comes from God, creator of the universe and of universal law, by which all men are bound. Indeed, in his very first sentence, the Watchman describes years gone by, when "God set Israel a statute and law by the hand of the father of all prophets, Moses, His faithful servant; God set shepherds over his people, seers among His community."[9] In contrast to the lofty Enlightenment ideal of autonomous man as his own sovereign, Erter constituted the maskilic intellectual as sovereign—entrusted with the apparatus of power, control, and leadership—over European Jewry. And indeed, in his descriptions of past and present Jewish political reality Erter evokes the divine authority of the prophets, "seers among His community," who "saw visions of God and beheld the divine; He placed His message in their mouths, and His word on their tongues, to preach to the House of Jacob, to speak to the House of Israel. . . . They were the people's teachers, leaders, chastisers and consolers."[10] The change in Jewish political theory wrought by Isaac Erter, heralding the constitution of a modern Jewish sovereign—if only within the confines of the utopian imagination of Hebrew literature—may be understood in light of Carl Schmitt's famous assertion, "All significant concepts of the modern theory of the state are *secularized theological concepts.*"[11]

Erter saw divine revelation as the source of Jewish law, as well as the source of the Watchman's sovereignty. In this, Erter followed in the footsteps of Moses Mendelssohn, whose influence was particularly strong among the Galician maskilim.[12] From a rationalist perspective, Mendelssohn considered Judaism a religious community, with an ethical identity common to all religions, and shared Lessing's view (expressed in *Nathan the Wise*) that "natural religion" may serve as a basis for tolerance between religions. Nevertheless, and despite his rational interpretation of the religious precepts, he continued to view the Sinaitic revelation to the Israelites as a historical event and the foundation of Jewish law.[13]

As noted above, Erter describes his own revelation experience as follows: "His image is before me when I behold the world and its fullness, the laws and cycles of its hosts. When my eyes rove over the face of this earth, when I gaze upon the array of order and change that the Creator established at the time of creation, then does my heart contemplate the loving-kindness, greatness, goodness, and wisdom of God."[14] This anti-deist revelation-by-gaze represents a dramatic shift in the very concept of revelation. The Watchman characterizes his contemplation of the wonders of creation as "His [God's] image is before me." God does not return his gaze ("God has never appeared to me eye to eye"), but it is a form of revelation nonetheless,[15] which he observes with his "eyes of flesh." The ancient form of revelation is no longer, but it has been replaced by a new, modern revelation, which draws its vocabulary from the realm of romantic imagination.

Romantic poetry is often described as an immediate—that is, unmediated—representation of the divine. The importance of a political theology based on the kind of revelation that constitutes the Watchman as sovereign thus lies in the immediacy between the Watchman's supervising gaze and the divine supervision or providence revealed by that gaze. The Watchman's proclamation of a Jewish state of emergency—the act that constitutes him as sovereign, observer, and supervisor of his people—is an expression of his consciousness as sovereign and, inasmuch as the narrator is the Watchman himself, is an articulation of self-consciousness. In other words, the moment at which he proclaims himself sovereign, on the basis of the unmediated revelation he has experienced, also marks the beginning of the Watchman's self-consciousness. It is thus the moment of mediation, of transition from consciousness to self-consciousness, from immediate knowledge of the divine to awareness of that knowledge, undermining its immediacy and therefore the validity of the revelation itself. It is this romantic and irresolvable paradox of the necessary separation of consciousness from the self-consciousness that negates it[16] that the satire's romantic narrative seeks to resolve.

The Watchman's goal is to resolve the paradox by overcoming the inner separation he experiences as sovereign. The dream in which Hasidut and Hokhmah (Hasidism and Wisdom) fight over who will crown the Watchman sovereign over the entire Jewish people on its behalf, is thus the stage on which it unfolds. In narrating this rift between two opposing political desires he hopes to transform his inner separation of consciousness as sovereign, from a separation between two allegorical representations into a symbolic representation of their unification under his absolute rule as the one and only sovereign of the Jewish people.

As Paul de Man has shown, however, this process of transforming abstract, mechanical, mediating allegory into a vital and concrete symbol—that is, a present and immediate revelation that eliminates the mediation between narrative signifier and divine signified—will never arrive at its destination as a symbol that binds them together through the romantic imagination they share. The fact that this process occurs over time, as the plot unfolds, makes the realization of its final goal impossible. The more time passes, the greater the gap and hence the need for allegorical mediation between the signifier and the signified of the moment of revelation. In other words, Erter's romantic attempt to reconcile the two opposing allegories through his satiric narrative gives rise to a growing but ultimately unsatisfiable desire, which renders the struggle between Hasidism and Haskalah a powerful vehicle for the creation of a national sovereign.

The separation may be resolved by means of what Geoffrey Hartman termed "religious myth" (following Hegel and Mircea Eliade), especially Judeo-Christian revelation (as in the case of the Watchman), which affords European consciousness a sense of history.[17] This myth may function as a timeless figure, capable of neutralizing the temporality of intellectual attempts to resolve the sovereign's inner separation of consciousness, by constituting the myth of the nation.

2

The main focus of "Hasidut ve-Hokhmah" is Erter's scathing criticism of Hasidism, rooted—as the title itself suggests—in "wisdom" (*hokhmah*). It is a quality that the hasidim are said to reject, as Joseph Perl remarks in his satire *Megaleh Temirin*, which preceded "Hasidut ve-Hokhmah" and served as a model for all subsequent anti-hasidic literary works: "For every man must cast aside all wisdom."[18] "Hasidut ve-Hokhmah" may be characterized in keeping with Schiller's definition of satire as a sentimental composition that rebels against the contrast between reality and the ideal, to the point of ahistorical despair of any utopia or solution:[19]

> The poet is satirical if he takes as his subject matter the distance from nature and the contradiction between the actual and the ideal.... He can accomplish this seriously as well as facetiously, with passion as well as levity, depending upon whether he dwells in the domain of the will or the intellect. The former happens by means of the censuring or pathetic satire, the latter by means of the amusing satire.... *Thus, the actual world in this case is necessarily an object of aversion,* but what is most important, the aversion must itself

spring in turn from the contrasting ideal. The aversion could also have a merely sensuous origin and be grounded solely in a need frustrated by the actual world.[20]

"Hasidut ve-Hokhmah" may thus be defined as a "censuring or pathetic satire," which, as actual political action, should change the real world for the better. It is a kind of satire that—unlike satire that levels its caustic criticism at the entire human race—leaves room for hope.

The binary approach of maskilic praiseworthiness versus hasidic reprehensibility is reflected in the literary contrast between maskilic satire and hasidic hagiography. In this sense, maskilic anti-hasidic satire may be seen as a direct response to the hasidic genre of the hagiographic tale, in keeping with Shmuel Werses's claim that maskilic literature was, in fact, forged by the hasidic literature it railed against.[21] Werses actually argues, citing Simon Dubnow's classic *Toldot ha-Hasidut* (History of Hasidism), that Haskalah literature played a "purely testimonial role, taking no active part in the conflict itself."[22] For a deeper understanding of the genre, however, we must explore the political function of maskilic anti-hasidic satire, written in the venerable tradition of anticlerical satire, which exposes the mendacity and hypocrisy of the clergy. Any attempt to define the political roles played by the rival genres must include a "symptomatic reading" of the texts, based on the tension between what they appear to be, literary works published for a Hebrew-reading public, and the deeper structures (including political interests) that lie beneath the surface. Exposing this tension between the readily apparent and the hidden elements in these satires will also reveal the poetic mechanism that affords them their political agency in the struggle against Hasidism.

It is the persona of the satirist assumed by the maskilic author that creates the apparent ("surface") satiric text. Exposing the tension between the surface structure of the satire and the political interests it conceals allows us to chart the poetic principles of the satire without falling into the historicist trap, which relates to the satirical text as if it were a historical document. In other words, the censure and denigration of the hasidim in maskilic anti-hasidic satire do not simply attest to maskilic attitudes to Hasidism. They also constitute a poetic mechanism that serves the political interest of the Haskalah, and since this interest requires a stark, dichotomous distinction between Hasidism and Haskalah, the former must be unequivocally vilified, with no room whatsoever for nuance or ambivalence.

The satirical effect of "Hasidut ve-Hokhmah" is the result, first and foremost, of the fact that the clash between the two allegorical figures, Hasidut and Hokhmah (Wisdom, representing the Haskalah), is a struggle for influence over the Watchman, to determine under whose auspices he will become sovereign over the Jewish people. Efforts of the Haskalah in that direction are understandable, as the Haskalah sought a sovereign capable of spearheading its efforts to resolve the Jewish Question through emancipation within the modern European state. The Jewish sovereign's political theology allows him to fight for the political status of European Jews, just as his civil sovereignty allows him to participate in the sovereignty of the European state. The efforts of Hasidut to recruit the Watchman, on the other hand, are soon revealed to be false, aimed only at co-opting him, in order to subvert his power and standing. This is due to the fundamental difference between the political theology of Hasidism and that of the Haskalah. Contrary to the civil sovereignty to which the Haskalah aspired, hasidic political theology rests on the figure of the tzadik as sovereign over the hasidic court and community. Unlike the state sovereignty advocated by the Haskalah, the sovereignty envisioned by Hasidism rejects the actualization forced upon it by the maskilim, while its political approach to the European state entails not civil integration but rather survival, avoidance, and withdrawal into the hasidic court. The temptations that Hasidut holds out to the Watchman are thus attempts at deception, garnering sharp satirical condemnation as evidence of ethical and political corruption.

3

The fundamental dichotomy at the heart of the satire is established in the title "Hasidut ve-Hokhmah" itself and in the epigraph from the book of Proverbs that follows. Rather than reveal that the struggle it describes is between rival political camps, Hasidism and the Haskalah, Erter chose—for obvious political reasons—to juxtapose Hasidism as a historical phenomenon and Wisdom as an ahistorical quality. This is made plain by the epigraph: "Say to wisdom, 'You are my sister,' and call discernment a friend. To keep you from a stranger-woman, from a smooth-talking alien woman."[23] In his commentary on verse 4, Meir Leib Weisser (Malbim) explains the difference between *binah* (discernment), the validity and authority of which are independent of historical circumstances, and the historical contingency of *hokhmah* (wisdom), rooted in the biological-historical bond of familial fraternity:

> Say to wisdom, "You are my sister." The bond of fraternity is a function of birth, while the affinity of friendship is a matter of choice. As we have already noted, humanity cannot discover the principles of wisdom alone, but they must be given to him by God—as the love of a sister is from God. While the human soul possesses all of the faculties that may support wisdom, the principles of wisdom [itself] are instilled in the human soul from the time of its creation, like a sister, related by birth. Discernment, on the other hand, is acquired on one's own, by inferring one thing from another. And that is why it is written, "Call discernment a friend," for it is like a friend with whom one becomes close by choice.[24]

This combination of contingency and ahistoricity—that is, of "Say to wisdom, 'You are my sister'" and "call discernment a friend"—afforded maskilic satire the independent and eternal authority of discernment, as well as that of the historical contingency of wisdom. The Haskalah movement in Galicia—unlike the Berlin Haskalah, which viewed Jews as universal citizens whose religious identity was a private matter—offered the religiously observant Galician Jews a historical and even a national collective identity. In so doing, the Haskalah adopted the political approach reflected in the biblical wisdom literature. Following the destruction of the First Temple and the Judean monarchy, biblical wisdom literature provided a political alternative to traditional Jewish sovereignty.

Erter sought to highlight the unique qualities of wisdom as an allegory for the Haskalah, by means of the distinction in the wisdom literature (for which the Haskalah had a particular affinity; witness Mendelssohn's well-known commentary on Kohelet) between wisdom (*hokhmah*) and discernment (*binah*). This distinction is especially evident in Job 28:12: "But wisdom where is it found, and where is the place of insight [discernment, *binah*]? Man does not know its worth."[25] Wisdom signifies the contingent, limited, and therefore imperfect knowledge of the maskil. The question "Wisdom where (*me-'ayin*) is it found?" decries the limits of human wisdom and its lack of authority to render knowledge absolute truth. Traditional exegesis offers a similar interpretation, reading the phrase as a statement rather than a question: "Wisdom comes from nothingness (*me-'ayin*)." The source of wisdom is nothingness, that is, its contingency stems from the fact that it is self-constituting—corresponding, from Erter's point of view, to the self-constitution of the autonomous subject of the maskil.

Discernment, on the other hand, represents absolute, unlimited, and ahistorical knowledge. The question regarding discernment is thus not "Where is it found?" but "Where is its place?" In other words, how can we know the way to absolute truth? For Erter, biblical "discernment" signifies ahistorical maskilic rationalism, which stands in contrast to the type of rationalism he prefers: the historical contingency of Galician Haskalah.

Erter favors the collective and therefore limited wisdom that signifies the Galician Haskalah, to the ahistorical discernment that would appear to signify the Haskalah of Berlin. The political act performed by Erter in his satire may therefore be defined as fierce opposition to the authority of the hasidic tzadik, which flows from the divine abundance (*shefa*) and thus carries the weight of absolute truth, that is, discernment. Through dissensus, which Rancière defines as the gap between the sensible and the intelligible,[26] Galician maskilic satire creates a distinction between its own commitment to the Jewish religion, which entails historical and contingent wisdom, and the absolute divine truth of the hasidic tzadik, which it decries and disparages. This is a manifestly political act, which includes both scathing criticism of Hasidism and the presentation of Galician Haskalah as a Jewish alternative. Hasidut and Hokhmah thus struggle with each other for influence, that is to say, control over the Watchman. Erter obviously prefers the authority and control of rational Hokhmah to that of irrational Hasidut. The degraded state of the tzadik's sovereignty attacked in the satire parallels the loss of monarchical authority following the destruction of the Temple, attested to in the biblical wisdom literature. The satirist's contempt for the tzadik's sovereignty reflects his belief in Hasidism's inability to deal with the Jewish Question, as outlined in "Tekhunat ha-Tzofeh." In contrast, he viewed the alternative sovereignty offered by maskilic wisdom—based on the historical contingency of the Jewish national collective—as the key to resolving the Jewish Question.

Due to the extreme and scathing nature of Erter's satire, the politics of Hokhmah and Hasidut are grounded in the absolute conflict between friend and enemy.[27] Their respective identities are the result of overdetermination, deriving both from the ahistorical and eternal aspects that classify them as friend or enemy and from the historical elements of their struggle in the actual arena of Jewish life in nineteenth-century Galicia.

In light of the above, we may understand Werses's assertion regarding the contribution of Hasidism to the forging of maskilic literature in the sense that the literary development of anti-hasidic satire as a political tool of the Haskalah entailed the constitution of Hasidism as an absolute enemy. The maskilim needed to present hasidim as excoriated and reviled subjects in order to deny the legitimacy of their presence as Jews in the European public sphere. They wielded satire as a political weapon, in an attempt to neutralize the tarnishing effect of Hasidism on the image of Jews in the eyes of Europeans, which they saw as an impediment to their goal of integrating Jews into European public space. It goes without saying that the satire's contemptuous portrayal of Hasidut's material wretchedness—outlandish clothing, lewdness, vulgarity, and unhygienic behavior, offending civilized sensibilities—serves to highlight the material portrait of the maskil as decent and pure, indicating a sensible and rational temperament.

The second part of the epigraph, "To keep you from a stranger-woman, from a smooth-talking alien woman," represents Hasidism as a lascivious and seductive woman, with "exposed ears and a prominent adam's apple."[28] The description of the figure of Hasidut, as observed by the Watchman, has autobiographical undertones[29]—witness the fact that the Watchman does not limit his characterization of the hasidic enemy to rational, universal arguments, such as its lack of wisdom and discernment. The Watchman's autobiographical voice also notes the intense seductiveness of Hasidism, which had threatened to cloud his rational judgment as a maskil. This subversion of propriety and refinement, as represented by Hokhmah, is conveyed by means of the grotesque figure of Hasidut,[30] which possesses both feminine and masculine characteristics.[31]

Hasidut presents herself as a deceiver in the service of the cult of Hasidism, of which she herself is an adherent: "I practice deceit in all my deeds, in order to pass substance on to my lovers and their storehouses to fill. All my secrets I will pass before you."[32] In contrast, Hokhmah appears as a respectable woman, "the serene and peaceful woman, with a crown [of shining stars] on her head," who appeals to the Watchman's sense of reason: "Amass learning. Gather knowledge. My reason I will pass before you."[33]

The political role assigned to maskilic anti-hasidic satire would thus appears to have been not only to undermine the legitimacy of the hasidic presence in the European public sphere, as an irrational element, but also to counteract the flagrant sexuality of the vulgar and "ludicrous woman,"[34] who—in the spirit of Jewish ethical (*musar*) literature—must be guarded against. As mentioned above, the maskilim saw the hasidim as a source of embarrassment in non-Jewish society, but also as a source of fear within Jewish society, due to the powerful attraction they held. Erter resorted to gender stereotypes in order to represent the dichotomous contrast between Hasidut and Hokhmah, not as a static and ahistorical phenomenon, but as the result of a process in which the Watchman for the House of Israel overcomes his forbidden desires, which threaten to undermine his role as political leader and supervisor of the Jewish people.

Erter places the Watchman on high, affording him a broad perspective of the entire nation, above and beyond its individual political groupings. It is the scathing criticism that the Watchman levels at the Jewish people as a whole that constitutes it as an imagined national unit, encompassing both Haskalah and Hasidism. The Watchman's critical, supervising gaze is a mechanism of control over the entity that he himself creates. Erter thus follows in the footsteps of Israel of Zamość, who, in his satire "Nezed ha-Dema" (A Pottage of Tears), published in 1773, rebuked his people from a high vantage point that allowed him to observe and address them and, in so doing, to constitute them as a single national unit: "Here I stand on a hilltop, to speak from booming thunder's hiding place, to call ruin and to cry destruction, to rage for the Lord's cause, to raise a banner on a high mountain, to command the Hebrews to listen."[35]

The first verse in Erter's epigraph to "Hasidut ve-Hokhmah" ("Say to wisdom, 'You are my sister,' and call discernment a friend") represents the idea of the maskilic struggle against Hasidism as rooted in the universal, normative, and egalitarian identity promoted by the Enlightenment. The second verse ("To keep you from a stranger-woman, from a smooth-talking alien woman"), on the other hand, represents a very different approach, stemming from a clear distinction between identities. In the passage from the first verse to the second, the author departs from the Enlightenment ideal of gender blindness to embrace identity politics, characterizing the Jewish woman signifying Hasidism as overtly sexual and therefore a threat to the male maskil.[36]

4

The two genres—maskilic satire and the hasidic hagiographic tale—represent different models of sovereignty. Erter's narrator, the Watchman, is a sovereign who, with his Olympian gaze, supervises and guides his people. He exercises his sovereignty by virtue of his commitment to the Enlightenment values of universal morality and the laws of the modern state, and judges those under his moral rule accordingly. The narrator of the hagiographic tale, on the other hand, is not bound by such values. Unlike the Watchman, who speaks as the sovereign, the hagiographic narrator speaks of his sovereign, the tzadik, whom he praises and exalts as a spiritual, religious, and political authority. It is the authority of the sovereign tzadik that supervises and guides the hasidic community and determines the laws of the hasidic court. Contrary to the Watchman's national sovereignty, the sovereignty of the tzadik is limited to what Martin Buber termed the hasidic *edah*, or community. Unlike Benedict Anderson's imagined national community, the hasidic edah is organized as a non-imagined community, that is, a community in which members know one another face to face, and control does not rely upon the abstract imagination of its subjects.

Both types of sovereignty, however, derive their authority from God. The tzadik is God's representative on earth who, by the flow of divine abundance, is able to establish the hasidic court as a theocratic polity over which he himself rules as sovereign: "The *tzadik* is, in the eyes of his followers, the highest authority, like a king to whom God has granted dominion over the world. This is stated explicitly in the book *Keter Shem Tov* [Crown of the Good Name; Zolkva (Zhovkva), 1793/4 (part 1); and Zolkva, 1794/5 (part 2)]."[37] At the same time, the moral authority of the Watchman also derives from God, albeit via the biblical prophets—Ezekiel, in Erter's case. This theological dimension plays a crucial role in the Watchman's mission, marking him as one who is in communion with divine providence, having experienced a kind of revelation. As in Judah Leib Mieses's anti-hasidic satire *Kin'at ha-Emet* (Zeal for the Truth),[38] the use of revelation in Erter's satires appears to draw directly on the political theology of Moses Mendelssohn who, as noted, never ceased to affirm the validity of the Sinaitic revelation as the absolute basis for Jewish law. Indeed, Erter alludes to the political role of revelation in Mendelssohn's thought, in the Watchman's remarks regarding his delight in "the books of two Moseses [Moses Maimonides and Moses Mendelssohn], who came to offer us their example, following our prophet Moses."[39] The Watchman is thus an expression of what Olga Litvak has termed "romantic religion," in which the figure of the prophet—fashioned through a romantic reading of Scripture—serves as a poetic model.[40]

In "Hasidut ve-Hokhmah," Hasidut seeks to present its own sovereignty as an alternative to maskilic sovereignty. Both types of sovereignty, however, offer a Jewish political solution to the Jewish Question, that is, a political order that purports to defend Jews from the violence that is directed against them, since the act of constituting sovereignty is, in fact, the act of proclaiming a state of emergency. In making such a proclamation, the sovereign assumes the responsibility to defend those he defines as his subjects, and in so doing must also identify the source of danger, that is, define the enemy.[41] The political theology of Hasidism constitutes the tzadkik as sovereign of the theocratic hasidic court, whose authority derives from God. Maskilic anti-hasidic satire therefore seeks to characterize the connection between the tzadik (the hasidic sovereign) and God as false or nonexistent. That is why Hasidut offers the following characterization of the hasidic institution of dynastic succession: "And eminent families marry into the lineage of the man of God."[42] The fact that the dynasty is portrayed as sanctifying God's name "in the eyes of the Children of Israel, by the prodigies and wonders they perform in a world of great [natural] order," merely reinforces the maskilic view regarding the theological breach between the tzadikim and God, since "[in such a world] the hand of God is not seen."[43]

The political theology behind the Watchman's actions is evident in Hokhmah's condemnation of hasidic greed and deception, which focuses on God as the source of Jewish intellectual authority, in the person of the persecuted maskil, for whom the Watchman is a paradigm: "Then hear me, my son! You are still innocent, a stranger to deceit. Your spirit balks at the larceny of holy scoundrels, and your soul loathes their duplicitous hearts. Heed this inner voice, for it is divine feeling that moves you. . . . Look to the men of renown that I, *Hokhmah*, daughter of God, have placed among you . . . who, like the prophets of old, expose the sins [of the people] and do not conceal them. Indeed, like those men of God, they too suffer their fill of insults and spittle, yet remain impervious to taunts and jeers."[44] In contrast, Hasidut describes the ridiculous behavior of the miracle-working tzadik, who serves as the hasidic sovereign: "And they act in the manner of the sons of Eli [1 Samuel 2], yet they are priests to God, whose secret they hold. . . . Eat and drink, dance and prance, sing and satisfy their hearts' every desire—this is what they do for as long as they walk the face of this earth. And they are shown great respect in their lives and in their deaths. They bequeath a fortune and the memory of a holy name to their sons after them, and eminent families marry into the lineage of the man of God."[45] Hasidut encourages the maskil to renounce his sovereign role as Watchman for the House of Israel, in favor of the hasidic sovereignty of the tzadik, arguing that hasidic corruption (which she celebrates) would soon resolve the personal financial difficulties he described in the satire's exposition,[46] as well as procuring further benefits and the adulation of the masses.[47] The Watchman, however, mocks Hasidut, whose attempt to ground the authority of the tzadikim in their reputation as miracle workers is in fact a parody of the constitution of a sovereign moral subject through divine revelation. The fact that Hasidut purports, through the tzadik, to establish rules and exercise control, based on a simulacrum of Enlightenment logic, is a disappointment to the Watchman:

> The ignorant have a passion for wondrous tales, and delight in the extraordinary. Before a child knows to spurn evil and to choose good, his nurse tells him marvelous stories, with which she lulls him to sleep on her lap when he cries. With the breath of her lips she creates new heavens and a new earth in the child's mind, producing creatures at will, to fill the world she has summoned from nothingness. And at her pleasure, she imposes her rule over the land she has fashioned with her words. And the child's parents and teachers instill this land in him, a world that stands firm not to be shaken, even in his old age. And when he grows up and becomes a man about the world, his eyes long to see the unusual, but fail to do so. He thus rejoices in every wonder, and is saddened when its causes are revealed to him. And he is vexed by the Creator of all things, for He established order in the world, and set its upheavals within the boundary of [natural] law.[48]

Like a mirror image of Hasidut's complaints regarding the enlightened order imposed by maskilic sovereignty, Hokhmah portrays the tzadik as a swindler and a charlatan. Nevertheless, Hokhmah creates an imaginary affinity with Hasidut, in order to increase her own power of seduction. She thus presents the Ba'al Shem Tov, the ultimate tzadik, as a pure figure and a worthy sovereign, sanctioned by God. She claims, however, that Hasidut corrupted him and led him astray, making him devious and deceitful, contrary to his true nature. The fact that the Ba'al Shem Tov's subjects lacked judgment allowed him to cheat them, against his better nature, to become an imitation of a tzadik, that is, a false sovereign: "For a heartless people has no use for words of wisdom, and they will call that which they do not understand, holy. In these ways of mine walked my firstborn, Israel [Ba'al Shem Tov], making a name for himself in the land. His hands did not perform the myriad wonders of which the *hasidim* chatter in the streets; his deeds were few, and nary a miracle among them. Only I, *Hasidut*, instilled cunning in the heart of my chosen one, my darling, so that his acts were filled with guile and his handiwork with ruses."[49]

## 5

Although the satirical genre would seem to dictate an inflexible dichotomy between Hasidut and Hokhmah, and indeed Hasidut is entirely without wisdom or reason, Erter chose to ascribe irrational sexual desire to both of his allegorical figures, as a kind of universal trait. Considering the blatant gender bias in "Hasidut ve-Hokhmah," it is no coincidence that the trait is ascribed to two women—allegories for Hasidism and Haskalah.

The legitimacy that Erter affords the representation of sexual desire, albeit in a negative light, illustrates a fundamental difference between the literary views of the Berlin Hebrew Haskalah and those of its Galician successor. The centrality of sexual desire in "Hasidut ve-Hokhmah" stands in stark contrast to the admonition by Naphtali Herz Wessely—a leading figure in the Berlin Haskalah—to the writers of *ha-Me'asef*: "Do not adopt poems of desire—words of lust and love—like some of the poetry of Immanuel [of Rome], and much of the poetry of the current poets of every nation. Put away poetry and literature and narrative that is inlaid with love—beloved of the heart's [evil] inclination and hated of the mind."[50]

In "Hasidut ve-Hokhmah," the Watchman, who is both protagonist and narrator of the sexual drama that unfolds in the satire, appears as a man forced to choose between licit and illicit sexuality. The anti-hasidic work encourages the maskil to favor wholesome meaningful sexuality while describing the process of his disengagement from forbidden desire. The choice is an allegory for the attraction Hasidism holds for the maskil. It is also an allegory for the bond that exists between the two factions, as members of a single people, despite their political differences. Just as Hasidut freely expresses her desire for the Watchman, so does Hokhmah. Although the sexuality of Hasidut is far more pronounced than that of the demure Hokhmah, the competition between them for the Watchman's passion is entirely symmetrical:

Two women, unlike the daughters of this world, came together to my tent, and both took hold of my arms—the one pulling me to her, and the other drawing me to her, each striving with all her might to take me from the other. When one prevailed, the other held me fast with every ounce of her strength, and as the first was about to defeat her, redoubled her efforts, both raising their voices: "He is mine," cried the one, "for it is me he has long desired. You shall not take him from me, for I will not let him go!" "No matter," replied the other, "He will never leave me."[51]

The symmetry becomes even greater when Hasidut presents herself as true Hokhmah ("for I am very wise"),[52] characterizing the Hokhmah present in the Watchman's dream as "Fatuity, standing there, to your right." The fact that the universalist Watchman is assigned a clearly male gender identity turns the maskilic satire's struggle against Hasidism into a political struggle between the sexes. The dimension of sexual desire in maskilic discourse—in contrast to the Enlightenment ideal of sublime and refined love—appears here as unbridled, transgressive passion, affording greater insight into the source of the satirical sovereign-narrator's authority. The Watchman's sexual attraction to Hasidut—an allegory for the seductive power of Hasidism in Galicia,[53] and the efforts that maskilim made to overcome it—results in his admonition to maskilim that they reject the hasidim, unequivocally and without hesitation, as legitimate candidates for the realization of the maskilic solution to the Jewish Question.

Classic attempts to address the Jewish Question, such as Lessing's *Nathan the Wise* and Mendelssohn's *Jerusalem*, considered the possibility of coexistence between the rival religions in the European public sphere, based on tolerance and the Enlightenment values of reason and morality. Beneath the surface of universal equality, however, lurked the threats of violence, passion, and aversion, resulting in irreconcilable difference and contrast. In *Jerusalem*, written after Lessing's death, Mendelssohn sought to rethink the universal concept of citizenship from the position of minority—tolerated by the majority, and an integral part of the modern, universal state.[54]

In contrast to the rational, universal, Enlightenment approach taken by the Hebrew Haskalah, Hasidism posed a radical challenge, as a political group that rejected the entire principle of a legitimate civil minority of individual citizens, whose collective interaction with the state must rely on the universal notion of tolerance. Contrary to the Haskalah, Hasidism presented itself in the European state as a Jewish collective that, in its passion and disquieting otherness, actually heightened the sense of difference, thereby threatening Enlightenment universalism. Hasidism greatly increased the emotional dimension of liminal Jewish existence, causing the state's interpellation of the Jews as individuals to actually strengthen their standing as a vibrant collective outside the state.

Amir Mufti, writing from a postcolonial perspective, described the dual nature of efforts to resolve the Jewish Question in terms of the instability created by the liminality of Jewish collective identity, as well as the indispensability of Jews as a minority, in order to avert the threat of abstraction that hangs over the modern state.[55] At the same time, the persistence of the Jewish Question rendered the isolation and liminality of the Jews in Europe, embodied in the figure of the wandering Jew, a source of potential violence against them, inasmuch as it threatened the fantasy of divided European romantic consciousness, to attain "Unity of Being."[56] It is thus no wonder that the flagrant otherness of the hasidim brought the maskilim, who had sought civil equality as a tolerated minority, to deploy the weapon of satire against them. In so doing, they hoped to neutralize this threat to their efforts to deny their liminal existence as Jews in European society. The choice of the maskilim to resort to the deadly and emotional medium of satire, imbued with hatred and repulsion, was determined by the political straits into which the hasidim had driven them. For the very same reason, Erter chose the figure of the maskilic Watchman to narrate his anti-hasidic satire, as one who identifies with the divided European romantic consciousness and therefore strives, unsuccessfully, to emerge from his liminality and isolation.

## 6

The adoption by the Galician maskilim of the aggressive, political genre of satire, which ran counter to maskilic values, may be understood in light of the explanation offered by Shmuel Feiner: "The special circumstances surrounding the maskilim's activity in Galicia, in the midst of a traditional Jewish society that was hostile to them, and in particular the dominant presence of the hasidic movement, did not allow them to develop a lukewarm, neutral and individualistic Haskala, like that in those regions of the empire where the Hasidim posed no threat."[57] The anti-hasidic satires written by Galician maskilim were inexorably linked to their political inferiority, relative to the strength of the hasidic movement in the province, as satire is a weapon of the weak. Conversely, in the early days of the Haskalah, before Hasidism appeared on the scene, Hebrew maskilim rejected the emotional and indecorous aggressivity of satirical writing. In Nahal ha-Besor (River of Good Tidings), published in 1783 by Hevrat Dorshei Leshon Ever (Society of Friends of the Hebrew Language) and attached to the first issue of *ha-Me'asef*, organ of the Hebrew Haskalah in Germany, Naphtali Herz Wessely cautioned writers to avoid the genre of satire: "Writings and tales of mockery by which to mock your brethren and their deeds in general or in particular, in the manner of satire (סאטירע)."[58] This is the same Wessely who, in "Petihat ha-Meshorer" (The Poet's Preface) to his *Shirei Tiferet* (Poems of Glory), sharply attacked the literary writing of "poems of wickedness, desire, lewdness, scoffing, drinking and so forth, [conceived] from the intensity that such feelings provoke in the hearts of their authors, of which Kohelet said, 'Better to hear the rebuke of the wise than for a man to hear the song of fools.'"[59] Earlier, Mendelssohn himself had expressed his opposition to satire, asserting that the only way to promote true enlightenment is through enlightenment.[60]

Some of the Berlin maskilim did, however, try their hands at satire, aiming their barbs at imposters (that is, those they did not consider true maskilim) and, naturally, at the rabbis who had declared all-out war against them and, in particular, against Naphtali Herz Wessely, author of the maskilic manifesto *Divrei Shalom ve-Emet*. Such were the satires of Aaron Halle-Wolfssohn and Isaac Euchel, or Saul Berlin, who wrote a satire against the rabbis, in Wessely's defense. Wessely himself, however, strongly opposed satirical writing, which he considered at odds with the ideals of Hebrew literature. Wessely the elitist could not abide a "low" genre like satire. The rise of Hebrew satire thus came as a response to the heightened political challenges posed by Hasidism.[61]

7

The principles of eighteenth-century aesthetics, as articulated in Immanuel Kant's *Critique of Judgment*, formed the basis of Wessely and Mendelssohn's aesthetic thought. Their rejection of satirical writing was thus primarily the result of their views regarding the distinction between aesthetic judgment, which is entirely disinterested, and interested judgment, rooted in reality and utility. Satire, which has a purpose beyond itself—the realization of specific political interests—lacks the disinterested freedom of aesthetic judgment as understood by Kant and Schiller. Furthermore, according to Kant, assent cannot be imposed in matters of beauty, nor can the recognition of beauty in one object be extended to others. Satire, on the other hand, not only aggressively seeks to impose assent regarding the aesthetic qualities of its political project but also demands that the single object of its attack be seen as an allegory for other, similar objects. Contrary to eighteenth-century aesthetics, which viewed the question of the actual existence of the aesthetic object with indifference and thus rejected desire as an aesthetic principle, satire presupposes the reality of its object. Indeed, the attack against the allegorical figure of Hasidut in "Hasidut ve-Hokhmah" is an emotional and desire-laden onslaught against Hasidism as an actual phenomenon.

While the conservative maskilim of Berlin adopted an aesthetic approach suited to the preservation of their political standing in the Prussian state, the Galician maskilim took a critical and revolutionary satirical approach. Meïr Letteris prefaced his Hebrew translation of Lucian's satire "Alexander the False Prophet" (based on Christoph Martin Wieland's German translation, and published in *ha-Tzfirah*) with the following remark: "All of Lucian's books are filled with understanding and knowledge. By means of mockery and ridicule he allows truth to go forth like the sun in its might."[62]

The depoliticization of art in the aesthetic thought of the Berlin Haskalah, which aspired to harmonious satisfaction in beauty, including the hope for universal assent in judgments of taste, is reflected in Wessely's characterization of the essence of poetry as "brief language that conveys a wise moral message, phrased in such a way as to stir the soul of all who hear it, causing their hearts to feel and their minds to understand all."[63] Isaac Euchel too, in his satire *Igrot Meshulam ben Uriyah ha-Eshtamo'i* (The Letters of Meshulam ben Uriah the Eshtamoi), defined the principles of poetry as "the pleasantness that the poet evokes in the soul of the listener . . . which favors the enhancement of virtue and raises the spirit above lesser opinions and thoughts."[64] Similarly, Mendelssohn's aesthetic approach fostered the good and the harmonious, by means of the (passive) contemplation of pleasantness and grace, harmony and perfection, in keeping with the notion that "the good is the product of good taste."[65] Schiller, on the other hand, posited an "ideal of grace (or beauty) based not on the conflict between the cognitive sense of duty and natural inclination, but on the *complete fusion of the two*. Schiller's ideal of beauty is the state of moral perfection in which moral behavior is not achieved by repressing the natural inclination, but by following it. It is the tendency of the heart itself that demands compliance with duty."[66] Wessely also wrote, in his preface to *Shirei Tiferet*, of the aesthetic ideal of harmony[67] and that "the soul will naturally choose to speak in poetry, for good or for ill, but not every soul has the ability to express its inner feelings in poetry."[68]

Such depoliticizing restraint gives rise to the moral fusion of emotion and intellect, which exists both beyond the senses (servants of the useful) and beyond the power of discernment (servant of the truth) and is self-sufficient and entirely devoid of any interest beyond itself. In contrast, Rancière defines the political as dissensus or disagreement, based on the gap between the sensible and the intelligible.[69] This gap is evident in the Galician anti-hasidic satires, which make a sharp distinction between acceptance of the fundamental principles of Jewish religion and theology, and absolute rejection and mockery of the false pretensions of the hasidic tzadik, who purports to realize, in his revolting and contemptible body, a direct connection with the divine, by means of the spiritual abundance that flows down to him. As Simon Halkin pointed out, Hokhmah does not fight against religion but against what she sees as a deviation from suitable Jewish religiosity.[70]

Unlike the harmonious didacticism that characterized the aesthetic approach of the Berlin Haskalah, Erter's satirical representation of the struggle between Hasidut and Hokhmah was meant to give offense—intensified by the use of allegory and radical abstraction. The satire destroys the wonder of the hasidic tale, by rejecting the concrete possibility of its premises. On the other hand, the Watchman's passage from the world of intellect and reason to the world of imagination and emotion is explained by means of a realistic background story. While reading Haskalah literature, he grows tired and passes to a state of sleep.[71]

In traditional, Jewish ethical (*musar*) literature, the process of entering a dream also entails a weakening of the soul's supervision over the body, as well as a rising of repressed emotions to the surface.[72] In other words, the Watchman, whose primary role is to supervise his people by means of his gaze, prepares himself for political action against the hasidim by entering a state of consciousness in which the control he exerts over his own body and the emotional basis of his political position is weakened. It is a moment of liberation, which allows him to witness the stormy, emotional confrontation between two opposing world views, engaged in political action against each other. The dream ensures that the Watchman's decision to choose Haskalah is not merely the product of rational consideration grounded in his reading of maskilic literature but also a romantic decision rooted in imagination, desire, and emotion.

Indeed, the context of the dream eventually turns the struggle between Hasidut and Hokhmah into an exciting battle between two unrealistic phenomena, undermining the truth of the hasidic story[73] and replacing it with humorous anecdotal writing.[74] The purpose served by the dream in Erter's satire thus appears to extend beyond the parameters of the genre. That is not to say that the ironic representation of Hasidut's words constitutes a shift in genre; it is, rather, part of process whereby maskilic preaching is extracted from her discourse, as her assertions are developed in Hokhmah's response to them. Erter uses the striking contrast between anti-hasidic satire and hasidic hagiography to brilliant poetic effect, as he brings it to a climax in which they effectively exist within the same genre. In a thoroughly logical poetic process, Erter constructs his satire as a continuous arc from ironic writing in the genre of hasidic hagiography to nonironic writing in the genre of maskilic hagiography.

The structure of "Hasidut ve-Hokhmah" is less a passage from genre to genre—from the satirical to the didactic, in the spirit of Wessely—than a dialectical process that ultimately dissolves all contrasts and concludes with the voice of the Watchman, who awakens from his dream and "sublates" (*Aufheben*) the drama he has just "witnessed":

> These words of wisdom astounded me and brought me to my knees before her [in contrast to *Hasidut*'s suggestion that he merely feign acceptance of Haskalah, publicly bending his knee to it],[75] to proclaim that you alone I desire. And like the shadows of the night flee before the sun rising in its might, so *Hasidut* shrank before the light of *Hokhmah* that waxed stronger as she spoke—the house filled with her light, and I awoke. But even after I had awoken, I raised my hands to the heavens and said: "I will forever conceive prudence, wisdom and discernment."[76]

Erter's narrator, the Watchman, functions as a parody of the dream interpreter, who cracks the allegorical code and explains all its hidden meanings. It is the Watchman who realizes, through his story, the ludicrous premise of the satire's structure of meaning: a struggle between Hasidism and the Haskalah transformed from a struggle between discernment and foolishness to a gendered clash between a chaste woman and a whorish siren. Indeed, later in the satire there is a scene rife with desire and sexual temptation, in which the two women, Hasidut and Hokhmah, seek to entice the Watchman, who serves both as narrator and as protagonist in the story.

8

The extensive use that Erter makes of the dream scene in "Hasidut ve-Hokhmah" greatly underscores the role of imagination and the loosening of rationalistic constraints in the satire, as well as its complex relationship with romanticism—which is, ultimately, the national romanticism typical of early nineteenth-century Galician Hebrew literature.[77]

In order to clarify this point, I would first like to draw attention to the similarity between hasidic sovereignty, based on the immanent presence of God, and the Mendelssohnian concept of sovereignty—Jewish sovereignty, which Mendelssohn believed could coexist with European sovereignty—based on the historical event of the Sinaitic revelation, at which the Torah and all of the religious precepts were given to the Jewish people. Alexander Altmann identified a tense dualism in Mendelssohn's thought, while Allan Arkush has referred to a contradiction between Mendelssohn's rational approach to the Jewish religion as a basis for citizenship founded on enlightenment, and his conception of religion as rooted in faith and revelation. David Sorkin, on the other hand, has denied the existence of any such contradiction, attributing Mendelssohn's thought to "religious enlightenment"—an approach based on a return to the Judaism of the Jewish philosophers of Andalusia and Italy, who advocated the study of Jewish textual tradition alongside interaction with the surrounding culture and rejected the view that the study of Kabbalah and Talmud should take precedence over study of Scripture and the Hebrew language. Sorkin's view has been criticized by Olga Litvak, who claims that he merely replicates the criticism of Western European Jews against their Eastern European counterparts and limits his position on the Haskalah as a whole to German Jewry and Mendelssohn. According to Litvak, Sorkin's view of Western European Judaism as more "authentic" leads him to ignore Eastern Europe, which gave rise both to Hasidism and to its own brand of Haskalah.[78]

Indeed, in contrast to Mendelssohn's balanced combination of the historical event of irrational revelation and Enlightenment rationality, which

Sorkin identifies with "religious enlightenment," Erter and the Galician maskilim offered a fundamentally romantic and historical model for Jewish identity, which also served as the basis for their attacks on Hasidism. Unlike Mendelssohn's civil and nonnational—that is, non-messianic—religious approach, they located their position as maskilim within a historical, romantic, national, and topical framework. The Berlin Haskalah constituted a religious Jewish identity exclusively for the private sphere, which sought only to conduct a rational and tolerant relationship with European history and religion, while the Galician maskilim constituted a historical Jewish identity that sought to bring Jewish presence into European public sphere. This historical Jewish identity posed a direct challenge to the aspiration of the Berlin maskilim to integrate into European history, as universal citizens. Contrary to the classic Enlightenment model of universal human identity embraced by the Berlin maskilim, the Galicians offered the possibility of a separate Jewish identity, with its own history and its own romantic, national foundation.

Erter's satires show the beginnings of national romanticism, with which a nationalist-Zionist scholar like Joseph Klausner clearly identified. Klausner's opinion of Erter's satires is evident in his assertion that "the form of the satires is that of the romantic vision: supernatural apparitions, dreams, and fantasies. Yet, the content of the satires is realistic." Klausner described the romantic aspect of the satires as a confession that combines romanticism and realism.[79]

Contrary to Klausner, Halkin rejected the idea of a synthesis between the rational and the irrational in Erter's satires. Halkin viewed the Watchman's autobiographical confession as unrelated to the satire itself or to its real-life author, Isaac Erter. To Halkin's mind, the confession is merely a background story not essential to the satire, which is, in itself, a schematic, abstract representation of life.[80] Uri Shoham takes a similar view and, in his analysis of "Hasidut ve-Hokhmah," goes as far as to dismiss the satirical element altogether, suggesting rather that the entire work—including the Watchman's confession—should be understood as allegory.[81]

From the perspective of the Galician maskilim, there was an inherent contradiction in Mendelssohn's Jewish identity project, between rationalism and revelation. Thus, rather than rejecting the satirical genre outright, as their Berlin counterparts had done, they offered a new, romantic solution to the contradiction. Contrary to the Kantian aesthetics of the Berlin maskilim, whereby the fact that beauty is not an independent concept precludes its imposition on readers as a truth, the Galicians' romanticism offered a political approach to beauty—conceived by the author and imposed on readers as an aesthetic value. The aesthetics of satire thus provided an appropriate response to the contradiction between rationalism and irrationality that they perceived in the Kantian aesthetics of Berlin.

The politics of the aggressive concept of beauty in anti-hasidic satire force the reader to accept its truth. Although its attacks are essentially rationalist arguments against the irrational aspect of Hasidism, they are also grounded in romantic aesthetics that no longer obey Wessely's harmonistic decorum. Galician satire also subverts and unsettles prevailing bourgeois propriety, as in Erter's scathing attack, in "Moznei Mishkal," against the deception of the rabbinate. In "Hasidut ve-Hokhmah," he mocks the tzadik's immediate connection with the divine—used by hasidim to justify the grave carnal sins of their leaders. Maskilic satire thus offers a literary solution to the contradiction they perceived in the Berlin approach—denouncing not only hasidic immorality, on the basis of universal and rationalist norms, but also the version of revelation embraced by Hasidism. The target of aggressive anti-hasidic satire was essentially the hasidic body, which the satirists presented as riddled with passions and desires, plagued with sexual corruption—to the point of committing explicitly forbidden acts. In illustrating this point, the maskilic satirists were not above occasional references to bodily fluids.

Erter's romantic approach allows him to use the linguistic structure of satire to bring the contradictory poles together, by creating a common discursive space, in which the Watchman's personal, autobiographical confession—that is, his Bildung as a maskil—plays a central role. It is the Watchman's voice in the surface text that creates the deep romantic structure that integrates the position of the rationalist critic with that of the autobiographical experience, embodying the satirical message in his personal confession. The stirrings of nationalism expressed by Erter's Watchman result from his position as a sovereign who is a critical supervisor, based on rational principles, but also one who derives his theological authority from revelation.

## 9

The maskilic attacks against the rabbis primarily concerned the fossilized structures of Jewish religious institutions and leadership. The struggle against

Hasidism, on the other hand (like the hasidic struggle against the Haskalah), was a conflict between two Jewish movements, representing opposing reactions to the political condition of Jews in the Modern Era. The passage from a feudalistic social and economic system to that of the modern capitalist state weakened the social fabric afforded by the *kahal*, that is, the institutions of the Jewish community. In this context, both movements grappled with the Jewish Question. What their respective solutions—emancipation and citizenship or survival within the European empire—had in common was their aspiration to political power in relations between Jews, as they sought protection in the European public sphere. Both solutions stipulated a clear distinction between the neutral public sphere and the private religious sphere. It was this approach that led the maskilim to advocate limiting Jewish religious existence to the private sphere—reflected in Mendelssohn's formula "German of the Mosaic faith" and, later, in the slogan "Be a man in the streets and a Jew at home," coined by Judah Leib Gordon in his 1863 poem "Hakitzah 'Ami."

Jürgen Habermas's classic thesis regarding the transformation of the public sphere, over the course of the eighteenth century, into a social sphere, distinct from the state, the economy, and the family, enabling individuals to relate to one another as private citizens discussing the common good.[82] In sharp contrast to Habermas's description, however, the state in which maskilim, hasidim, and non-Jewish citizens interacted was not a secular space, free of religious and gender bias, but was decidedly Christian and male, considering that "religion is neither merely private, for instance, nor purely irrational. And the public sphere is neither a realm of straight-forward rational deliberation nor a smooth space of unforced assent."[83]

And indeed, from a Jewish perspective, the distinction between the private and public spheres was perhaps something to aspire to but clearly no more than an unattainable fantasy, as parts of Jewish religious identity would always stand out in the essentially Christian, European public sphere. The relationship between the spheres thus offered little in terms of finding a solution to the Jewish Question.

The conservative Berlin maskilim sought to preserve the existing political order, to make the Protestant distinction between the private and the public sphere a permanent state of affairs, thereby ensuring that Christian belief in God would remain a private matter. In light of this separation between the private and the public sphere, Hasidism—which lacked a public presence in Berlin—posed no threat to the maskilic project of integrating Jews into the European empire. That is why only a very small number of

Berlin maskilim who, like Mendel Lefin, had moved from Berlin to Galicia resorted to anti-hasidic satirical writing. It was the visible presence of the hasidim in the public sphere in Galicia—which undermined the fantasy of separation between the public and the private sphere—that led the Galician maskilim to embrace the genre of anti-hasidic satire.

The Berlin maskilim, on the other hand, considered satire an inferior and dangerous genre, capable of disrupting the prevailing separation between the spheres, which maintained the static, antirevolutionary aesthetic refinement they advocated. Wessely's criticism of satire, published in "Nahal ha-Besor," may thus be seen as a kind of warning against the political power of satire to upset public serenity and the stability of the separation between the spheres: "lest your good admonitions be as traps in the eyes of those who hear them and as thorns in the sides of those who seek them." Following Charles Taylor's critique of Habermas's myth of the Enlightenment, which distinguishes between the religious and the nonreligious,[84] Wessely's words may be seen as a warning against any attempt to undermine his fantasy of a sharp distinction between the Doctrine (*Torah*) of God, which pertains to the private religious sphere, and the Doctrine of Man, which pertains to the neutral public sphere.[85]

Wessely thus preached depoliticization, cautioning that satire might contribute to the creation of political contrast in the eyes of the maskilic reader.[86] The political that Wessely rejected was that of the totalitarian state (exemplified in Carl Schmitt's dichotomous characterization of the political in terms of friendship and enmity),[87] rather than a concept of the political in line with Habermas's critique of Schmitt, in the name of the universality of democracy and the moral order of the modern state.

In this sense we may draw upon Habermas's opposition to political theology to better explain the Berlin Haskalah's opposition to the political in the public sphere of an absolute regime, the Christianity of which it denied.[88] The opposition of the maskilim was, in effect, Jewish opposition to the political theology of the Christian state. Surprisingly, it was a kind of opposition that the hasidim could also embrace, within the intimate context of the hasidic court and its sovereign, the tzadik.

## 10

The theological perspective that brought about the collapse of the maskilic distinction between the private and the public sphere ultimately raised the question of the Jewish citizen's physical, corporeal presence in the public sphere. The universal and disinterested Kantian approach to aesthetics espoused by the Berlin maskilim served as a political and aesthetic point of departure for the Galician maskilim. Through the crude political and literary weapon of satire, they had actually begun to address the postcolonial dilemma of the universal and autonomous subject at the heart of hegemonic Enlightenment aesthetics, versus the physical subject as an embodiment of emotion and intellect. The satirical attacks against the hasidim (subjects of the European colonials and their maskilic emissaries) spanned the gap between the dilemma's extremes—abstract universality and serenity, and emotion-laden physical particularism—by applying universalist aesthetics to the physicality of the body that experiences pain and pleasure.

David Lloyd derives the category of the universal subject of the Enlightenment not from political autonomy but from the aesthetic principle, which he characterizes as discourse on the human body that registers pleasure and pain. He addresses the central question in postcolonial theory: How can we sustain a notion of human subjectivity that lays claim to the universality and representativeness that underlie Western aesthetics and ethics, while viewing human beings as actual physical expressions rather than as autonomous agents of cultural representation? Lloyd contrasts Kant's universal aesthetic, which transcendentalizes the physical body, with Edmund Burke's location of the universality of aesthetic judgment in the sensible body itself. Postcolonial political criticism rests on the universal aesthetic and on the development of its progressive narrative by the sensible body.

Lloyd argues that the claim for the universal validity of artistic taste owes more to physicality than to human universality. In other words, universal reason does not suppress or erase the corporeal or the physical. In practice, he believes, no distinction can be made between the characteristics of art, the material objects, and their impact on the body as an organ of feeling that raises questions of form, taste, and aesthetic judgment. The individual is, therefore, not the autonomous subject of the Enlightenment but a subject that is also subordinated to nature and desire, needs and impulses. Following Frantz Fanon, Lloyd considers the impact of the colonial body on the body of the native and the violence inflicted on it.[89]

This kind of political impact appears with a vengeance in "Hasidut ve-Hokhmah," as a violent and vulgar satirical attack on the hasidic body—repulsive and contemptible, due to its attempt to undermine the principle of division between the genders, between the private and the public sphere. In this, Erter demonstrates his loyalty to the Western European bourgeois ethos, also reflected in Herz Homberg's *Imrei Shefer* (Goodly Words; 1802). According to this ethos, there is a clear distinction between the protected, private sphere—domain of the domestic woman, the emotional and intuitive "angel in the house"—and the public sphere, province of the male provider and maskil,[90] who may also act as a political subject. "Hasidut ve-Hokhmah" thus attacks the reversal of traditional gender roles, whereby Hasidut, in all her coarse and blatant sexuality, is markedly present in the public sphere, while the wise and refined Hokhmah actually confines herself to the private sphere. By means of this reversal, Erter illustrates to his readers how Hasidism subverts the Enlightenment bourgeois distinction between the public and the private sphere. Erter presents the repulsively ostentatious presence of Hasidism in the public sphere as that of a Jewish religious sect that the maskilim wish to confine within the boundaries of Jewish space.

The very appearance of the hasidim in the general, public sphere, however, rendered them a political subject, active in the imperial political arena and, as such, a threat to the political project of civil integration advocated by the Haskalah. This is the logic behind maskilic attempts, like those of Herz Homberg, to penetrate the very heart of the hasidic court, practices, and way of life—to impede their harmful presence in the European public sphere by combating the ills within the hasidic court itself.

Alongside the conservatism of the Berlin maskilim, we find the insular politics of survival espoused by the hasidim of Austria-Hungary, which gave rise to the genre of hasidic hagiography—in praise of the tzadik, that is, the hasidic sovereign, who offered a revolutionary alternative to the maskil, emissary of the imperial sovereign, Watchman, and observer, as described in Erter's satire by the figure of Hokhmah: "Your eyes will behold the demise of a great dominion and the birth of a new kingdom; the passing of a land and the foundation of another in its place."[91] The politics of citizenship embraced by the Galician maskilim led them to create Hebrew literature that wielded the weapon of satire, in order to uproot that which posed a threat to their chances of integration, as Jews, into the Austro-Hungarian Empire.

In the early nineteenth century, in eastern Galicia, there arose a circle of maskilim born after the annexation of Galicia, previously a part of Poland, to the Austrian Empire. The members of this group, located primarily in the cities of Brody, Lvov, and Tarnopol, saw themselves as loyal citizens of Austria. The enlightened, absolutist regime of Emperor Joseph II adopted a reformist policy with regard to the Jews, including the efforts of Homberg to develop a network of modern Jewish schools.[92] The Galician maskilim saw themselves as agents of the imperial authorities, who treated the hasidim like colonized subjects of the Crown. Postcolonial criticism of the Enlightenment has included accusations of Eurocentrism (Western European contempt for the Eastern European backwardness of the hasidim; rejection of cultural difference and moral relativity (disregarding Hasidism's unique qualities, considering it a retrograde religious movement), painting colonial subjects as "primitive" or "savage" (labels applied to the hasidim); and a belief in the progressive nature of colonial conquest, disguised as civilization and education to reason (the civilization of irrational Hasidism through the violence of enlightenment and progress).[93]

Dipesh Chakrabarty described this political aspect of colonialist Enlightenment, noting that basic "concepts such as citizenship, the state, civil society, public sphere, human rights, equality before the law, the individual, distinctions between public and private, the idea of the subject, democracy, popular sovereignty, social justice, scientific rationality" are all part and parcel of European Enlightenment. Chakrabarty argues that these concepts necessarily entail a "universal and secular vision of the human"—in contrast to the kind of ideological reality indicated by David Sorkin. The nineteenth-century "enlightened colonizer" (in this case the maskil, in relation to the hasidim), however, "both preached this Enlightenment humanism at the colonized and at the same time denied it in practice."[94] And indeed, the maskilim preached the principles of Enlightenment while employing belligerent, antidemocratic, and underhanded tactics, such as humiliation and informing, against the hasidim. The goal of the maskilim was to deny the hasidim any legitimate existence, by virtue of their sovereign gaze, which they turned against them in the form of satirical violence.

A postcolonial perspective, which criticizes the violence inherent in imposing the principles of colonial Enlightenment on the colonized, would thus characterize hasidic politics as a struggle over appropriate modes of resistance to the maskilim, emissaries of the empire. From the point of view of the Galician maskilim, such resistance, which sought to undermine their efforts to normalize the hasidic "savages," jeopardized the political path they had chosen, by means of which they had hoped to resolve the Jewish Question. The maskilim sought to realize—for themselves and for all Jews, including the hasidim—the civil ideal of improving their status and ultimately obtaining emancipation within the Austrian Empire. The purpose of maskilic anti-hasidic satire was undoubtedly to damage the image of the hasidim in the eyes of Jews, to the point of rendering them outcasts. The maskilim thus hoped to thwart hasidic ambitions to determine the nature of Jewish presence in the imperial domain, which could undermine their own goal of Jewish integration and citizenship. At times the maskilim complemented their satirical denigrations of the hasidic presence in the public sphere with panegyrics to rulers such as Napoleon, the tsar, or the Austro-Hungarian emperor. Just as maskilic satire was a mirror image of hasidic hagiography, so too maskilic panegyrics were a mirror image of the abuse the hasidim leveled at the maskilim.

II

In eliminating the distinction between private religion and public citizenship and denigrating the hasidim, maskilic satire recruited the maskilic individual to its collective project—a project no longer based entirely on the Enlightenment principle of universal identity. The maskilic project, in fact, proposed a new kind of Jewish identity, which entailed the abstraction of an imagined national community. The Watchman's blatant aversion to the hasidic body effectively eliminated it and extricated it from the closed space of the hasidic court, thereby ultimately allowing it to join the abstraction of imagined nationality.

The act of eliminating the hasidic body created an abstract imagined community in the shared space beyond the confines of the hasidic court. The construction of this imagined community is rendered possible by a process of transcendentalization, which not only eliminates spatial differences but also erases physical, ethnic and religious boundaries between Jews (hasidim and maskilim alike), paving the way for the development of a distinct national identity. In other words, rather than representing the Jewish body through mimesis, anti-hasidic satire expressed a new kind of maskilic, romantic approach, which valued the truth of imagination above that of reason.[95]

The significance of the Jewish body—of contemptible Hasidut on the one hand and laudable Hokhmah on the other—is expressed by means of a romantic outburst of positive, formative emotions. The fundamental contrast between abstract allegory and tangible, concrete romanticism is mediated by the Jewish theological ground they share. Romanticism is also present in the allegory of the hasidic body, which the allegory of wisdom (the Haskalah) rejects. Through post-satirical romantic irony, however, as in Jonathan Swift's *Gulliver's Travels,* every rational act that seeks to free itself from the body appears as a kind of dangerous illusion of purity.[96]

In "Hasidut ve-Hokhmah," all of this is recounted by the Watchman, whose ethnic and religious identity is transformed, by means of the allegorical struggle between Haskalah and Hasidism, into a Jewish national identity—the romantic creation of maskilic anti-hasidic satire. The allegory in "Hasidut ve-Hokhmah" provides the arena for the struggle between Hasidism and the maskilim, whom it presents as surrogates and collaborators of the imperial state. Allegories are generally expressions of imperial power, embodied in public monuments and statues put on display for all to see, shaping public space and leaving no doubt as to who rules and exercises authority. In "Hasidut ve-Hokhmah," it is the Watchman who is supposed to control the private sphere, as a means to controlling the public sphere. Yet, the allegorical figure of Hasidut presents Hasidism from a postcolonial perspective, actually appropriating imperialist allegory in order to oppose it.[97] Allegory undermines imperial power by articulating it from within the experience of oppression. This is the context of Fredric Jameson's famous assertion, in his controversial article "Third-World Literature in the Era of Multinational Capitalism," that the dominant figurative mode in third-world literature is necessarily that of national allegory as an act of resistance, since "the story of the private individual destiny is always an allegory of the embattled structure of the public . . . culture and society."[98]

The romantic nationalism behind the allegory in "Hasidut ve-Hokhmah" is thus rooted, first and foremost, in the tension between the consciousness and physical representation of each of its three characters. The first is, of course, the Watchman, whose autobiography serves as an exposition for the entire satire. Yehuda Friedlander, in his commentary on "Hasidut ve-Hokhmah," notes that the contrast between Hasidut and Hokhmah, which unfolds during the dream, is a development of the story of the Watchman's life, as described in the exposition. In his dream, Hasidut promises to resolve his need for money, while Hokhmah offers to slake his thirst for wisdom.[99]

A crucial part of the exposition is Erter's recourse to the genre of hasidic hagiography—to portray a paragon of maskilic virtue. Erter tells of the Watchman's significant encounter with the maskil who had rented a room in his father-in-law's house. The revelation, earlier in the narrative, that the father-in-law was a swindler, underscores the honesty of the maskil, by contrast. The maskil is presented as the Watchman-narrator's mentor and is probably an allusion to Joseph Tarler, whom Erter met in his youth, when he was still a hasid. As a result of their meeting, Erter abandoned Hasidism in favor of the Haskalah and under the guidance of Tarler (who subsequently converted to Christianity) perused maskilic literature as well as works of medieval Jewish philosophy.[100]

The autobiographical aspect of the Watchman's voice in "Hasidut ve-Hokhmah," as in Erter's other satires, rests largely on the epistolary genre in which it was written, as a communication between two real people: Isaac Erter, present in the text as the Watchman, and *Kerem Hemed* editor Samuel Leib Goldenberg, to whom it is explicitly addressed. Rhetorically, contrary to the interpretations of Menucha Gilboa and Uri Shoham,[101] there would appear to be no distinction between the nonfictional Erter and the satire as fiction. In fact, the satirical text attempts to construct nonfictional truth—capable, by virtue of its authority as Truth, of mounting a successful attack against the true, nonfictional hasidic tale.[102]

The satirical genre is clearly suited to this literary purpose, whereby the allegory in "Hasidut ve-Hokhmah" is the product of a broader metaphor, constructed—in its referent and in the object of its attack—as truth. This truth affords validity to the biographical satirist's political intervention in the actual balance of power between maskilim and hasidim.

Indeed, the political role of the exposition in "Hasidut ve-Hokhmah," in which the Watchman tells his life story, is to create the effect of absolute truth essential to effecting real political change. The Watchman's story includes his early marriage, at the age of thirteen, the passing of his wife only a year later, the second wife his relatives "laid in my bosom, in her place," the father-in-law who swindled him, and his ensuing financial difficulties. The Watchman identifies all these elements with the collective biography of "the children of our people who reside in the land of Poland."[103]

Further support for the concrete nature of the satire's political aims can be found in its focus on material matters, so prominent in the exposition, in which the Watchman, the satire's narrator, recounts his financial woes: "The money ran out of my pocket, but the desire to strive for great things did not depart from my heart, for from the days of my youth I despised being considered as one of the common people."[104] This appears to allude to Numbers 23:9: "For from the tops of the crags do I see them. Look, a people that dwells apart, amongst the nations is not reckoned."[105] By means of this allusion to

Balaam's curse, famously transformed into a blessing, the Watchman signals both his own lofty position, at "the tops of crags," from which he supervises his people, and his identity as a satirist whose sharp criticism of the hasidim aims to bring about their complete transformation, thereby also transforming his satirical curse into words of praise that will serve as an alternative to hasidic hagiography. The Watchman's loneliness and lack of "reckoning" among his people highlights his adversarial consciousness opposite the hasidim, which informs his satirical logic.

The Watchman never ceases to "strive for great things." In addition to his financial disappointment, he becomes disillusioned by the false miracles of the hasidim, leading to spiritual and religious dissatisfaction with Hasidism itself—expressed in typical maskilic fashion, in terms of light and darkness: "And my soul refused to believe the miracles performed by the thousands, without support, as opposed to ancient times when, in order to free the treasured people from the iron forge and sustain them in the desert for forty years, God entrusted but a few of His wonders to His faithful servant [Moses]. And I have read their books, and they are all cloud and fog, secreted in darkness and wrapped in shadow. The light of my understanding could not illuminate such obscurity. I touched the cloud with my hands, felt the darkness."[106] Nevertheless, the fact that the Watchman is the autobiographical narrator of Erter's satires means that his self-representation—mediated by his language—always entails a figurative shift away from the literal self-signification of autobiography.[107] This figurative shift appears to undermine the Watchman's ability to serve in the authoritative political role of sovereign narrator, who recounts the satire as autobiography, as he possesses the national gaze.[108]

The instability of this extratextual reality is apparent in the specularity of the satirical text. The Watchman's gaze at Hokhmah, which entails, as in the Lacanian mirror stage, complete identification with her, as a maskil, as well as differentiation from her the moment he recognizes that they are indeed separate. This is the case with Hokhmah, but also with the Watchman's adversarial interaction with Hasidut. The instability is also a mark of the satirical effect resulting from the unconscious self-irony of Hasidut. Ironic language, however, splits the subject in two: an empirical self that is unaware of its own inauthenticity, because it naively believes the language in which it exists to be transparent; and an emiprical self that knows it exists only in language and is therefore aware of its own inauthenticity.[109] The existence of the empirical self of Hasidut is mediated by allegorical language, rendering it inauthentic. Hasidut's use of allegorical speech is thus postfigurative, the speech of an inauthentic self, unaware of its own falseness. On the other hand, the self knows that it is allegorical—that is, exists only through the medium of allegorical language. Hasidut thus knows that her empirical self is inauthentic, that she herself is a mere illusion, that she is lying.

Romantic irony is bound by a similar contradiction, which prevents irony—that is, the gap between saying and said—from developing an ironic, satirical-critical position. That is because any attempt by the hasid to locate the ironic position of the maskil opposite and outside his experiential, empirical self demands that he pass through the linguistic medium that forces him back to an internal, linguistic position, which precludes the location of an ironic position opposite and outside his empirical self.

A political reading of Hasidut's monologue as satire, however, eliminates the instability and self-destruction of irony (which is both aware and unaware that she is lying in relation to extralinguistic reality), choosing to understand Hasidut's words as allegory (with no illusions that it represents the actual world), that is, as speech that is aware of its own falseness/allegory but cannot be otherwise. Allegory is always a story that, in the act of narration, creates a gap or shift between its signifiers and its signified, resulting in ironic distance from the context in which they exist. Any political judgment that denounces violence and hypocrisy through irony locates itself outside that judgment. It is the political that interrupts the ironic cycle of destruction and construction, by invoking an external authority, such as prophecy, divine inspiration, or revelation, which allows it to locate itself outside the context it denounces.[110]

Hasidut is aware of the fact that her speech in praise of immoral and fraudulent tzadikim is false, but she is politically committed to uttering these falsehoods. In other words, the political effect of maskilic satire is achieved through Rancière's dissensus (the separation between the sensible and the intelligible), which the irony of the Watchman wields against Hasidut, while distinguishing the empirical phenomenon of Hasidut from the linguistic-allegorical representation by which she is mediated to her readers. Dissensus, by means of this distinction, reveals the inauthenticity of Hasidut, that is, the pretense, deception, and masquerading of the tzadikim, exposed by the maskilic satires. On the other hand, despite her awareness of the falseness of her allegorical speech, as a linguistic phenomenon, which always exists at a distance from the reality it describes, she has no choice but to communicate in that fashion.

Viewed in this light, the question of the existence of an extratextual reality (the reality of Galician Hasidism, in this case), which is a necessary condition for the political effect of satire, is by no means trivial. There can be no certainty that the formidable mechanism of satire is not brought to bear here on figurative, linguistic creations rather than on actual hasidim, who may or may not exist. The answer would seem to lie not in refuting the doubt, which remains valid so long as there is no way of examining the political beyond its linguistic representation, but in the distinction between the justification of the political act and the significance of its efficacy. The Watchman, who constitutes his imagined national community by his gaze, does so under conditions of uncertainty regarding the existence of the nation that he is constituting. Nevertheless, following Paul de Man, the constitution of a nation is the constitution of sovereignty, while sovereignty is a mechanism that employs and justifies violence. The control that the Watchman exerts over his people entails the potential of violence, whether at the hands of the Watchman himself or at the hands of his surrogates. Masikilic anti-hasidic satire was a violent response to the real threat posed by the hasidim—their ostensible appearance as an allegory of a larger collective, which rendered them a political force with which the maskilim had to contend.

And the hasidim were indeed a growing political force, in relation to the maskilic minority in Galicia. Although the ironic linguistic representation of the Watchman does not initially afford a decisive political victory, the violent circumstances in which the literary struggle between hasidic hagiography and maskilic satire developed did make way for such a victory, predicated on the necessity of Hasidut as an allegory. This necessity, opposite the necessity of Hokhmah as an allegory, transforms the figurative, linguistic confrontation between them into a political struggle between two sovereign authorities, Hokhmah and Hasidut, with the victory of the one over the other laying the foundations for the constitution of Jewish national sovereignty.

## 12

The proximity between the rival camps in Erter's satire is evinced by his allegorical figures, Hokhmah and Hasidut. Although the narrator (the Watchman) denounces the figure of Hasidut and praises that of Hokhmah, Hasidut is the richer and more captivating character.

The appeal of Hasidut would appear to stem from the way in which her true, ugly face is revealed. As a prophet who has experienced revelation, the Watchman possesses remarkable powers of observation, which he trains on the entire Jewish people, within which he identifies the hasidim as swindlers and charlatans. His penetrating gaze reveals the shocking truth behind Hasidut's misleading external appearance, the mask of deception she uses to conceal her crimes. At the same time, the Watchman himself is repulsed by what he sees.[111]

The deceit displayed by Hasidut and revealed by the Watchman is self-incriminating. She speaks of herself and her values with unconscious self-irony. The Watchman's rationalist act of unmasking thus unfolds as a kind of game, in which the reader is exposed to the irony of the satire that mocks Hasidut for making a mockery of herself. The duality of the language with which Hasidut presents herself is thus a source of schadenfreude, as the deluded Hasidut becomes entangled in her own web.

Contrary to the autonomy of the sovereign Watchman, the hasid who sings the tzadik's praises is subordinate to the sovereignty of the tzadik. The authority of the tzadik does not derive from the universal value system of the Enlightenment, which creates a common, human identity. On the contrary, it is a clear example of identity politics, based not on equality and universal identity but on differences between particular collectives. The Watchman possesses the self-consciousness of a sovereign. This also extends, however, to the invalidation of the sovereignty of the hasidic tzadik, as tainted by fraud and imposture—a theme found, for example, in a letter by Nachman Krochmal and especially in the satires of Joseph Perl.[112]

The epistolary genre plays an important role in the Watchman's autobiographical account of Hokhmah's criticism of Hasidut, which heightens the narrator's aversion to Hasidut, to the point of disregarding her entirely. In so doing, the Watchman is able to create a synthesis between praise and condemnation. Hokhmah attacks Hasidut in order to praise the Haskalah, and Hasidut attacks Hokhmah in order to praise Hasidism. Ultimately, however, satire and praise converge to interpellate the reader as a model maskil, made privy to the correspondence between two maskilim. This interpellation is achieved by the satirical text, which represents the reality to which the Watchman awakens. Erter concludes this complex composition with the phrase "Here end the words of your friend," thereby creating a direct link to the material reality of the satire as a letter—the form given to it by *Kerem Hemed* editor Samuel Goldenberg, much to Erter's satisfaction.[113]

## 13

As noted above, the political purpose of the anti-hasidic satires was the removal of the hasidim from the European public sphere, where their presence and actions threatened to undermine the maskilic solution to the Jewish Question: the integration of Jews who were identified as such into sovereign European-Christian space. Indeed, as Erter's allegorical figure Hokhmah notes, the Watchman observes the Jews throughout the European sphere:

> At your pleasure, my son, I will place you on the cherub of my spirit and fly with you to the end of the earth. And you will behold seas and deserts, rivers and forests, rocky heights that reach the clouds, mighty mountains girded with flaming torches, wondrous creations divine and human that bring joy to all who see them. And you will be amazed at the host of human variety and legions of man's diversity, in language, government and belief, and in the customs and mores of their lands.
>
> Or you will be borne on the wings of the wind, soaring to the beginning of time, skipping the generations, and you will see men emerging from hollows of rock and stone, and from the depths of the forests, wandering like wolves of the plains, without a society, as they begin to build towns and establish polities lands and kingdoms. Men of renown will appear before you, heroes who perform feats of courage to rescue their brothers from the jaws of wild animals; men who willingly sacrifice their lives that their homelands might rule![114]

The Watchman's goal is the radical negation of Hasidism, to which end he enlists the extreme and destructive genre of satire. Following Shmuel Werses's remark that "the literature of the Haskalah indirectly attests to the powerful attraction that Hasidism held, even sweeping up a part of the maskilic camp itself,"[115] the political role of anti-hasidic satire may be defined as a concerted effort to convince maskilic readers that their fears of the hasidim are unfounded. The far-reaching satirical humiliation of the hasidim was intended to discredit them in the eyes of all maskilim, thereby ensuring their exclusion from the society of Jews—recognized by the imperial authorities, if only to grant them access to state educational institutions for the sake of their intellectual improvement. Krochmal offers some insight into the relationship between the maskilim and the authorities in this matter: "Nevertheless, if it is true that this abomination and villainy occurred, as the hypocrites here prattle and boast, that you were threatened with excommunication, and harassed to hand over many of your books to be burned, you should avenge yourself of them, and especially that village teacher, and assail them with the legal instruments afforded by his excellency the governor."[116] This suggestion of recourse to the imperial governor in order to strike at the hasidim shows that the political goal of anti-hasidic satire was to assure the maskilic readership that the political alternative offered by the hasidim for Jewish existence within the empire was entirely without basis. Anti-hasidic satire was meant to convince maskilic readers that the hasidim were best avoided altogether, as they had nothing to contribute to the all-important project of emancipation. The scathing criticism of the hasidim in the satires was meant to arouse the readers' negative feelings against them, to the point of recoiling from them as Jews who might otherwise have been partners in the struggle for emancipation, while allaying any fears of a supposed hasidic threat to the vision of emancipation and integration. Indeed, as Hasidut concludes her attempt to seduce the narrator, he is stunned at first but immediately declares that there was, in fact, nothing new in her characterization of the hasidim: "And I was stunned, my soul distraught. From the beginning I had known, the *hasidim* [*mithasdim*: lit. those who pretend to be saintly] are fools, and their rabbis ignorant and devoid of understanding."[117]

The narrator was stunned not because he had discovered anything new about the hasidim but because he had suddenly developed a new, far more critical awareness of the things he had already known. It is with this dramatic awakening that Erter effectively constitutes his protagonist as the Watchman for the House of Israel, transforming his identity—from waverer between Hasidism and Haskalah to gazing observer of his people, a critical supervisor who ultimately constitutes them as a nation.

The conflict between the Watchman and the people stems from the moral criticism typical of the national intellectual:[118] "Like those men of God [the prophets], they too suffer their fill of insults and spittle [Isaiah 50:6], and, like them, these intellectuals [lit. men of spirit] remain impervious to taunts and jeers. They risk their lives in order to convey to the people their desire for knowledge, and to eradicate from among them all poison and foolishness, even if its root is gnarled with age. To them you shall look up, my son!"[119] This passage also entails a rhetorical shift—from the narrator's ironic account of Hasidut's self-incriminating words to the Watchman's direct, biting satire. When Hokhmah begins her rebuttal to Hasidut's harangue, the Watchman highlights her gaze as it catches his own, characterizing her as one whose speech—like his—is the product of an enlightened, supervising gaze: "With her eyes, the serene and peaceful woman, with a crown [of shining stars] on her head, read my thoughts, laughed at the failure of her counterpart, opened her mouth and said."[120]

As noted, anti-hasidic satire was a political act that complemented and reinforced the efforts of the maskilim, under the aegis of the imperial authorities, to revolutionize the lives of the hasidim and their leaders, that they might, ultimately, join the maskilic project of integration into the empire. Satire was particularly suited to this political task, in light of its ability to hold up a binary picture of reality: black versus white, reprehensible versus praiseworthy. Satire thus lends itself to Carl Schmitt's classic definition of the political as a sharp and often violent distinction between friend and enemy.[121] The practical significance of Schmitt's definition of the political is all-out war, with no possibility of dialogue or compromise, a battle to the death. For the maskilim this meant that nothing less than the complete elimination of their hasidic rival would do—with the goal of denying the hasidim legitimacy in the European public sphere, in order to ensure the success of maskilic project of integration. This is also the source of the Berlin Haskalah's rejection of the satirical genre. The warning expressed by Mendelssohn and Wessely against the politicization of literature was directly related to the aspirations of the Berlin maskilim, who feared that such literary battles would undermine the clear separation between the private nature of the sphere in which religion is practiced and the political nature of the public sphere dominated by the state.

As a Jewish political philosopher, Mendelssohn defended the validity of this separation of religion and state, but only with regard to the period of exile that followed the destruction of the Hebrew state. This is, however, precisely the distinction that anti-hasidic satire sought to change. Anti-hasidic satire played an important role in Jewish efforts to transform the relationship between the Jewish religion and the Christian state. The maskilic attacks against the hasidim were attacks against fellow Jews, lest they jeopardize Jewish integration. In other words, they rejected Mendelssohn and Wessely's view that Jewish religious existence remain in the private, nonpolitical domain, and that political action be limited to furthering the integration of Jews into the European public sphere. Through the medium of satire, the Galician maskilim sought to take political action against Hasidism as a public expression of the Jewish religion, that is to say, against the nature of their presence in the European public sphere. Political, anti-hasidic satire thus served the Galician maskilim in their efforts to remove the division created by the Berlin maskilim between their Jewish religion and the European-Christian state. In Galicia, anti-hasidic satire moved Hebrew literature away from the political conservatism of the Berlin Haskalah, creating a romantic, revolutionary, and political body of literature that prepared the ground for the development of national politics.[122]

This nationalism, of course, had no interest whatsoever in Jewish settlement in the Land of Israel, and hence in Zionism or any form of proto-Zionism. Erter's nationalism was that of a national minority under the protection of the imperial authorities—as expounded in two of his later works. The first of these is the unfinished "'Aliyat Damesek" (Damascus Affair), on the Damascus Affair of 1840. Erter, like many Jews around the world, expressed national solidarity with the Jews of Damascus, who had been accused of ritual murder.[123] The second text is "Kol Kore li-Vney Yisra'el Toshvei Eretz Galitzyah" (Appeal to the Children of Israel Residing in the Land of Galicia),[124] in which Erter—like Perl in *Boḥen Tzadik* (1838), which advocated Jewish agricultural settlement in the Crimea—called upon the Jews of Galicia to form a national association for the training of Jewish farmers (Galizischer Jüdischer Ackerbau-Verein), with the goal of promoting Galician Jewish productivity on their native soil.

It was Baruch Kurzweil who identified colonialism as the connection between Joseph Perl's struggle against Hasidism and his support for Jewish settlement under the auspices of the empire: "While Gans, Zunz and their friends practically made the plan to establish 'colonies' contingent upon another goal, the destruction of rabbinism, Perl linked his colonizing hopes to the destruction of Hasidism."[125] In other words, Kurzweil saw hasidic resistance to the empire and its maskilic surrogates as an expression of anti-colonialism. This was Kurzweil's understanding of the political position of Hasidism in Europe. Where the Land of Israel was concerned, however, Perl feared that the colonial project might itself become hasidic. From his opposition to Jewish settlement there, as described by Kurzweil ("Perl saw the Land of Israel as a dangerous center of Jewish mysticism"), we may infer that he would have opposed later Jewish colonialism as well, inasmuch as "Perl did not dream of a Jewish state. Of course he would have rejected a secular version of the messianic idea and, with a little imagination, his satirical treatment of hasidic immigration to Palestine may be rendered incredibly topical. The spiritual relationship between the Holy Land and the diaspora has not changed." Kurzweil's own implied anti-Zionism is reflected in his remark that "immigration (*'aliyah*) to the Land of Israel was not voluntary then either, but was [as it is now] a matter of necessity."[126]

The Watchman undergoes a radical transformation during the course of the satire—from a sovereign, prophetic figure, observing and guiding his people, based on the moral authority afforded by universal reason, to a romantic figure, bound by visions and imagination.

Erter's biblical-linguistic point of departure was the universalist *Be'ur* project (German translation and maskilic commentary on Scripture) undertaken by Moses Mendelssohn and other maskilim, in which they sought to break free of rabbinical supervision and authority. Erter's romantic use of biblical language went beyond the rationalist-universalist use to which the Berlin Haskalah had put it, showing early signs of the Galician maskilic tendency to draw upon aggadic and midrashic language as well.[127]

## 14

In the satire's exposition, Erter sets the stage for a negative analogy between the two Jewish women in the narrator's life—both plain and sexually unappealing—and the sexual drama that unfolds in his dream. In both cases, one woman replaces another. In the first case, the narrator's first wife dies and is replaced by a second wife, "laid in my bosom, in her place," as a result of cruel fate and oppressive social norms. In the second case, which lies at the heart of the satire, the Watchman, torn between sexual desire and reason, is forced to choose between the two allegorical women, Hasidut and Hokhmah. By means of an emotional confession, the Watchman constitutes his authority as a rational critic, attacking the deception and corruption of the hasidim, based on bitter personal experience. His own trials and tribulations serve as a justification for his satirical criticism. Grounding the satiric mode in such a confession represents a romantic, literary solution to the inherent contradiction the Galician maskilim identified in the ideas of the Haskalah. This contradiction came to light in the wake of the conflictual encounter between the maskilim and the harsh physical reality that prevailed among Galician Jews, culminating in the physical encounter with the growing strength of Hasidism in Galicia, epitomized (from a maskilic perspective) in the deceitful, promiscuous, and immoral hasidic body.

In 1823, Letteris published a Hebrew translation of Lucian's satire "Alexander the False Prophet"—a satirical description of a fraudulent miracle worker, ultimately exposed by men of truth.[128] This satire, among others by Lucian, appears to have had an important influence on Erter, if only because of its contemporary relevance. As Letteris notes:

> If you, dear reader, were to take one of his works and replace the names of well-known men of his time with those of men still living, whom you know for certain follow the same path, then you would be surprised to see and you would be satisfied that this work was written yesterday and not in ancient times. You may do the same with the work I have placed before you today . . . and should the reader find those in our times as well, who are its equals in manner and in deed, causing his former respect for them to be replaced by contempt, the fault is not mine, nor can he hold it against me.[129]

It was probably Letteris's rationalist approach to the failings of modern Jewish society that led him to relate to Lucian's satire as an anti-hasidic work,[130] in which Alexander is excoriated as a miracle worker of the same stripe as the Ba'al Shem Tov.[131] Letteris thus expanded the boundaries of Hebrew literature beyond the Jewish religious context, while omitting Lucian's references to Epicurus,[132] in order to render the satire less specific to the pagan world and more universally applicable, across religions (monotheistic and pagan alike), ages, and cultures. Erter's criticism of the hypocritical religiosity of the targets of his satire clearly parallels Lucian's demytholigization of the world of pagan legend, while his idealist position corresponds to Lucian's sober Greek pragmatism. The lasting impression of Lucian's satires on the sixteenth-century Reformation[133] may explain their influence on the Galician maskilim, in light of the fact that Jewish civil identity embraced by the Berlin Haskalah ("German of the Mosaic faith") was grounded in the Protestant distinction between the public and the private sphere—the latter being the domain in which true religious faith exists.

## 15

Hasidut attempts to seduce the Watchman with an unabashed description of hasidic corruption, which she presents as normative behavior. Hasidut's words ironically assume the casuistic style of religious texts. She goes as far as to act as a procurer, suggesting that the Watchman, as a corrupt tzadik, might take advantage of women who come to him with fertility problems. She tells him that he himself might impregnate them—after having taken their money: "And if a woman be barren and come to you to open the seal of her womb, you shall lay your hand on her, and on your hand she shall lay her silver. From the blessings of your mouth she will not conceive a child, unless she is blessed by your loins, and you will have exacted a high price from her in return for her child. And should she conceive, the blessings of breasts and womb shall be your portion."[134] The extreme sexual vulgarity employed by Erter in this passage appears to draw upon Letteris's "Alexander," which includes the following description of the false oracle: "And Alexander amassed great wealth, enjoying success wherever he went. And he lay with the women who came to consult with him, if he found them attractive, and it was an honor in their eyes, that a holy man such as he desired their company."[135] Here we find one of the fundamental differences between the Hebrew satires of the Berlin Haskalah and those of the Galician maskilim. Compare Erter's blatant description of the sexual act to the relatively delicate words of warning that the dubious scholar Mordecai[136] offers his grandson Meshulam in Euchel's *Igrot Meshulam ben Uriyah ha-Eshtamo'i*: "He who eats bread without washing his hands, it is as if he lay with a prostitute, as it is written 'For a whore's price is no more than a loaf of bread.'"[137] As Meir Gilon notes with regard to the satires of the Hebrew Haskalah and general Enlightenment in Germany: "As for the approach of exponents of the Enlightenment—Jews and non-Jews alike—to the erotic, theirs was no less puritan than that of their conservative opponents."[138]

The coarseness of Erter's language further highlights the role of the narrator's gender identity in determining his political actions. The fact that the universalist Watchman possesses a distinct gender identity renders the maskilic struggle against Hasidism, in the satire, a political struggle between male and female. The element of sexual desire (as opposed to the Enlightenment ideal of sublime and refined love) in maskilic discourse—which, in the satire, assumes the form of vulgar, forbidden, and transgressive lust—offers a more precise understanding of the source of the sovereign Watchman's authority.

The political role played by sexual desire in the gender struggle between Hasidism and Haskalah is in fact a product of the struggle between two rival political theologies. On the one hand, theocratic Hasidism is organized around the hasidic court and views the tzadik as the sovereign representative of God on earth. On the other hand, the Haskalah seeks to obtain imperial citizenship—a form of sovereignty also based on divine right—for the Jews. Unlike the hasidic subject of Jewish theocracy, however, the maskilic subject serves a Christian sovereign. It was on the basis of this political stance that conservative rabbis accused the maskilim of assimilation—that is, theo-political assimilation, not necessarily entailing intermarriage.

The Jewish nature of the maskilic goal of emancipation—that is, citizenship that would allow them to take part in Christian sovereignty—produced a political conflict between two sources of authority for Jewish sovereignty: a maskilic source, within the framework of Christian sovereignty, and a hasidic source, within the framework of theo-political autonomy. In the mind of the maskil, these divergent political theologies gave rise to a conflict between the two sovereignties—the Christian and the Jewish. The clearest expression of this conflict may be found in the thought of Moses Mendelssohn, whose utopian goal of a religiously neutral European public sphere (based on a Protestant distinction between the public and the private domain) led him to advocate coexistence between the sovereignties. It was Mendelssohn's utopian subject, which he defined by means of the civil identity "German of the Mosaic faith" (but effectively "Christian of the Mosaic faith"), that led to Johann Kaspar Lavater's famous challenge that he convert to Christianity and thereby resolve the inherent contradiction in his identity.

The political role played by the Watchman, the speaker in Erter's anti-hasidic satire, may thus be defined as the action of a unified maskilic subject aimed at dividing the hasidic unity between the revelation and reality achieved within the body of the tzadik, by means of dissensus, that is, the separation between the sensible and the intelligible. The politics of dissensus employed in the maskilic satire is based on a sharp distinction between transcendent divine authority, which the maskilim by no means denied, and the utter rejection of the way in which hasidic immanentism received base, contemptible, false, and morally uninhibited expression.

The maskilic solution to the Jewish Question, as understood through the genre of anti-hasidic satire, was thus, in effect, a political act, intended to remove the hasidic body from Jewish-European space, as a threat to the integration efforts of the Haskalah. By undermining the legitimacy of the political theology behind the body of the hasidic tzadik, maskilic satire sought to eradicate the shameful and dangerous physical presence of Hasidism in the public sphere, which the maskilim hoped to constitute as a joint Jewish-European space, free of contradiction or conflict.

In place of the lascivious, transgressive hasidic body, Erter's maskilic satire offers a weak and refined Jewish body. It is a body that has failed to earn a living from physical labor, which it rejected in favor of spiritual development as a maskil. In this, Erter's Watchman resembles Lucian, in "The Dream," who rejected the manual labor of sculpture in order to pursue the ideal of spiritual refinement. Although the self-representation of Erter's narrator is marked by physical and sexual weakness, the fact that the Watchman ultimately prefers the romanticism of the imaginative power of revelation to maskilic rationalism indicates that his current weakness is in fact a void that will, at some point in the future, be filled with national passion. This would explain the Watchman's ongoing appeal. Although created in the early nineteenth century, Erter's narrator continued to accompany and inspire Hebrew literature for generations. In identifying the sources of Jewish weakness and ineffectuality, Erter also offered hope and the desire for national growth and triumph. The pattern is repeated in the "revival literature," beginning in the late nineteenth century, penned by members of a national minority whose Zionist aspirations led them to envisage the sovereign power of a people in its homeland, realizing their national desire in its messianic body. Even A. B. Yehoshua's forest ranger, in the story "Facing the Forests" (1968), may be seen as a reincarnation of the Watchman—his physical and spiritual weakness signifying the longing for Jewish sovereignty as an abrogation of the moral responsibilities entailed in its realization.[139]

Chapter 4

# The Politics of the Hasidic Story in the Russian Empire

I

Stephen Howe defined an empire as "a large political body which rules over territories outside its original borders. It has a central power or core territory—whose inhabitants usually continue to form the dominant ethnic or national group in the entire system—and an extensive periphery of dominated areas."[1] When the boundaries between the center and the periphery are blurred—whether culturally or geographically—the result is a kind of "internal colonialism," that is, a hybrid situation in which the center remains culturally and politically dominant while seeking to educate the internally colonized in its ways. In the case of the Russian Empire, the hybridity of the relationship between the dominant core and the dominated periphery stemmed from the religious and ethnic heterogeneity of the polity—considered a given by Russian leaders, who devised a series of categories for the classification and division of the empire's subjects, contributing, in turn, to the practice of differentiated governance.[2]

Over the course of the nineteenth century, the Russian Empire underwent a shift in its conception of alterity, which it defined in increasingly ethnic rather than religious terms.[3] With the ascension of Tsar Nicholas I, in 1825, a massive campaign was launched to integrate the Jews—who had enjoyed relative freedom since 1804—into Russian society. To understand the empire's political relationship with its Jewish subjects, we must begin with the partitions of Poland in the late eighteenth century. The series of partitions, which ultimately brought about the disappearance of Polish sovereignty, also led to the absorption of large numbers of Jews in the three neighboring empires of Russia, Prussia, and Austria, all ruled by enlightened absolute monarchs. The maskilim—the westward-looking scholars of the Jewish Enlightenment or Haskalah, who advocated a model of Jewish imperial citizenship—believed that the monarchs' commitment to the safety and well-being of their subjects should be reciprocated with abiding loyalty, above any religious or corporate identity.[4]

Following the third partition of Poland, in 1795, hundreds of thousands of Jews suddenly found themselves under Russian rule. For the Russian authorities, who had previously restricted Jewish settlement throughout most of the empire, these Jews of the Pale were an unknown quantity. The Russian authorities, in line with Enlightenment ideals, sought to transform the Jews, by regulatory means, from members of a religious cultural community to subjects capable of contributing to the welfare of the empire and its citizens. The reforms of the 1860s and the Polish uprising of 1863 were critical moments for the Russian Empire's rethinking of its administrative policies.[5] Following the Crimean War (1855), the empire embarked upon a path of Westernization and modernization. Eight years later, the Polish uprising put an end to these attempts at liberalization, replacing them with a nationalist agenda that aspired to state unity. The previous, imperial political model, based on cooperation with local elites, was replaced by policies of assimilation and Russification. The lack of democratic institutions, however, meant the "segmented" modernization of Russia resulted in the nationalization of local populations rather than their integration.[6]

The absolutist administration saw the existence of autonomous corporate Jewish communities as a threat to central control, and therefore sought to limit or even revoke their independence. The basic attitude of the Russian authorities to the Jews may perhaps be summed up in the words of comte de Clermont-Tonnerre, an advocate of Jewish emancipation in France: "The Jews should be denied everything as a nation but granted everything as individuals."[7] Essentially, however—like the Enlightenment philosophers described by Edward Said, who took a humane position on the management of the colonies but did not dispute the fundamental superiority of the white race[8]—the enlightened Russification of the Jews was accompanied by a perception of the Jews as an inferior race.[9]

Russian public opinion demanded that Jews acquire the Russian language—a demand that the Jewish maskilim readily embraced. The question of language was strongly linked to economic issues, however. The fact that a large number of Jews made their living from the production and sale of alcohol by state concession did more to promote education and the dissemination of the Russian language among the Jews than any of the coercive measures instituted by the government of Nicholas I.[10]

The authority of the *kahal*, or autonomous Jewish community council, had been severely weakened in the aftermath of the Chmielnicki persecutions of 1648–49, and the hasidic leadership began to bypass or even supplant the kahal, in interactions between the Jews and the state.[11] The hasidim lived in separate corporations, as autonomous communities. In financial matters, for example, the various hasidic "courts" (communities) acted in the capacity of prestatal corporative bodies, controlled by their respective tzadikim.[12] As a result of their obvious ethnic alterity, occasional disregard for the law,[13] and the fact that the hasidic courts tended to operate in the manner of a "state within the state," the hasidim were widely perceived as a threat (or "internal enemy")[14] of Russian society, against which it sought to defend itself.

While the hasidim trod carefully for fear of the empire's watchful eye, the maskilim actively embraced the empire and its practices, adopting its colonial gaze and accompanying "regime of truth."[15] Just as in the history of colonialism the regime of truth determined who was a "normative" European,[16] so too the Russian imperial authorities determined who was a "normative" Russian. The Jews were measured against this standard and were expected to change in order to resemble it. Ultimately, the imperial goal (which was not free of contradictions) was to turn the Jews from "them" into "us."[17]

All of this changed in 1825, with the ascension of Tsar Nicholas I (known as the "Iron Tsar")—notoriously cruel and despotic in his policies toward the Jews, whom he considered "backward, superstitious, isolated, dirty, parasitic, and unproductive."[18] Alongside increasingly centralist tendencies, Nicholas I launched a broad campaign of intervention in the lives of the Jews, aimed at freeing them from the fanaticism to which he believed them to be in thrall, in order to turn them into productive members of society.[19] The methods employed by the campaign included, first and foremost, interference in Jewish education and the conscription of Jews into the Russian Army. Conscription also had an educational purpose: integration of the Jewish recruits—and through them, their families—into Russian society. Despite the government's declarations (not always credible) of its commitment to freedom of religion, both of these methods were widely perceived by the Jews as attempts to convert them to Christianity.[20] Indeed, of all the measures mandated by the tsar, forced conscription (including of children under the age of eighteen) had the greatest impact on the lives of Jews in the Russian Empire.[21] The steps taken by Nicholas I were typical of empire: seeking to control the population through mechanisms of surveillance and intrusion into previously autonomous spheres. Such mechanisms often target even the most trivial aspects of everyday life,[22] such as clothing. In fact, in 1844 the Russian government imposed a tax on distinctive Jewish dress, soon followed by a similar decree in Poland. Ironically, the Russian style the Jews were forced to adopt eventually came to be identified specifically with Jews, as in the case of the so-called "Jewish hat."[23]

Unlike the maskilim, who aspired to emancipation—that is, to a Jewish political existence that would entail participation in imperial sovereignty—hasidic theology rejected all forms of political or civil involvement with the state, leading the hasidim to engage in a struggle for political survival. The struggle was exacerbated in 1844 with the abolition of the kahal in the Russian Empire,[24] leaving the hasidim even more exposed to the regime's encroachments and Russification efforts. They were thus forced to develop defense mechanisms to safeguard their continued existence as an autonomous Jewish community.

2

Hasidism produced a wealth of theological and homiletic literature, most notably in the genre of the hasidic tale, which served as a bridge between the elite of hasidic society and the hasidic masses. Indeed, more than 150 booklets of hasidic tales were published between the 1860s and 1914—cheaply and carelessly printed, making them accessible to the poorer classes.[25] According to Simon Dubnow, hasidic literature was, in fact, "geared to the tastes of the masses."[26] It was thus popular literature read by ordinary Jews—contrary to the elitist maskilic literature of the time, published in low-circulation periodicals and books aimed at a very narrow readership.[27]

In 1875, Jacob Kaidaner published a collection of hasidic tales, entitled *Sipurim nora'im* (Tales of Awe),[28] at a time when hasidic narrative literature was enjoying a resurgence—following publication of *Kehal Hasidim* (Hasidic Congregation, 1864),[29] by Michael Levi Rodkinson (Frumkin). In the book, Kaidaner implies that he had met the founder of the Habad hasidic movement, Shneur Zalman of Liadi, as well as his disciple Aaron HaLevi of Staroselye (who would later cause a split in Habad). Kaidaner's involvement with Habad only began in earnest, however, under the leadership of Dovber Shneuri (the second rabbi of Habad, known as the "Middle Rebbe"), during a six-month stay in the town of Lubavitch (Lyubavichi). Kaidaner would appear to have been a follower (*hasid*) of Shneuri's successor, Menahem Mendel Schneersohn (known as the *Tzemah Tzedek*),[30] and it was probably at this time that he wrote *Sipurim nora'im*.

Kaidaner's text attests to the political juncture at which it was written. As it was clearly intended, first and foremost, for the adherents and supporters of the hasidic movement, it falls into the category that Joseph Dan calls "inter-hasidic literature."[31] In the preface, however, Kaidaner lists three types of intended reader:[32] maskilim—ardent supporters of Jewish emancipation, which the hasidim actively resisted; mitnagdim—the extreme opponents of Hasidism who hounded the hasidim, even going as far as turning them in to the authorities[33]—to whose objections the book purports to respond; and hasidim—the book's primary audience.

Due to the particular rivalry between Hasidism and the Haskalah, the maskilic reader may very well have ranked just below the hasidic reader in the author's mind. After all, just as Hasidism served maskilic literature as a foil for its own development,[34] so too Hasidic literature was forged, if only in part, in response to the Haskalah. Beyond polemics, Kaidaner would also undoubtedly have hoped to win over some of the more moderate maskilic readers. Indeed, there was a pronounced divide between moderate and radical maskilim in matters concerning the Jewish religion and acceptance of Russian culture.[35] Further support for the idea that Kaidaner was specifically addressing maskilim may be found in the extensive communication that took place between hasidim and maskilim, with each group writing about the other and reading its works.[36] It also stands to reason that a hasidic writer would focus on maskilic readers, as the Haskalah was considered Hasidism's foremost rival—witness the fact that hasidim and mitnagdim set aside their differences, in early nineteenth-century Galicia, to combat the common threat of the Haskalah.[37] As Shmuel Feiner wrote, "The Hassidic movement was regarded as the traditional enemy of the Haskalah in Eastern Europe, and from the time of Salomon Maimon, Joseph Perl, Judah Leib Mieses, Isaac Erter, Isaac Baer Levinsohn, Nachman Krochmal and others, became associated with a set of negative stereotypes, expressing a social and ideological antithesis to the future envisioned by the *maskilim*. The relationship between *hasidim* and *maskilim* was viewed in dichotomous terms."[38]

At the political heart of the conflict between Hasidism and the Haskalah lay the question of Jewish emancipation. The maskilim considered the hasidim enemies of emancipation, as they did not merely fail to support it but actively fought against it. As part of their struggle against Hasidism, the maskilim showed enthusiastic support for the regime's program of Russification. In the words of Isaac Baer Levinsohn: "We are commanded by God to love the people and the king in whose land we reside . . . and nothing arouses a person to love a people and a land more than the perfect knowledge of the language of that people . . . , which is why it is right and good to adopt the language of the land as one's own language."[39] Consequently, the hasidim regarded the maskilim as collaborators and adopted a twofold strategy: vehemently opposing the Haskalah and, at the same time, seeking ways to mitigate conflict with the imperial authorities through cooperation and even participation in the government's reformist schemes.[40] Both sides, in fact, sought to maintain good relations with the authorities, while leveraging those relations against the other.

The resulting situation might best be described as one of uneasy coexistence, with neither side managing to impose its will on the entire community.[41] We must bear in mind that the maskilim did not merely pursue the Enlightenment objective of individual rights, but also sought collective rights for Jews—not only for themselves but for the entire Jewish community. They wished to transform traditional Jewish society, not abandon it. Maskilim and hasidim alike supported the continued existence of corporate Jewish communities—to which end each side developed alternative autonomous bodies to the kahal, abolished in Russia in 1844. The hasidim had their communities, led by the tzadikim, while the maskilim had their circles.[42]

Given their respective stances vis-à-vis the empire—the maskilim joining forces with the authorities against the hasidim, and the hasidim opposing the imperial regime but cooperating with it nonetheless—the struggle between Hasidism and the Haskalah may be understood in terms of protonationalism versus nonnationalism. In aspiring to civil emancipation within the empire for all Jews without renouncing Jewish distinctiveness, the Haskalah effectively embraced a proto-national position. In rejecting emancipation and the empire, on the other hand, seeking only to maintain its own way of life, Hasidism espoused a nonnational approach.[43]

The hasidic nonnationalism position and resistance to emancipation is apparent, inter alia, in the predominantly oral nature of hasidic culture—described by Moshe Rosman as follows: *"Hasidism was essentially an oral cul-*

*ture*. The organization and conduct of Hasidic life was largely a matter of oral tradition. This tradition was passed on from father to son and veteran to novice. Spreading of the doctrines was done through personal encounter and face-to-face teaching. The oral *derashah* (homily) served an important social purpose in *binding* the group together; it was not initially viewed as a spiritual legacy to be carefully recorded."[44] The hasidic tale was thus recounted by the tzadik or other witness-narrator and passed down from generation to generation.[45] The hasidic author—the bridge between the spoken and the written word[46]—therefore underscored the fact that his was not an autonomous work of belles-lettres meant to be read in private but rather a form of premodern literature intended to be recounted and performed in public.[47] In this sense, hasidic literature stands in sharp contrast to contemporary belles-lettres—that is, original works, written in a national literary language and serving as the basis for a national literature.[48]

The hasidic tale thus differs from proto-national maskilic literature in that the author's perspective is not that of an individual writer making up a story but of a writer who is a link in a narrative chain, performing a text that belongs to a collective that also reads it as a collective.[49] In other words, the hasidic author is not the Enlightenment ideal of the autonomous artist but a heteronomous storyteller subordinate to the collective and, what is more, to the tzadik and to God. That is why Jacob Kaidaner does not identify himself by name in *Sipurim nora'im*, offering only the merest hint at the very end of his preface:

> I shall not place my name at the head of these writings of mine, for I have no desire for such things. It is not for my own honor that I have composed this volume, but to show that Israel is not bereft in these generations that have witnessed God's wonders. It is truth I desire and it is therefore truth my mouth utters and words of honesty my lips speak, as Heaven is my witness, *selah*. And all who seek truth shall find sense and divine pleasure in these words of truth. Do not ask my name, for it is hidden [Judges 13:18] and concealed. Your light will burst forth [*y-v-k-a*] like the dawn [Isaiah 58:8].[50]

The author's collectivist literary perspective ("It is not for my own honor that I have composed this volume")—typical of "minor literature"[51]—would appear to stem, at least in part, from the theocentrism of hasidic theology, which places God rather than the individual at the center.[52] Once again, Kaidaner was not writing belles-lettres, which, particularly in the wake of romanticism and nationalism, ascribed considerable cultural importance to authors as individuals. In contrast to maskilic literature, which developed primarily in the European genres of satire, the novel, and the long poem,[53] the hasidic author Kaidaner wrote folktales, with the purpose of praising and immortalizing the tzadikim—"to attest to the greatness of Hasidism in general, and of Habad in particular, in both exoteric and esoteric matters."[54] The tales are meant to ensure that the deeds of the tzadikim are not forgotten. As Kaidaner notes in his preface to *Sipurim nora'im*, "I have long been fiercely jealous for the holiest ones, whose memory is nearly forgotten."[55]

The hasidic community of storytellers, readers, and listeners may thus be defined—in contrast to Benedict Anderson's imagined national community (1999)—as a *non-imagined* and therefore *nonnational* community. Such intimate groups (comprising a tzadik and his followers) were in fact "face-to-face" communities.[56] Witness, for example, the way in which Kaidaner begins a tale of a young man who came to see R. Shneur Zalman of Liadi: "My brothers and friends, pay heed to the [following] wondrous tale."[57] This opening denotes a concrete situation, in which the story is told to a concrete audience.

Unlike national time, which Anderson defines as homogenous time anonymously and simultaneously shared by members of an imagined community,[58] the time that informs hasidic literature is religious, binding a community whose members are personally acquainted with one another. It is divine time that governs all things, enabling a particular tzadik to act in a particular place and influence events on behalf of a particular person in an entirely different place, distant in time and space. In the story of the young man and R. Shneur Zalman, it was R. Shneur Zalman who acted at the synagogue in Liadi on behalf of a particular young man, whose enemies, the non-Jewish sorcerers, were killed by means of a repeated biblical verse:

> The young man went home, and as he journeyed, felt almost completely well. When he approached his destination, the Jews who lived near the high-ranking official said to him: "Have you heard what happened near your inn? The non-Jew who lives near you, near the inn, the one who runs the mill—he and his wife met a sudden death, in an instant, and neither had fallen ill in the slightest beforehand." And he asked them, "On what day did this happen?" And they re-

plied, "On the morning of the holy Sabbath." And he told them that he had sensed it in Liadi, during the chanting of the Torah. When he returned home, his wife told him about it as well. And they knew that the event had occurred at the very moment when our holy Rabbi read out the verse, "For there is no divining in Jacob [and no magic in Israel] [Numbers 23:23]." And the time of their [the foreigner and his wife's] deaths was none other than the moment at which [the rabbi] repeated the verse several times.[59]

Contrary to generalizing, abstract national time, religious time is concrete and specific, and only affects one whom the tzadik has decided it will affect. For example, it was not the Ba'al Shem Tov's intention to impart the ability to attain a state of devequt to every single Jew, only to a limited circle of intimates, known by scholars as the "Besht's circle":[60]

It was . . . [the] spontaneous relationship of each individual to the *Ẓadik* that fashioned the Hasidim into a community. Even if they visited their *Ẓadik* only once a year, meeting him or even being near him that one time was sufficient to sustain the Hasidim for the entire year. While away from the *Ẓadik*'s physical presence, the Hasidim would recount his teachings and relate details of his biography in order to maintain the sense of contact. This allowed the Hasidic community to exist even though its membership was widely dispersed. But communal cohesion was only a side benefit; the dispersed community was never organized in any fashion. Everything derived from the spontaneous relationship that each individual felt toward the head of the community. No intermediary came between the Hasid and his *rebbe*.[61]

The fact that the protagonist of the hasidic tale is usually a concrete tzadik[62] also stands in contrast to the imagined abstraction of national community, which produces the common, future-oriented national time that Anderson identifies with the rise of the novel. The tzadik in the hasidic tale—R. Shneur Zalman, in this case—is constructed as a mythological hero, thereby sanctifying the story.[63] A further essential component of the tale, however, is a member of the rabbi's flock, a certain "exceptional young man, financially dependent on his father-in-law," and the place in which the events unfold is precisely marked in hasidic space: "in the vicinity of Liadi," that is, where the rabbi himself resides.[64]

While the maskilic writers, following European literary models, produced works of fiction—thereby contributing to the initial phases of the construction of an imagined national community—the hasidic authors, who drew upon Jewish folk narrative, such as the legends of the saints, magic tales, and wisdom novellas, presented their tales as "unadulterated truth."[65] A clear expression of the latter approach can be found in the fact that the narrator in the story of the young man and R. Shneur Zalman is presented as a witness-narrator, who has firsthand knowledge of the events he describes and is well acquainted with the young man's life: "Until, in the course of time, his father-in-law's fortunes declined, and the young man was forced to engage in matters of trade."[66] He is also an omniscient narrator, who knows the young man's heart and mind: "As he journeyed through the forest near Liadi, he remembered how he used to spend [the holiday] with the rabbi [R. Shneur Zalman], and was deeply saddened. Then, in an act of self-sacrifice, he abandoned the wagon and all of its merchandise in the forest."[67]

This focus on the young man's consciousness within the narrative sequence produces the effect of a firsthand account—further reinforced by the portrayal of R. Shneur Zalman as intimately acquainted with the young man's innermost thoughts: "The rabbi, rest his soul, said to his pleasant son, the great rabbi, our teacher Rabbi Dovber: 'This young man is called a hasid by [virtue of] immense self-sacrifice.'"[68] In terms of the narrator's epistemic hierarchy, it is clear that his presence as a witness relies, theologically, on the profundity of the rabbi's knowledge—that is, his ability to know even things that are hidden. Kaidaner further stresses this point, adding that "it was a wonder in the eyes of his son the rabbi, for he knew that [his father] had not exchanged a single word with the young man."[69] So too when R. Shneur Zalman instructs that the young man should be called fifth to the reading of the Torah scroll, although "he clearly did not even know that he [the young man] had arrived."[70]

The tzadik is thus a figure who provides definite information not only about knowable events in the present or the past but also (by relying on God's will) about hidden things and future events—as, for instance, when he tells the young man, "God willing, the wagon and its merchandise will be found perfectly intact."[71] The fact that Kaidaner's narrator is a witness-narrator, whose authority ultimately derives from the theological-hasidic authority of the tzadik, effectively makes the tzadik the author of the tale, shaping and guiding the narrator while also appearing as a character in the story itself. It is only by virtue of the tzadik-author's knowledge of hidden things that the narrator is able to perceive the inner workings of the characters' minds. The hasidic tale thus eliminates the rhetorical distinction between witness-narrator and omniscient narrator and, ultimately, between narrator and author as well.

Regarding the absence of common, imagined national time in Hasidism, Immanuel Etkes wrote: "The Besht had no plan! He did not work toward any sort of final date or event of a revolutionary cast."[72] Etkes thus defines the nonnational underpinnings of hasidic practices. It is a position that saw complete redemption in the improvement of Jewish life in the diaspora.[73] To use the term coined by Gershom Scholem, Hasidism countered national teleology with a sort of "neutralized messianism."[74] In contrast to Ben Zion Dinur, who wrote copiously about messianic elements in the hasidic movement,[75] Scholem argued that the movement actually distanced itself from the idea of national redemption, which views human history as an arena in which one may act by means of messianic force,[76] to further national-political goals. The messianism that persisted in Hasidism was, rather, a vision for the future, accompanied by the belief that redemption may not be hastened.[77] As Simon Dubnow remarked regarding the messianism expressed in the "Besht's Epistle" (a letter from the Ba'al Shem Tov to his brother-in-law, R. Gershon of Kitov),[78] "The national element is canceled out by the religious element."[79]

While Hasidism indeed took a dim view of Jewish nationalism, mid-nineteenth-century Russia saw the development of another movement—the Hebrew Haskalah, which transcended local community, to act across regions. Initially, these activities consisted primarily of reciprocal visits and personal ties, lacking a trans-local framework or an established movement with a clear center and periphery. This rendered even the identification of Isaac Baer Levinsohn as the movement's leader in Russia no simple task.[80] Such attempts were, in effect, the stirrings of proto-nationalism, furthered over the course of the nineteenth century by the establishment of institutions such as the Society for Promoting Enlightenment among Jews in Russia (known by its Russian acronym, OPE)—founded in 1863 as, first, the national representative body of Russian Jews[81]—and by the maskilic approach to Judaism as a historical religion. This nascent nationalism is apparent, for example, in Levinsohn's views on the Hebrew language,[82] which he calls the "bond of religion and lifeblood of the nation," uniting "all of our brethren of the diaspora, scattered to the four winds." Furthermore, he argues that every nation has its own particular language that sets it apart from other nations, and that as "Hebrews," the Jews' should be Hebrew.[83] It was not until the 1850s and '60s, however, that Hebrew became a distinct national issue—in the writings of Judah Leib Gordon, for example, although Gordon's support for the Hebrew language was mitigated by his commitment to the Russification of the Jews.[84]

As a newly founded cultural institution, maskilic Hebrew literature sought to act as a moral "watchman"—an aspiration reflected in the title of Erter's series of satires, *Ha-Tzofeh le-Veit Yisra'el* (The Watchman of the House of Israel; an allusion to Ezekiel 3:17). Although the maskilic writers' authority did not derive from revelation,[85] the theological component of their work, in the sense of a link to historical Judaism, is clearly apparent in such biblical allusions. It is also evident in the fact that they did not merely criticize the people (for example, for embracing Hasidism) but also sought to lay the foundations for a national identity based on a new understanding of Scripture and a redefinition of the Hebrew language as embodied in and exemplified by the Bible. This new understanding of Scripture was twofold: recognizing its sacredness but also relating to it as a corpus of Jewish national literature—viewed through the prism of nostalgia for the national independence which the maskilim believed the Jewish people enjoyed in biblical times, and to which they aspired to return.[86] Hence the ambivalence of the maskilim toward the secularization of the new Hebrew literature. Although they had taken Hebrew out of the synagogue and made it a part of everyday life—keenly aware of the role of literature in constituting national identity—its connection to the Bible preserved the theological basis of maskilic nationalism. The fact that the process of maskilic secularization was never completed, or even advocated by a majority of maskilim, meant that the proto-nationalism that Hasidism encountered was, in reality, a hybrid that had never abandoned the sacred and religious components of its language and literature.

The dichotomy between hasidic and maskilic literature was thus dulled considerably, as the Haskalah that had not abandoned religion was not unequivocally opposed to Hasidism's pronounced religiosity. Furthermore, the hasidim considered the hasidic tale itself an integral part of divine worship, a quintessentially religious act, capable of gathering the "holy sparks" and achieving *tikun* (restoration).[87]

3

As outlined briefly above, Kaidaner tells the story of a young hasid forced to abandon his religious studies in order to earn a living as a merchant when his father-in-law, who had previously supported him, suffers financial ruin. One day, he decides to leave his wagon with all his wares in the forest, in order to spend the holiday of Shavuot with R. Shneur Zalman of Liadi. At the holiday's end, the rabbi informs him that he will find his wagon and merchandise just as he left them. The young man complains to the rabbi that he is no longer able to study and pray as he once did, due to the burden of earning a living. The rabbi advises him to find a village inn, where his wife may run the tavern while he spends his time immersed in study and prayer.

The young man returns to the forest, and all is indeed as the rabbi had said it would be. He is observed by a high-ranking government official who had noticed the abandoned wagon and is eager to hear his story. When the official hears of the rabbi's advice, he informs the young man that he just happens to have such an inn and will gladly rent it to him and even lend him any money he may need to cover his initial costs. Although he is warned that the inn is under the spell of two sorcerers who live nearby, he places his faith in the rabbi's counsel and rents the inn. The venture is a great success, and he is soon able to repay the official's loan.

Six months later, he falls ill and, realizing that his illness is the work of the sorcerers, goes to see the rabbi. He arrives in Liadi on the eve of the Sabbath and is so weak that he is unable to go to the synagogue until the next morning. During the service, as per the rabbi's instructions, the young man is called fifth to the reading of the weekly portion from the Torah scroll. As he approaches the podium, the rabbi glows with fervor, becoming "a flaming torch" as he reads the verse "For there is no divining in Jacob and no magic in Israel,"[88] which he repeats a number of times with great devotion. By the end of the Sabbath, the young man begins to feel better and is assured by the rabbi that all will be well. With the rabbi's blessing, the young man returns home, where he discovers that the sorcerer and his wife suddenly died—as it turned out, at the very moment the rabbi had recited the verse in the synagogue. The young man went on to become very wealthy and remained devoted to Torah study all his days.

The choice of the Jewish innkeeper as a protagonist reflects a trend in Polish literature—the stereotyped depiction of the demonic Jewish innkeeper who, through the sale of liquor, acts as an intermediary between Jews and non-Jews.[89] The non-Jewish government official who facilitates the young man's rental of the inn represents the hasidic theological concept of tikun (restoration)—realized in the story through the cooperation between the authorities (represented by the official) and the hasidim to defeat the sorcerers. Indeed, the official who had wondered at the sight of a wagon standing unattended in the forest for three days was very impressed by the young man's explanation ("and it was a marvel in his eyes"),[90] thereby effectively accepting the authority of the tzadik as an authentic miracle worker. So too the official's offer of an inn to rent as well as a loan to get the young man started bring the tzadik's advice to fruition, making the government official an emissary of the tzadik.

The empire is thus represented in the story as an ally of Hasidism, while the inn leased by the young man embodies the way in which the hasidim perceived their relationship with the empire—as a framework that enables their survival without having to renounce their religious autonomy (as renters they make no claims of ownership over Russian space). In turn, the empire, represented by the official, affirms the divine authority of the tzadik. Thus, under the tzadik's aegis, the story manages to realize a flexible and complex relationship between the Russian authorities and the Jews, who are part of the empire and wish to survive within it, despite the threat of Russification. Kaidaner's story also establishes the young man as a paradigm of those Jews charged with negotiating with the empire on behalf of their coreligionists—following the convention in hasidic tales that non-Jewish kings and noblemen have virtually no contact with ordinary Jews, instead dealing exclusively with Jewish tenants, big community leaders, court advisers, or community rabbis.[91]

Indeed, in the story of the young man and R. Shneur Zalman, contact between the hasidim and the non-Jewish inhabitants of the empire is controlled and supervised by the tzadik, so that even where there is danger, the young man is sure to come to no harm. The words "For there is no divining in Jacob and no magic in Israel" recited by the rabbi to protect the young man and his family from the non-Jewish sorcerers are uttered in the Bible by the non-Jew Balaam, whose blessings protected the Jews against the evil designs of Balak, king of Moab. Thus, when the local Jews warn the young man of the danger in leasing this particular inn, he replies: "I do not fear the sorcerers, for the holy rabbi has ordained that I shall make a living in this way. Would the holy rabbi grant me a livelihood that would cause my death? God forbid that any evil should come from him."[92]

The ambivalence of the hasidic survivalist stance vis-à-vis the Russian authorities is reflected in aspects of the official's behavior that are not directly addressed in the story. For example, the official must have been aware of the danger posed by the inn when he offered it to the young man, yet he said nothing. It is also clear that he had not taken any steps to have the sorcerers removed. As a matter of fact, he was probably thrilled at the opportunity to rent a cursed inn that no one else wanted. Perhaps he had faith in the tzadik's ability to resolve the problem, although this explanation is unlikely, as a hagiographic text such as this would certainly have celebrated the fact. What the story actually seems to imply is that as beneficial and religiously significant as cooperation with the non-Jewish empire may be, the politics of survival demand a certain amount of distance and caution.

The degree of hostility found in the maskilic anti-hasidic satires is unparalleled in hasidic literature, which chose a more subversive path—combining opposition to the Haskalah with attempts to make the hasidic tale and its politics more accessible to the maskilic reader. This complex hasidic approach to the Haskalah may also shed light on hasidic interaction with the Russian Empire, since the hasidim viewed the maskilim as agents of the empire as well as coreligionists. Ultimately, however, the gap between the two movements in such matters was not unbridgeable, as both advocated Jewish autonomy and the continued existence of corporate Jewish communities. This affinity between the movements is illustrated, for example, in Kaidaner's portrayal of the high-ranking official, which resembles depictions of imperial officials in maskilic literature.

The Habad tale (of which Kaidaner's story is one) may be seen as an integral part of material religious life, with those involved in the world of action and engaged in public service[93] obeying the dictates of Habad theosophy through the story.[94] Like the hasidic tale in general, it is based on the mythic contrast between good and evil (the official and the sorcerers, in Kaidaner's story), rooted in anthropocentric kabbalistic dualism.[95] Accordingly, human history is understood as the story of cosmic tikun, after which the Jewish people will be redeemed as a necessary outcome of the redemption and restoration of God.[96] In Kaidaner's story, the young man abandons the material wagon because it is the expression of the divine in physical matter. He later returns to its materiality, as "the revealed semblance of reality and its true infinite essence—that are defined as *Yesh* [being] and *'Ayin* [nothingness], reflect the double meaning of existence in which everything embodies itself and its opposite. . . . However, each of these opposites changes its essence fundamentally and incessantly—the infinite yearns to be manifest in the finite, and the finite aspires to be enveloped again in the infinite."[97]

Rabbi Shneur Zalman himself, as he appears in this tale, "annihilates" himself in prayer, realizing the Habad ideal of *avodah be-vittul* (worship in self-annihilation). "The goal of such worship is the annihilation of being into nothingness, the effacement of each person's separate being, and its reinclusion within the Divine. . . . The concept of self-annihilation is meant to express the consciousness that one is esteemed as nought before the divine source. *Bittul* reflects the human relation to reality as devoid of autonomous essence, because the divine abundance provides life and being at every instance."[98] In helping the young man obtain a livelihood and bringing about the deaths of his enemies through prayer, R. Shneur Zalman imbues mundane affairs with divine meaning.

There are a number of elements in the story that reflect the subversive ambivalence of the hasidic reaction to the Haskalah. For example, at the very heart of the story is a young hasid who earns his living as a merchant. This would appear to be an attempt to find common ground with maskilic readers. Although the maskilim advocated the "productivization" of Jews and criticized those who engaged in commerce, such activities (as opposed to complete "unproductivity") enjoyed a degree of tolerance. Even Levinsohn, who advocated Jewish labor in agriculture, did not reject commerce outright.[99] In general, "Levinsohn presented his model of Haskalah in such a way as to allow the Eastern European Jew to live 'in both worlds' at once."[100] Another aspect of the tale's continuous debate with the maskilic reader appears at the end, when the pupil becomes a wealthy man and remains true to his studies and prayers. In this, the story refutes the Haskalah claim that Scripture studies prevent the integration of the hasidim into the labor market. Another attempt to engage maskilic readers appears at the very end of the story, when the young man is said to have become both very wealthy *and* a faithful student of the Torah. This seems to be an attempt to refute maskilic criticism that Torah study prevents the hasidim from joining the labor force.

Most of all, however, the story seems to seek legitimacy in the eyes of the reader—the maskilic reader in particular—by contrasting the magic of the tzadik and that of the non-Jewish sorcerer and his wife. Magic is common in Hasidism, and magic contests are a frequent theme in hasidic tales,[101] while the Haskalah was contemptuous of all magic, miracle workers, and folk healers. Kaidaner thus seeks to paint R. Shneur's action—causing the sorcerers' death by reciting the verse "For there is no divining in Jacob and no magic in Israel"—as "white magic," drawing upon the holy forces of God and the angels, rather than "black magic," considered illegitimate sorcery.[102] This approach is particularly interesting in light of R. Shnuer Zalman's well-known disdain for the cult of the tzadik and the expectation that the tzadik will provide his followers with material assistance—performing miracles, resolving financial woes, healing the sick, and making the barren fruitful.[103] Indeed, in another story Kaidaner denounces magical practices,[104] and in yet another defends the Ba'al Shem Tov against accusations of having performed magic by means of sacred names.[105] The hasidic struggle for legitimacy is particularly evident in the storyteller's intentional choice of a verse from Balaam's blessing, which actually stresses the fact that the Israelites do not practice sorcery. Kaidaner's attempt to legitimize R. Shneur Zalman's magic—whether by virtue of the verse he employs or by contrast with the sorcery performed by the non-Jews whose death he causes—should thus be seen in light of maskilic criticism of the irrational, magical practices of the hasidim—in Judah Leib Mieses's *Kin'at ha-Emet* (Zeal for the Truth, Vienna, 1828), for example, or Erter's *Ha-Tzofeh le-Veit Yisra'el* (The Watchman for the House of Israel, Vienna, 1858).[106]

The use of "white magic" to combat non-Jewish sorcerers[107]—generally identified in hasidic tales with wicked officials or representatives of the church—should also be seen in the context of hasidic survival strategies, as members of a persecuted minority within the Russian Empire, offering them some comfort and hope.[108]

4

The strongest manifestation of the battle between Hasidism and the Haskalah in Kaidaner's tales can be found in the very language he employs: a combination of Hebrew and Yiddish. While Yiddish was widely denigrated by maskilim as "ugly,"[109] their actual attitude to the language was far more ambivalent or, as Shmuel Werses described it (paraphrasing a talmudic expression), "the right hand rebuffs while the left hand beckons."[110] The attitudes of miskilim to Hebrew were far less ambiguous. The Haskalah had developed a "high," largely biblical form of Hebrew, which they termed "pure language," rejecting all forms of contamination, whether from Yiddish or Aramaic, as in the traditional rabbinic style.[111]

Hasidic literature—more specifically, hasidic tales and hagiographies—had no such qualms about the "purity" of language and freely mixed Hebrew and Yiddish in a non-diglossic fashion, hardly distinguishing between high and low registers. In Kaidaner's case, this was certainly also a result of the heterogeneous and dialogic nature of his linguistic performance—in contrast to the monologic character of maskilic literature. Hasidic Hebrew style was so influenced by Yiddish that Shmuel Niger referred to the language of Rabbi Nahman of Bratslav's tales as "Yiddishized Hebrew,"[112] a hybrid that undermined the maskilic aspiration to create a homogenous "pure language" with a single clear origin. This Hebrew-Yiddish hybrid threatened to undermine the maskilic project of creating a "pure," homogenous national language with a single clear origin.

The two positions were not entirely adversarial, however. Despite its ambivalent attitude to Yiddish and despite its support for Russification, the Haskalah shared Hasidism's attitude of linguistic resistance to the empire. For example, Rabbi Shneur Zalman of Liadi used the sacred tongue (echoing maskilic devotion to Hebrew) as a tool of resistance against imperial oppression, changing the language of his lessons to Hebrew in response to the restrictive statues of 1804—although his intention was certainly to effect change through the mystical properties of the language.[113]

The Hebrew literature created by the authors of the hasidic tales constituted Hebraic continuity rooted in Yiddish. Unlike the mitnagdim, who simply incorporated Yiddish words directly into the Hebrew text,[114] thereby demonstrating their indifference to the question of Hebrew literature, the hasidim created a Hebrew-Yiddish continuum: a dialogic language in the Bakhtinian sense—that is, a polyphony that unifies consciousnesses (Yiddish and Hebrew) without positing unitary knowledge.[115] As Mikhail Bakhtin stresses, every word is directed at another, every utterance has an addressee. Within the framework of linguistic dialogism, however, the "otherness" addressed by the speaker is not singular but merges with the singular speaker in dialectic transcendence.

Bakhtin points out that the center, which creates meaning, encounters otherness not as something absolute and stable but rather from a perspective of relativity. In other words, the center is dependent on the other for its existence, and therefore produces only the illusion of presence. The self is dialogic, relative: its meaning is the product of an ongoing process, not a finished thing. The fact that meaning is generated by dialogue suggests a struggle between different meanings. This clash of events of meaning is part of the conflict between "self" and "other."[116]

Bakhtin called this this polyphony of social and discursive forces "heteroglossia." The term marks the social and cultural conditions that generate meaning out of the mélange of different languages. At any given moment, powerful, yet unstable, factors exist that make the utterance of a meaningful word possible—a meaning that may change if the word is spoken at a different time or in a different place. Unlike structuralism, which seeks to uncover inherent patterns in language, all utterances are heteroglossic in Bakhtin's view, because they are "shaped by forces whose particularity and variety are practically beyond systematization."[117]

Shmeruk and Werses describe hasidic language and its ties to Yiddish in their discussion of Perl's satirical parody of hasidic texts.[118] Hasidic Hebrew is characterized by parataxis (extensive use of the *vav* conjunction), pleonasm (use of the *vav* conjunction to introduce a temporal clause that comes after the main clause), and disagreement in gender and number between nouns, verbs, and adjectives—all establishing Yiddish within Hebrew. Yiddish is also integrated in hasidic Hebrew in the following ways: "1. Yiddish explanations of features of local reality; 2. idiomatic expressions borrowed from Yiddish; 3. expressions particular to polemical speech; 4. Hebrew idioms incorporated into Yiddish; 5. spelling of Hebrew words based on Yiddish pronunciation."[119]

Shmerok and Werses also point out the use of the Hebrew definite article following Yiddish rather than Hebrew usage (*ha-shenei yo'atzim*, in place of *shenei ha-yo'atzim* [the two advisers]; *mekhashef ha-aher* in place of *ha-mekhashef ha-aher* [the other sorcerer]); matching adjectives to the Yiddish gender of the modified noun (*be-atzvut gadol* [with great sadness]); gendering adverbs (changed to adjectives in Hebrew) as in Yiddish (*na'aseh ha-medinah male* [Yid. *ful*] *gazlanim* [the country became full of thieves]); changing the Hebrew preposition *le* (to) to *al* (on)—translating the Yiddish *oyf*; using the *kal* or *pi'el* constructions with *et atzmo* (himself) where the Yiddish *zikh* would be used (*ve-shakhvu et atzmam* [lay (themselves) down]); dropping the *vav* in words ending in *vav-tav*, as per their Yiddish pronunciation (*apikors't* [pron. *apikorses*], in place of *apikorsut* [heresy]).

This mixture of Yiddish and Hebrew is emblematic of the paradoxical hasidic conception of reality ("everything embodies itself and its opposite") and of the view that divine sparks can be found even in the lowest estates and among the simplest and the least educated. The hasidic text thus combines the "low" and the profane with the "high" and the sacred—mundane Yiddish with the Holy Tongue (just as physical matter was mixed with divine fragments or sparks as a result of the cosmic "breaking of the vessels"). In this way, Hebrew remains religiously charged even as it is combined with Yiddish. This approach is typical of the Habad movement from its inception, rooted in the famous letter written by the Ba'al Shem Tov to his brother-in-law, R. Gershon of Kitov.[120]

This stood in sharp contrast to the scorn heaped on Yiddish by the maskilim, whose neoclassical orientation led them to favor the use of Russian over a language they considered inferior.[121] The hasidic tale thus undermined the credibility and aesthetic authority of the idea of a "pure" language. "The Haskalah's newfound bilingualism reflected, above all, the duality of its approach to the empire. Indeed, [the *maskilim*] hoped that identification with the centralized state would supplant premodern collective identity, leaving the language of ritual and spirituality to be purified and purged of its so-called perverted and defective layers."[122]

Hasidic literature may thus be described as a "minor literature,"[123] inasmuch as it was deterritorialized in relation to the "major literature" of the Haskalah. It was the literature of a religious rather than a national community and assumed a position against the proto-national "major" literature of the Haskalah. Kaidaner deterritorialized Hebrew by creating a literary language that heterogeneously and fluently combined Hebrew and Yiddish. His Hebrew is often a translation that preserves the original language, and his use of Yiddish loanwords (calques) reflects the fact that hasidic dialogue and discourse were generally conducted in Yiddish, as opposed to hasidic writing, which was primarily in Hebrew. The following are a few examples of Kaidaner's Hebrew-Yiddish style (also reflecting some of the characteristics pointed out by Werses and Shmeruk) in the story of the young man and R. Shneur Zalman:[124]

1. *Pa'am nasa al ha-yerid* (once he went to the fair): The Hebrew preposition *el/le* is replaced with the preposition *al* (a translation of the Yiddish *oyfn*).
2. *Ve-darko hayah linso'a al Hag ha-Shavu'ot* (it was his custom to travel [to the tzadik for the holiday of Shavuot]): Again, the preposition *al* (rather than *el* or *le*) is a translation of the Yiddish *oyfn*.
3. *Ad she-noda lo ha-mesir't* [pron. *Mesires*] *nefesh shelo* (until he discovered his self-sacrifice): The *vav* in the *vav-tav* ending of the word *mesirut* is dropped, writing the word as it is pronounced in Yiddish. The lack of gender agreement between the subject and the verb, as well as the placement of the definite article, also reflect Yiddish rather than Hebrew usage.
4. *Ve-ahar zeh ra'ah eikh she-ba ha-avrekh el ha-agalah* (and then he saw the young man approach the wagon; lit. how the young man approached the wagon): This is a direct translation from the Yiddish, *er hot gezen vi s'iz gekumen der avrekh*.

It was Joseph Klausner who praised Hasidic language precisely for these inconsistencies (as opposed to those who dismissed it as Yiddishized Hebrew), arguing that they proved it was a living language.[125] Hasidic language is nondiglossic but, at the same time, diglossic—using low Yiddish for high intellectual purposes and high Hebrew for a low literary genre. Rather than as an aberration, Lewis Glinert sees this as a step toward linguistic modernity: "using a single language in a multiplicity of functions." In this way, hasidic language contributed to the emergence of a Modern Hebrew vernacular (used by the hasidim alongside Yiddish) and to the prestige of Yiddish.[126]

In combining Yiddish and Hebrew, hasidic language combines oral and written language as well. Itamar Even-Zohar argues that there is indeed a hierarchical diglossia in the hasidic tale, with each language serving a different purpose: the primary language compensates for what it lacks by using the secondary language, whether directly or through loan translations.[127] This would seem to indicate that the hasidic text does not in fact employ the secondary language, Yiddish, in its own right but merely uses it to fill the lacunae of the primary language. There is another possibility, however, and that is that the secondary language, rather than complementing the primary language and compensating for its deficiencies, in fact further destabilizes the system, creating a heterogeneous language. Dan Miron suggests that hasidic literature was, in fact, "a bilingual Jewish literature, whose essential character was non-diglossic, or almost non-diglossic, namely, a literature in which the two Jewish languages functioned within a framework where the high-low, sharply etched binarism became blurry and diffuse."[128]

Following Miron, the language of Kaidaner's hasidic tales may be said to be the product of the encounter between premodern textuality and modernity in the form of maskilic literature. The hasidic text is subject to the subversive power of Yiddish, which generates an unrestrained, deterritorialized discourse that undermines the proto-nationalist function of Hebrew in Haskalah literature. I deliberately write proto-nationalist and not nationalist, because the neoclassical gap between sensual intent and linguistic outcome also exists in maskilic literature (later bridged, for example, in the synthetic language of Shalom Jacob Abramovitsh [Mendele Moykher-Sforim], as well as in Hayim Nahman Bialik's romantic-nationalist language).

The Haskalah disparaged hasidic speech. Joseph Perl, for example, in *Megaleh Temirin*, mocks the hasidim, whom he describes as "unable to write the Holy Tongue properly and, like simpletons, routinely make errors and mistakes."[129] Upon closer examination, however, we discover that the "errors and mistakes" in the Hebrew of the hasidic tale are the result of the destabilizing power of Yiddish, which creates an unruly, deterritorialized text, thereby disrupting the proto-national function of Hebrew in maskilic literature. If "politics consists in reconfiguring the distribution of the sensible which defines the common of a community, to introduce into it new subjects and objects, to render visible what had not been, and to make heard as speakers those who had been perceived as mere noisy animals,"[130] then the discourse of the hasidic tale strove to unsettle the "linguistic purity" of the emerging proto-nationalist Hebrew of the Haskalah.

Dan Miron remarked, in reference to the *shibutz* ("inlay" or "mosaic") style in maskilic literature,[131] "the controlling power of meaning in the linguistic organization of the utterance is rather limited, sometimes being reduced to the selection of units that appear to be roughly appropriate and to stringing these units syntactically together" "without there being a link between these units and the one-off meaning which they effect."[132] In this process of insertion and syntactic integration, there would appear to be some parallel between maskilic and hasidic literature—an affinity reinforced by the reverence that both the Haskalah and Hasidism had for the Hebrew language.[133] Thus, despite the stark contrasts between hasidic and maskilic language, the two languages also bear a degree of resemblance to each other, in their aversion to nationalist unification and romantic homogeneity.

In the course of its transition toward nationalism, the Haskalah also changed its attitude to the Russian-Hebrew diglossia it had developed under imperial rule. As Israel Bartal wrote, "In the age of emerging nationalisms under multicultural empires, adopting the language of the imperial center was a significant political act, clearly reflecting the tension between the Jews and their environment, which demanded that they adopt the local national language.... Modern Jewish nationalism introduced a strange and innovative concept to the traditional Jewish collective—a single language for all purposes; in other words, abolishing diglossia."[134]

Hasidic nonnationalist language took a different but not antithetical path. On the one hand the hasidim (especially Habad) emphasized diglossia and made a clear distinction between the Holy Tongue and the national "Zionist language,"[135] while preserving Yiddish as a spoken, secular language. In their literature, however, rather than abolishing diglossia by eliminating one of the two languages—as the nationalists had done with Yiddish or the Yiddishists had done with Hebrew—they reduced the diglossia itself to the point where Yiddish and Hebrew became intertwined. The result was a heterogeneous language, which constantly undermined the "major," homogenous, exclusive, national language.

Chapter 5

# The Politics of *Sefer Hasidim* by Micha Yosef Berdichevsky

I

In 1900, Micha Yosef Berdichevsky published four books of prose fiction and four books of essays. In that same year, he also published a ninth volume, *Sefer Hasidim*, a collection of stories and nonfiction pieces, most of which he had collected from hasidic literature, in particular from *In Praise of the Baal Shem Tov*, but also from *Hasidic Ethical Wills* and *Shalom 'al Israel* by Eliezer Zvi Zweifel.[1] Like other writers—for example, Y. L. Peretz, Yehuda Shteynberg, Martin Buber, and Sh. Y. Agnon—Berdichevsky reworked hasidic texts and adapted them for a modern Jewish literature.

In *Sefer Hasidim*, which was written in the summer and autumn of 1894,[2] Berdichevsky created a neoromantic Hebrew literary work in the spirit of the fin-de-siècle; within that framework he nationalized the hasidic text and inserted it into Zionist national culture.[3] *Sefer Hasidim* "reflects the influence of the Symbolist-Romantic climate in European culture, which Berdichevsky actively pursued during the period of his studies in Germany and Switzerland." Furthermore, "as a native son of the city of Medzhybizh, the cradle of Hasidism, and as someone who had since childhood soaked up the legacy of his family, which always prided itself on its close connections with the dynasty of the Baal Shem Tov, Berdichevsky revealed throughout his life a deep affinity to the world of Hasidism, an affinity that reveals itself in scores of his essays and stories."[4]

In the sketch "On Hasidism," which he sent to the editor of the journal *ha-Magid*—reacting to the negative criticism from the hasidic community in the wake of the publication of chapters from *Sefer Hasidism* in *Sifrei sha'ashu'im*, edited by Isaac Fernhof[5]—Berdichevsky explicitly wrote that "the Hasidic movement is, in my opinion, a revelation of great and lofty power that acts at the depths of the national soul and arouses the spirit of life in our dry bones."[6] With these words he acknowledges the influence of *Moreh nevuchei ha-zman* (Guide for the Perplexed of the Time) by Rabbi Nachman Krochmal, first published in 1851, which stressed the spiritual weight of myth, "whose main principle is the meaning of the heart, and its purpose is to instill in the people's thoughts devotion, morals, and good beliefs, for the individual and for the group."[7]

Indeed, the Hasidic text was at its origin a nonnationalist, religious text. In Berdichevsky's hands the hasidic text received a new national makeover by his preserving its religious content. In this way, Berdichevsky was not dissimilar to Ahad Ha'am (who also strove for modern nationhood, but without national Jewish sovereignty), who wrote in his 1902 article "Resurrection of the Spirit" about Hasidism: "Despite all of its erosion, Hasidism still contains here and there significant ideas impressed with *Hebrew originality*, more than we would be able to find in the literature of the '*haskalah*.'"[8]

But how exactly to place the religious hasidic text in relation to nationalism, that is, in relation to modern sovereign Jewish existence, which was so important to Berdichevsky? Talal Asad in his discussion of the history of religion maintains that nationalism in fact has religious roots.[9] Even further he argues against accepting the simplicity of the secularization thesis, whereby national progress entails the historical transition from religion to secularism. Even though nationalist secularism sees itself in opposition to God, in fact it is not detached from God; secular nationalism is often very close to divinity, whose absence is quite present in its conception.[10]

Preservation of religious content from hasidic texts is opposed to the Nietzschean motto "In order to build an altar, you need to destroy an altar," which Berdichevsky declares at the beginning of his essay "Old Age and Adolescence" (1899). This motto, which elicited sharp criticism from Shmuel Leib Zitron,[11] shows that Berdichevsky did not talk only about the destruction of religion but rather also about the construction of sanctity. According to Avner Holtzman, "We need to recognize that the Nietzschean content was integrated within an independent conception that included a strong basis of renewed nostalgia for the tradition of Israel."[12] Even though the hasidic text was originally not a national text, it is important not to allow the religiousness of the hasidic text to blind us to its nationalizing function; we need to avoid reading the hasidic text in the light of its nationalism.[13]

2

The translator, according to Jacques Derrida, following Walter Benjamin, has an obligation to the original. The original does not require a faithful reproduction; rather, "it gives itself within its own transformation."[14] Indeed, in the terms of Gilles Deleuze and Félix Guattari.[15] Berdichevsky in his nationalizing act of translation changed the status of hasidic literature within the Hebrew literature of the period of national renaissance, from a "minor literature" to a hegemonic "major literature," which imagined itself, in the end, as a literature for a Jewish state. At the fin de siècle hasidic literature stood opposite the literature of the Haskalah, which offered itself as a model of a major literature. But Berdichevsky overcame his opposition to the minor hasidic text and translated it into a universal major-literature model.

It's possible that the hasidic text might best be understood, first and foremost, in terms of what Deleuze and Guattari called "the deterritorialization of language," that is, as a wild, unkempt language that is not organized in the simple forms of a crystalized, homogeneous style. Because of this, Jacob Elbaum argued in the matter of the hasidic story that "even if the language stutters, the stammer is located principally in the grammar of the language, and we shouldn't conclude presumptively from that about the creative power (or lack of power) of the writer." Elbaum continued that it is possible to find in the hasidic story "a mélange of languages and styles: Biblical phrases, language structures derived from the sages, Aramaisms and Yiddishisms."[16] Joseph Klausner, who also defended the language of the hasidim, defined it as a "natural language" and preferred it to the language of the maskilim because of its "vitality."[17]

Berdichevsky himself, after going back on his original excitement about Hasidism, as reflected in *Sefer Hasidim*,[18] articulated for some years the linguistic and structural minorness of the hasidic text when speaking about the mix of names, fictional tenses, and repetitions and contradictions: "This mix is present in all the tales. Here there are complete stories, stories that are almost Biblical in their completeness and flow of language: and there, there is no order . . . and no flow of events. . . . Sometimes the narrator speaks in the first person, other times in the third. Sometimes he repeats what was already told, sometimes contradicts himself, or begins and does not finish."[19] In *Sefer Hasidim*, Berdichevsky domesticated the minor text. Through the means of the national subject, he formulated a linguistic territorialization for the hasidic text that "normalized" its language for inclusion in a major Hebrew literature. Indeed, in 1908, eight years after the publication of *Sefer Hasidim*, Berdichevsky was involved, together with Joseph Hayim Brenner, in a struggle against the minor literature of Hebrew writers from Galicia, like Isaac Fernhof and Re'uven Fahn, and in favor of a major Hebrew literature that both Berdichevsky and Brenner were working to establish.[20]

Berdichevsky articulated this process of creating a major literature through violent control of a synthetic literary language, which had developed to a certain extent at that time within the hegemonic language of the new Hebrew literature. In the words of Ziporah Kagan, at the base of this language stood "an eclectic style that united several linguistic strata—layered and distinct 'linguistic streams'—into one language. This was a language made up of an *unparalleled* combination of Biblical Hebrew, the language of wisdom literature, medieval Hebrew, and more."[21] In a process that Deleuze and Guattari would call the reterritorialization of language, Berdichevsky therefore translated the minor language of *In Praise of the Baal Shem Tov*, and of other hasidic texts, into the suitable language of the major literature.

Another expression of minorness can be understood within the identity of the author of the hasidic text. Berdichevsky transformed the anonymous, folk text of the hasidim, whose authorship was, so far as anyone knew, collective, into a text by an individual author, the type who stood at the center of literary creativity within the period of national renaissance. *In Praise of the Baal Shem Tov* does include stories by Rabbi Dov Ber Melinitz, but over the decades that separated the oral version of the tales and their publication in 1815, and in light of the fact that several versions of the stories are known (in Yiddish versions too), and considering the role of the printers in organizing these versions[22]—from all these factors it's clear that the function of the book's author was not individual but collective. In the story of the revelation of the Ba'al Shem Tov, for instance, there are two versions: one by Dov Ber Melinitz and the other by the printer Israel Jaffe.[23]

In the words of Moshe Rosman, it's necessary to notice a sharp distinction between the context of the authorship of *In Praise of the Baal Shem Tov* and the context of its printing.[24] Indeed, it is necessary to add that the provenance of transmission of these texts is not always clear, and the texts themselves appear originally in print as if they had been passed down from the mouth of some or other tzadik. An obvious objection to the significance and authority of the original hasidic text comes from the fact that most books about Hasidism from the first generations were written by students who attributed the writings to their rabbis. It is known, for example, that the stories of the acts of Rabbi Nachman from Bratslav are actually texts by his pupil, Rabbi Nathan Sternhertz, and were transmitted in Yiddish, only later being translated into Hebrew.

In order to translate the minor hasidic text into a major text Berdichevsky employed a device similar to that in his stories from the same period, where he gave the protagonist his own given name, Michael, and placed in the center of the story an original, individual character. As someone born in Medzhybizh, the Ba'al Shem Tov's hometown, Berdichevsky placed at the beginning of *Sefer Hasidim* an autobiographical article called "The Soul of the Hasidim." In this, Berdichevsky created a place for an autobiographical author who helped create a major national literature that places at its center the autonomous individual.[25] Indeed, according to Holtzman, the autobiographical position in "The Soul of the Hasidim" is "Berdichevsky's first conscious attempt to give his own biographical material an artistic function and place it at the intersection of national and mythic meaning."[26] Like the autobiographical foundation, which focuses on the individual and exists beyond any particular belonging, a universalism gives power to Berdichevsky's fiction, the origin of which is the European Enlightenment and which subjugates under the hegemony of the nation different identities that do not naturally coexist. This power is what harnesses the collective hasidic text in *Sefer Hasidim* to the creation of a major national literature.

In fact, objections to this version of nationalism arose, and this neohasidic tendency was harshly attacked by Shai Horowitz and Moshe Lieb Lilenblum.[27] In spite of which, Berdichevsky nevertheless was one of the founders of a national paradigm within the center of Hasidism. Indeed, since the beginning of the twentieth century the study of Hebrew hasidic literature has worked to blend this literature, one way or another, with the national Zionist project, by emphasizing the universal humanistic foundations that anchored Jewish law.[28]

Individualism is the basis of Berdichevsky's thought; as Nicham Ross writes: "Writing about Hasidism in the new Hebrew literature presented it as the inspiration for national attention to the spiritual universe of the individual."[29] It seems that Berdichevsky's stance coincides with the trend that crystalized in Simon Dubnow's research of Hasidism three decades later: Dubnow presented Hasidism as the uprising of individualistic essence after the demise of Sabbateanism, in an attempt to show that Hasidism converted national redemption into personal redemption.[30] It also seems that Berdichevsky was deeply impressed by the hasidic idea of minimalism, which sees in the reader who is exposed to the hasidic text an individual who regards the concept of "sparks" as belonging to individual people in their present life.[31] Berdichevsky's thought posits at its center the "desire for life" which beats within the soul of the Jewish individual and which is supposed to materialize through aesthetic experience, which allows a synthesis between both the subjective feelings of the artist and general human reality, as well as between physical and spiritual life.[32] According to Berdichevsky, the "loyal poet" is the one *"whose soul and the external world combine within him into one thing* and they create one thing."[33] The aesthetic appearance of these hasidic notions manifests itself in Berdichevsky in the image of the lonely young Jewish man. Thus, Brenner in his article "Mediations of an Author" regarded this manifestation in Berdichevsky as the beginning of a period of Hebrew prose at the beginning of the century.[34]

The fierce conflicts that were typical of Berdichevsky's thought and literary creativity intensified the strong effect of autonomy in his subject, through what Simon Halkin called "the pain of Jewish historicism," which emphasizes the importance of the individual as opposed to any generalization of Judaism as a religious or moral idea.[35] Dan Miron pointed out a similar process that developed at the same time in Hayim Nahman Bialik's poetry: "This is how Bialik used the prophetic mask to separate his 'I' from the collective national identity, and that is how the mask became the central means for forming his national poetry. This poetry did not in fact come to 'express' the people, to give an outlet to their sufferings and outcries of thousands of years; rather, it changed the people to extract it forcefully from the quagmire of static spiritual reality it was in".[36] As we've seen, in 1900, simultaneously with the publication of *Sefer Hasidim*, Berdichevsky also published collections of stories in which he established the national subject in the form of the concrete universal. This was also his point of departure in the national translation of Hasidism, as Gershom Sholem would claim years later: "The original contribution of Hasidism to the treasure of religious thought ... was intertwined with the way in which it understood values of the life of the individual: general ideas became individual moral values."[37]

This is then the literary basis for the national subject that Berdichevsky continuously groomed in his philosophical and literary work. Even when he rejected the Zionist establishment, and even when he claimed that Zionism was already too late,[38] and even when he doubted the possibility of settling the land.[39] Berdichevsky still believed in the Jewish universal individual as a national foundation. And even if at times he became weary of Jews as such,[40] he always maintained a universal radical negation of the diaspora.[41] It is interesting that Brenner, in his article "The Image of the Zionist Immigrant in Our Literature" (1919), characterized Yehoshua-Nathan, the protagonist of Berdichevsky's story "The Exit," who abandons the diaspora and emigrates to Eretz-Israel, as doing this as an individual for himself and not for the collective.[42]

The particular national identity of the concrete universal was based for Berdichevsky on universalist justifications. That is how things are, for example, in the novella "Two Camps," in which, according to Miron, the protagonist transforms from a state of chaos and blindness to a state of exerting his individual will within the conflictual two-camp existence in which he lives and in which he establishes himself. In other words, on one hand, he is a universal individual disconnected from his past or any social group; on the other, he has a will that has no realization except within the framework of a certain collective.[43] This is a clear example of the "concrete universal," which even when it is informed by the particular will acts from within a great conflict embodied by the deep universal commitment of the individual, meaning the universality of any person in the world.

In his discussion of what Hasidism means for him, Berdichevsky emphasized its "lyrical imagery,"[44] meaning the universal aesthetics he experienced while he worked on the hasidic texts. Berdichevsky's universalism is nicely expressed in the introduction to *Sefer Hasidim*, where he translated the pantheistic ideas inherited from Hasidism and romanticism, in which there is no place devoid of god,[45] an autonomous universal stance. In his words, "Humanity is the sum of all creation and its outcome from beginning to end,"[46] and thus, paradoxically, it is in fact the individual who eventually establishes the national culture.

A poignant example of Berdichevsky's establishment of an autonomous moral and individual subject by means of the individual's turbulent interiority is shown in the story "Redemption," included in *Sefer Hasidim*, with the character of Rabbi Rafael of Bersher, whose deep morality refused to lie even to save one Jewish soul; to prevent moral turpitude, Rabbi Rafael requested that God take his life instead.[47] Berdichevsky published his version of the story already in 1892 under the title "The Death of a Tzadik,"[48] and it is possible to assume that he heard the famous story about the life and death of Rabbi Rafael from the rabbi's disciples when he stayed in Bersher in the years 1887–89. In order to understand the way in which Berdichevsky worked the story in *Sefer Hasidim*, it is interesting to compare his version with the canonic one that appears in the hasidic book *Letters of Eliyahu*, by Eliyahu Lerman, published in 1894. "As brought forth in the Gemorrah (Nida 36) there was a rabbi who said to his wife 'prepare my shroud' and died before it was his time. And so it came to pass in our lifetime (of the righteous Rabbi Rafael of Bericht, of blessed memory) who was afraid he would be forced to tell a lie and was very cautious of it and said about himself even the hairs of my *payos* have no hint of prevarication in them. And he lay on the ground and rested his soul."[49] As opposed to Lerman's succinct rendition, Berdichevsky formed his story through broad psychological characterizations of Rabbi Rafael of Bersher, using internal and external monologues to reflect an individual, autonomous subject. For example: "No! He won't perform this abomination, he won't do it. . . . But the blood of the Jew will be on him? And the wife? And her children? . . . And suddenly he woke up and jumped from his bed, his face in a state of horror, and he called out with a great cry: Lies! Monster! Satan! Get out of my house! Get out, vermin! Beware, do not touch me. . . . Oh your smell is in my nose, you reek, poison, and suffocate. Be gone! Get out!"[50]

3

Secularism includes within it religious meaning through the connection to nationality. That is to say, the national arena is the site where secularism and theology converge and where the hybridity of national theology materializes. This duplicity of the national text was well identified by Berdichevsky, who described it in the preface to his collected essays called *Ba-derekh* (On the Way; 1922); there, he discusses *Sefer Hasidim*, which had been published more than twenty years before. The hasidic story, according to Berdichevsky, is a sacred text, but he himself did not turn to it for strictly religious reasons. The implication is that Berdichevsky supposedly secularized the hasidic story, but in reality the theological infrastructure of the hasidic text was not obscured at all. The product of the marriage of religion and secularism, according to Berdichevsky's retrospective description, is "religious fancy clothes," which were "like wings for my soul."[51]

Hasidism is thus a broker between the Jewish religion and nationality: in other words, the national translation uses religion for its own purposes, exploiting the mechanism of national universalization of religion, which is exposed here in its entirety. Berdichevsky translated the Hasidic idea of devotion into national universal truth, by which "a person should feel who he is and what he is."[52] He also translates the hasidic idea of proliferation of materiality into the principle of enlightenment, which sees the human as the center of everything.[53] The romantic artist-author creates the spiritual infrastructure for the realization of this process of nationalizing the hasidic text, by projecting new light on things, a light whose origin is in a religious mystical drive.[54]

It seems that what attracted Berdichevsky to Hasidism was actually its dialectical relationship with tradition,[55] and thus in his article "The World of Israel," published in *ha-Melitz* in 1890,[56] he focused on the subjective religious experience, which presents Hasidism as an alternative to the normative halakhic system. At first glance, it seems like a simple translation based on the autonomous subjective model of nationality, which Antonio Gramsci pointed out contributes to the ethical state by virtue of being moral.[57] In truth, Berdichevsky produces a dynamic moral subject that despite being heteronomic, meaning subjected to religion as well, presents itself as autonomous and universal. Berdichevsky's translation proves the argument that Martin Buber would make in 1906, namely, that Hasidism turned mysticism into an ethos.[58] This ethos was created by, among other things, the act of telling stories,[59] and this act produces narratives that organize a collective, narratives that sometimes—as with Rabbi Nachman from Bratslav or the stories of Rabbi Israel of Rogin—also have [theoretical] strength.[60]

The autonomous subject of Berdichevsky is characterized by deep hybridity. It is quite possible that Berdichevsky meant, by leaning on Hasidism and on its immanent and pantheistic infrastructure, to also contribute to the establishment of the sanctity of the autonomous mystical individual, since he sought to bestow on the heteronomic religious authority, which he did not wish to abandon, a measure of autonomy that fits the cultural model of nationality. It seems that Berdichevsky was of the same mind that Buber would take years later concerning the role of storytelling in the establishment of the collective and in turning to the hasidic community. Buber would present Hasidism as canceling the distinction between the heteronomic and the autonomous.[61] In his words, "'moral' deeds are, by definition and by nature, no less religious than 'religious' deeds."[62] Those are the deeds that bring holiness to the world.[63]

The autonomous heteronomic structure of the subject in *Sefer Hasidim* thus reflects the movement between the religious pole and the secular pole. In his discussion of Zionism Yehuda Shenhav has shown, following Bruno Latour, that modernity includes two systems of conflicting principles: "The first, known as 'hybridization,' mixes 'non-homological' and distinct elements. The second, known as 'purification,' creates separate ontological zones with no continuity between them."[64] Only when hybridization and purification are both in motion do they give rise to the modern as a category of praxis and discourse. Zionism, according to Shenhav, "hybridizes the secular with the religious, while at the same time it obscures these hybridization practices, thus purifying nationalism (the very product of hybridization) and treating nationalism and religion as two separate spheres of action"—purifying a hybridization of primordialism (religion, old Jew) and modernity (secularism, new Jew).[65] These words illuminate the role of Hasidism as mediator between religion and secularism and as creating, even temporarily, "pure" nationalism with religious roots.

## 4

What was the social context in which the hasidic story was authored and told? Rosman writes, "Hasidism was mainly an oral culture. Hasidic life was organized and practiced largely from an oral tradition, which was passed from father to son, from a veteran Hasid to a novice. The knowledge of Hasidism was disseminated through personal contact and face-to-face instruction. The oral sermon served a supremely social role: it was the unifying glue of the group rather than especially at the beginnings of Hasidism a spiritual legacy worthy of precise notation."[66] The hasidic story was told from the mouth of the tzadik himself or from the mouth of a witness storyteller. Through the generations it passed orally until finally it was written down. The last storyteller is the bridge between oral literature and written literature.[67] The oral infrastructure of the hasidic text, which found expression in the preference for oral telling over written form,[68] resulted in a sloppiness in the editing and of hasidic books,[69] but it mainly determined the audience of this story as a group whose numbers were limited.

And as mentioned above, this community can be characterized as a "face-to-face community."[70] Indeed, the Ba'al Shem Tov did not seek to instill devotion in every person of Israel, and his intended audience "was made up of a small group of close followers, known in the literature as 'the circle of the Ba'al Shem Tov.'"[71] Even the Ba'al Shem Tov's commitment to "all of Israel," which appears mainly in a letter that he sent to his brother-in-law Rabbi Gershon of Kitov,[72] has no pan-national messianic trajectory;[73] it was only relevant to the limited community of the Ba'al Shem Tov's inner circle,[74] who circulated the letter from one person to another. The fact that the protagonist of the hasidic story is usually a certain tzadik[75] also stands in opposition to Benedict Anderson's concept of imagined community—a national community that creates a common national time facing the future—in which Anderson places the roots of the novel. Emmanuel Etkes wrote about the possibility of a common imagined national time: "The Baal Shem Tov has no plan! He does not strive to any date or event of a revolutionary nature"[76]—and this, in effect, he defined as the nonnational infrastructure of hasidic practices.

In opposition to the imagined national community, which places fictional literature at its center, as can be seen in the literature of the Haskalah, hasidic literature is "only a symbolic repetition of the deeds of the *tsadikim* (by retelling the story) which may cause the actual occurrence of that appearance in reality."[77] The story is believable only if it is based on a chain of oral and written delivery,[78] and as such it gets reprinted and constantly reworked, as is common in folk stories.[79] Hasidic literature is distinct from national literature in that the stance of the author is not one of an individual author who puts together the fictional story from imagination; rather, a single author's contribution is a minor phase in a long chain of retelling of a text that belongs to the collective.

A literary expression of the non-imagined aspect of the community in which the hasidic story was created is the specificity of the hasidic text in naming names and places, probably in order to prevent reading it as a fictional literary text; the hasidic story presents itself as telling completely factual truth even when it relates miracles. Berdichevsky, on the other hand, in his work editing and refashioning the hasidic stories, encouraged reading the hasidic text (when it is not autobiographical) as a fictional text. This is especially obvious in the great anthology of the works of the fathers of Hasidism, on which Berdichevsky toiled for several years after publishing *Sefer Hasidim*. In compiling this anthology, which Berdichevsky never completed and never published,[80] he disguised places, names, and details of reality,[81] and by doing so encouraged his audience to read the text as fictional.

Hasidism adopted the principle of pneumatic leadership, which opposed Rabbinic leadership,[82] and therefore the folk storytelling of the hasidic story established a limited mystical community.[83] Buber called this community by the name "the Hasidic ethnicity," a community in which the tzadik acts as an intermediary between the community and god.[84] The Bratslav hasidic group gained the moniker "kibbutz," which is to say a community whose members personally know one another; the people consolidates itself around a core band of members, which the Ba'al Shem Tov called "my band,"[85] and only afterward, on this basis, could the tzadik take on an intermediary role between the people and all of Israel.[86] Followers of a charismatic tzadik were bound to him and to one another through a mystical attachment,[87] and sometimes, in the hasidic milieus that were led by order and hierarchy, they used "letters of contact" and notes in order to connect between the hasid and the tzadik.[88]

Ada Rapoport-Albert has discussed the proliferation and the divisions of the hasidic movement into multiple centers and separate groups already in the days of the Ba'al Shem Tov and not just after the death of his disciple Dov Ber, the Maggid of Mezhirech.[89] Rivka Dvir-Goldberg has commented on the internal politics—which were not pan-national—of the specific milieus of different tzadikim, which might have been the end-all of the hasidic story.[90] Most interesting is that evidence of the lack of nationality in hasidic consciousness is seen in the immigration of hasidism to the Land of Israel, which was not tied to national aspiration to rule territory but was conducted for religious reasons. This immigration, which created what Israel Bartal called "exile in the land,"[91] was typified by the preference of the diaspora over the Land of Israel.

Gershom Scholem objected to the Zionist interpretations of early hasidic theories, such as the interpretation of Ben Zion Dinur, which includes criticism of life in exile by the "universal subject" of Zionism. As an example of the neutralization of messianism by Hasidism, Scholem quoted the Maggid of Mezhirech, who said: "It is easier to achieve the holy spirit and unification with god in the diaspora than in the Land of Israel."[92] In spite of all this, in his nationalistic translation of *Sefer Hasidism*, Berdichevsky imagines a national community as his intended audience, which he establishes using his autobiographical subject, with its universalist dimensions. The imagined national time, common to all members of the community (who do not know one another), is involved with a common messianic national teleology on whose horizon, distant as it may be, stands the national state. This is the place to mention that the basis of Berdichevsky's opposition to Ahad Ha'am was Ahad Ha'am's surrender of the idea of national redemption in the name of the idea of a spiritual center.[93]

Against this national teleology Hasidism positioned, in the famous words of Scholem, a kind of neutralized messianism.[94] Dinur went to great lengths to identify messianic elements in Hasidism,[95] but Scholem claimed that Hasidism separated itself from the idea of national redemption, which sees history as created by humanity, a space for action through messianic power in order to advance national political aims.[96] In hasidic thought, messianism is a vision of what's to come, which cannot be hastened; in other words, a vision that does not demand immediate fulfillment.[97] Dubnow, in analyzing the messianic concept in the letter of communication of the Ba'al Shem Tov states explicitly that "the national element in canceled by the religious element."[98]

Isaiah Tishbi took a different view and showed that for many rabbis and disciples of the new Hasidism messianic trajectories existed side by side with opposing trajectories. Tishbi noted that messianic elements exist in a letter the Ba'al Shem Tov wrote to his brother-in-law Rabbi Gershon of Kitov; in the writings of students of the Maggid of Mezhirech; and in the writings of Rabbi Jacob Joseph of Poland. In the teachings of the Maggid, however, it's possible to see a neutralization of messianism.[99] Tishbi summarized his complex stance on messianism in Hasidism with these words: "After the teachers of Hasidim relinquished . . . they focused on developing a religious and moral theory in new directions. They did not negate messianic trajectories, nor did they reach a 'neutralization' of messianism as Scholem claimed; several of them even positioned the messianic idea and the aspiration to hasten its realization as the center of their spiritual world, and used it as a dominant element in the religious and moral theory of the new Hasidism."[100] In spite of all this, it seems that in the eyes of Berdichevsky, as in the eyes of other neo-hasidic authors,[101] stood a homogeneous and unified image of Hasidism that was based on "neutralizing messeanism," as Scholem would later call it. Messianism, when it exists, looks to the Land of Israel. Therefore it is possible to add that for the question of the actual political place of diaspora Jews, meaning in the Russian Empire and the Austro-Hungarian Empire, Hasidism, as opposed to the Jewish Enlightenment, never aspired to emancipation; and therefore when this aspiration failed, Hasidism also did not develop a stance toward national auto-emancipation.

A particularly salient example of Berdichevsky's nationalizing activity in his translation of the hasidic text is the story "A Candle of Light" (Ner lema'or) which is a reworking of the famous story by the son of Rabbi Adam in *In Praise of the Baal Shem Tov*.[102] This hasidic story, which most likely was not written by the ascribed author but rather is the product of the publisher, Rabbi Israel Jaffe,[103] seeks to attribute superhuman powers to the Ba'al Shem Tov[104] and thus deals with the question of inheritance by preferring the holy spiritual heir to the biological one.[105] Elbaum bases his reading of the story on the hermeneutic principle of the hasidic preference for the hidden over the revealed, which is its opposite: "The Baal Shem Tov and the son of Rabbi Adam represent opposites. In the revealed realm, in the public's eyes, the son of Rabbi Adam is infinitely greater than the Baal Shem Tov, whereas in the hidden realm it is the opposite. The Baal Shem Tov and the son recognize this, and the narrator includes us in their knowledge of this, which he does with a touch—and perhaps with even more than a touch—of irony."[106]

Berdichevsky accepted the basic narrative structure of the story about the son of Rabbi Adam. First and foremost he placed at the center of the story a person who lives alone and who does not know his own holiness; in his loneliness the man embodies a Dionysian character, which represents the tragic and heroic ethos from the writings of Nietzsche.[107] Berdichevsky translated the sacred hasidic foundation—which Yitzhak Bacon exaggerated to such an extent that he saw in the story an analogy devised by Berdichevsky between himself and the Ba'al Shem Tov[108]—into a national text at whose center is the reception of writings from Rabbi Adam, which is described against the background of the national aspiration to occupy the land. From this description it is implied that the exposure and transmission of these writings to the Ba'al Shem Tov would result in ending the cycles of occupation and exile, and therefore they're analogous to a renewed conquering of the land.

Berdichevsky added this story to another story about Rabbi Adam, in which Rabbi Adam sends his son to the town of Akop, where the Ba'al Shem Tov resides, in order to hand him the sacred writings. The original text in *In Praise of the Baal Shem Tov* says that Rabbi Adam passed away after commanding his son to hand the writings to the Ba'al Shem Tov; the death of Rabbi Adam as well as the description of the son's travel to Akop are relayed briefly: "And before his death he commanded his son here under his hand are writings that are the secrets of the torah, but you are not worthy of them but rather you should look for this town called Akop, there you will find a man who is called Israel Ben Eliezer who is about fourteen years of age and you will give him the writings because they belong to the root of his soul if you are worthy for him to teach you that is good."[109] On the other hand, in Berdichevsky's *Sefer Hasidim* the matter is described as a rite of initiating the son and obliging him to swear that he will follow through with the transmission:

> And he called his only son, his precious son, a young disciple, and commanded him and said: when I shall pass on you should take these sacred writings from safe keeping and rise and go from town to town and give them to Israel Ben Eliezer, because they belong to him and to the root of his soul . . . and if you are fortunate enough for him to take you under his wing you shall pour water on his hands, and be happy—and his son responded:
> —I shall do as you said.
> —Swear to me!
> And he swore. And he finished speaking to him and grew weary and passed away in his old age. And nobody knows his grave.[110]

The saying "and nobody knows his grave," which ends the description, echoes the image of Moses, who sees the land from afar and cannot reach it. The inverted analogy to Moses, which is established here as an analogy to the biblical story of conquering the land, is obvious; according to this analogy what is about to come—the giving of the writings to the Ba'al Shem Tov by Rabbi Adam's son—is analogous to the national acquisition of the land.

In Berdichevsky's text Rabbi Adam's son tracks down the Ba'al Shem Tov and bestows upon him the holy writings. He watches the Ba'al Shem Tov read these writings at night, "studying as if between pillars of fire."[111] And as to their study together, the original story in *In Praise of the Baal Shem Tov* emphasizes their studies of the Gemorrah as well as practical Kabbalah, whereas Berdichevsky plays down halakhic learning and discusses their studies using a mystical generalization: "And they secluded themselves there many days, and discussed secrets and secrets of secrets."[112]

In the process of translating this story about Rabbi Adam's son, Berdichevsky vacillates between two conflicting trajectories—mystification, on the one hand, and realism, on the other.[113] On the one hand, he omitted a large part of the realistic context of the original story. The reason for this was the penchant in Berdichevsky, who aspired to create a holy text, to play down, much in the spirit of Hasidism, the mundane in favor of the spiritual. Berdichevsky also repeats the Lurian expression that appears in *In Praise of the Baal Shem Tov* and characterizes the writings as belonging to the Ba'al Shem Tov's "root of his soul."[114] It seems therefore that Berdichevsky, who created a modernist hasidic text in the spirit of the European symbolists whose writings he was reading at the time,[115] also acted in accordance with hasidic norms and amended his texts toward a mystical sanctification, which blurs the distinction between signifier and signified.[116] On the other hand, in specific sections that depict an interpersonal encounter dealing with holy things, the description tends toward realism by emphasizing the humanity of the characters. Hence the moment that Rabbi Adam commands his son to hand over the writings to the Ba'al Shem Tov is depicted in *In Praise of the Baal Shem Tov* in brief, whereas Berdichevsky offers a dramatization of this event and concludes the description with a dialogue between father and son.[117]

Between the story about Rabbi Adam's son in *In Praise of the Baal Shem Tov* and Berdichevsky's retelling of it, there is at least one other text—*Revelation of the Hidden*, by Joseph Perl, published in 1819. This is a belittling, parodic text about Hasidism and the language of its literature, in which Perl acted, according to Shmuel Werses, as a satirical editor.[118] Perl's book was one of the central texts in the struggle between the Haskalah and Hasidism, which lasted the length of the nineteenth century and was characterized by the dependence each side had on the other, in order to sharpen its stance.[119] The Jewish Enlightenment, as is known, came out against what it identified in Hasidism as an uneducated attraction to magic and sorcery.[120] In the preface to Perl's *Revelation of the Hidden*, as in *In Praise of the Baal Shem Tov*, the story appears about the writings of Rabbi Adam that the Ba'al Shem Tov himself deposited into the hands of their guardian.[121] But for Perl the uncovering of these writings is accompanied by a sarcastic ridicule of miracles and metaphysical events, which climaxes when the guardian hands over to the narrator a page of Rabbi Adam's writings that has the power to turn him invisible.[122] Perl's story seeks to debunk the stronghold of Hasidism in by undermining the idea of the holiness of the source in Hasidism, by depicting the writings of Rabbi Adam as a magical object and the hasidim as complete idiots.[123]

It appears that Berdichevsky sought to rehabilitate the status of the hasidic original after the heavy blow it received from the Enlightenment version, and indeed in his preface to *Sefer Hasidim* he repents and reverses course from his own Enlightenment attitude toward Hasidism.[124] As opposed to Perl's mocking rationalism, Berdichevsky presents a national version that bestows great respect on the sanctity of the original text and on supernatural events. It is true that he changed the story of discovering the writings—instead of a miraculous opening of the rock, it was the rain that broke it apart[125]—but he left in place the dream that revealed to Rabbi Adam what to do with the writings. In his paper "Witness to Hasidism" that Berdichevsky sent to the editor of *ha-Magid*, as mentioned above, he defined Perel's *Revelation of the Hidden* as a mere joke; in truth, he claimed, "our eyes shall see great people who sat in the highest realms." He also emphasized his own place, as the reworker of hasidic legends, as one of the "today's authors, meaning the national ones."[126] Even in his paper "From the Lives of the Hasidim," published in *ha-Shiloah* in 1897, where he reviews Ezriel Nathan Frenk's book on Hasidism, Berdichevsky attacks the author for continuing the war of the Jewish Enlightenment on Hasidism and calls for a representation of Hasidism in the national spirit; according to Berdichevsky's individualistic and autonomous outlook, the national spirit must only depict "the 'typical' and the *intrinsic* in them [in the Hasidism], meaning only those elements and facets in their lives that are different from ours."[127]

As mentioned, Berdichevsky's translation seeks to emphasize the autonomy of the acting characters. The ending of his story "A Candle of Light" is based on the story "Death of the Son" in *In Praise of the Baal Shem Tov*, the last of the stories that Berdichevsky reworked in *Sefer Hasidism* into one story. In this story Rabbi Adam's son died due to a failure of his mystical powers, which caused the Angel of Fire to descend instead of the Angel of Torah, as the son had requested of the Ba'al Shem Tov. Berdichevsky changed the hasidic original completely. In both texts Satan is involved, but in the hasidic original he possesses Rabbi Adam's son while he is taking a nap, whereas with Berdichevsky he replaces the light that comes from the sky (which does not burn what's down below) with a light that "eats up and destroys with the tongue of its flame the entire house and the city around it."[128] In the first text, the catastrophe happens due to human weakness, reflected in the theurgic act, the sleepiness of Rabbi Adam's son; in the second text, theurgy fails due to an external element—Satan. Rabbi Adam's son and certainly the Ba'al Shem Tov himself, says Berdichevsky, act with great force and realize their human autonomy up to the horrible phase of Satan's external intervention. The ability to activate spiritual force is therefore independent and autonomous and has the power to serve the collective, which may be of national magnitude.

## 5

For Berdichevsky, nationalizing the text of the unimagined hasidic community could not have been that clear cut. As Carl Schmitt wrote, "All significant concepts of the modern theory of the state are secularized theological concepts."[129] Talal Asad suggested extending this distinction to nationalism as well,[130] and by so doing brings us closer to the possibility offered by Homi Bhabha—to illuminate the structure of national discourse by two opposing means of signifying the nation. Bhabha discussed the basic ambivalence of national discourse, which is divided between "pedagogy," meaning a transparency and immediacy of the signification of the nation, and "performativity," meaning a renewable noncontinuous performance of signifying the nation.[131] Pedagogy of the nation is smooth and unproblematic, and may be characterized as a hidden and almost automatic signification of the nation as secular and homogenous; whereas performativity, which is the *act* of signification, uncovers by definition its complex texture and its heterogeneous action with many obstacles, an action that cannot get away from the religion embedded in the language as symbolic praxis. Berdichevsky, through the act of translating the hasidic text, builds a secular object of nationality as a practice that uses language saturated with theological meanings. This insight is well apparent in the stance of Dov Sadan, who objected to seeing the secular historiography of Hebrew literature as national literature and claimed that Hebrew literature includes religious streams, exactly like hasidic literature.[132]

This ambivalence of the holy and the secular is clearly apparent in the nationalizing translation of the hasidic text, since, according to Bhabha, "we should remember that it is the 'inter'—the cutting edge of translation and negotiation, the *in-between* space—that carries the burden of the meaning of culture."[133] And indeed translation as a hybrid political act complicates the identity of the translated text. Since it is involved in a betrayal of its ostensibly secular goals, it breaks apart the coherence of the translation and creates an ambivalent and undecided text.[134]

The hybridity of holiness and secularism is achieved by the sanctity of the hasidic text since, as Scholem determined, "the story of the deeds of the holy men became a new religious value, and has a celebration of religious rite."[135] Joseph Dan saw in the hasidic story a hagiographic text, a holy and sanctifying text that contains sparks of holiness.[136] According to Scholem, the hasidic story, as an exemplary holy text, is untranslatable.[137] But Berdichevsky, as mentioned above, translates the hasidic tale not into one of complete secularism but rather one of a new hybrid holiness. In truth, Berdichevsky wrote a new holy text based on Hasidism's rejection of the dry halakhic text, a rejection that is articulated by pantheistic language, mystical abstraction, and the idea of tangible labor. The double hasidic attitude is described in a paper by Rabbi Jacob Joseph of Poland: "A complete man must achieve two kinds of learning every day, as did Isaac Luria Ashkenazi, first he should learn the halakha by argumentation in order to break the shells and to remove the black clothing from the bride and adorn her with the holy clothes of the torah and then he should study the second course to attach himself to the internal realms of the torah without any clothing."[138] Berdichevsky subscribed to this attitude, which reads the halakha as mystical—and in the name of the idea that Arthur Green identified in Rabbi Nachman of Bratslav as a "complementary attitude, not an oppositional one, to the common secular attitude,"[139] he wrote a text that, like the hasidic text, sanctifies secularity "by uncovering its god-like potential."[140]

As opposed to Scholem, who claimed that it is impossible to translate the holy text, Walter Benjamin claimed that it is only in the holy texts that "meaning has ceased to be the watershed for the flow of language and the flow of revelation. Where the literal quality of the text takes part directly, without any mediating sense, in true language, in the Truth, or in doctrine, this text is unconditionally translatable."[141] Ostensibly, Scholem and Benjamin contradict each other, but if we understand that Benjamin hinges the possibility of translation on a strict demand for the exclusivity of sacred language, we could say that their stances are complementary. In the wake of Benjamin's words, Derrida claimed that the holy text enfolds within it an event of non-meaning. This is non-meaning, which exists in pure form outside wordiness, and because of that is sacred. In the holy text meaning is transmitted from the stream of language to the stream of revelation and is present as a text, as an absolute that does not communicate or say anything is outside the event of translation itself.[142]

Michal Ben-Naftali also discussed the lack of meaning of the holy,[143] by quoting Scholem's words on the kabbalists: "The fact that god expressed his own presence, even if this expression is distant and unachievable to man, is important to them far more than any 'meaning' that this expression may communicate to a man. In their conception, the torah is a complete entity which precedes any human interpretation since even the deepest one is by nature forever a lesser proportion to the perfect nature devoid of any particular meaning of divine revelation."[144] When Berdichevsky writes in the preface to *Sefer Hasidim*, "The Soul of the Hasidim," on his entrance into the hasidic world, he tells of "a hall where I learned to sanctify myself and to dedicate all my actions and ways to god."[145] One of the stories, "I am Prayer," which is in its entirety a mystical description of a revelation, emphasizes the pure holiness that is devoid of meaning. Berdichevsky sanctifies the mundane by awarding the status of the language of revelations to mundane language. This is the language of a holy text, a language that transmits the sanctity of revelations without carrying a definite meaning that can be transmitted.

Derrida's criticism of Benjamin's belief in the existence of a pure and harmonic language that can be related in translation and of his belief in the binary distinction between translation and original[146] allows us to uncover the hybridity of holiness and secularism in Berdichevsky's texts. Ehud Luz discussed the paradox in Berdichevsky's stance toward religion when he wrote about Berdichevsky's article "On the Question of the Past" (1902): "The greatest revolutionary of Hebrew literature, the greatest rebel against the authority of 'the books' in general and the oral law specifically, is seeking an objective anchor in tradition. This is the paradox: in order to express his longing for a pure subjective religious experience, which is not mediated by heavy tradition, Berdichevsky uses linguistic expressions that immediately raise for the reader the memory of the historic revelation in Sinai."[147] "In this way," wrote Fishel Lachover, "which has religion in it, but not belief, not even that which can be found by non-believers, Berdichevsky instituted the non-continuity in our history. There is no lineage of one Kabbalah, of one tradition."[148] What Berdichevsky found so compelling in Hasidism was, as mentioned above, its dialectic relationship to tradition,[149] as he wrote in his article "The World of Israel" (1890),[150] which focuses on the subjective religious experience Hasidism offers as an alternative to the normative halakhic system, through what can be called "the ecstatic system that expresses 'the engraving on the tablets.'"[151]

6

Berdichevsky's text is within the realm of a national theology that establishes major literature, the literature of a sovereign people, and relies on political theology for its authority. Schmitt defined the sovereign as someone with the power to declare a state of emergency and suspend the rule of law.[152] Suspending the rule of law is a dictatorial act, since the state of emergency is outside the normally valid legal order, and at the same time dependent on it, since it is responsible for the decision whether the entire constitution may be suspended.[153] Sovereignty is " the highest, legally independent, underived power";[154] the status of the sovereign who declares a state of emergency is analogous to the status of the god.[155]

Sovereignty is based, then, on divine authority, and therefore also on the theological tradition of the nationality in which it exists. Scholem wrote on the theological basis of Zionism in his famous letter to Franz Rosenzweig of 26 December 1926, where he claimed that the secularization of the Hebrew language within the framework of the realization of Zionism was not a done deal. The Hebrew language cannot be completely secular, and using it for secular needs involves suppression. The theological infrastructure of the language of Zionism, Scholem claimed, meaning the religious layer that stands at the base of the language and remains embedded in its words, its grammar, and the meaning of its expressions, is a hidden and suppressed power that will eventually break to the surface.[156] Indeed, the theological role of the politics of sovereignty of the text that Berdichevsky wrote is the political basis of the sovereign national translation of hasidic theology.

In order to explain the political nature of hasidic theology in Berdichevsky's version, one must also examine the deep gnostic dimension of his thought. Scholem rejected gnosis as a creative element in Hasidism;[157] on the other hand, he claimed that the great thinkers in Hasidism used the conceptual world of gnosis and copied from it in their papers on man and man's path to god.[158] Hasidism sees the evil in the divine as an exile in which the sparks reside. The sparks in the Lurian Kabbalah are a result of the "breaking of the vessels," and they are meant to be redeemed by man.[159] By so doing, by sanctifying the existent and by bringing up sparks, the jurisdiction of the religious act, which begins with man and his decision to be devoted to the god, is enlarged.[160] It appears that the sparks strengthen or emphasize, by their very existence, the basic gnostic principle of an immanent god who rejects the transcendental god.

Berdichevsky's critical attitude toward religious law and his preference for an immediate personal religious experience brought Yotam Hotam, in his paper on the gnostic foundation of Zionism, to point out that rejecting the transcendental god enables Berdichevsky to channel an immanent god: "The vitalistic dichotomy is here at its zenith with the political conclusion which is parallel to modern gnostic strategy—the return to the political framework (of a people on its land) is a rediscovery of an 'original' Jewish existence, of a hidden immanent nature, and the demise of a diasporic existence, which is a victim of halakhic law and the authority of the transcendental god."[161] Hotam explains Berdichevsky's theo-political-Zionist use of Hasidism as an immanent gnosticism, which is expressed "in the ordering authority of the 'national will.' This authority focuses on the national-political popularization of a gnostic theological pattern: on the one hand, diaspora, halakha, and a transcendental god, all of which must be denounced, and on the other hand, the immanent, the natural, the self, all of which are expressed in the political way of life to which one must return."[162]

In the political theological spirit, Berdichevsky's national theology is based on the violence through which the sovereign exacts his authority. Indeed, immediately after pointing out the hybridity of religious motivation in *Sefer Hasidim*, Berdichevsky turned to discuss the violent facet of the ramifications of his translation, which can be described in postcolonial terms as a violent act.[163] In fact, Berdichevsky rejected the possibility that the religion that is supposed to serve sovereign nationality would materialize without violence. For him, political theology is the only way that religion might be preserved in the national discourse:

> And I turned and saw after that, that we built ourselves too many ladders to the sky, for we are too spiritual and that the spirit is eating my tribesmen's backbone and makes us powerless. Then I had the idea of a change of values within us, a change of value about everything we had; and I sought to banish the rule of spirit and coronate the material, to reclaim our force and courage, to make us into people who know life and are not just religion-abiding Levites. Once again I saw that there is no individual without a community; a family cannot find its way without land to occupy, there is no people without a land. I rejected the conditions of diaspora for a generation now and sought to unite the people with its erstwhile abode, even if I had been distant from the actors and the actions within us, the lot of them.[164]

Berdichevsky's Nietzschean shift in values is focused on the creation of Jewish sovereignty by violent means, using "force and courage" based on political theology. This violence is expressed first and foremost in occupying a territory, since "a family cannot find its way without land to occupy, there is no people without a land." Berdichevsky wrote in the same spirit in his paper "Land," which was originally published in Brenner's *ha-Me'orer*, about the Sabbath that unites the secular and the holy in a "Hebrew and material" life: "Even the mitzvahs which by law are not contingent on the land, were given in the land and their power is in the land. A material and spiritual independent-national culture cannot survive without a national element of a territory."[165]

Nationalism for Berdichevsky is the violent arm of the autonomous individual. In his German paper "A Clarification," which was translated by S. Herberg, he clearly phrased the Gordian knot between the autonomous individual and territorial nationalism, using British colonialism as a model: "If each individual would attempt to make his life a national life and to lay down the foundation to his own home, this would create a homeland for others who would always come to a place where there is a 'crisis.' . . . Under the Basel Congress, with its innocent wish to establish a safe haven in a public way, I am envisioning a society whose establishment is not a generous gift, but rather like the Indian eastern society which is working at great energy to acquire its own land."[166]

7

In the second part of *Sefer Hasidim*, called "Legends," Berdichevsky brought together eight stories that depict the life of the Ba'al Shem Tov according to *In Praise of the Baal Shem Tov*.[167] "Two Worlds," the first story in the second part, tells of Eliezer, who in *In Praise of the Baal Shem Tov* is mentioned to be the father of the Ba'al Shem Tov.[168] In Berdichevsky's story, Eliezer is a Jew from Volokhia, the owner of a hotel, who is abducted while wailing for the diaspora and is sold as a slave, and later, after advising "one of the most important people in the kingdom" how to defend against the enemies of the kingdom, ascends to become a nobleman.[169] And here, in Berdichevsky's version, after Eliezer has proved his expertise in the ways of defending against the foreign occupiers, he creates an inverted political analogy between "thus the land is blessed for him, all of its enemies are defeated, is calm and fruitful without menace"[170] and his national frustration in view of the deplorable state of Jerusalem: "And he will remember and revel when he sees this city rebuilt, and the city of god is humiliated to the lowest level"[171]—a frustration that expresses in actuality his longing for the reestablishment of a Jewish political theology.

Berdichevsky did not stop at doubling the length of the story in *In Praise of the Baal Shem Tov*. He added more details about the man's life and about his wife, and also noted that "a man resides in their home, half slave, half free man, who serves every guest and accompanies him on his way when there is danger."[172] He also added spatial descriptions, which contribute a mystical atmosphere to the story. But mainly he added lengthy descriptions of the relationship of the Ba'al Shem Tov with his father and thus enlisted the motif of dynastic patriarchy to serve the national story. Furthermore, in the story that appears in *In Praise of the Baal Shem Tov*, Eliezer confesses to the woman he received from the king and reveals that he is a Jew,[173] whereas in Berdichevsky's version, the Jew defines himself as a "Hebrew" and the place from which he was abducted is called the "Land of the Hebrews"[174]—a direct reference to the biblical story of Joseph addressing the chief cupbearer in prison, "For indeed I was stolen away out of the Land of the Hebrews."[175] Although the exposition of the story mentions that Eliezer came from Volokhia, where he was abducted, Berdichevsky contradicts his original storyline and emphasizes that he is actually talking about the new Jew—"the first Hebrew," as he is called in his famous article "Destruction and Building"[176]—who comes from the Land of Israel, where in the future the Hebrews would rule.

Berdichevsky's national teleological element thus bestows on his narrative representations a substantial measure of violence, which is embedded in a nationality that aspires to sovereignty. The strongest expression of this violence is the forceful takeover of territory defined as national: god guides Eliezer and instructs him how the kingdom could overcome its enemies. It seems that here Berdichevsky followed the Yiddish original in *In Praise of the Baal Shem Tov*, which expands on this matter and details "how to establish the armies, they needed much wisdom to carry out the war."[177]

Elbaum claimed that the hasidic language had not yet formed into a unified synthetic language,[178] and therefore it could not serve the violent vitalism of the desire to rule over a national territory. As already mentioned, Berdichevsky domesticated the minor text of *In Praise of the Baal Shem Tov*, and in the name of a unified national subject he created a linguistic territorialization that abolishes deterritorialization, flattens the heterogeneity of hasidic language, and "normalizes" it. In this way, Berdichevsky transforms the hasidic story into a territorial, national story whose foundation is political theology.

# Appendix

# Isaac Erter, "The Plan of the Watchman"

From Isaac Erter, *Ha-Tzofeh le-Veit Yisra'el* [Watchman for the House of Israel], ed. Yehuda Friedlander (Jerusalem: Mosad Bialik, 1996), 61–63.

> Son of man, I have appointed thee a watchman unto the house of Israel; and when thou shalt hear a word at My mouth, thou shalt give them warning from Me. (Ezekiel 3:17)

From the time God placed law and rules for the people of Israel in the hands of the father of all prophets, Moses, His faithful servant, the Lord raised up shepherds from among His people, seers within His community; they saw visions of God, and caught sight of the Almighty; He placed His speech in their mouths, and His word upon their tongues, to exhort the house of Jacob, to impart His message to the House of Israel. From on high God opened the doors of His heavens to them, and showed them all His glory and contented them with his image when they were in a wakeful state. He unrolled the upcoming days before them as if He were unfurling a scroll and revealed the hidden treasures of the times before their eyes. Strong was the love of God's people in their heart, they were the teachers of this people, and they made it happy, afflicted it and comforted it. With fiery law they purified the kidneys and heart of bad thoughts and deceptive ideas, and the breath of their lips was a burning wind for every evil man and fool, the rod of their mouths struck the land when its inhabitants were corrupted, and ministers, priests and the nobles of the land could not hide from the whip of their tongues. And in times of sorrow they spoke to the hearts of their people, and comforted them, they foretold pleasant futures and strengthened the hearts of those lacking hope.

More than two thousand years ago prophecy was sealed off, and the eye of no human who walks on the land of this earth has seen divine visions. The kingdom of Israel declined as it failed to harken to the voice of its seers, realm was lost, there ceased to be a ruler and king for Jacob. Innumerable sufferings and hundreds of years of torment did not atone for the House of Israel's sin and for its mutiny in defying the words of the Lord's prophets. Now the soul of the people has crumbled under its guilt and with an oppressed heart it regrets its former crimes, but the windows of the heavens will no longer be torn open, and the windows of heaven have been sealed, never to be opened again.

And yet today there are many among the people who see, who say that the windows of the heavens are sealed yet translucent and through them the heavenly sights can be seen. These people are too weak to do anything desirable, and have an arm like God to create sons of gods and angels of the Lord. With a movement of the lips they create an angel, and with a wrinkle of the tongue a seraph. God's heart is in their hands as the watercourses, they turn whither they will, with the raising of their hands they bring to life and with the breath of their lips they kill, and apart from them God will not establish His dominion over the earth. They removed the government from his shoulder, and so that he should have delight at all times they placed a queen at his right hand, a wife and a concubine. The visionaries pronounce such harmful and erroneous words and even write them in a book, and the people of Israel, a people that long ago learned to harken to the voice of seers, listens with open ears and hears.

And I will not set my face like flint, to say to my people, "I too am one of the prophets," and attribute to myself the glory of the divine seers. The name of my God is too holy to me for me to utter something that He has not commanded. I am not a seer, I am not a prophet, but I am watching you, House of Israel. God has never made Himself visible to me eye to eye, but every time I contemplate to envision the world and its fullness and the laws of the movement of its heavenly bodies, the image of God is before my eyes. Every time my eyes wander over the face of this earth, every time I consider the changes, and the arrangements that its Creator has placed in it since its inception, my heart reflects on God's grace, His greatness, goodness and His wisdom: then my hand grasps the inkstand, and that which stirs within my heart passes to my pen, to open also the ear of my people to these lessons.

# Notes

### INTRODUCTION

1. Dan Ben Amos and Jerome R. Mintz, eds., *In Praise of the Baal Shem Tov* (*Shivhei ha-Besht*), trans. Dan Ben Amos and Jerome R. Mintz (Lanham: Rowman and Littlefield, 2004), 35–36 (translation slightly modified—H.H.).
2. Jonatan Meir, *Ḥasidut medumah: 'Iyunim bi-Khetavav ha-satiriyim shel Yosef Perl* (Jerusalem: Mossad Bialik, 2013), 31.
3. Immanuel Kant, "An Answer to the Question: What Is Enlightenment?," in *Practical Philosophy*, ed. and trans. Mary J. Gregor (Cambridge: Cambridge University Press, 1999), 11–12; Michel Foucault, "What Is Enlightenment?," in *The Foucault Reader*, ed. Paul Rabinow, trans. Catherine Porter (New York: Pantheon Books, 1984), 32–50.
4. Shmuel Werses, "Ha-Hasidut be-Einei sifrut ha-Haskalah: Min ha-Pulmus shel Hasidei Galitzyah," in *Megamat ve-Tzurot be-Sifrut ha-Haskalah* (Jerusalem: Magnes, 1990), 91.

### CHAPTER I

1. Nathan Sternhartz, *Šivḥei ha-Ran* [Praises of R. Nahman] (Betar Illit: Machon Even Shtiya, 2008), 29.
2. According to the commentary in the 2008 edition of *Šivḥei ha-Ran*, 29; so too Arthur Green, *Tormented Master: A Life of Rabbi Nahman of Bratslav* (Tuscaloosa: University of Alabama Press, 1979), 65.
3. Ora Limor, "Mekomot kedoshim ve-'Aliyah la-Regel," in *'Aliyah la-Regel: Yehudim, Notzrim, Muslemim*, ed. Ora Limor, Elchanan Reiner, and Miriam Frankel (Raanana: Open University, 2006), 44.
4. Ada Rapoport-Albert, *Hasidim ve-Shabta'im, Anashim ve-Nashim* (Jerusalem: Zalman Shazar Center, 2014), 86–94.
5. Sternhartz, *Šivḥei ha-Ran*, 25.
6. Ibid., 28.
7. Ibid.
8. Ibid.
9. Ibid., 26–27.
10. Ibid., 32.
11. Ibid., 39.
12. Ibid.

13. Ibid., 61.
14. Ibid., 56.
15. Ibid., 61.
16. Ibid., 36–37.
17. Rapoport-Albert, *Hasidim ve-Shabta'im*, 95.
18. Victor Turner, *Dramas, Fields and Metaphors: Symbolic Action in Human Society* (Ithaca: Cornell University Press, 1974) 195–97.
19. Ibid., 168–70, 201–3.
20. Rapoport-Albert, *Hasidim ve-Shabta'im*, 97.
21. Lila Abu Lughod, *Dramas of Nationhood: The Politics of Television in Egypt* (Chicago: University of Chicago Press, 2005), ix, 19.
22. Ilya Luria, *Edah u-Medinah: Hasidut Habad ba-Imperiyah ha-rusit 1828–1883* (Jerusalem: Magnes, 2006), 44.
23. Moshe Rosman, *Founder of Hasidism: A Quest for the Historical Ba'al Shem Tov* (Berkeley: University of California Press, 1996,) 139.
24. Zeev Gries, *Sefer, Sofer ve-Sipur be-Reshit ha-Hasidut* (Tel Aviv: Hakibbutz Hameuchad, 1992), 12, 23–27.
25. Gershom Scholem, *On the Mystical Shape of the Godhead: Basic Concepts in the Kabbalah* (New York: Schocken, 1991), 125.
26. Dov Sadan, *Avnei Bedek̲: Al Sifrutenu, Mosadah va-Agafeha* (Tel Aviv: Hakibbutz Hameuchad, 1962), 29; Jacob Elbaum, "Ha-Besht u-Veno shel R' Adam: 'Iyun ba-Sipur mi-Shivhei ha-Besht," *Mehkarei Yerushalayim be-Folk̲lor yehudi* 2 (1982): 74.
27. Gershom Scholem, *Ha-Shalav ha-'aharon: Mehkarei ha-Hasidut shel Gershom Scholem*, ed. David Assaf and Esther Liebes (Jerusalem: Am Oved and Magnes, 2008), 15.
28. Martin Buber, *Be-Pardes ha-Hasidut* (Jerusalem: Mosad Bialik and Dvir, 1979), 22–23, 32.
29. Immanuel Etkes, *The Besht: Magician, Mystic, and Leader*, trans. Saadya Sternberg (Waltham, MA: Brandeis University Press, 2005), 195–99.
30. Rachel Elior, *Herut 'al ha-Luhot* (Tel Aviv: Ministry of Defense, 1999), 178.
31. Ibid., 15, 37.
32. Samuel A. Horodezky, *Zikhronot* (Tel Aviv: Dvir, 1957), 58, 65.
33. Rapoport-Albert, *Hasidim ve-Shabta'im*, 23–41.
34. Rivka Dvir-Goldberg, *Ha-Tzadik ha-Hasidi ve-Armon ha-Livyatan: 'Iyun be-Sipurei Ma'asiyot mi-pi Tzadik̲im* (Tel Aviv: Hakibbutz Hameuchad, 2009), 39–52.
35. Joseph Dan, *Ha-Sipur ha-hasidi* (Jerusalem: Keter, 1975), 55.
36. Sternhartz, *Šivḥei ha-Ran*, 25.
37. Ibid.
38. Leviticus 19–20.
39. Ibid., 20:24.
40. Green, *Tormented Master*, 69.
41. Ibid.
42. Ibid., 61.
43. Ibid., 77.
44. Ibid., 76.
45. Mendel Piekarz, *Hasidut Braslav* (Jerusalem: Mosad Bialik, 1995), 100.
46. Ibid., 88.
47. Ibid., 124, 126.

48. Ibid., 126.
49. Turner, *Dramas, Fields and Metaphors*, 166; Limor, "Mekomot kedoshim," 34.
50. Michel Foucault, "Of Other Spaces: Utopias and Heterotopias," in *Rethinking Architecture: A Reader in Cultural Theory*, ed. Neil Leach (New York: Routledge, 1997), 332.
51. Sternhartz, *Šivḥei ha-Ran*, 25.
52. Ibid., 42.
53. Ibid., 45.
54. Ibid., 68.
55. Ibid., 68–69.
56. Ibid., 40.
57. Limor, "Mekomot kedoshim," 6, 11.
58. Ibid., 6.
59. Ken Frieden, "Literary Innovation in Yiddish Sea Travel Narratives, 1815–24," *Poetics Today* 35, no. 3 (2014): 375–76.
60. Sternhartz, *Šivḥei ha-Ran*, 40.
61. Psalm 107:29–30.
62. Rapoport-Albert, *Hasidim ve-Shabta'im*, 100.
63. Limor, "Mekomot kedoshim," 40.
64. Ibid.
65. R. Nahman Bratslav, *Sefer Ha-Middot* [The Book of Moral Qualities] (Jerusalem: Nekuda Tova, 2010), 213.
66. Exodus 15:4.
67. Genesis 4.
68. Micah 7.
69. Nancy Sinkoff, "Strategy and Ruse in the Haskalah of Mendel Lefin of Satanow," in *New Perspectives on the Haskalah*, ed. Shmuel Feiner and David Sorkin (London: Littman Library of Jewish Civilization, 2001), 95; Rivka Schatz Uffenheimer, *Hasidism as Mysticism: Quietistic Elements in Eighteenth-Century Hasidic Thought* (Princeton: Princeton University Press 1993), 344.
70. Schatz Uffenheimer, *Hasidism as Mysticism*, 368.
71. Babylonian Talmud, *Bava' batra'* 74a.
72. Psalm 104; R. Nahman Bratslav, *Liqquṭei Moharan ha-mevo'ar* [The Collected Teachings of R. Nahman, with Commentary], vol. 2 (Betar Illit: Machon Even Shtiya, 2002), lesson 17, chapter 8.
73. Bratslav, *Liqquṭei Moharan*, lesson 17, chapter 8.
74. Martin Cunz, *Die Fahrt des Rabbi Nachman von Brazlaw ins Land Israel (1798–1799)* (Tübingen: J. C. B. Mohr, 1997), 83.
75. Bratslav, *Liqquṭei Moharan*, lesson 73.
76. *Bava Kamma*, 17a.
77. Cunz, *Die Fahrt des Rabbi Nachman von Brazlaw ins Land Israel*, 93.
78. Dan, *Ha-sipur ha-hasidi*, 187.
79. Sternhartz, *Šivḥei ha-Ran*, 27; Ken Frieden, "Neglected Origins of Modern Hebrew Prose: Hasidic and Maskilic Travel Narratives," *AJS Review: The Journal of the Association for Jewish Studies* 33 (2009): 19.
80. Hannan Hever, *'El ha-Hof ha-Mekuveh* (Jerusalem: Van Leer Institute and Hakibbutz Hameuchad, 2007).
81. Ibid.

82. Green, *Tormented Master*, 67.
83. Ibid., 82.
84. Margaret Cohen, *The Novel and the Sea* (Princeton: Princeton University Press, 2010), 4.
85. Ron Margolin, "Belief and Heresy in the Teachings of Bratslav Hasidism based on Nathan Sternharz' *Liqquṭei Halakhot*" (master's thesis, University of Haifa, 1991), 73–79.
86. Rebbeca Wolpe, "The Sea and the Sea Voyage in Maskilic Literature" (Ph.D. diss., Hebrew University of Jerusalem, 2011), 256.
87. Ibid., 136.
88. Frieden, "Neglected Origins," 18–19; Sinkoff, "Strategy and Ruse," 95–96.
89. Margolin, "Belief and Heresy," 64.
90. R. Nahman Bratslav, *Kol Sipurey Rabbi Nachman mi-Bratslav* [Complete Stories of Rabbi Nachman of Bratslav], ed. Zvi Mark (Tel Aviv: Yedi'ot Aharonot and Mosad Bialik, 2014), 212–18.
91. Immanuel Etkes, "Introduction: Between Change and Tradition," in *Isaac Baer Levinsohn, A Testimony in Israel*, ed. Immanuel Etkes (Jerusalem: Zalman Shazar Center, 1977), 13.
92. Wolpe, "The Sea and the Sea Voyage," p. vi; Gary B. Ferngren, ed., *Science and Religion: A Historical Introduction* (Baltimore: Johns Hopkins University Press, 2002), 163.
93. John Gascoigne, "Physico-Theology," in *Encyclopedia of the Enlightenment*, ed. Alan Charles Kors, vol. 3 (Oxford: Oxford University Press, 2003), 278.
94. David B. Ruderman, *Jewish Thought and Scientific Discovery in Early Modern Europe* (Detroit: Wayne State University Press, 2001), 30.
95. Frieden, "Neglected Origins," 35.
96. Frieden, "Literary Innovation," 376.
97. Margolin, "Belief and Heresy," 56.
98. Haim Liberman, *'Ohel Raḥal* (New York: Empire Press, 1980), 69–73.
99. Margolin, "Belief and Heresy," 60, 69; Shmuel Feiner, *Milḥemet Tarbut: Tenu'at ha-Haskalah ha-yehudit ba-Me'ah ha-19* (Jerusalem: Carmel, 2010), 98–99, 103, 111–15.
100. Zohar Shavit, "Literary Interference between German and Jewish-Hebrew Children's Literature during the Enlightenment: The Case of Campe," *Poetics Today* 13, no. 1 (1992): 41–61.
101. Moses Mendelssohn-Frankfurt, *Metsi'at ha-'Aretz ha-ḥadashah* [Discovering the New Land] (Altona: self-pub., 1807).
102. Frieden, "Literary Innovation," 358–59; Wolpe, "The Sea and the Sea Voyage," pp. vi–vii.
103. Wolpe, "The Sea and the Sea Voyage," 59.
104. Isaac Euchel, "'Iggerot Mešullam ben 'Uriyyah ha-'Eštamo'i" [The Letters of Meshullam b. Uriyyah the Eshtemoi], in *Studies in Hebrew Satire*, vol. 1 (*Hebrew Satire in Germany: 1790–1797*), ed. Yehuda Friedlander (Tel Aviv: Papyrus, 1979 [1789]), 42; Wolpe, "The Sea and the Sea Voyage," 60.
105. Wolpe, "The Sea and the Sea Voyage," 38.
106. Limor, "Mekomot kedoshim," 13.
107. Mendelssohn-Frankfurt, *Metsi'at ha-'Aretz ha-ḥadashah*, "Introduction," 3.
108. Feiner, *Milḥemet Tarbut*, 99–100.
109. Frieden, "Literary Innovation," 363–64; Feiner, *Milḥemet Tarbut*, 99–101; Piekarz, *Hasidut Braslav*, 28.

110. Joseph Weiss, *Mehkarim Be-hasidut Bratslav,* ed. Mendel Piekarz (Jerusalem: Mosad Bialik, 1995), 62; Feiner, *Milhemet Tarbut,* 99.

111. Piekarz, *Hasidut Braslav,* 27.

112. Yonatan Ben Harosh, "Bein Nigun ha-Shtikah li-Kedushat ha-Dumiyah: Ha-Yahas la-Kefirah be-Mishnatam shel R. Nahman Mi-Bratslav ve-R. A. I. Kook," *Akdamot* 19 (2007): 4–5.

113. Frieden, "Neglected Origins," 6; Chone Shmeruk, *Ha-kri'ah Le-navi'* (Jerusalem: Hebrew University and Zalman Shazar Center, 1999), 68.

114. Wolpe, "The Sea and the Sea Voyage," 118.

115. Mendelssohn-Frankfurt, *Metsi'at ha-'retz ha-hadashah,* 6.

116. Ibid., 98.

117. Ibid., 14 and 24.

118. Euchel, "'Iggerot Mešullam ben 'Uriyyah ha-'Eštamo'i," 43

119. See, for example, the maskilic Hebrew expressions of support for Napoleon, Baruch Mevorach, *Napoleon ve-Tekufato: Reshumot ve-'Eduyot 'ivriyot shel Beney ha-Dor* (Jerusalem: Sifriyat Dorot and Mosad Bialik, 1968), 9.

120. Hillel Zeitlin, *Rabbi Nachman mi-Bratslav: Tza'ar ha-'Olam ve-Kisufey Mashiyah* (Jerusalem: Orna Hess, 2006), 51–52.

121. R. Nahman Bratslav, *Śiḥot Ha-Ran* [Conversations of R. Nahman] (Jerusalem: Nekuda Tova, 2010), 117, 148.

122. Sternhartz, *Šivḥei ha-Ran,* 29.

123. Yehuda Liebes, "Ha-Hidush shel Rabbi Nahman Mi-Bratslav," *Da'at* 45 (2000): 92.

124. Green, *Tormented Master,* 300.

125. Weiss, *Mehkarim be-Hasidut Bratslav,* 116.

126. Wolpe, "The Sea and the Sea Voyage," 15–16.

127. Mendelssohn-Frankfurt, *Metsi'at ha-'Aretz ha-hadashah,* 73.

128. Ibid., 85.

129. Ibid., 86.

130. Ibid., 160–61.

131. Wolpe, "The Sea and the Sea Voyage," 164, 314.

132. Frieden, "Literary Innovation," 36; Haim (Haikl) Hurwitz, *Tsofnas Paneyekh* [He Who Explains Hidden Things] (Berdichev: Israel Bek, 1817), 1–2.

133. Wolpe, "The Sea and the Sea Voyage," 279.

134. Ibid.

135. Ibid., vi.

136. Ibid., 289.

137. Weiss, *Mehkarim be-Hasidut Bratslav,* 110.

138. Zeitlin, *Rabbi Nachman mi-Bratslav,* 51.

139. Sternhartz, *Šivḥei ha-Ran,* 44.

140. Ibid., 25.

141. Ibid., 26.

142. Ibid.

143. Ibid.

144. Mevorach, *Napoleon ve-Tekufato,* 14; Franz Kobler, *Napoleon and the Jews* (New York: Schocken, 1975), 49–103.

145. Simon Schwarzfuchs, *Napoleon, the Jews and the Sanhedrin* (London: Routledge and Kegan Paul, 1979), 169–70.

146. Zeitlin, *Rabbi Nachman mi-Bratslav*, 73.
147. Mevorach, *Napoleon ve-Tekufato*, 72–73.
148. Ibid., 7–9.
149. Ibid., 15.
150. Sternhartz, *Šivḥei ha-Ran*, 52.
151. Immanuel Etkes, *Rabbi Shneur Zalman of Liadi: The Origins of Chabad Hasidism* (Waltham, MA: Brandeis University Press, 2015), 208–58.
152. Ibid., 223.
153. Sternhartz, *Šivḥei ha-Ran*, 31.
154. Samuel A. Horodezky, *'Olei Ṣiyyon* (Tel Aviv: Department for Youth Affairs of the World Zionist Organization and Gazit, 1947), 164.
155. Green, *Tormented Master*, 72.
156. Ibid., 31–32.
157. Ibid., 32.
158. Ibid., 41.
159. Ibid.
160. Y. L. HaCohen Fishman, *Sarey ha-Me'ah: Rashumot ve-Zikhronot*, vol. 6 (Jerusalem: Mosad Ha-Rav Kuk and Achiasaf, 1956(, 130.
161. Jonah 1:15.
162. Sternhartz, *Šivḥei ha-Ran*, 41.
163. Piekarz, *Hasidut Braslav*, 59–71.
164. Zvi Mark, *The Scroll of Secrets: The Hidden Messianic Vision of R. Nachman of Breslav* (Brighton, MA: Academic Studies Press, 2010).
165. John Eade and Michael J. Sallnow, *Contesting the Sacred: The Anthropology of Pilgrimage* (Urbana: University of Illinois Press, 2000), 7.
166. Gershom Scholem, "The Neutralization of the Messianic Element in Early Hasidism," in *The Messianic Idea in Judaism and Other Essays on Jewish Spirituality* (New York: Schocken, 1995), 179.
167. Ben Zion Dinur (Dinburg), "Reshitah shel ha-Hasidut ve-Yesodotehah ha-Sotsiyaliyim ve-ha-Meshihiyim," in *Perakim be-Torat ha-Hasidut u-ve-Tuldotiha*, ed. Avraham Rubinstein (Jerusalem: Zalman Shazar Center, 1977), 53–121.
168. Scholem, "The Neutralization of the Messianic Element," 183.
169. Avraham Rubinstein, "'Igeret Ha-Besht Le-R. Gershon mi-Kotov," *Sinai* 67 (1970): 134.
170. Simon Dubnow, *Toldot ha-Hasidut 'al Yesod Mekorot Rishonim, Nidpasim u-Khitvei Yad* (Jerusalem: Dvir, 1967), 62–63.
171. For a prime example, see Eliezer Schweid, *Moledet ve-Eretz Ye'udah* (Tel Aviv: Am Oved, 1979), 93–105.
172. Mark, *The Scroll of Secrets*, 165–67.
173. Jonatan Meir, "Megilat setarim: Hazono ha-meshihi ha-sodi Shel *R. Nahman Mi-Bratslav*," *Zion* 75, no. 1 (2010): 16.
174. Benedict Anderson, *Imagined Communities: Reflections on the Origin and Spread of Nationalism* (London: Verso, 2003).
175. Etkes, *The Besht*, 152.
176. Ibid., 79.
177. Rubinstein, "'Igeret Ha-Besht Le-R. Gershon mi-Kotov," 129–39; Etkes, *The Besht*, 83–84.

178. Etkes, *The Besht*, 111.
179. Ibid., 112, my emphasis.
180. Tova Cohen, "Ha-Hasidut ve-Eretz Yisra'el: Aspekt nosaf shel ha-Satirah be-Megaleh Temirin," *Tarbiz* 48, nos. 3–4 (1979): 337.
181. Green, *Tormented Master*, 83–84.
182. Limor, "Mekomot kedoshim," 34.
183. Nathan Sternhartz, *Ḥayyei Moharan* [The Life of R. Nahman] (Jerusalem: Machon "Torah Netzach" Breslov, 1996), 70.
184. Sternhartz, *Ḥayyei Moharan*, 351; Weiss, *Meḥkarim be-Hasidut Bratslav*, 175.
185. Green, *Tormented Master*, 84.
186. Ibid., 68–69; Weiss, *Meḥkarim be-Hasidut Bratslav*, 103.
187. Limor, "Mekomot kedoshim," 20.
188. Eade and Sallnow, *Contesting the Sacred*, 8–9; Ora Limor and Elchanan Reiner, "Petaḥ davar," in *'Aliyah la-Regel: Yehudim, Notzrim, Muslemim*, ed. Ora Limor and Elchanan Reiner (Jerusalem: Open University and Yad Izhak Ben-Zvi, 2005), 11.
189. Margolin, "Belief and Heresy," 53–54.
190. Yoad Eliaz, *Eretz/Text* (Tel Aviv: Resling, 2008), 67–82.
191. Mark, *The Scroll of Secrets*, 156.
192. Jacques Rancière, "Discovering New Worlds: Politics of Travel and Metaphors of Space," in *Travellers' Tales: Narratives of Home and Displacement*, ed. George Roberton et al. (London: Routledge 1994), 29–30.
193. Shlomo Berger, "Keri'ah Di'asporit shel Ti'urei Masa' le-Eretz Yisra'el bi-Yidish min ha-Me'ah ha-17," in *Lir'ot ve-Laga'at*, ed. Yitzhak Hen and Iris Shagrir (Raanana: Open University, 2011), 287–96.
194. R. Nahman Bratslav, *Liqquṭei Moharan ha-mevo'ar* [The Collected Teachings of R. Nahman, with Commentary], vol. 3 (Betar Illit: Machon Even Shtiya, 2002), lesson 78.
195. Ibid.
196. Rapoport-Albert, *Hasidim ve-Shabta'im*, 111. For a similar discussion in *Ḥayyei Moharan* 1, 31, see Rapoport-Albert, *Hasidim ve-Shabta'im*, 115; and on the connection between the "non-knowledge" ('i yedi'ah) of *pešiṭut* and *qaṭnut*, as an ideal [in contrast to the rationalism of the maskilim with whom he was in touch in Uman (Piekarz, *Hasidut Braslav*, 21–55)], as well as "Seder ha-Nesi'ah," in Sternhartz, *Šivḥei ha-Ran*, chap. 20, pp. 1–2; chap. 33, pp. 34–35; *Ḥayyei Moharan* 2, 42, 43, see Rapoport-Albert, *Hasidim Ve-shabta'im*, 115–25.
197. Sternhartz, *Šivḥei ha-Ran*, 27.
198. Ibid.
199. Avraham Rubinstein, *Shivḥei ha-Besht* (Jerusalem: Reuven Mass, 2005), 59.
200. Sternhartz, *Šivḥei ha-Ran*, 29.
201. Ibid.
202. Mark, *The Scroll of Secrets*, 179.
203. Sternhartz, *Šivḥei ha-Ran*, 26.
204. Ibid., 26–27.
205. Rapoport-Albert, *Hasidim ve-Shabta'im*, 96.
206. Mark Verman, "Aliyah and Yeridah: The Journeys of the Besht and R. Nachman to Israel," in *Approaches to Judaism in Medieval Times*, vol. 3, ed. David R. Blumenthal (Chico, CA: Brown University and Scholars Press, 1988), 162.
207. Sternhartz, *Šivḥei ha-Ran*, 41.
208. Wolpe, "The Sea and the Sea Voyage," 20.

209. Israel Halpern, *Ha-'aliyot ha-rishonot shel ja-Hasidim le-Eretz Yisra'el* (Jerusalem: Schocken, 1947), 21.

210. Sternhartz, *Šivḥei ha-Ran*, 26.

211. Moshe Idel, "Eretz Yisra'el hu' Hayut mi-ha-Boreh: 'Al Mekomah shel Eretz Yisra'el ba-Hasidut," in *Eretz Yisra'el ba-Hagut ha-yehudit ba-'Et ha-ḥadashah*, ed. Aviezer Ravitsky (Jerusalem: Yad Izhak Ben-Zvi, 1998), 258.

212. Ibid., 259–60.

213. Ibid., 263.

214. Ibid., 265–66.

215. Alon Goshen-Gottstein, "Eretz Yisra'el be-Haguto shel Rabbi Nahman mi-Braslav," in *Eretz Yisra'el ba-Hagut ha-yehudit ba-'et ha-ḥadashah*, ed. Aviezer Ravitsky (Jerusalem: Yad Izhak Ben-Zvi, 1998), 291–94.

216. Ibid., 281, 278, 285, 287.

217. Mark, *The Scroll of Secrets*, 175.

CHAPTER 2

1. Isaac Erter, *Ha-Tzofeh le-Veit Yisra'el* [Watchman for the House of Israel], ed. Yehuda Friedlander (Jerusalem: Mosad Bialik, 1996), 61–63. The first English translation of Erter's text can be found in the appendix.

2. Ezekiel 3:17.

3. Ezekiel 3:18–19.

4. Ezekiel 3:20–21.

5. Dan Miron, *Ha-rofeh ha-medumeh: Iyunim ba-Sifrut ha-yehudit ha-klasit* (Tel Aviv: Hakkibutz Hameuchad, 1995), 12.

6. Michel Foucault, *Discipline and Punish: The Birth of the Prison*, trans. Alan Sheridan (Oxford: Vintage, 1979).

7. Martin Jay, *Downcast Eyes: The Denigration of Vision in Twentieth-Century French Thought* (Berkeley: University of California Press, 1994), 382–84, 393.

8. Simon Halkin, *Mavo le-Siporet ha-'Ivrit, Reshimot lefi Hartsaotav shel S. Halkin*, ed. Sophia Hillel (Jerusalem: Mifal ha-shekufal, Hebrew University, 1955), 208; emphasis in the original.

9. Galicia was a region north of the Carpathian Mountains, defined as such by the Austrians, who ruled over it from 1772 to 1918.

10. George L. Mosse, *Confronting the Nation: Jewish and Western Nationalism* (London: Brandeis University Press, 1993), 132.

11. Jonathan Culler, "Anderson and the Novel," ed. Jonathan Culler and Pheng Cheah, *Grounds of Comparison: Around the Work of Benedict Anderson* (London: Routledge, 2003), 32–39.

12. Uri Shoham, *Ha-Mashma'ut ha-aheret: Min ha-Mashal ha-alegori ve-'ad ha-Sipur ha-parari'alisti* (Tel Aviv: Makhon Kats, Tel-Aviv University, 1982), 99.

13. The vision in Ezekiel 3, as well as the vision of the divine chariot in Ezekiel 1.

14. Carl Schmitt, *Political Theology: Four Chapters on the Concept of Sovereignty*, trans. George Schwab (Chicago: University of Chicago Press, 2005).

15. Such political messianism, representing national sovereignty, can be found in Ezekiel 38, when God calls upon the prophet to deliver a prophecy regarding the war of Gog and

Magog, at the End of Days, after which (according to the Babylonian Talmud, in Sanhedrin 97a), the Messiah will appear: "And the word of the Lord came to me, saying: Son of man, set your face toward Gog of the land of Magog, the chief prince of Meshech and Tubal, and prophesy against him. . . . And it will come to pass on that day, when Gog will come against the land of Israel, said the Lord God, that My fury will rise up in My nostrils. For in My jealousy and in the fire of My wrath I have spoken. Surely on that day there will be a great shaking in the Land of Israel. . . . And I will call for a sword against him throughout all my mountains, said the Lord God: Every man's sword will be against his brother. And I will plead against him with pestilence and with blood; and I will cause to rain upon him, and upon his bands, and upon the many people that are with him, an overflowing shower, and great hailstones, fire, and brimstone. Thus I will magnify Myself and sanctify Myself; and I will make myself known in the eyes of many nations, and they will know that I am the Lord" (Ezekiel 38:123). Ezekiel 33 makes a clear connection between the watchman and the war of Gog and Magog: "Son of man, speak to the children of your people and say to them: When I bring the sword upon a land, if the people of the land take a man from among them, and set him for their watchman: If when he sees the sword come upon the land, he blows the trumpet and warns the people" (Ezekiel 33:23). It is likely that Erter, in adopting the term "Watchman of the House of Israel" also had the following Talmudic passage in mind: "The Holy One, blessed be He, was about to make Hezekiah the Messiah and Sennacherib Gog and Magog" (Sanhedrin 94:1; *Yalkut Shimoni*, Isaiah 9, sec. 415).

16. Schmitt, *Political Theology*.

17. Simon Halkin, *Muskamot u-Mashberim be-Sifrutenu* (Jerusalem: Mosad Bialik, 1980), 44.

18. Re'uven Fahn, *Kitvei Re'uven Fahn*, part 2: *Pirkei Haskalah* (Stanisławów: Dorshei ha-Universita ha-Ivrit bi-Yerushalayim, 1937), 137.

19. Foucault's postmodern critique of the Enlightenment reveals the cognitive, historical, contingent, and ephemeral elements at the basis of Enlightenment universalism: "This entails an obvious consequence: that criticism is no longer going to be practiced in the search for formal structures with universal value, but rather as a historical investigation into the events that have led us to constitute ourselves and to recognize ourselves as subjects of what we are doing, thinking, saying. In that sense, this criticism is not transcendental . . . in the sense that it will not seek to identify the universal structures of all knowledge or of all possible moral action, but will seek to treat the instances of discourse that articulate what we think, say, and do as so many historical events" (Foucault, "What Is Enlightenment?," 45–46). See also in the introduction to this book.

20. Azmi Bishara, foreword to *Ha-Neorut—Proyekt sh-lo Nishlan? Shesh Masot al Meorut u-Modernizm*, ed. Azmi Bishara (Tel Aviv: Hakkibutz Hameuchad, 1997), 21.

21. Jay, *Downcast Eyes*, 389.

22. Erter, *Ha-Tzofeh le-Veit Yisra'el*, 62.

23. Indeed, the sovereign subject of Zionism, realized years later in the State of Israel as a "Jewish and democratic state," was justified by means of Jewish theological principles that lie at the root of Zionism. See: Amnon Raz-Krakotzkin, "Ha-Shiva el ha-Historia shel ha-Gueoula," in *Ha-Zionut ve-ha-Hazarah la-Historia: Ha'arakha me-hadash*, ed. Shmuel Noah Eisenstadt and Moshe Lisk (Jerusalem: Yad Izhak Ben-Zvi, 1999); Hannan Hever, *Be-Hoach ha-El, Teologia ve-Politika ba-Sifrut ha-Ivrit ha-modernit* (Tel Aviv: Hakkibutz Hameuchad, Van Leer Institute, 2014). First and foremost among these is the principle of separation between Jews, as the Chosen People, and non-Jews. It is for this reason that Zionist theology

demanded a separate space for Jews in Palestine, distinct from Palestinian space. The tragic consequence of this Zionist theology of space was the Nakba, the ethnic cleansing of Palestine, that accompanied the establishment of the State of Israel. Furthermore, some 125 years after the publication of Erter's first satire, the Jewish sovereignty of the State of Israel was constituted in response to the state of emergency created by the Jewish Holocaust and the state of emergency declared by the British Mandatory government in Palestine (a state of emergency that is still in effect in Israel to this day). The sovereign who declares the state of emergency is also the one who defines the anomalous or exceptional as such (Schmitt, *Political Theology*, 6). In the Jewish state, this implies the legal "exceptionalization" of the non-Jew, that is, the Palestinian. Since in Schmitt's view "all significant concepts of the modern theory of the state are secularized theological concepts" (ibid., 36), the concept of the sovereign—the one who declares the state of emergency—is analogous to that of the miracle, which establishes divine sovereignty over political theology (ibid., 3639).

24. Antony Angie, *Imperialism, Sovereignty, and the Making of International Law* (New York: Cambridge University Press, 2005), 148; Wendy Brown, *Walled States, Waning Sovereignty* (New York: Zone Books, 2010), 22, 26, 53, 119; Yehuda Shenhav, *Beyond the Two-State Solution: A Jewish Political Essay* (London: Polity, 2012), 149–53.

25. Raz-Krakotzkin, "Ha-Shiva el ha-Historia shel ha-Gueoula," 31, 34.

26. Étienne Balibar, *Race, Nation, Class: Ambiguous Identities*, trans. Chris Turner (London: Verso, 1991).

27. Shalom HaCohen, "Al Mahbarot Bikurei ha'Itim," *Bikurei ha'Itim* 1 (1821) : 4. Such nonteleological proto-nationalism appeared long before Peretz Smolenskin's nationalism of the 1870s, Hovevei Tziyon (Lovers of Zion) nationalism of the 1880s, and, of course, the founding of the World Zionist Organization in 1897. Erter himself, in the period following his return from medical school in Budapest in 1829, wrote explicitly nationalist texts. In 1840, for example, the Jews of Damascus were falsely accused of having murdered a Christian monk and his servant, eliciting a wave of European Jewish solidarity with the Jews of the Middle East. Erter took part in this constitution of imagined national community (which also included a contribution by Heinrich Heine) with an essay entitled "Megilat Damesek" (The Scroll of Damascus). In this essay Erter creates a Jewish national historical continuum by viewing the events of his day in Damascus in the context of Haman's persecution of the Jews in the biblical Scroll of Esther (in Isaac Erter, *Ha-Tzofeh le-Veit Yisra'el* [Watchman for the House of Israel] [Tel Aviv: Machbarot Lesifrut, 1952], 195–97).

28. Dan Miron, *From Continuity to Contiguity: Toward A New Jewish Literary Thinking* (Stanford: Stanford University Press, 2010), 184.

29. Erter, *Ha-Tzofeh le-Veit Yisra'el*, 62.

30. Miron, *From Continuity to Contiguity*, 184–85.

31. Mordechai Eliav, *Ha-Hinuch ha-yehudi Be-Germania bi-Mei ha-Haskala ve-ha-Emantsipatsia* (Jerusalem: Ha-sochnut ha-yehudit le-Eretz Yisra'el, 1960), 2; Yitzchak Julius Guttmann, *Ha-Philosophia shel ha-Yahadut* (Jerusalem: Mosad Bialik, 1953), 268–69.

32. Moshe Pelli, *Bikurei ha-Itim—Bikurei Haskalah: Mafteah mu'ar le' Bikurei ha-Itim, Ktav ha'Et shel ha-Haskalah ba- Galicia* (Jerusalem: Magnes, 2005), 51, 67.

33. Joseph Klausner, *Historyah shel ha-Sifrut ha-'Ivrit ha-hadashah*, vol. 2 (Jerusalem: Achiasaf, 1952), 323, 328, 331.

34. Like the windows of Solomon's Temple, as described in 1 Kings 6:4.

35. Erter, *Ha-Tzofeh le-Veit Yisra'el*, 62.

36. Ibid., 62–63.

37. Shoham, *Ha-Mashma'ut ha-aheret*, 87.

38. Haim Weiss, *"U-ma she-patar li ze lo patar li ze": Kriah be-Masechet ha-Halomot she-ba-Talmud ha-bavli* (Beer Sheva: Dvir, Machon Hekshariml and Ben-Gurion University, 2011), 40–41.

39. Menucha Gilboa, *Mivnim u-Mashmauiot: Iyunim be-Sifrut ha-Haskalah* (Tel Aviv: Ekad, 1977), 16.

40. Erter, *Ha-Tzofeh le-Veit Yisra'el*, 69.

41. See the author's letter to the editor dated 7 Tevet 5581 (12 December 1820), in Erter, *Ha-Tzofeh le-Veit Yisra'el*, 212.

42. Ibid., 64–70.

43. Yehuda Friedlander, foreword to Isaac Erter, *Ha-Tzofeh le-Veit Yisra'el* [Watchman for the House of Israel], ed. Yehuda Friedlander (Jerusalem: Mosad Bialik, 1996), 7; Klausner, *Historyah shel ha-Sifrut ha-'Ivrit ha-hadashah*, vol. 2, 326.

44. Joseph Chotzner, "Isaac Erter: A Modern Hebrew Humourist," *Jewish Quarterly Review* 3, no. 1 (October 1890): 106.

45. The appearance of *Bikurei ha-Itim* marked the passage of the Haskalah from its declining center in Berlin to Galicia (Fahn, *Kitvei Re'uven Fahn*, 103); Joseph Klausner, *Historyah shel ha-Sifrut ha'Ivrit he-hadashah*, vol. 1, *Mavo klali: Dor ha-Me'asfim (1781–1820)* (Jerusalem: Hevra le-Hotza'at Sefarim al-yad ha-Universita ha-Ivrit, 1930), 180–257. As early as the late eighteenth century, maskilim began to converge on Vienna, which they established as a leading center of maskilic thought and culture—radiating to Galicia and serving as a point of reference for the Galician adherents of the movement. For example, in 1793 the Italian maskil Samuel Aaron Romanelli abandoned the Prussian capital (already in decline as a maskilic center) for Vienna, where the Haskalah was just beginning to flourish. The preeminent founder of the Galician Haskalah, Mendel Lefin of Satanov (1749–1826), arrived in the region in 1808 (Rachel Menkin, "Ha-Herem be-Lemberg bi-Shenat 1816: Ravrevanut maskilit ve-Historyo-grafyah yehudit," *Zion* 73, no. 2 [2008]: 174); Raphael Mahler, *Divrei Yemei Yisrael: Dorot aharonim*, vol. 1, book 4: *Reshit ha-Haskalah be-Eropah ha-mizrahit* (Merhavyah: Sifriyat Poalim ve-ha-kibtrz ha-artzi Hashomer Hatzair, 1956), 71, while the town of Brody, where Erter lived, was the most important maskilic center of the three large Jewish communities in Galicia: Lvov/Lemberg, Tarnopol, and Brody.

All of this took place amid the reforms enacted by Joseph II of Austria—including the Edict of Toleration (1782), which granted civil rights to Austrian Jews. Joseph was an enlightened absolute ruler and champion of religious tolerance, inspired by Frederick the Great of Prussia and other figures in the European Enlightenment (particularly Voltaire). Joseph's rule over the Habsburg Empire lasted from 1780 to 1790, during which time he sought to establish a church that would not interfere in state affairs, presenting a centralist, reformist position against the power of the Catholic Church. Contrary to his mother, Empress Maria Theresa, he favored tolerance of religious minorities, granting civil rights to Jews and Protestants. See Moshe Eliyahu Gonda, *Mediniyut ha-Sovlanut ha-Datit shel Yosef ha-sheni be-Hungaryah* (Tel Aviv: Eked, 1976). Joseph's benevolence toward the Jews resulted, inter alia, in the establishment of Hebrew publishing houses in Vienna. The first of these was owned by a Christian by the name of Kurzbeck, with whom Romanelli found work as a proofreader until 1798. Romanelli was subsequently replaced by the Galician-born grammarian and maskil Judah Leib Ben Ze'ev, who later took a proofreading position at Anton Schmid's Hebrew publisning house. See Fahn, *Kitvei Re'uven Fahn*, 29, 51; Andrei S. Markovits, "Introduction: Empire and Province," *Nation Building and the Politics of Nationalism: Essays on an Austrian Galicia*, ed. Andrei S. Markovits and Frank E. Sysyn (Cambridge, MA: Harvard Ukrainian Research Institute, 1982); Moshe Pelli, "Ha-Malbahad ha-Nohri Anton Schmid: Madpis Sifrei Kodesh ve-Sifrei Haskalah," in *Ha-Sifria shel Tnuat ha-Haskalah: Yetziratah shel Republicat ha-Sfarim ba-Hevra ha-yehudit ba-Merhav ha-dover Germanit*, ed. Shmuel Feiner, Zohar Shavit, Natalie Naimark-Goldberg, and Tal kogman (Tel Aviv: Am Oved, 2014), v.

Like the Berlin Haskalah before it, the Galician Haskalah sought to improve the cultural behavior, hygienic standards, education, working conditions, and productivity of the Jews and, in particular, to encourage them to learn German, the official language of the Habsburg Empire. The Congress of Vienna settlement (1815) brought political stability to Galicia, and young maskilim born after the partition of Poland took this new state of affairs—a powerful Austrian bureaucracy and the existence of German schools for Jews—for granted.

46. Reuben Brainin, "Issac Ereter (Toldotav ve-Tzurato ha-sifrutit)," *Kol kitvei Brainin*, vol. 1 (New York: Ha-va'ad le-hotza'at Kol kitvei Reuven Ben Mordechai Brainin, 1923); Klausner, *Historyah shel ha-sifrut ha-'ivrit ha-hadashah*, vol. 2, 326.

47. Klausner, *Historyah shel ha-Sifrut ha-'Ivrit ha-hadashah*, vol. 2, 324–27.

48. Shmuel Feiner et al., "Mavo," in *Ha-sifria shel Tnuat ha-Haskalah: Yetziratah shel Republicat ha-sfarim ba-Hevra ha-yehudit ba-Merhav ha-dover Germanit*, ed. Shmuel Feiner, Zohar Shavit, Natalie Naimark-Goldberg and Tal kogman (Tel Aviv: Am Oved, 2014), 9.

49. Baruch Kurzweil, *Be-Ma'avak al-Erkei ha-Yahadut* (Tel Aviv: Schocken, 1969), 73.

50. Jonatan Meir, *Hasidut medumah: 'Iyunim bi-Khetavav ha-satiriyim shel Yosef Perl* (Jerusalem: Mossad Bialik, 2013), 26.

51. Eliyahu Stern, "Reforming the Rabbinic Canon and the Shaping of Modern Eastern European Jewry" (lecture, Textual Unities Conference, Yale University, 7 October 2013).

52. Feiner et al., "Mavo," 28–29; Robert Darnton, *The Literary Underground of the Old Regime* (Cambridge, MA: Harvard University Press, 1982); Robert Darnton, "What Is the History of Books?," in *The Kiss of Lamourette: Reflections in Cultural History* (New York: Norton, 1990).

53. Gonda, *Mediniyut ha-Sovlanut ha-datit shel Yosef ha-sheni be-Hungaryah*, 59–86.

54. Raphael Mahler, *Hasidut ve-ha-Haskalah* (Merhavyah: Sifriyat Poalim ve-ha-kibtrz ha-artzi Hashomer Hatzair, 1961), 133–54.

55. Erter, *Ha-Tzofeh le-Veit Yisra'el*, 68.

56. Halkin, *Mavo le-Siporet ha-'Ivrit*, 166.

57. Shoham, *Ha-Mashma'ut ha-aheret*, 87.

58. Erter, *Ha-Tzofeh le-Veit Yisra'el*, 66–67.

59. Simon Halkin, *Zramim ve-Tzurot ba-Sifrut ha-Ivrit ha-hadashah*, vol. 1, *Prakim be-Sifrut ha-Haskala u-bi-Sifrut Khibat Tzion* (Jerusalem: Mosad Bialik, 1984), 169.

60. There is also probably some truth to the suggestion that Erter had shown a certain affinity for Hasidism in his youth (Chotzner, "Isaac Erter: A Modern Hebrew Humourist," 107).

61. Erter, *Ha-Tzofeh le-Veit Yisra'el*, 69. In terms of religious commitment, Erter, and the Galician maskilim in general (Mahler, *Hasidut ve-ha-Haskalah*, 6065), followed in the footsteps of their Berlin predecessors, who not only remained faithful to Jewish beliefs and observance but, according to David Sorkin, espoused an ideal of "religious enlightenment" (not to be confused with "Christian Enlightenment"). See Mahler, *Hasidut ve-ha-Haskalah*, 69; David Sorkin, *The Berlin Haskalah and German Religious Thought Orphans of Knowledge*

(London: Valentine Mitchell, 2000); David Sorkin, *The Religious Enlightenment: Protestants, Jews and Catholics from London to Vienna* (Princeton: Princeton University Press, 2008). German maskilim like Naphtali Herz Wessely, author of *Divrei Shalom ve-Emet* (Words of Peace and Truth), would often stress their allegiance to Jewish religious tradition (Halkin, *Zramim ve-Tzurot ba-Sifrut ha-Ivrit ha-hadashah*, 170–71). Indeed, in the process of comparing the various weights mentioned in "Moznei Mishkal," the satirical narrator resorts to theological distinctions between them: "Among their number were fear of God and hypocrisy—true belief and superstition" (Erter, *Ha-Tzofeh le-Veit Yisra'el*, 67). Similarly, in "Hasidut ve-Hokhmah" (Hasidism and Wisdom), Erter underscores his own religious commitment, inasmuch as his narrator tells of the maskil who instructed him to read not only the writings of Moses Mendelssohn but also the writings of Maimonides (Erter, *Ha-Tzofeh le-Veit Yisra'el*, 73).

62. Klement Kaps and Jan Surman, "Postcolonial or Post-Colonial? Post(-)Colonial Perspectives on Habsburg Galicia," *Historyka Studia Metodologizne* 42 (2012): 7–35.

63. Chotzner, "Isaac Erter: A Modern Hebrew Humourist," 109.

64. This softer, incipient form of nationalism—that is, Jewish proto-nationalism—thus began to develop in the *early* nineteenth century, rather than in the *late* nineteenth century, as generally assumed. See Jacob Katz, *Leumiut yehudit: Masot u-Mehqarim* (Jerusalem: Hasifriya hatzionit, 1978), 7; regarding Galician Jews, in particular, see Joshua Shanes, *Diaspora Nationalism and Jewish Identity in Habsburg Galicia* (New York: Cambridge University Press, 2012), 19.

65. Hedva Ben-Israel, *Be-shem ha-Uma, Masot u-Ma'amrim al Leumiut ve-Tzionut* (Jerusalem: Hebrew University, 2004), 10–16.

66. Erter, *Ha-Tzofeh le-Veit Yisra'el*, 67–68.

67. Erter, *Ha-Tzofeh le-Veit Yisra'el*, 68.

68. See *Yeshu'ot Ya'akov* (Zhovka, 1809), image 1.

69. Meir Balaban, *Shalshelet ha-Yahas shel Mishpahat Orenshtien-Brode* (Warsaw: Hahevra le-hafatsat madaei ha-Yahadut be-Polania, 1931), 32; Rachel Menkin, "Maskilei Lemberg ve-Eretz Y'isra'el: Al Parashah lo yedu'ah mi-Shnat 1816," *Katedra* 130 (2008): 47. On Joseph Perl's criticism of Orenstein in *Bohen Tzadik* (Investigating a Righteous Man), see Meir, *Hasidut medumah*, 176–77.

70. On the question of Orenstein's responsibility for the affair, see Menkin, "Ha-Herem be-Lemberg bi-Shenat 1816," 179, 182–84, 196.

71. For the full text of the notice, see ibid., 197–98.

72. Nancy Sinkoff, *Out of the Shtetl: Making Jews Modern in the Polish Borderlands* (Brown Judaic Studies, no. 336) (Hanover, NH: Brown University Press, 2004), 221.

73. David Sorkin, *Moses Mendelssohn and the Religious Enlightenment* (Berkeley: University of California Press, 1996), 114–17.

74. Meir, *Hasidut medumah*, 176.

75. Balaban, *Shalshelet ha-Yahas shel Mishpahat Orenshtien-Brode*, 3031; Menkin, "Maskilei Lemberg ve-Eretz Y'isra'el," 38, 44, 47; Menkin, "Ha-Herem be-lemberg bi-Shenat 1816," 173, 187, 196; Meir, *Hasidut medumah*, 177–82.

76. Balaban, *Shalshelet ha-Yahas shel Mishpahat Orenshtien-Brode*, 30; Menkin, "Ha-Herem be-lemberg bi-henat 1816," 175.

77. Erter also alludes to his excommunication in another satire, "Tashlikh" (Cast Off), published in 1840 (Erter, *Ha-Tzofeh le-Veit Yisra'el*, 104). See also Brainin, "Issac Ereter (Toldotav ve-Tzurato ha-sifrutit)"; Klausner, *Historyah shel ha-Sifrut ha'Ivrit he-hadashah*, vol. 2, 325–26.

Baruch Kurzweil wrote about the satirist as avenger in his essay on the satire of Joseph Perl, attributing the phenomenon to disappointment at the discrepancy between the world of childhood and that of empirical reality. This stands in contrast to Kant's famous definition of enlightenment as a release from immaturity to maturity, and it highlights the romanticism at the heart of Perl and Erter's work, as typical examples of the Hebrew Haskalah. See Olga Litvak, *Haskalah: The Romantic Movement in Judaism* (New Brunswick, NJ: Rutgers University Press, 2012). Following Schiller, Kurzweil recognizes a degree of sentimentalism in Perl's satire (Kurzweil, *Be-Ma'avak al-Erkei ha-Yahadut*, 5861), eventually leading to the nationalist sentimentality of late nineteenth-century "Hibbat Zion" poetry.

78. Menkin, "Maskilei Lemberg ve-Eretz Y'isra'el," 49.

79. Henry Sussman, *Around the Book: Systems and Literacy* (New York: Fordham University Press, 2011), 24, 21.

80. Walter Benjamin, "Theses on the Philosophy of History," in *Illuminations*, trans. Harry Zohn (New York: Schocken Books, 2007), 254.

81. Benedict Anderson, *Imagined Communities: Reflections on the Origin and Spread of Nationalism* (London: Verso, 2006).

82. Mahler, *Divrei Yemei Yisrael*, vol. 1, book 4, 194–208.

83. Erter wrote his satire in the spirit of Mendelssohn's enlightened hermeneutics, which postulated that the process of signification is one of rational abstraction ("wisdom"), which leads to irrational objectification, thereby causing the signifier to appear as a thing, an object of idolatry, which, as in the story of the golden calf, then replaces divine law (Moses Mendelssohn, *Yerushalayim: Ktavim ktanim be-'Inyanei Yahdut ve-Yehudim*, trans. S. Herberg and Y. L. Baruch (Tel Aviv: Massada and "Le-gvulam" with the participation of Mosad Bialik, 1947), 116–17; Amos Funkenstein, "Ha-Torah ha-medinit shel ha-Emantsipatsyah ha-yehudit mi-Mendelssohn ad Herzl," in *Tadmit ve-Toda'ah historit ba-Yahadut u-be-Svivstah ha-tarbutit* (Tel Aviv: Am Oved, 1991), 206. In other words, rather than the book-object signifying sanctity, it becomes sacred in its own right. Following Mendelssohn, Erter depicts Orenstein's religious book from an Enlightenment perspective, seeking a mechanism capable of interrupting the vicious cycle of abstraction and objectification; providing a way out, through the demystification of the sign (Amir Mufti, *Enlightenment in the Colony: The Jewish Question and the Crisis of Postcolonial Culture* [Princeton: Princeton University Press, 2007], 49), that is, liberation from the sign that has become a fetish.

According to Mendelssohn, the remedy for such fetishization lies in the "ceremonial law," inasmuch as it pertains to practices and actions rather than to imagery and signs, and is therefore more conducive to abstraction and symbolic interpretation (Mendelssohn, *Yerushalayim: Ktavim ktanim be-'Inyanei Yahdut ve-Yehudim*, 116, 124; Funkenstein, "Ha-Torah ha-medinit shel ha-Emantsipatsyah ha-yehudit mi-Mendelssohn ad Herzl," 206–7). In "Moznei Mishkal," on the other hand, the fetish is demystified by means of the brutal physical treatment of Orenstein's book—a commentary on the *Shulhan Aruch*, the very epitome of the law. In describing the violence to which the book is subjected in the name of rationalism and universal morality, Erter makes the tearing of the book of the law into a law in its own right, based on the moral rationalism of the Hebrew Haskalah. The maskilic war against the rabbinate was thus a holy war, that is, a political struggle rooted in theology.

In "Pirkei ha-Zahav" (Golden Chapters; "Gilgul Nefesh" [Transmigration of a Soul], 1845), a parody of Hippocrates' *Aphorisms* (*Pirkei Ipokrat*, in Hebrew), Erter's narrator gives short shrift to the fetishization of books, offering the following advice to physicians: "Buy endless books, clothe them in leather coats of reddened ram skins, gild their spines and edges, place them in a case, and lock them up forever, never to read them. But place closed but transparent windows on your cases, that the people might behold the glory of your many books and proclaim that your wisdom is without end" (Erter, *Ha-Tzofeh le-Veit Yisra'el*, 161–62).

84. Funkenstein, "Ha-Torah ha-medinit shel ha-Emantsipatsyah ha-yehudit mi-Mendelssohn ad Herzl," 208.

85. Erter, *Ha-Tzofeh le-Veit Yisra'el*, 65.

86. Robert Cover, "Obligation: A Jewish Jurisprudence of the Social Order," in *Law, Politics, and Morality*, ed. Michael Walzer (Princeton: Princeton University Press, 2006).

87. Hannah Arendt, *The Origins of Totalitarianism* (Cleveland: Meridian, 1962), 274–75.

88. Jacob Katz, *Et lahkor ve-Et lehitbonen* (Jerusalem: Zalman Shazar Center, 1999), 101–10.

89. Gershon David Hundert, *Ge'ula ktana u-me'at Kavod, ha-Hevra ha-yehudit be-Polin-Lita ba-Me'ah ha-shmonah-esrei* (Jerusalem: Zalman Shazar Center, 2008), 67.

90. The leading maskil of his day, whom Erter knew well during the time he spent in Lemberg/Lvov (1813–1816). See Chotzner, "Isaac Erter: A Modern Hebrew Humourist," 108.

91. Mahler, *Hasidut ve-ha-Haskalah*, 59, 67; Nancy Sinkoff, "Bein Historiah le-Halahah: Ha-Mikre shel Yosef Perl," in *Ha-Haskala li-Gvaneha: 'Iyyunim hadashim be-Toldot ha-Haskala u-ve-Sifruta*, ed. Israel Bartal and Shmuel Feiner (Jerusalem: Magnes, 2005).

92. Micha Yosef Berdichevsky, *Ketavim*, vol. 14, *Sipurim 1905–1913* (Tel Aviv: Hakkibutz Hameuchad and Beit Sholem Aleichem, 2014), 55–56.

93. Ibid., 58.

94. See Numbers 19:19.

95. Berdichevsky, *Ketavim*, 60–61.

96. Ibid., 55–56.

97. Yotam Hotam, *Gnosis moderni ve-Tsiyonut: Mashber ha-Tarbut, Filosofyat he-Hayim ve-Hagut le'umit yehudit* (Jerusalem: Magnes, 2007), 182.

98. Berdichevsky, *Ketavim*, 56–57.

99. Karl Marx, *Capital: Critique of Political Economy*, vol. 1, trans. Ben Fowkes (Harmondsworth: Penguin Classics, 1982), 163–77.

100. Georg Lukács, *History and Class Consciousness*, trans. Rodney Livingstone (Cambridge, MA: MIT Press, 1971).

101. Homi Bhabha, "The Other Question," in *The Location of Culture* (London: Routledge, 1994), 66–84.

102. Jonatan Meir, "Yosef Perl, Rabi Natan me-Nemirov ve-Hamtza'at 'ha-Sfarim ha-kdoshim'," in *Ha-Sifria shel Tnuat ha-Haskalah: Yetziratah shel Republicat ha-Sfarim ba-Hevra ha-yehudit ba-Merhav ha-dover Germanit*, ed. Shmuel Feiner, Zohar Shavit, Natalie Naimark-Goldberg, and Tal kogman (Tel Aviv: Am Oved, 2014).

103. Shlomo Avineri, *Mishnato ha-hevratit ve-hamedinit shel Karl Marx* (Tel Aviv: Hakkibutz Hameuchad, 1976), 120.

104. Slavoj Žižek, "How Did Marx Invent the Symptom?," in *Mapping Ideology*, ed. Slavoj Žižek (London: Verso, 1994), 296–97.

105. Ibid., 300–303.

106. Ibid., 303.

107. Ran HaCohen, "Germanit be-Otiot Ivryiot: Kama he-Arot al Ma'arehet Ktiva hibridit," in *Ha-Sifria shel Tnuat ha-Haskalah: Yetziratah shel Republicat ha-Sfarim ba-Hevra*

*ha-yehudit ba-Merhav ha-dover Germanit*, ed. Shmuel Feiner, Zohar Shavit, Natalie Naimark-Goldberg, and Tal kogman (Tel Aviv: Am Oved, 2014), 460.

108. Ibid., 463.

109. Ibid., 465.

110. Bhabha, "The Other Question," 72; Homi Bhabha, "Introduction: The Location of Culture," in *The Location of Culture* (London: Routledge, 1994), 12.

111. Eric Hobsbawm, "Petah Davar," in *Lehamtzie Uma: Anthologiah*, ed. Yossi Dahan and Henry Wasserman (Raanana: Open University, 2006), 7.

112. Jacques Derrida, *Margins of Philosophy*, trans. Alan Bass (Hemel Hempstead: Harvester Wheatsheaf, 1982).

113. Described by Bialik in his essay "Mendele u-Shloshet ha-Krakhim" (Mendele and the Three Volumes), which also revolves around the weighing of books—an allusion to Erter's "Moznei Mishkal." See Hayim Nahman Bialik, *Divrei Sifrut* (Tel Aviv: Dvir, 1961), 186.

114. Bialik, *Divrei Sifrut*, 190; Sadan, *Avnei Bedek: 'Al Sifrutenu, Mosadah va-Agafeha* (Tel Aviv: Hakibbutz Hameuchad, 1962), 32–33. Where Erter's satirical language becomes lampoonery, it subverts its own linguistic stability and integrity. While Erter's style is dominated by biblical language (see Friedlander, foreword to *Ha-Tzofeh le-Veit Yisra'el*, 147), which he, like other maskilim, consciously chose in order to set himself apart from the rabbinate (Ilan Eldar, *Ba-Derh la-Ivrit ha-hadasha: Mi-Mendelssohn ad Mendele* [Jerusalem: Carmel, 2014], 206), it is somehow disrupted or discordant. This is because Erter's satirical language is, in fact, halfway between the biblical style of Haskalah literature (which created a clear divide between the reality represented and the language used to represent it) and the national realistic style that developed in Hebrew literature in the second half of the nineteenth century. The realistic style was a synthesis of biblical and Rabbinic Hebrew, and its beginnings are identified with the publication of the story "Be-Seter Ra'am" (In the Secret Place of Thunder; 1886), by Mendele Moykher-Sforim. There is a clear sense, in Erter's writing, that language is no longer entirely divorced from reality, inasmuch as his use of biblical phrasing is tempered by an avoidance of high, literary language (Eldar, *Ba-Derh la-Ivrit ha-hadasha*, 124).

115. Bialik, *Divrei Sifrut*, 189.

116. Ibid., 187.

117. Ibid., 191–92.

118. In his essay "Yotzer ha-Nusah" [Creator of the *Nusah*], Bialik discusses Mendele's contribution to the development of a "strong and brave literature" (Bialik, *Divrei Sifrut*, 204).

119. Mendelssohn, *Yerushalayim: Ktavim ktanim be-'Inyanei Yahdut ve-Yehudim*, 101.

120. Erter, *Ha-Tzofeh le-Veit Yisra'el*, 61–63.

121. Klausner, *Historyah shel ha-Sifrut ha-'Ivrit he-hadashah*, vol. 2, 339.

122. David Sorkin, "Haskalah ve-Emantzipatzia: Doh beinaim," in *Ha-Sifria shel Tnuat ha-Haskalah: Yetziratah shel Republicat ha-Sfarim ba-Hevra ha-yehudit ba-Merhav ha-dover Germanit*, ed. Shmuel Feiner, Zohar Shavit, Natalie Naimark-Goldberg, and Tal Kogman (Tel Aviv: Am Oved, 2014), 73–75.

123. Eliav, *Ha-Hinuch ha-yehudi be-Germania bi-Mei Ha-haskala ve-ha-Emantsipatsia*, 39–51.

124. Herz Homberg, a maskil associated with Moses Mendelssohn, was appointed supervisor of elementary schools in Galicia by Joseph II in 1787. In 1812, he published the Jew-

ish catechism *Bne-Zion: Ein religiös-moralisches Lehrbuch für die Jugend israelitischer Nation* (Augsburg).

125. Shanes, *Diaspora Nationalism*, 22.
126. Mahler, *Hasidut ve-ha-Haskalah*, 25.
127. Shmuel Ettinger, "Ha-Yehudim bi-Tzvat ha-Haskalah," *Zmanim* 3 (1980): 52–53.
128. Raphael Mahler, *Divrei Yemei Yisrael: Dorot aharonim*, vol. 1, book 3: *Eropah ha-mizrahit* (Merhavyah: Sifriyat Poalim ve-ha-kibtrz ha-artzi Hashomer Hatzair, 1955), 34–46.
129. Mahler, *Hasidut ve-ha-Haskalah*, 61, 67.
130. Judah ben-Jonah Jeitteles, "Li-Frantz ha-rishon," *Bikurei ha-Itim* 3 (1823): 117–19.
131. Judah ben-Jonah Jeitteles, "Hadashim mi-karov bau," *Bikurei ha-Itim* 7 (1826): 45–49.
132. Pelli, *Bikurei ha-Itim: Bikurei Haskalah*, 47, 53, 55, 81.
133. Markovits, "Introduction: Empire and Province," 12.
134. Klausner, *Historyah shel ha-Sifrut ha-'Iivrit he-hadashah*, vol. 2, 323–24; Friedlander, foreword to *Ha-Tzofeh le-Veit Yisra'el*, 7.
135. Yoav Peled, "Mi-Teologia le-Sotziologia: Marks ve-ha-Emantzipatzia shel ha-Yehudim," *Teoria u-Vikoret* 6 (1995): 46–47.
136. Coined by Judah Leib Gordon in his 1863 poem "Hakitzah 'Ami" (Awake My People).
137. Judith Butler and Gayatri Chakravorty Spivak, *Who Signs the Nation-State?* (New York: Seagull Books, 2010), 19.
138. Mufti, *Enlightenment in the Colony*, 27, 38–39, 41, 43, 51–53.
139. Funkenstein, "Ha-Torah ha-medinit shel ha-Emantsipatsyah ha-yehudit mi-Mendelssohn ad Herzl," 199.
140. Ibid., 200.
141. Markovits, "Introduction: Empire and Province," 9–10, 15.
142. Butler and Spivak, 2010, *Who Signs the Nation-State?*, 108–9.
143. Yehuda Shenhav, "Halalei Ribonut, he-Harig u-Matsav ha-Herum—Le'an ne'elmah ha-Historia ha-imperialit," *Teoria u-Vikoret* 29 (2006): 16.
144. Weiss, *"U-ma she-patar li ze lo patar li ze,"* 53.
145. Erter, *Ha-Tzofeh le-Veit Yisra'el*, 69.
146. Shmuel Feiner, *Mahapehat ha-Neorut: Tnuat ha-Haskalah ba-Meah ha-18* (Jerusalem: Zalman Shazar Center, 2002).
147. Larry Wolff, *The Idea of Galicia: History and Fantasy in Habsburg Political Culture* (Stanford: Stanford University Press, 2010), 29. In this context, it is worth noting Rachel Menkin's conclusion that the idea that Herz Homberg (see note 125) was widely resisted and reviled by Galician Jews is, in fact, a later view developed primarily by the historian Gershon Wolff, rather than a faithful representation of the response to his writings and work in Galicia at the time (Rachel Menkin, "Naphtali Herz Homberg: Ha-Dmut ve-ha-Dimui," *Zion* 71, no. 1 [2006]: 153–202). Scholars have largely misunderstood the implications of Homberg's *Bne-Zion* catechism, seeing it as a heretical attempt to teach "religion," rather than a response to government requirements regarding Jewish instruction, in which the author—in the spirit of Mendelssohn's *Jerusalem*—distinguished between "universal morality" (governing human relations) and religion (pertaining to the relationship between humans and God, with "natural religion" serving as the basis for morality). Seen in this light, we are able to appreciate the political significance of the partial rejection of the book by Gali-

cian Jews. Although the truths that Homberg stated in *Bne-Zion* (a work intended for the civil education of the Jews of the Habsburg Empire) were universal truths, stemming from "natural religion," the book also included Jewish sources, in keeping with the Mendelssohnian view that the separation between religion and the public sphere need not be absolute (Rachel Menkin, "The Moral Education of Jewish Youth: The Case of Bne Zion," in *The Enlightenment in Bohemia: Religion, Morality, and Multiculturalism*, ed. Ivo Cerman, Rita Krueger, and Susan Reynolds [Oxford: Voltaire Foundation, 2011], 273, 276, 279–80, 284–85, 292–93; Sorkin, "Haskalah ve-Emantzipatzia: Doh beinaim," 69–70). It would thus appear, contrary to the later and extremely negative image of Homberg, that Galician Jews did not actually harbor deep hostility toward the man or his catechism. In fact, *Bne-Zion* offered them the possibility of bridging the gap between Jewish civil existence in the European public sphere—ostensibly religiously neutral—and particular Jewish presence in that sphere.

The Berlin Haskalah dealt with this conflict by trying to downplay its significance—promoting belief in the idea of tolerance, for example. The Galician maskilim, on the other hand—unlike Mendelssohn, who made a clear distinction between civil and religious duties, with the intention of turning the Jewish community into a voluntary organization with weak sovereignty and no power of enforcement (David Sorkin, *The Transformation of German Jewry, 1780–1840* [Oxford: Oxford University Press, 1987], 70–72)—struck an intermediate position, between the aspiration to universal citizenship and preserving the rights and authority of the Jewish collective. This intermediate position explains the conflicted views of Galician Jewish intellectuals such as Mendel Lefin and the moderate and religiously observant maskil Joseph Perl, who devoted most their energy to the fight against the hasidim and their courts (Mahler, *Hasidut ve-ha-Haskalah*, 157–86), while objecting to the dismantling of the *kahal* (the traditional Jewish communal authority) by the absolutist government. The Galician maskilim thus adapted to the transitional political situation that resulted from Joseph II's Edict of Toleration, attempting to accommodate both the civil existence of Jews and their existence as Jews in the public sphere of the empire. Legally, the kahal had been abolished, yet the Edict of Toleration allowed Jewish communities to raise taxes—indicative of a degree of Jewish autonomy (Sinkoff, *Out of the Shtetl*, 218–19, 240). Elections for Jewish communal institutions were also permitted, but an edict from 1810 made the right to vote contingent upon knowledge of the German language (Shanes, *Diaspora Nationalism*, 25).

148. See Dan Miron, "Al Aharon Volfson ve-Ma'hazehu 'Kalut Da'at u-Tzeviut'" (Reb Hanokh ve-Reb Yosefch), in *Rabi Aharon Volfson, Kalut da'at u-Tzeviut* [Reb Hanokh ve-Reb Yosefch], ed. Dan Miron (Tel Aviv: Siman Kriah, 1977), 6–10.

149. Reuven Michael, *Ha-ktiva ha-historit ha-yehudit: Me-ha-Renesans ad ha-Et ha-hadasha* (Jerusalem: Mosad Bialik, 1993), 131–33.

150. Mahler, *Divrei Yemei Yisrael: Dorot aharonim*, vol. 1, book 3, 11–49.

151. Shmuel Werses, "Ha-Hasidut be-einei Sifrut ha-Haskalah: Min ha-Pulmus shel Hasidei Galitzyah," in *Ha-Dat ve-ha-Hayim: Tenu'at ha-Haskalah ha-yehudit be-mizrah Eropah*, ed. Immanuel Etkes (Jerusalem: Zalman Shazar Center, 1993), 45, 47.

152. Ibid., 52.

153. Mahler, *Hasidut ve-ha-Haskalah*, 87–131; Abraham Jacob Brawer, *Galicai ve-Yehudieha: Mehkarim be-Tuldot Galicia ba-Meah ha-shmonah-esrai* (Jerusalem: Mosad Bialik, 1965), 182.

154. Menkin, "Maskilei Lemberg ve-Eretz Y'isra'el," 31–32.

155. Ibid., 32–34.

156. Pelli, *Bikurei ha-Itim: Bikurei Haskalah*, 21.

157. Eric Hobsbawm, *Nations and Nationalism Since 1780: Programme, Myth, Reality* (Cambridge: Cambridge University Press, 1990).

158. The idea of "the Jew within the Empire" embodies the dilemma faced by the maskilim ever since Mendelssohn: the desire of members of a minority to integrate into the majority and at the same time remain distinct. It is the same contradictory political structure that gave rise, in the wake of the French Revolution, to romantic "nation-thinking," which stresses the cultural uniqueness of the collective over the abstract universalism of the Enlightenment (Mufti, *Enlightenment in the Colony*, 68–70). Maskilic proto-nationalism may thus also be explained in light of the romantic spirit that came to characterize the Haskalah in general and the Galician Haskalah in particular. This Jewish romanticism was in fact a response to the rise of romantic nationalism in Europe that followed the Napoleonic Wars, which rejected the Jews, as it strove to revive the past and its symbols. Western European politicians would certainly have preferred to relate to the Jews in their respective countries as individual members of a religious group. The fact that the Jews possessed their own ancient historical and literary tradition, however, forced these politicians to see them as a distinct ethnic community committed to its own cultural heritage—that is, as a kind of nationalism. This, in turn, reinforced Jewish self-identification as a transnational collective—as did the doomed attempts by non-Jewish advocates of emancipation to weaken solidarity and contacts between the Jewish community within the emancipated state and Jewish communities in other countries (Jacob Katz, *Ha-Yetziah min ha-Getto: Ha-Reka ha-hevrati la-Emantzipatzia shel ha-Yehudim, 1770–1870* [Tel Aviv: Am Oved, 1985], 193–94, 202, 208–9).

159. See Menkin, "Ha-Herem be-Lemberg bi-shenat 1816," 187–90.

160. Bhabha, "The Other Question," 74–75.

161. Bhabha, "Introduction," 116.

162. Ambivalently mimicked by Homi Bhabha, allowing him to write from a nonintellectual, non-Western standpoint; Robert Young, *White Mythologies: Writing History and the West*, 2nd ed. (London Routledge, 2004), 197–98.

163. Arendt, *The Origins of Totalitarianism*, 230.

164. Mufti, *Enlightenment in the Colony*, 40.

165. Katie Trumpener, *Bardic Nationalism: The Romantic Novel and the British Empire* (Princeton: Princeton University Press, 1997), 22–23.

166. Funkenstein, "Ha-Torah ha-medinit shel ha-Emantsipatsyah ha-yehudit mi-Mendelssohn ad Herzl," 209.

167. Mahler, *Divrei Yemei Yisrael: Dorot aharonim*, vol. 1, book 4, 71–73.

168. Menkin, "Ha-Herem be-Lemberg bi-shenat 1816," 182, 197.

169. Erter, *Ha-Tzofeh le-Veit Yisra'el*, 212.

170. Fahn, *Kitvei Re'uven Fahn*, 104; Shmuel Feiner, *Milhemet Tarbut: Tenu'at ha-Haskalah ha-yehudit ba-Me'ah ha-19* (Jerusalem: Carmel, 2010), 4952; Pelli, "Ha-Malbahad ha-Nohri Anton Schmid: Madpis Sifrei kodesh ve-Sifrei Haskalah," 144–49.

171. For example, the review of Joseph Perl's *Megaleh Temirin*, published under the pseudonym of Peli, attributed to Solomon Judah Leib Rapoport (1832, 175–81; see Klausner, *Historyah shel ha-Sifrut ha-'Ivrit he-hadashah*, vol. 2, 283).

172. Judah ben-Jonah Jeitteles, *Bnei ha-Neurim: Kolel Meshalim, Mihtamim, Imrei Musar ve-Hohma, Hadut, u-Melitzot Musar*, vol. 1 (Prague, 1821), 88.

173. Ibid., 116.
174. Meïr Halevi Letteris, "Be-or Kitvei ha-Kodesh," *ha-Tzfirah* 1 (1823): 58.
175. Lucian, "Toladot Alexander mi-Abonoteichus Navie Sheker," trans. Meïr Halevi Letteris, *ha-Tzfirah* 1 (1823): x; Jonatan Meir, "Lucianus ha-ivri," *Dehak* 5 (2015): 295–304.
176. Menucha Gilboa, "'Ha-Tzfirah shel Meïr Halevi Letteris ke-Kovetz lohem," in *Sadan: Mehkarim le-sifrut*, vol. 1 (Tel Aviv: Tel Aviv University, 1984), 77–84.
177. Letteris, "Be-or Kitvei ha-Kodesh," 13.
178. Mahler, *Hasidut ve-ha-Haskalah*, 60–62.
179. Gilboa, "'Ha-Tzfirah shel Meïr Halevi Letteris ke-Kovetz lohem," 81.
180. Another text that contributes to the proto-nationalist character of *ha-Tzfirah* is an unsigned, ostensibly anonymous piece entitled "Igeret Hitnatzlut" (Letter of Apology) (see in Letteris, *ha-Tzfirah* 1 (1823): 42–53). The piece was undoubtedly written by Rabbi Nachman Krochmal, and it condemned religious attacks against him for having defended a Karaite Jew whom he considered a true maskil. In the Karaites Krochmal saw a group of maskilim who also espoused nationalist ideals (Gilboa, "'Ha-Tzfirah shel Meïr Halevi Letteris ke-Kovetz lohem," 85). Theologically, the author recognizes the fact that the Karaites may not conform to the norms of rabbinic, Talmudic Judaism, but, from a modern nationalist perspective, he sees no reason they should not be considered part of the Jewish collective.
181. Feiner, *Mahapehat ha-Neorut*, 71–79.
182. Werses, "Ha-Hasidut be-einei Sifrut ha-Haskalah," 45.
183. Pelli, *Bikurei ha-Itim: Bikurei Haskalah*, 23.
184. Joseph Perl, *Megaleh Temirin* (Vienna: A. Strauss, 1819).
185. Moshe Pelli, "The Impact of Deism on the Hebrew Literature of the Enlightenment in Germany," *Eighteenth-Century Studies* 6, no. 1 (1972): 35–59.
186. Meïr Halevi Letteris, "Hakdama le-Isaac Erter," in *Ha-Zofeh le-Veit Yisrael* (Vienna: 1858), 16; Meïr Halevi Letteris, *Mihtavei Bnei Kedem* (Vienna, 1866), 110–11.
187. Halkin, *Mavo le-Siporet ha-'Ivrit*, 160.
188. Shoham, *Ha-Mashma'ut ha-aheret*, 79–87.
189. Halkin, *Mavo le-Siporet ha-'Ivrit*, 191.
190. Erter, *Ha-Tzofeh le-Veit Yisra'el*, 18.
191. Žižek, "How Did Marx Invent the Symptom?," 326, 330.
192. Bhabha, "The Other Question," 80.
193. Amir Benbaji and Hannan Hever, "Mavo: Historiyah sifrutit u-Vikoret ha-Sifrut," in *Sifrut u-Ma'amad: Likrat Historiografiyah politit shel ha-Sifrut ha-Ivrit ha-hadasah*, ed. Amir Benbaji and Hannan Hever (Jerusalem: Van Leer Institute and Hakkibutz Hameuhad, 2014), 20–21.
194. Žižek, "How Did Marx Invent the Symptom?," 306.
195. Ibid., 320–21.
196. Brainin, "Issac Ereter (Toldotav ve-Tzurato ha-sifrutit)," 268–80.
197. Žižek, "How Did Marx Invent the Symptom?," 310.
198. Ibid., 315.
199. Ibid., 315–16.
200. Ibid.
201. Gill Deleuze and Félix Guattari, *Kafka: Towards a Minor Literature*, trans. Dona Polan (Minneapolis: University of Minnesota Press, 1986).
202. Mufti, *Enlightenment in the Colony*, 13.

203. Moshe Pelli, *Sugot ve-Sugiot ba-Sifrut ha-Haskala ha-Ivrit: ha-Genre ha-maskili ve-Avizareihu* (Tel Aviv: Hakibbutz Hameuchad, 1999), 148–49.
204. Shmuel Werses, "'Gilgul Nefesh' shel Isaac Erter be-Gigulo le-Yiddish," *Mi-Lashon el Lashon: Yetzirot ve-Gilguleihem be-Sifruteinu* (Jerusalem: Magnes, 1996), 229.
205. Pelli, *Sugot ve-Sugiot ba-Sifrut ha-Haskala ha-Ivrit*, 200.
206. Ibid., 200–201.
207. Joseph Klausner, *Kitzur ha-Historyah shel ha-Sifrut ha-'Iivrit ha-hadashah*, vol. 1, ed. Benzion Netanyahu (Jerusalem: Mada, 1954), 218.
208. Ibid., 215.
209. Ibid., 212.
210. Halkin, *Zramim ve-Tzurot ba-Sifrut ha-Ivrit ha-hadashah*, 185.
211. Ibid., 175.
212. Ibid., 176–77.
213. Fredric Jameson, "Third-World Literature in the Era of Multinational Capitalism," in *The Jameson Reader*, ed. Michael Hardt and Kathi Weeks (Oxford: Blackwell, 2000).
214. Pelli, *Bikurei ha-Itim: Bikurei Haskalah*, 63.
215. Jay, *Downcast Eyes*, 393.
216. Erter, *Ha-Tzofeh le-Veit Yisra'el*, 169.
217. Anderson, *Imagined Communities*.
218. Pelli, *Bikurei ha-Itim: Bikurei Haskalah*, 48.
219. Mendelssohn *Yerushalayim: Ktavim ktanim be-'Inyanei Yahdut ve-Yehudim*, 129.
220. Ibid., 133, 137.
221. Ibid., 138.
222. Peled, "Mi-Teologia le-Sotziologia," 48.
223. A case in point is that of *Mehkarei Eretz* (Studies of the Land; 1814), a biblical geography of the Land of Israel by Salomon Löwisohn (1789–1821)—a Hebrew maskil of the Habsburg Empire (born in Hungary, he lived in Prague and Vienna, where he worked as a proofreader for Anton Schmid). Although Löwisohn presented his book as an expression of the national hopes of the Jewish people to be released from the tribulations of exile and to return to its historical homeland, the Galician Hebrew writer Re'uven Fahn (on the subject of Fahn's non-Palestinocentric nationalism, see Hannan Hever, *'El Ha-Hof Ha-mekuveh* (Jerusalem: Van Leer Institute and Hakkibutz Hameuchad, 2007), writing more than century later, not only highlighted the fact that the book was published at the same time as the founding of the "Sanhedrin" in Napoleonic France (as a political tool to oversee Jewish life in France) but, as a Galician Hebrew writer, also declared that the Jews had no ambition to settle in the land of their fathers, only to attain equal rights in the diaspora (Fahn, *Kitvei Re'uven Fahn*, 62, 67).
224. Paul de Man, *Blindness and Insight* (Minneapolis: University of Minnesota Press, 1983), 209.
225. Ibid., 211.
226. Jay, *Downcast Eyes*, 406.
227. Erter, *Ha-Tzofeh le-Veit Yisra'el*, 68–69.
228. Dustin Griffin, *Satire: A Critical Reintroduction* (Lexington: University of Kentucky Press, 1994), 6–39, 64–70.
229. Jacob Samuel Bick, "El Maskilei Benei 'Ami," *ha-Tzfirah* 1 (1823): 76.
230. Joseph Perl, *Bohen Tzadik* (Prague, 1838), 100–105.

231. Erter, *Ha-Tzofeh le-Veit Yisra'el* (1952), 198–202; Klausner, *Historyah shel ha-Sifrut ha-'Ivrit he-ḥadashah*, vol. 2, 329.

CHAPTER 3

1. "Hasidut ve-Hokhmah" was Erter's second satire, following "Moznei Mishkal" (published in *Bikurei ha-Itim* 2 [Vienna, 1822]: 166–69) and followed in turn by "Telunot Sani ve-Sansani ve-Semangelof" (The Complaints of Sani, Sansani, and Semangeloff, *Kerem Ḥemed* 3 [Prague, 1838]: 106–11), "Ha-Tzofeh le-Veit Yisra'el—Tashlikh" (The Watchman for the House of Israel—*Tashlikh*; Prague, 1840), and "Ha-Tzofeh le-Veit Yisra'el—Gilgul Nefesh" (The Watchman of the House of Israel—Transmigration of a Soul; Leipzig, 1845). As noted, all of these satires appeared in the volume *Ha-Tzofeh le-Veit Yisra'el* (Vienna, 1858), edited by Meïr (Max) Letteris and published after Erter's death. Letteris prefaced the collection with Erter's programmatic essay "Tekhunat ha-Tzofeh," written in 1823, shortly after the publication of "Moznei Mishkal," in which he outlined the figure of the Watchman for the House of Israel, who serves as a narrator in the satires—a narrator who observes the objects of the satire from a position of superiority, which affords him privilege, authority, and power.

2. Isaac Erter, *Ha-Tzofeh le-Veit Yisra'el* [Watchman for the House of Israel], ed. Yehuda Friedlander (Jerusalem: Mosad Bialik, 1996), 71.

3. Ibid.

4. Ibid., 72.

5. Ibid.

6. Ibid., 73.

7. It is a hegemonic gaze capable of inflicting severe punishment, such as the publication of a violent anti-hasidic satire, for any deviation from the moral norms and standards it dictates. The totality of the Watchman's gaze brings its sovereign power to bear upon "the stable and opaque surface of the body," that is, the material that he observes (Martin Jay, *Downcast Eyes: The Denigration of Vision in Twentieth-Century French Thought* [Berkeley: University of California Press, 1994], 382–84, 393). In effect, the Watchman constitutes himself as sovereign over the entire Jewish people, distinguishing between its positive and negative elements, that is, between the Haskalah and Hasidism. It is only from the lofty position of Watchman for the House of Israel—one who both expresses and supervises the mores and morals of the people—that he is able to appoint himself ruler. Self-appointment to a position of rulership over an entire group of people is contingent upon a determined set of material conditions that not only justify such an act but actually demand it. This realization lies at the heart of Carl Schmitt's definition of sovereignty, a product of his trenchant criticism of the Weimar Republic and its liberal political thought, eradicated with the rise of the Nazis to power in Germany.

8. Erter, *Ha-Tzofeh le-Veit Yisra'el*, 62.

9. Ibid., 61.

10. Ibid.

11. Carl Schmitt, *Political Theology: Four Chapters on the Concept of Sovereignty*, trans. George Schwab (Chicago: University of Chicago Press 2005), 36.

12. Moshe Pelli, *Bikurei ha-Iitim: Bikurei Haskalah: Mafteah mu'ar le' Bikurei ha-'Iitim, Ktav ha-Eet shel ha-Haskalah ba- Galicia* (Jerusalem: Magnes, 2005), 51, 67.

13. Mordechai Eliav, *Ha-Hinuch ha-yehudi Be-Germania bi-mei ha-Haskala ve-ha-Emantsipatsia* (Jerusalem: Ha-Sochnut ha-yehudit le-Eretz Yisra'el, 1960), 2; Yitzchak Julius Guttmann, *Ha-Philosophia shel Ha-Yahadut* (Jerusalem: Mosad Bialik, 1953), 268–69.

14. Erter, *Ha-Tzofeh le-Veit Yisra'el*, 62–63.

15. Uri Shoham, *Ha-Mashma'ut ha-aheret: Min ha-Mashal ha-alegori ve-'ad ha-Sipur ha-parari'alisti* (Tel Aviv: Makhon Kats, Tel Aviv University, 1982), 87.

16. Geoffrey H. Hartman, "Romanticism and 'Anti-Self-Consciousness,'" in *Romanticism*, ed. Cynthia Chase (London: 1993), 46.

17. Ibid., 46–48.

18. Joseph Perl, *Megaleh Temirin*, ed. Jonatan Meir (Jerusalem: Mosad Byalik, 2013 [1819]), 503.

19. Baruch Kurzweil, *Be-Ma'avak al-Erkei ha-Yahadut* (Tel Aviv: Schocken, 1969), 58, 60.

20. Friedrich Schiller, "Naive and Sentimental Poetry," in *Essays*, ed. Daniel O. Dahlstrom and Walter Hinderer (New York: Continuum, 1993), 205–6.

21. Shmuel Werses, "Ha-Hasidut be-Einei Sifrut ha-Haskalah: Min ha-Pulmus shel Hasidei Galitzyah," in *Megamat ve-Tzurot be-Sifrut ha-Haskalah* (Jerusalem: Magnes, 1990), 91.

22. Ibid., 93.

23. Proverbs 7:4–5; translation R. Alter.

24. Erter, *Ha-Tzofeh le-Veit Yisra'el*.

25. Translation R. Alter.

26. Jacques Rancière, *Aesthetics and Its Discontents*, trans. Steve Corcoran (Cambridge: Polity Press, 2009).

27. Schmitt, *Political Theology*.

28. Erter, *Ha-Tzofeh le-Veit Yisra'el*, 75.

29. Werses, "Ha-Hasidut be-Einei Sifrut ha-Haskalah," 236.

30. Yehuda Friedlander, "Mavo," in Isaac Erter, *Ha-Tzofeh le-Veit Yisra'el*, ed. Yehuda Friedlander (Jerusalem: Mosad Bialik, 1996), 26.

31. Tova Cohen, *Ha-ahat Ahuvah ve-ha-ahat Senu'ah: Ben Metsi'ut le-Vidyon be-Te'ure ha-Ishah be-Sifrut ha-Haskala* (Jerusalem: Magnes and the Hebrew University, 2002), 72. Erter's work is thus in keeping with the misogynistic streak in Galician maskilic satire—notably in Perl's *Megaleh Temirin*. This misogyny is characterized by the social conceptualization of female types—hasidic women in Perl's satire (Cohen, *Ha-ahat Ahuvah ve-ha'ahat Senu'ah*, 64–71), and the allegorical figures of Hasidut and Hokhmah in Erter's work. Such misogynistic typification was a new phenomenon that went beyond earlier criticism of women in general, as in the case of "the ludicrous woman" (*ha-ishah ha-nil'eget*) in "Nezed ha-Dema" (A Pottage of Tears), by Israel ben Moses ha-Levi of Zamość (1700–72) (Cohen, *Ha-ahat Ahuvah ve-ha'ahat Senu'ah*, 59–64).

32. Erter, *Ha-Tzofeh le-Veit Yisra'el*, 24.

33. Ibid., 83.

34. Cohen, *Ha-ahat Ahuvah ve-ha'ahat Senu'ah*, 37, 52–56.

35. Israel of Zamość, *Nezed ha-Dema* (1773), preface.

36. In order to effect this passage from Enlightenment universality to identity politics, Erter takes, as a point of departure, the standard maskilic discourse of rational, scientific knowledge, in which the figure of Hokhmah promises to instruct the Watchman, in order to provide him with the necessary ammunition for his struggle against the hasidim. As

Erter remarks in his notes to "Hasidut ve-Hokhmah," Hokhmah expounds authoritatively and in considerable detail on the various areas of scientific knowledge, including: "algebra, geometry, architecture, military tactics, mechanics, hydraulics, optics, astronomy, natural history, physics, psychology, aesthetics, [and] logic." The list concludes with "metaphysics [and] ethics," which Hokhmah describes as "beyond discernment." This appears consistent with a deistic worldview ("Note the boundary that God has set"), although the context is that of the revelation event experienced by the Watchman (and described in "Tekhunat ha-Tzofeh"), and Hokhmah herself criticizes hasidic attempts to subvert this maskilic revelation, for fear that "the cloud will be lifted from the House of Israel" (Erter, *Ha-Tzofeh le-Veit Yisra'el*, 85–87).

37. Raphael Mahler, *Hasidut ve-ha-Haskalah* (Merhavyah: Sifriyat Poalim ve-ha-Kibtrz ha-artzi Hashomer Hatzair, 1961), 109.

38. Judah Leib Mieses, *Kin'at ha-Emet* (Vienna: 1828), 29–38; Shmuel Feiner, *Haskalah ve-Historiah: Toledotha shel Hakarat he-Avar yehudit modernit* (Jerusalem: Zalman Shazar Center, 1995), 141.

39. Erter, *Ha-Tzofeh le-Veit Yisra'el*, 52.

40. Olga Litvak, *Haskalah: The Romantic Movement in Judaism* (New Brunswick, NJ: Rutgers University Press, 2012), 31.

41. Schmitt, *Political Theology*.

42. Erter, *Ha-Tzofeh le-Veit Yisra'el*, 77.

43. Ibid.

44. Ibid., 81–82.

45. Ibid., 77.

46. Ibid., 78–79.

47. Ibid., 80–81.

48. Ibid., 75–76.

49. Ibid., 76.

50. Naphtali Herz Wessely, "Mihtav," *Ha-Me'assef* 1, no. 1 (1783): 8.

51. Erter, *Ha-Tzofeh le-Veit Yisra'el*, 74.

52. Ibid., 75.

53. Werses, "Ha-Hasidut be-Einei Sifrut ha-Haskalah," 103.

54. Amir Mufti, *Enlightenment in the Colony: The Jewish Question and the Crisis of Postcolonial Culture* (Princeton: Princeton University Press, 2007), 43.

55. Ibid., 54, 60, 68.

56. Hartman, "Romanticism and 'Anti-Self-Consciousness,'" 47.

57. Feiner, *Haskalah ve-Historiah*, 108.

58. Wessely, "Mihtav," 8.

59. Naphtali Herz Wessely, *Shirei Tiferet* (Berlin, 1789), vi. The internal quotation is from Kohelet 7:5.

60. Jeremy Dauber, *Antonio's Devils: Writers of the Jewish Enlightenment and the Birth of Modern Hebrew and Yiddish Literature* (Stanford: Stanford University Press, 2004), 88.

61. Erter's Watchman is, in effect, an aggressive, emotional, and radical Galician version of the enlightened narrator of Mendelssohn's *Kohelet Musar* (Preacher of Morals), the first Hebrew periodical, published in 1755, in the European Enlightenment tradition of the "moral weekly." Such publications served readers as an alternative to preachers and clerics, with the voice of the writer—that is, the voice of reason—replacing that of the man of the cloth, as a theological and moral guide for society. The moral weeklies offered readers lives

of happiness and spiritual perfection no less than religion and the church did. Unlike those who advocated coexistence between the church and Enlightenment morality, Mendelssohn was wary of religious preachers. Mendelssohn, like Erter after him, employed irony to establish the standing of the modern, autonomous, moral subject of the Jewish intellectual writer, distinct from religious institutions and closer to the people. Both writers also made use of the epistolary genre. There is, however, a clear difference between them. While Mendelssohn used subtle irony against the preachers and traditional moral literature (Meir Gilon, *Kohelet Mussar le-Mendelssohn al Reka Tekufato* [Jerusalem: Israeli Academy of Science and Humanities, 1979] 140–45), Erter, in the act of constituting the subject of the Watchman, resorted to the aggressive irony of satire—in response to the radical political circumstances surrounding the bitter conflict between Haskalah and Hasidism.

62. Meïr Halevi Letteris, "Tekhunat ha-Tzofeh," *Moznei Mishkal* (1823): 13–14.

63. Wessely, *Shirei Tiferet*, v.

64. Issac Euchel, "Igrot Meshulam ben Uriyah ha-Eshtamo'i," *ha-Me'asef* 6 (1790): 349.

65. Fischel Lachover, *Toldot ha-Sifrut ha-'Ivrit ha-hadashah*, vol. 1 (Tel Aviv: Dvir. 1966), 58–59.

66. Nili Mirsky, foreword to *Al Shira naivit ve-santimentalistit: Al ha-Nisgav*, by Friedrich Schiller, trans. David Aran (Tel Aviv: Sifriyat Poalim, 1985), 7–13.

67. Wessely, *Shirei Tiferet*, xii.

68. Ibid., v.

69. Rancière, *Aesthetics and its Discontents*.

70. Simon Halkin, *Mavo le-Siporet ha-'Ivrit, Reshimot lefi Hartsaotav shel S. Halkin*, ed. Sophia Hillel (Jerusalem: Mifal ha-shekufal, Hebrew University, 1955), 205.

71. Erter, *Ha-Tzofeh le-Veit Yisra'el*, 73.

72. Yakir Englander, *Ha-Guf ha-Gavri ha-haredi-lita'i: Be-Sifrut ha-Musar u-ve-Sipurei ha-Tzadilim* (Jerusalem: Magnes, 2016), 40.

73. Hannan Hever, "The Politics of Form of the Hassidic Tale," *Dibur* 2 (2016): 57–73.

74. Werses, "Ha-Hasidut be-Einei Sifrut ha-Haskalah," 96.

75. Erter, *Ha-Tzofeh le-Veit Yisra'el*, 81.

76. Ibid., 87.

77. Menahem Brinker, *Estetika ke-Torat ha-Bikoret: Sugiot ve-Tahanot be-Toldoteiha* (Tel Aviv: Oneversita Meshudert, 1982), 114.

78. Litvak, *Haskalah*, 66–71.

79. Joseph Klausner, *Historyah shel ha-Sifrut ha-'Ivrit ha-hadashah*, vol. 2 (Jerusalem: Achiasaf, 1952), 332.

80. Simon Halkin, *Zramim ve-Tzurot ba-Sifrut ha-Ivrit ha-hadashah*, vol. 1, *Prakim be-Sifrut ha-Haskala u-Visifrut Khibat Tzion* (Jerusalem: Mosad Bialik, 1984), 172–73.

81. Shoham, H*a-Mashma'ut ha-aheret*, 89, 92–105. In effect, the interpretations offered by Halkin and Shoham reflect the hegemonic Zionist narrative, which views the rise of Zionism as a response to the violent outbreaks of antisemitism in the 1880s, marking the collapse of the ahistorical rationalism of universalist Haskalah. According to the Zionist narrative, it was only at that critical point that the Jews entered European history as a distinct, Jewish phenomenon, when the inability of universal identity to protect the Jews against European violence compelled them to renounce their aspiration to emancipation. Klausner's Zionism, on the other hand, was that of Ahad Ha'am—far more interested in the spiritual fate of the Jews than in their physical well-being. He therefore ascribed little importance to external and material influences on national thought and saw no reason why Erter,

writing in the early nineteenth century, could not have developed a national, romantic approach. Klausner thus understood the various components of Erter's work in a unifying, organic light, combining emotional, personal confession with the rationalist criticism of satire. Unlike Halkin and Shoham, whose structural distinction between the two elements stemmed from their association of the appearance of national literature with the hegemonic, Zionist timetable, Klausner was able to identify Jewish national literature as early as the first part of the nineteenth century. An even more extreme example is offered by the historiographical position of H. N. Bialik, also a faithful disciple of Ahad Ha'am, who named Moses Hayim Luzzatto (Ramhal), who wrote in the first half of seventeenth century, as the harbinger of Jewish national literature.

82. Jürgen Habermas, *The Structural Transformation of the Public Sphere: An Inquiry into a Category of Bourgeois Society*, trans. Thomas Burger and Frederick Lawrence (Cambridge, MA: MIT Press, 1989 [1962]).

83. Eduardo Mendieta and Jonathan Vanantwerpen, "Introduction," in *The Power of Public Sphere*, ed. Eduardo Mendieta and Jonathan Vanantwerpen (New York: Columbia University Press. 2011), 1.

84. Ibid., 6.

85. Naphtali Herz Wessely, *Mivhar Ketavim*, ed. Gedaliah Elkoshi (Jerusalem: Avar, 1952).

86. Wessely, "Mihtav."

87. Schmitt, *Political Theology*.

88. Mendieta and Vanantwerpen, "Introduction," 1–5.

89. David Lloyd, "The Pathological Sublime: Pleasure and Pain in the Colonial Context," in *The Postcolonial Enlightenment: Eighteenth-Century Colonialism and Postcolonial Theory*, ed. Daniel Carey and Lynn Festa (Oxford: Oxford University Press, 2013), 71–76.

90. Cohen, *Ha-ahat Ahuvah ve-ha'ahat Senu'ah*, 32–34.

91. Erter, *Ha-Tzofeh le-Veit Yisra'el*, 84.

92. Feiner, *Haskalah ve-Historiah*, 105–7.

93. Daniel Carey and Lynn Festa, "Introduction: Some Answers to the Question—What Is Postcolonial Enlightenment?," in *The Postcolonial Enlightenment: Eighteenth-Century Colonialism and Postcolonial Theory*, ed. Daniel Carey and Lynn Festa (Oxford: Oxford University Press, 2013), 8.

94. Dipesh Chakrabarty, *Provincializing Europe: Postcolonial Thought and Historical Difference* (Princeton: Princeton University Press, 2000), 4.

95. Brinker, *Estetika ke-Torat ha-Bikoret*, 71. In this sense, the relationship between romanticism and Enlightenment was not wholly antithetical but also entailed a degree of cooperation and even identification—in terms of radical criticism as well as Bildung, that is, the education of the public. The potential conflict between these two goals (educating the public about principles that are themselves subject to radical criticism) led early romantics to transform the Enlightenment. The destructive power of criticism unleashed by the Enlightenment was compensated for through imagination and the aesthetic affirmation of community and of the principle of reason in the public sphere (Fredrick C. Beiser, *The Sovereignty of Reason: The Defense of Rationality in the Early English Enlightenment* [Princeton: Princeton University Press, 1996], 318–26, esp. 319 and 325).

96. Claire Colebrook, *Irony* (New York: Routledge, 2004), 89.

97. Stephen Slemon, "Post-Colonial Allegory and the Transformation of History," *Journal of Commonwealth Literature* 23, no. 1 (1988): 157–58.

98. Fredric Jameson, "Third-World Literature in the Era of Multinational Capitalism," in *The Jameson Reader*, ed. Michael Hardt and Kathi Weeks (Oxford: Blackwell, 2000), 320.

99. Friedlander, "Mavo," 25.

100. Ibid., 7, 73.

101. Menucha Gilboa, *Mivnim u-Mashmauiot: Iyunim be-Sifrut ha-Haskalah* (Tel Aviv: Ekad, 1977), 12–13; Shoham, *Ha-Mashma'ut ha-aḥeret*, 79–105.

102. Hever, "The Politics of Form of the Hassidic Tale," 57–73.

103. Erter, *Ha-Tzofeh le-Veit Yisra'el*, 71

104. Ibid., 72.

105. Translation R. Alter.

106. Erter, *Ha-Tzofeh le-Veit Yisra'el*, 73.

107. Paul de Man, *Allegories of Reading* (New Haven: Yale University Press, 1979).

108. "For just as autobiographies, by their thematic insistence on the subject, on the proper name, on memory, on birth, eros, and death, and on the doubleness of specularity, openly declare their cognitive and tropological constitution, they are equally eager to escape from their coercions of this system. Writers of autobiographies as well as writers on autobiography are obsessed with the need to move from cognition to resolution and to action, from speculative to political and legal authority" (ibid., 922).

109. Paul de Man, *Blindness and Insight* (Minneapolis: University of Minnesota Press, 1983), 214.

110. Colebrook, *Irony*, 108–10, 121; de Man, *Blindness and Insight*.

111. My analysis of the political position of the Watchman's maskilic gaze at the hasidim relies, inter alia, on Shai Ginsburg's introduction to his translation of Paul de Man's essay "Autobiography as De-facement."

112. Also written in the epistolary genre, popular among maskilim, see: Werses, "Hahasidut be-Einei Sifrut ha-Haskalah," 96. In his letter, Krochmal writes: "And do not concern yourself, my dear, with the greatness and majesty with which they exalt and praise their leaders, as the latter command them to do, as if one of them were a king or prince of Israel. Only fools and children are blinded by such things. In the eyes of the discerning *maskil*, such 'greatness' is neither a mark of honor nor of glory, but only of shame and disgrace." Krochmal immediately goes on to disparage Rabbi Levi Isaac of Berditchev (Nachman Krochmal, *Moreh Nevuhei Ha-zman* [Berlin: Iyanut, 1924], 417; *Kerem Hemed* 1 (1833).

113. Erter, *Ha-Tzofeh le-Veit Yisra'el*, 87. Maskilic writing in the epistolary genre parallels the actual letters exchanged by the maskilim, some of which appear in the volumes edited by Meïr Letteris. The premise that they sought to create some sort of "republic of letters" in this fashion (Feiner, *Haskalah ve-Historiah*, 111) ignores the fact that the writers were personally acquainted with one another, and therefore lacked the dimension of an imagined community. The epistolary genre also drew upon the popular genre of letter-writing manuals (including model letters). Although considered a noncanonical genre, such *Briefsteller* developed a style of modern Hebrew prose, which approached that of the literary canon in the manual *Ketav Yosher* (Epistle of Righteousness; Vienna, 1821), by the Galician poet Shalom HaCohen, editor of *Bikurei ha-Itim*. This Hebrew Briefsteller, ordered from HaCohen by Anton Schmid, the Viennese publisher who published the bulk of Galician Hebrew literature, revealed the failure of the Berlin Haskalah to expand literary Hebrew beyond the biblical stratum. The practical purpose of the Briefsteller, on the other hand, forced authors to draw upon a variety of Hebrew, linguistic sources (Judith Halevi-Zwick, "Ha-Irgonim ha-ivri'im shel ha-Meah ha-shes-esrei," Dapim le-Meḥkar be-Sifrut 7 [1990]: 103–7).

114. Erter, *Ha-Tzofeh le-Veit Yisra'el*, 83.
115. Werses, "Ha-Hasidut be-Einei Sifrut ha-Haskalah," 91.
116. Krochmal, *Moreh Nevuhei Ha-zman*, 417; *Kerem Hemed* 1.
117. Erter, *Ha-Tzofeh le-Veit Yisra'el*, 82.
118. Lloyd, "The Pathological Sublime," 71–76.
119. Erter, *Ha-Tzofeh le-Veit Yisra'el*, 83.
120. Ibid., 82.
121. Schmitt, *Political Theology*.
122. Krochmal himself (a leading light of the Galician Haskalah), in his own historio-philosophical writings, acted "as a man of modern Hebrew literature in its transitional period between rationalism and romanticism; and also as the harbinger of modern Jewish nationalism" (Feiner, *Haskalah ve-Historiah*, 157). There can be no doubt that the first stirrings of nationalism among the Galician maskilim—clearly reflected, for example, in Meïr Letteris's poem "Yonah Homiyah" (Letteris, *ha-Tzfirah* 1 [1823], 2–4)—also contributed to the development of a particularly Jewish, rather than universal, historical and historiographical consciousness, including portraits of Jewish historical figures and analogies from Jewish history (Feiner, *Haskalah ve-Historiah*, 128).
123. Isaac Erter, "Alilat Damesek," in *Ha-Tzofeh le-Veit Yisra'el* (Tel Aviv: Mahbarot le-Sifrut, 1972), 195–97.
124. Ibid.
125. Kurzweil, *Be-Ma'avak al-Erkei ha-Yahadut*, 92.
126. Ibid., 94–95.
127. Dauber, *Antonio's Devils*, 98. Erter appears to have been influenced by Solomon Loewisohn's *Melitzat Yeshurun* (The Rhetoric of Jeshurun, 1816)—the Hebrew Haskalah's preeminent work on poetics, which highlighted the biblical sublime, the nonrational romantic imagination, and biblical allegory. In fact, Erter uses "pure" biblical language to place a physical, flesh-and-blood man at the center of his satire—a man riddled with fears of the seductive/castrating hasidic "femme fatale," clearly demonstrating that the Watchman's political motivation stems directly from his gender identity.
128. Lucian, "Toladot Alexander mi-Abonoteichus Navie Sheker," trans. Meïr Halevi Letteris, *ha-Tzfirah* 1: 13–42; Jonatan Meir, "Lucianus ha-ivri," *Dehak* 5 (2015): 278–304.
129. Meïr Halevi Letteris, foreword to "Toldot Alexander mi-Abonoteichus Navie Sheker," by Lucian, trans. Meïr Halevi Letteris, *ha-Tzfirah* 1 (1823), 14, 20; Meir, "Lucianus ha-ivri," 297, 301.
130. Meir, "Lucianus ha-ivri," 303.
131. Lucian, "Toladot Alexander mi-Abonoteichus Navie Sheker," trans. Jonatan Meir, *Dehak* 5 (2015): 280.
132. Werses, "Ha-hasidut be-Einei sifrut ha-Haskalah," 232–34.
133. Ibid., 222, 236–37.
134. Erter, *Ha-Tzofeh le-Veit Yisra'el*, 79.
135. Lucian, "Toladot Alexander mi-Abonoteichus Navie Sheker," 290.
136. Yehuda Friedlander, *Perakim ba-Satirah ha-ivrit* (Tel Aviv: Papirus, 1979), 27–28, 37–38.
137. Isaac Euchel, "Igrot Meshulam ben Uriyah ha-Eshtamo'I," in *Studies in Hebrew Satire*, vol. 1, *Hebrew Satire in Germany: 1790–1797*, ed. Yehuda Friedlander (Tel Aviv: Papyrus, 1979), 46. The internal quotation is from Proverbs 6:26; translation R. Alter.

138. Meir Gilon, "Ha-satira ha-ivrit bi-Tekufat ha-Haskalah be-Germania: Anatomiah shel Mehkar," *Zion* 42, no. 3 (1987): 225.

139. Hannan Hever, *'El ha-hof ha-mekuveh* (Jerusalem: Van Leer Institute and Hakibbutz Hameuchad, 2007).

CHAPTER 4

1. Stephen Howe, *Empire: A Very Short Introduction* (Oxford: Oxford University Press, 2002), 14.

2. Jane Burbank, Mark von Hagen, and Anatolyi Remov, foreword to *Russian Empire: Space, People, Power, 1700–1930*, ed. Jane Burbank, Mark von Hagen, and Anatolyi Remov (Bloomington: Indiana University Press, 2007), 8.

3. Paul Werth, "Changing Conceptions of Difference, Assimilation, and Faith in the Volga-Kama Region, 1740–1870," in *Russian Empire: Space, People, Power, 1700–1930*, ed. Jane Burbank, Mark von Hagen, and Anatolyi Remov (Bloomington: Indiana University Press, 2007), 169–95.

4. Mordechai Zelkin, "Ha-Haskalah ha-yehudit u-She'elat ha-Otonomiyah," in *Kehal Yisra'el: Ha-Shilton ha-atzmi le-Dorotav*, vol. 2, *Ha-'Et ha-hadashah*, ed. Israel Bartal (Jerusalem: Zalman Shazar Center, 2004), 157.

5. Burbank, von Hagen, and Remov, *Russian Empire*, 11.

6. Sviatoslav Kaspe, "Imperial Political Culture and Modernization in the Second Half of the Nineteenth Century," in *Russian Empire: Space, People, Power, 1700–1930*, ed. Jane Burbank, Mark von Hagen, and Anatolyi Remov (Bloomington: Indiana University Press, 2007). The situation was essentially that of an imperial power striving to turn a multiethnic polity into a nation-state. To that end, it sought to resolve the contradiction between imperial integrity and ethnic diversity, by attempting (unsuccessfully, for the most part) to "normalize" members of non-Russian ethnicities—Russifying them to fit the empire's national ideal. This transition from imperial to national paradigm allows us to draw analogies from the state's attitude to Muslims to its attitude to Jews (Elena Campbell, "The Muslim Question in Late Imperial Russia," in *Russian Empire: Space, People, Power, 1700–1930*, ed. Jane Burbank, Mark von Hagen, and Anatolyi Remov (Bloomington: Indiana University Press, 2007).

7. Israel Bartal, "Ha-Otonomiyah ha-yehudit ba-'Et ha-hadashah: Ma nimhak? ma nosaf?," in *Kehal Yisra'el: Ha-shilton ha-'atzmi le-Dorotav*, vol. 2, *Ha-'et Ha-hadashah*, ed. Israel Bartal (Jerusalem: Zalman Shazar Center, 2004), 10–11.

8. Edward Said, *Culture and Imperialism* (New York: Vintage Books. 1994), 241.

9. The Russian Empire's ambivalent position with regard to the nationalization of non-Russians, vacillating between national and imperial principles (Kaspe, "Imperial Political Culture and Modernization in the Second Half of the Nineteenth Century," 458), created a hybrid relationship between the monarchs' reliance on imperial dynasticism and their acceptance of expressions of nationalism in the context of modern colonial imperialism (Frederick Cooper, *Colonialism in Question, Theory, Knowledge, History* [Berkeley: University of California Press, 2005], 153–58). This policy suited both the hasidim, who sought recognition as corporative religious communities within the empire, and the maskilim, whose goal of emancipation without renouncing particular Jewish identity was well served by the conservative nationalist policies pursued by Alexander II and amplified by Alexander III, which

preserved relative ethno-political stability throughout the empire (Kaspe, "Imperial Political Culture and Modernization in the Second Half of the Nineteenth Century," 488).

10. Yehuda Slutsky, *Ha-'Itonut ha-yehudit-rusit ba-Me'ah ha-19* (Jerusalem: Mosad Bialik, 1970), 1819.

11. Eli Lederhendler, *The Road to Modern Jewish Politics* (Oxford: Oxford University Press, 1989), 40–47.

12. Israel Bartal, "Pinsk shel ma'la ve-Pinsk shel mata: Hasidim u-Maskilim, Metsi'ut u-Vidyon," in *Mi-Vilna le-Yerushalayim: Mehkarim be-Toldoteihem ve-Tarbutam shel Yehudei mizrah Eropa—Mugashim le-Profesor Shmuel Werses*, ed. David Assaf, Avner Holtzman, Chava Turniansky, Shmuel Feiner, and Yehuda Friedlander (Jerusalem: Magnes, 2002), 60.

13. Ilya Luria, *'Edah u-Medinah: Hasidut Habad ba-Imperiyah ha-rusit 1828–1883* (Jerusalem: Magnes, 2006), 36, 38; for example, in the case of smuggling, see Lederhendler, *The Road to Modern Jewish Politics*, 61–64.

14. Michel Foucault, *"Society Must Be Defended": Lectures at the Collège de France 1975–1976*, trans. Arnold I. Davidson (New York: Picador, 2003).

15. See Lederhendler, *The Road to Modern Jewish Politics*, 90.

16. Ann Laura Stoler, *Carnal Knowledge and Imperial Power: Race and Intimate in Colonial Rule* (Berkeley: University of California Press, 2010), 13.

17. In 1804, Tsar Alexander I (r. 1801–25) granted the Jews relative freedom, in an attempt to integrate them into Russian society. To that end, the "Statute Concerning the Organization of the Jews" was legislated, granting each subgroup within the Jewish community the right to build its own synagogues and choose its own rabbis, on condition that a common kahal retain overall authority in each town. At the same time, however, the statute deprived rabbis of the power of excommunication (*herem*) for the violation of religious norms and beliefs (Simon Dubnow, *Toldot ha-Hasidut al Yesod Mekorot rishonim, nidpasim u-khitvei yad* (Jerusalem: Dvir, 1967), 278.

18. John D. Klier, "State Policies and the Conversion of Jews in Imperial Russia," in *Of Religion and Empire: Missions, Conversion, and Tolerance in Tsarist Russia*, ed. Robert P. Geraci and Michael Khodarkovsky (Ithaca: Cornell University Press, 1993), 97.

19. Michael Stanislawski, *Tsar Nicholas I and the Jews: The Transformation of Jewish Society in Russia 1825–1855* (Philadelphia: Jewish Publication Society of America, 1983), 49–101.

20. Klier, "State Policies and the Conversion of Jews in Imperial Russia," 93, 99–102.

21. Stanislawski, *Tsar Nicholas I and the Jews*, 16, 31. These young conscripts were known as "cantonists."

22. Termed "the intimacies of empire" by Ann Stoler, *Carnal Knowledge and Imperial Power*, xxxv.

23. Raphael Mahler, *Ha-Hasidut ve-ha-Haskalah* (Merhavia: Sifriyat Poalim and Hakibbutz Haartzi Hashomer Hatzair, 1961), 239–41.

24. Israel Bartal, *Kozak u-Vedui: 'Am' ve-'Eretz' ba-Leumiyut ha-yisra'elit* (Tel Aviv: Am Oved, 2007), 161.

25. Eli Yassif, *The Hebrew Folktale: History, Genre, Meaning* (Bloomington: Indiana University Press, 1999), 371, 380.

26. Dubnow, *Toldot ha-Hasidut al Yesod Mekorot rishonim, nidpasim u-khitvei yad*, 384.

27. Joseph Dan, *Ha-Sipur ha-hasidi* (Jerusalem: Keter, 1975), 38–39.

28. Kaidaner, whose name appears to derive from the Lithuanian city of Keidan in the Kovno (Kaunas) district, where he was probably born (Gedaliah Nigal, foreword to Jacob Kaidaner, *Sipurim nora'im: Sipurim shel Ish Habad*, ed. Gedaliah Nigal [Jerusalem: Carmel,

1992], 13–29 lived in Vilkomir in the Rasein (Raseiniai) district. He was also the author of *Matzref ha-Avodah* (Crucible of Divine Service)—known too as *Vikuha Rabah* (Great Debate)—first published anonymously during the author's lifetime at Koenigsberg in 1858), by Dov Ber Segalovich (Haim Meir Hillman, *Beit Rabi* [Berdichev: Sheftil, 1902], 33; Nahum Lamm, *Torah li-Shmah: Be-Mishnat Rabi Hayyim mi-Volozhin u-ve-Mahsevet ha-Dor* [Jerusalem: Mosad ha-rav Kook, 1972], 208–18; Nigal, foreword to *Sipurim nora'im*, 13). According to Yehoshua Mondschein ("Ha-Sfarim 'Mitzraf Avodah' ve-Vikuha rabah'," *Alei Sefer 5* [1978]: 169), Kaidaner's real name was Jacob Bachrach. As Gedalyah Nigal points out, this is supported by the closing phrase of the author's preface to *Matzref ha-Avodah*, which forms the acrostic "Jacob Bachrach" (Nigal, foreword to *Sipurim nora'im*, 14–15).

*Sipurim nora'im* has appeared in some ten editions, including in 1892, 1894, 1913, 1957, 1988, 1992, and 2007. On the title page of the first edition (1875), Kaidaner is referred to as having already passed away, although we have no information regarding his date of death or birth. Since *Sipurim nora'im* includes a eulogy for Menahem Mendel Schneersohn of Lubavitch (known as the *Tzemah Tzedek*; Jacob Kaidaner, *Sipurim nora'im: Sipurim shel Ish Habad*, ed. Gedaliah Nigal [Jerusalem: Carmel, 1992], 136–38), who passed away in 1866, the tales appear to have been written after that time and probably a number of years before 1875 (Nigal, foreword to *Sipurim nora'im*, 19).

29. Dan, *Ha-Sipur ha-hasidi*, 34, 189–95.
30. Nigal, foreword to *Sipurim nora'im*, 16–17; Hillman, *Beit rabi*, 213.
31. Dan, *Ha-sipur ha-Hasidi*, 236.
32. Jacob Kaidaner, *Sipurim nora'im* (Jerusalem: N.p., 1957), 3. The preface does not appear in later editions.
33. Mordechai Teitelbaum, *Ha-Rav mi-Ladi u-Mifleget Habad*, vol. 1 (Warsaw: Tushiah, 1910), 72–81.
34. Shmuel Werses, "Ha-Hasidut be-Einei Sifrut ha-Haskalah: Min ha-Pulmus shel Hasidei Galitzyah," in *Ha-Dat ve-ha-Hayim: Tenu'at ha-Haskalah ha-yehudit be-mizrah Eropah*, ed. Immanuel Etkes (Jerusalem: Zalman Shazar Center, 1993), 45.
35. Shmuel Feiner, *Milhemet Tarbut: Tenu'at ha-Haskalah ha-yehudit ba-Me'ah ha-19* (Jerusalem: Carmel, 2010), 156–57, 231–64; Stanislawski, *Tsar Nicholas I and the Jews*, 114. One example of a moderate maskil is Eliezer Zweifel, whose book *Shalom 'al Israel* (Peace on Israel; 1868) was an attempt to find common ground between Hasidism and the Haskalah. Zweifel's elder, Isaac Baer Levinsohn, also known for his moderate positions, believed that the Haskalah was firmly rooted in Jewish tradition—a view taken even further by Samuel Joseph Fuenn, who developed an approach that Shmuel Feiner terms "religious Haskalah" (Feiner, *Milhemet Tarbut*, 111, 150–80, 181–230).
36. Feiner, *Milhemet Tarbut*, 102–7.
37. Dubnow, *Toldot ha-Hasidut al Yesod Mekorot rishonim, nidpasim u-khitvei yad*, 317.
38. Shmuel Feiner, "Ha-Mifneh be-Ha'arakhat ha-Hasidut: Eliezer Zweifel ve-ha-Haskalah ha-metunah," in *Ha-Dat ve-ha-Hayim: Tenu'at ha-Haskalah ha-Yehudit be-mizrah Eropah*, ed. Immanuel Etkes (Jerusalem: Zalman Shazar Center, 1993), 338.
39. Isaac Baer Levinsohn, *Te'udah be-Yisra'el* (Jerusalem: Zalman Shazar Center 1977), 39–40. The hasidim waged their own war against the maskilim, portraying the Haskalah—in works such as *Sipurei Kedoshim* (Tales of the Saints; 1866) and *Kehal Hasidim*—as a dangerous threat, beguiling readers with its tempting books, while the hasidic tzadikim rabbis stand fast against them (Eli Yassif, *Sipur ha-'Am ha-'Ivri: Toldotav, Sugav u-Mashma'uto* (Jerusalem: Mosad Bialik, 1994), 430–31.

40. Luria, *'Edah u-Medinah*, 13.

41. Mordechai Zelkin, *Be-'Alot ha-Shahar: Ha-Haskalah ha-Yehudit ba-Imperiyah ha-rusit ba-Me'ah ha-19* (Jerusalem: Magnes, 2000), 284–89.

42. Israel Bartal, "Ha-Otonomiyah ha-yehudit ba-'Et ha-hadashah: Ma nimhak? Ma nosaf?," in *Kehal Yisra'el: Ha-Shilton ha-'atzmi le-Dorotav*, vol. 2, *Ha-'et ha-hadashah*, ed. Israel Bartal (Jerusalem: Zalman Shazar Center, 2004), 11–13. Although the maskilim supported the regime in its campaign against the hasidim and traditional Judaism in general, they had no desire to cut themselves off from their Jewish base or to assimilate into the Russian-Polish intelligentsia and thus remained, by and large, an integral part of traditional Jewish society. For example, "From its inception, the process of 'maskilization' experienced by the city's [Vilna] youth went hand in hand with the traditional way of life, rather than in the direction of detachment from it" (Zelkin, "Ha-Haskalah ha-yehudit u-She'elat ha-Otonomiyah," 150–54, 265). This approach is also reflected in Levinsohn's "*Te'udah be-Yisra'el*," which posited that there was no contradiction between Torah and enlightenment.

43. As a result of the conflict between Hasidism and the Haskalah, the hasidic tale came to function as alternative Hebrew literature to the literature of the Haskalah.

44. Moshe Rosman, *Founder of Hasidism: A Quest for the Historical Ba'al Shem Tov* (Berkeley: University of California Press, 1996), 139.

45. The oral basis of Hasidic tales, which led to a preference of speech over writing (Shlomo Haramati, *Sod Siach: Dibur 'Ivri be-Me'ot 1619* [Tel Aviv: Yaron Golan, 1992], 118–25), also resulted in a lack of interest in the editing and publication of hasidic books. Above all, however, it limited its audience to the narrow community of hasidic listeners. As Immanuel Etkes notes, the Ba'al Shem Tov did not seek to impart devekut to each and every Jew; rather, his intended audience "consisted of a narrow band of associates—the group to which scholarship gives the label 'the Besht's circle.'" Immanuel Etkes, *The Besht: Magician, Mystic, and Leader*, trans. Saadya Sternberg (Waltham, MA: Brandeis University Press, 2005), 152.

46. Michal Oron, "Ha-Ishah ke-Mesaperet ba-Sipur ha-hasidi: Tahsis sifruti 'o Shimurah shel Masoret? 'Iyun be-Sipuro shel S. Y. Agnon 'Etrogo shel 'Oto Tzadik,'" in *Mi-Vilnah le-Yerushalim: Mehkarim be-Toldotehem u-ve-Tarbutam shel Yehudei merkaz Eropah, mugashim le-Profesor Shmuel Werses*, ed. David Assaf, Israel Bartal, Avner Holtzman, Chava Turniansky, Shmuel Feiner, and Yehuda Friedlander (Jerusalem: Magnes, 2002), 514.

47. Daniel Boyarin, "Placing Reading: Ancient Israel and Medieval Europe," in *The Ethnography of Reading*, ed. Jonathan Boyarin (Berkeley: University of California Press, 1993), 13.

48. The fact that the hasidic tale was typically presented as having originated from the tzadik himself or from some other witness-narrator, and subsequently transmitted orally from generation to generation, is a further expression of hasidic opposition to the emancipatory and nationalist character of maskilic literature.

49. Boyarin, "Placing Reading," 13.

50. Jacob Kaidaner, *Sipurim nora'im* (N.p.: N.p., 2007), 15–16. The word *yivka* (burst forth) in the closing quotation is an anagram of the author's first name, Ya'akov (spelled *y-a-k-v*, in Hebrew; Nigal, foreword to *Sipurim nora'im*, 14).

51. Gilles Deleuze and Félix Guattari, *Kafka: Towards a Minor Literature*, trans. Dona Polan (Minneapolis: University of Minnesota Press, 1986).

52. Rachel Elior, *Torat Ha-elohut Ba-dor Ha-sheni Shel Hasidut Habad* (Jerusalem: Magnes, 1982).

53. Dan Miron, *From Continuity to Contiguity: Toward a New Jewish Literary Thinking* (Stanford: Stanford University Press, 2010), 62.

54. Nigal, foreword to *Sipurim nora'im*, 26.
55. Kaidaner, *Sipurim nora'im* (2007), 14.
56. Lila Abu-Lughod, *Dramas of Nationhood: The Politics of Television in Egypt* (Chicago: University of Chicago Press, 2005), ix, 19.
57. Kaidaner, *Sipurim nora'im* (2007), 124.
58. Benedict Anderson, *Imagined Communities: Reflections on the Origin and Spread of Nationalism* (London: Verso, 1999).
59. Kaidaner, *Sipurim nora'im* (2007), 26–27.
60. Etkes, *The Besht: Magician, Mystic, and Leader*, 152.
61. Jacob Katz, *Tradition and Crisis: Jewish Society at the End of the Middle Ages*, trans. Bernard Dov Cooperman (Syracuse: Syracuse University Press, 2000), 209.
62. Dan, *Ha-sipur ha-Hasidi*, 55.
63. Ibid., 8, ¹.
64. Kaidaner, *Sipurim nora'im* (2007), 124.
65. Yassif, *The Hebrew Folktale*, 402.
66. Kaidaner, *Sipurim nora'im* (2007), 124.
67. Ibid.
68. Ibid.
69. Ibid.
70. Ibid., 126.
71. Ibid., 124.
72. Etkes, *The Besht: Magician, Mystic, and Leader*, 112.
73. Mahler, *Ha-hasidut ve-ha-Haskalah*, 302.
74. Gershom Scholem, "The Neutralization of the Messianic Element in Early Hasidism," in *The Messianic Idea in Judaism and Other Essays on Jewish Spirituality* (New York: Schocken, 1995).
75. Ben Zion (Dinburg) Dinur, "Reshitah shel ha-Hasidut ve-Yesodotehah ha-sotsiyaliyim ve-ha-meshihiyim," *Be-Mifneh ha-Dorot: Mehkarim ve-'Iyunim be-Reshitam shel ha-Zemanim ha-hadashim be-Toldot Yisra'el* (Jerusalem: Mosad Bialik, 1955).
76. Scholem, "The Neutralization of the Messianic Element in Early Hasidism," 183.
77. Avraham Rubinstein, "'Igeret ha-Besht Le-R. Gershon Mi-kotov," *Sinai* 67 (1970): 134.
78. On the Besht's Epistle, see Etkes, *The Besht: Magician, Mystic, and Leader*, 79–97.
79. Simon Dubnow, *Toldot ha-Hasidut 'al Yesod Mekorot rishonim, nidpasim u-khitvei yad* (Jerusalem: Dvir, 1967), 62–63.
80. Zelkin, *Be-'Alot ha-Shahar*, 113–31, 139–40, 143–44.
81. Lederhendler, *The Road to Modern Jewish Politics*, 113–18.
82. Levinsohn, *Te'udah be-Yisra'el*.
83. Azriel Shochat, "Yahasam shel ha-maskilim be-rusyah 'el ha-lashon ha-'Ivrit," in *Sefer Avraham Even-Shoshan*, ed. Ben-Zion Luria (Jerusalem: Kiryat Sefer, 1985), 363.
84. Ibid., 392–97.
85. Miron, *From Continuity to Contiguity*, 58–59.
86. Ibid., 60.
87. Dan, *Ha-sipur ha-hasidi*, 16–17.
88. Numbers 23: 23.
89. Magdalena Opalski, *The Jewish Tavern-Keeper and His Tavern in Nineteenth-Century Polish Literature* (Jerusalem: Zalman Shazar Center, 1986), 11–14.

90. Kaidaner, *Sipurim nora'im* (2007), 125.
91. Yassif, *The Hebrew Folktale*, 404.
92. Kaidaner, *Sipurim nora'im* (2007), 125.
93. Rachel Elior, *The Paradoxical Ascent to God: The Kabbalistic Theosophy of Habad Hasidism*, trans. Jeffrey M. Green (Albany: State University of New York Press, 1993), 31.
94. The hasidic tale is both sacred and sanctifying and, like anything in any place at any time, according to the theosophy of Habad, may serve as a point of departure for human contemplation of the divine essence, since "everything in the world is imbued with divine vitality" (Elior, *The Paradoxical Ascent to God*, 13). Furthermore, like anything in the world, the tale comprises both existence (*yesh*) and contraction (*tzimtzum*), as all things simultaneously embody themselves and their opposite. As Rachel Elior explains, each of these aspects conditions the other, "for at their root, the phenomena visible to man, the *Yesh*, or corporeality, are dependent on the divine '*Ayin* [nothingness], from which they draw their vitality and substance. In contrast, the *divine 'Ayin* is *dependent* on the modification that limits the *corporeal Yesh* for its discerned manifestation: *Yesh*, as a form, a limitation, or a conceivable contraction (*tzimtzum*), is the revealed expression of the divine '*Ayin*" (ibid., 26).
95. Dan, *Ha-sipur ha-hasidi*, 11–14.
96. Ibid., 16–17.
97. Elior, *The Paradoxical Ascent to God*, 33–34.
98. Ibid., 143.
99. Levinsohn, *Te'udah be-Yisra'el*, chap. 64.
100. Zelkin, *Be-'Alot ha-Shahar*, 19, 157, 219.
101. For example, in Rodkinson's *Kehal Hasidim*, see Dan, *Ha-sipur ha-Hasidi*, 204–6; Yassif, *The Hebrew Folktale*, 400–401.
102. Nigal, foreword to *Sipurim nora'im*, 7.
103. Dubnow, *Toldot ha-Hasidut al Yesod Mekorot rishonim, nidpasim u-khitvei yad*, 239–41.
104. Kaidaner, *Sipurim nora'im*, 35.
105. Ibid., 37–38; Nigal, foreword to *Sipurim nora'im*, 32.
106. Shmuel Werses, *Hakitzah 'Ami: Sifrut ha-Haskalah be-'Idan ha-Modernizatzyah* (Jerusalem: Magnes, 2001), 383.
107. Nigal, foreword to *Sipurim nora'im*, 44.
108. Ibid., 9.
109. Lewis Glinert, "The Hassidic Tale and the Sociolinguistic Modernization of the Jews of Eastern Europe," in *Ma'aseh Sipur: Mehkarim ba-Siporet ha-yehudit, mugashim le-Yoav Elstein*, ed. Avidov Lipsker and Rella Kushelevsky (Ramat Gan: Bar Ilan University Press, 2006), x.
110. Werses, *Hakitzah 'Ami*, 238–80.
111. Chone Shmeruk and Shmuel Werses, foreword to Yosef Perl, *Ma'asiyot ve-'Igrot mi-Tzadikim 'amitiyim u-me-Anshei Shelomeinu*, ed. Chone Shmeruk and Shmuel Werses (Jerusalem: Israeli Academy of Sciences, 1969), 42.
112. Shmuel Niger, *Bleter Geshichte fun der Yidisher Literatur*, ed. H. Leivick (New York: Congress for Yiddish Culture, 1952), 146.
113. Naftali Loewenthal, "Hebrew and the Chabad Communication Ethos," in *Hebrew in Ashkenaz: A Language in Exile*, ed. Lewis Glinert (Oxford: Oxford University Press, 1993), 182.
114. For an example of this kind of language, see Dubnow, *Toldot ha-hasidut al Yesod Mekorot rishonim, nidpasim u-khitvei yad*, 249.

115. Michael Holquist, *Dialogism: Bakhtin and His World* (London: Routledge, 1990), 14–39.
116. Ibid.
117. Ibid., 69–70.
118. Published by Werses and Shmeruk as *Ma'asiyot ve-Igrot mi-Tzadikim 'amitiyim u-mi-Anshei Shelomeinu* (Stories and Letters from True *Tzadikim* and from Our Own People; 1969).
119. Ibid., 50–51.
120. Loewenthal, "Hebrew and the Chabad Communication Ethos," 168–72; on the Besht's Epistle, see Etkes, *The Besht: Magician, Mystic, and Leader*, 79–97.
121. Israel Bartal, "Mi-Du-Leshoniyut masortit le-Had-Leshoniyut le'umit," *Shvut* 15 (1992): 186–87.
122. Ibid., 188.
123. Deleuze and Guattari, *Kafka*, 1986.
124. I would like to thank Professor Moshe Taub for bringing these examples to my attention.
125. Joseph Klausner, *Historyah shel ha-Sifrut ha-'ivrit ha-hadashah*, vol. 2 (Jerusalem: Achiasaf, 1952), 310–11.
126. Glinert, "The Hassidic Tale and the Sociolinguistic Modernization of the Jews of Eastern Europe," xi, xvii, xx.
127. Itamar Even-Zohar, "Le-Verur Mahutah ve-Tafkidah shel Leshon ha-Sifrut ba-Diglosyah," *Hasifrut* 2, no. 2 (1970): 286–302.
128. Miron, *From Continuity to Contiguity*, 279.
129. Joseph Perl, *Megaleh Temirin* (Vienna: A. Strauss, 1819), 2.
130. Jacques Rancière, *Aesthetics and Its Discontents*, trans. Steve Corcoran (Cambridge: Polity Press, 2009), 25.
131. On the *shibutz* style in maskilic literature, see Moshe Pelli, "On the Role of Melitzah in the Literature of Hebrew Enlightenment," in *Hebrew in Ashkenaz: A Language in Exile*, ed. Lewis Glinert (Oxford: Oxford University Press, 1993).
132. Miron, *Bein Hazon le-'Emet: Nitzanei ha-Roman ha-'ivri ve-ha-yidi ba-Me'ah ha-19* (Jerusalem: Mosad Bialik, 1979), 28–29; quoted in Pelli, "On the Role of Melitzah in the Literature of Hebrew Enlightenment," 101.
133. Shochat, "Yahasam shel ha-Maskilim be-Rusyah 'el ha-Lashon ha-'Ivrit," 353–430.
134. Bartal, "Mi-Du-Leshoniyut masortit le-Had-Leshoniyut ke'umit," 190.
135. Ibid., 192.

CHAPTER 5

1. Micha Yosef Berdichevsky, *Sefer Hasidim: Agadot, Partsufim, ve-Hizionim* (Warsaw: Toshia, 1900); Micha Yosef Berdichevsky, *Mahbarot Hazon: Sefer Hasidim (1899), Ma'amarot (1903)* (Holon: Bet Dvora Ve-Emmanuel, 1983) (facsimile publication); see also Martina Urban, *The Aesthetic of Renewal: Martin Buber's Early Representation of Hasidism as Kulturkritik* (Chicago: University of Chicago Press, 2008), 48.
2. For this point, see Avner Holtzman, "Sefer Hasidim: Nekudat ha-Motsa la-Siporet shel M. Y. Berdichevsky," in *Hakarat Panim: Masot 'al Micha Yosef* (Tel Aviv: City of Holon and Reshafim, 1994), 31.

3. Shmuel Werses, *Sipur ve-Shorsho: 'Iyunim be-Hitpathut ha-Prozah ha-'Ivrit* (Ramat Gan: Hebrew Writers Association of Israel and Masada, 1971), 104, 107; Urban, *The Aesthetic of Renewal*, 48; Nicham Ross, *Masoret ahuvah ve-senu'ah: Zehut Yehudit modernit ve-Ketivah neo-hasidit be-fetah ha-Me'ah ha-'esrim* (Beer Sheva: Ben-Gurion University Press, 2010), 487.

4. Holtzman, "Sefer Hasidim: Nekudat ha-Motsa la-Siporet shel M. Y. Berdichevsky," 27.

5. Werses, *Sipur ve-shorsho*, 108–9.

6. Micha Yosef Berdichevsky, "'Al Derekh ha-Hasidut," *ha-Magid* 6, no. 32 (19 August 1897).

7. Nachman Krochmal, *Moreh Nevuhei ha-Zman* (Berlin: Iyanut, 1924), 242; see also Urban, *The Aesthetic of Renewal*, 48.

8. Ahad Ha'am, "Tehiyat ha-Ruah," in *Kol Kitvei Ahad Ha-'am* (Tel Aviv: Dvir, 1953), 180; emphasis added.

9. Talal Asad, *Formations of the Secular* (Stanford: Stanford University Press, 2003), 189.

10. Ibid., 1.

11. See Avner Holtzman, *'El ha-Kera' she-ba-Lev: Micha Yosef Berdichevsky—Shnot ha-Tzsmihah (1887–1902)* (Jerusalem: Mosad Bialik, 1995), 167.

12. Ibid., 179.

13. One prominent example of this position is Ben Zion Dinur, who saw in Hasidism a messianic movement; see Ben Zion (Dinburg) Dinur, "Reshitah shel ha-Hasidut ve-Yesodotehah ha-sotsiyaliyim ve-ha-meshihiyim," in *Be-Mifneh ha-Dorot* (Jerusalem: Mosad Bialik, 1955), 81–277. Other scholars from the Jerusalem School of Jewish History joined Dinur's position and characterized Hasidism as a harbinger of Zionism, to such an extent that it gave "partial permission from Jewish tradition for the state of Israel and to the ethos established in it," according to Moshe Rosman in his article "Psak Dinah shel ha-Historiographia ha-yisra'elit 'al ha-Hasidut" (*Zion* 74 [2009]: 144, 149); see also Rachel Elior, *Herut 'al ha-Luhot* (Tel Aviv: Ministry of Defence, 1999), 256.

14. Jacques Derrida, "Des tours de Babel," in *Difference in Translation*, ed. Joseph F. Graham (Ithaca: Cornell University Press, 1985), 209–48.

15. Gilles Deleuze and Félix Guattari, *Kafka: Towards a Minor Literature*, trans. Dona Polan (Minneapolis: University of Minnesota Press, 1986).

16. Jacob Elbaum, "Ha-Besht u-Veno shel R' Adam: 'Iyun ba-Sipur mi-Shivhei ha-Besht," *Mehkarei Yerushalayim be-Folklor yehudi* 2 (1982): 69.

17. See Shlomo Haramati, *Sod Siach: Dibur 'Ivri be-Me'ot 16–19* (Tel Aviv: Yaron Golan, 1992), 116.

18. See Shmuel Werses, "Ha-Hasidut be-'Olamo shel Berdichevsky le-'or Hiburo shenignaz," in *Micha Yosef Berdichevsky: Mehkarim ve-Te'udot*, ed. Avner Holtzman (Jerusalem: Mosad Bialik, 2002), 251–57 ; Ross, *Masoret ahuvah ve-senu'ah*, 68–69, 321.

19. Micha Yosef Berdichevsky, "Le-Torat ha-Harkhev ve-ha-Tsimtsum," *Ha-'Atid* 5 (1924) : 152.

20. Hannan Hever, *Producing the Modern Hebrew Canon: Nation Building and Minority Discourse* (New York : NYU Press, 2002), xxx.

21. Ziporah Kagan, "Tzefunot ve-Agadot le-Berdichevsky: Bein 'Ibud le-Yetzirah," *Mehkarei Yerushalayim be-Folklor Yehudi* 13–14 (1991–92): 256.

22. Joseph Dan, *Ha-Sipur ha-hasidi* (Jerusalem: Keter, 1975), 64–68; Moshe Rosman, *Ha-Besht: Mehadesh ha-Hasidut* (Jerusalem: Zalman Shazar Center, 1999), 199; Immanuel Etkes, *Ba'al ha-Shem: Ha-Besht—Magiyah, Mistikah, Han'hagah* (Jerusalem: Zalman Shazar Center, 2000), 239–45.

23. Etkes, *Ba'al ha-Shem*, 249–50.
24. Rosman, *Ha-Besht: Mehadesh ha-Hasidut*, 255.
25. Fischel Lachover, *Toldot ha-Sifrut ha-'Ivrit ha-hadashah*, vol. 3, part 2 (Tel Aviv: Dvir, 1953), 84–85.
26. Holtzman, *'El ha-Kera' she-ba-Lev*, 196.
27. S. Y. Horowitz, "Ha-Hasidut ve-ha-Haskalah," *Ha-'Atid* 2 (1923): 29–99 (second printing); Samuel A. Horodezky, *Zikhronot* (Tel Aviv: Dvir, 1957), 84–89.
28. This is also the position of Joseph Dan; see Dan, *Ha-Sipur ha-hasidi*, 1.
29. Nicham Ross, "'Al Even ahat ve-'al ma-she-tahtehah: Gilgulah shel Agadah mi-'Shivhei Ha-Besht' 'ad Sh. Y. Agnon," *Mehkarei Yerushalayim Be-Folklor Yehudi* 26 (2009): 42.
30. Simon Dubnow, *Toldot ha-Hasidut 'al Yesod Mekorot rishonim, nidpasim u-khitvei yad* (Jerusalem: Dvir, 1967), 62; Elior, *Herut 'al ha-Luhot*, 16.
31. Avraham (Arthur) Green, "Hasidut," in *Leksikon ha-Tarbut ha-yehudit bi-Zmanenu*, ed. Avraham Shapira (Tel Aviv: Am Oved, 1993), 211, 213.
32. Ross, *Masoret ahuvah ve-senu'ah*, 345–46.
33. Micha Yosef Berdichevsky, *Kitvei Micha Yosef Bin-Gurion (Berdichevsky): Ma'amarim* (Tel Aviv: Dvir, 1960), 172. Here and later in the chapter all emphases appear in the original.
34. Yitzhak Bacon, *Ha-Tsa'ir ha-boded ba-Siporet ha-'Ivrit, 1899–1908* (Tel Aviv: Tel Aviv University—Student Union, 1978), 13.
35. Simon Halkin, "Geulah 'aniyah ke-zo," in *Hagut ve-Siporet bi-Yetsirat Berdichevsky*, ed. Ziporah Kagan (Haifa: Haifa University, 1981), 16.
36. Dan Miron, *Hadashot me-Ezor ha-Kotev* (Tel Aviv: Zemorah Bitan, 1993), 472.
37. Gershom Scholem, *Ha-Shalav ha-'aharon: Mehkarei ha-Hasidut shel Gershom Scholem*, ed. David Assaf and Esther Liebes (Jerusalem: Am Oved, 2008), 17; Ross, *Masoret ahuvah ve-senu'ah*, 365–67.
38. Halkin, "Geulah 'aniyah ke-zo," 22.
39. Nurit Govrin, *Dvash mi-Sela'* (Tel Aviv: Ministry of Defence, 1989), 20.
40. Ehud Luz, "'Al shtei Tfisot shel Kedushah be-Ma'amarav ha-mukdamim shel Micha Yosef Berdichevsky," in *Mi-Saviv la-Nekudah: Mehkarim hadashim 'al M.Y. Berdichevsky, Y.Ch. Brenner ve-A. D. Gordon*, ed. Avner Holtzman, Gideon Katz, and Shalom Ratsabi (Sde Boker: Ben-Gurion University of the Negev, 2008), 27–28.
41. Halkin, "Geulah 'aniyah ke-zo," 25.
42. Govrin, *Dvash mi-Sela'*, 18–19.
43. Dan Miron, *Bo'ah Laylah* (Tel Aviv: Dvir, 1987), 191–227.
44. Berdichevsky, *Kitvei Micha Yosef Bin-Gurion (Berdichevsky): Ma'amarim*, 770.
45. Luz, "'Al shtei Tfisot shel Kedushah be-Ma'amarav ha-mukdamim shel Micha Yosef Berdichevsky," 26.
46. Berdichevsky, *Mahbarot Hazon*, 7.
47. Werses, *Sipur ve-Shorsho*, 108; Nachman Hoberman, "Ha-Admor Rabbi Rafael mi-Bersher," *Ha-'Avar* 1 (1953): 106–8.
48. The story was published in *Otsar ha-Sifrut* 4 (1892). See also Berdichevsky, *Ketavim*, vol. 3, ed. Avner Holtzman and Yitzhak Kafkafi (Tel Aviv: Hakibbutz Hameuchad, 1998), 103–6.
49. Eliyahu Lerman, *Mikhtavei Eliyahu* (Berdichev: Haim Yaakov Sheftil, 1894), 16–18.
50. Berdichevsky, *Mahbarot Hazon*, 62.
51. Berdichevsky, *Kitvei Micha Yosef Bin-Gurion (Berdichevsky): Ma'amarim*, 375.
52. Berdichevsky, *Mahbarot Hazon*, 8.

53. Ibid., 9.
54. Luz, "'Al shtei Tfisot shel Kedushah be-Ma'amarav ha-mukdamim shel Micha Yosef Berdichevsky," 17.
55. Elior, *Herut 'al ha-Luhot*, 269.
56. Micha Yosef Berdichevsky, *Ketavim*, vol. 2, ed. Avner Holtzman and Yitzhak Kafkafi (Tel Aviv: Hakibbutz Hameuchad, 1996), 318–34.
57. Antonio Gramsci, *'Al ha-Hegmoniyah: Mivhar mi-tokh 'Mahbarot ha-Kele'*, trans. Alon Altras (Tel Aviv: Resling, 2009).
58. Martin Buber, *Be-Pardes ha-Hasidut* (Jerusalem: Mosad Bialik and Dvir, 1979), 106; Elior, *Herut 'al ha-Luhot*, 112.
59. Elior, *Herut 'al ha-Luhot*, 38.
60. Rivka Dvir-Goldberg, *Ha-Tzadik ha-hasidi ve-Armon ha-Livyatan: 'Iyun be-Sipurei Ma'asiyot mi-pi Tzadikim* (Tel Aviv: Hakibbutz Hameuchad, 2009), 142–43.
61. Buber, *Be-Pardes ha-Hasidut*, 110–11.
62. Ibid., 115.
63. Ibid., 122.
64. Yehuda Shenhav, "Modernity and the Hybridization of Nationalism and Religion: Zionism and the Jews of the Middle East as a Heuristic Case," *Theory and Society* 36 (2007): 3.
65. Ibid., 3–4.
66. Rosman, *Ha-Besht: Mehadesh ha-Hasidut*, 181.
67. Michal Oron, "Ha-Ishah ke-Mesaperet ba-Sipur ha-hasidi: Takhsis sifruti 'o Shimurah shel Masoret? 'Iyun be-Sipuro shel S. Y. Agnon 'Etrogo shel 'Oto Tzadik'," in *Mi-Vilnah le-Yerushalim: Mehkarim be-Toldotehem u-ve-Tarbutam shel Yehudei merkaz Eropah, mugashim le-Profesor Shmuel Werses*, ed. David Assaf, Israel Bartal, Avner Holtzman, Chava Turniansky, Shmuel Feiner, and Yehuda Friedlander (Jerusalem: Magnes 2002), 514.
68. Haramati, *Sod Siach*, 118–25.
69. Zeev Gries, *Sefer, Sofer ve-Sipur be-Reshit ha-Hasidut* (Tel Aviv: Hakibbutz Hameuchad, 1992), 12, 23–27.
70. Lila Abu Lughod, *Dramas of Nationhood: The Politics of Television in Egypt* (Chicago: Chicago University Press, 2005), ix, 19.
71. Etkes, *Ba'al ha-Shem*, 163.
72. Ibid., 88.
73. Avraham Rubinstein, "'Igeret Ha-besht le-R. Gershon mi-Kotov," *Sinai* 67 (1970): 120–39; Etkes, *Ba'al ha-Shem*, 92–93.
74. Etkes, *Ba'al ha-Shem*, 120.
75. Dan, *Ha-Sipur ha-hasidi*, 55.
76. Etkes, *Ba'al ha-Shem*, 121.
77. Eli Yassif, *Sipur ha-'Am ha-'Ivri: Toldotav, Sugav u-Mashma'uto* (Jerusalem: Mosad Bialik, 1994), 403.
78. Ibid., 405.
79. Ibid., 408.
80. Werses, "Ha-Hasidut be-'Olamo shel Berdichevsky le-'or Hiburo she-nignaz," 18; Ross, *Masoret ahuvah ve-senu'ah*, 320–21.
81. Werses, "Ha-Hasidut be-'Olamo shel Berdichevsky le-'or Hiburo she-nignaz," 248–49.
82. Scholem, *Ha-Shalav ha-'aharon*, 214.

83. Dov Sadan, *Avnei Bedek: 'Al Sifrutenu, Mosadah va-Agafeha* (Tel Aviv: Hakibbutz Hameuchad, 1962), 29; Elbaum, "Ha-Besht u-Veno shel R' Adam," 74. And for the mystical community see Scholem, *Ha-Shalav ha-'aharon*, 15.

84. Buber, *Be-Pardes ha-Hasidut*, 22–23, 32.

85. Etkes, *Ba'al ha-Shem*, 209–13. On the Hasidic community and its sources before the period of the Ba'al Shem Tov, which flourished as an oppositional alternative following the break-up of the Jewish public and the weakening of the authority of its leadership, see Dinur, "Reshitah shel ha-hasidut ve-yesodotehah ha-sotsiyaliyim ve-ha-meshihiyim," 104–70. On the community and the surroundings, see Haviva Padaya, "Le-Hitpathuto shel ha-Degem ha-hevrati-kalkali ba-Hasidut: Pidyon, ha-Havurah ve-ha-'Aliyah le-Regel," in *Dat ve-Kalkalah*, ed. Menachem Ben Sasson (Jerusalem: Zalman Shazar Center, 1995), 311–73.

86. Elior, *Herut 'al ha-luhot*, 178.

87. Ibid., 37.

88. Horodezky, *Zikhronot*, 58, 65. The aim for interpersonal connection brought about the creation of the role of the broker, someone who was tasked with seeing to these connections despite the obstacles that stood in the way. It has been written of the Habad circle that "the deep meaning that the Hasids attached to personal connections with the rabbi and the difficulty of pilgrimage brought forth a new phenomenon: the returning narrator—a pilgrim who reconstructs for his community what he saw and heard in the rabbi's circle during the pilgrimage" (Ilya Luria, *'Edah u-Medinah: Hasidut Habad ba-Imperiyah ha-rusit 1828–1883* [Jerusalem: Magnes, 2006], 44).

89. Ada Rapoport-Albert, "Ha-Tnu'ah ha-hasidit aharei Shnat 1772: Retsef Mivni ve-Temurah," *Zion* 55 (1990): 201–8.

90. Dvir-Goldberg, *Ha-Tzadik ha-hasidi ve-Armon ha-Livyatan*, 39–52.

91. Israel Bartal, *Galut ba-Aretz: Yishuv Eretz-Yisra'el beterem Tsiyonut* (Jerusalem: Hasifriyah Ha-tsiyonit, 1994), 15.

92. Scholem, *Ha-Shalav ha-'aharon*, 304–5.

93. Halkin, "Geulah 'aniyah ke-zo," 17–18.

94. Scholem, *Ha-Shalav ha-'aharon*, 5.

95. Dinur, "Reshitah shel ha-Hasidut ve-Yesodotehah ha-sotsiyaliyim ve-ha-meshihiyim," 194–70.

96. Scholem, *Ha-Shalav ha-'aharon*, 286.

97. Rubinstein, "'Igeret Ha-Besht le-R. Gershon mi-Kotov," 134.

98. Dubnow, *Toldot ha-Hasidut 'al Yesod Mekorot rishonim, nidpasim u-khitvei yad*, 32–62.

99. Isaiah Tishbi, "Ha-Ra'ayon ha-meshihi ve-ha-Magamot ha-meshihiyot be-Tzmihat ha-Hasidut," *Zion* 32 (1967): 24, 45.

100. Ibid., 45.

101. Israel Bartal, "Sekularyzacja Zydowskiej Duchowosci: Chasydyzm Ponownie Odnaleziony," in *Duchowosc Zydowska w Polsce*, ed. M. Galas (Cracow: Jagiellonian University, 2000), 190.

102. Avraham Rubinstein, *Shivhei Ha-Besht* (Jerusalem: Reuven Mass, 2005), 44–45.

103. Ross, "'Al Even ahat ve-'al ma-she-tahtehah," 46. On the sources of the story, see Chone Shmeruk, *Sifrut Yidish be-Polin* (Jerusalem: Magnes, 1981), 146–99.

104. Dan, *Ha-Sipur ha-hasidi*, 82.

105. Ross, "'Al Even ahat ve-'al ma-she-tahtehah," 28.

106. Elbaum, "Ha-Besht u-Veno shel R' Adam," 67. On the Hasidic hermeneutic principle of preferring the hidden over the revealed, see Elior, *Herut 'al ha-Luhot*, 143.
107. Ross, *Masoret ahuvah ve-senu'ah*, 497.
108. Bacon, *Ha-tsa'ir ha-boded ba-Siporet ha-'ivrit, 1899–1908*, 33.
109. Rubinstein, *Shivhei Ha-Besht*, 44.
110. Berdichevsky, *Mahbarot Hazon*, 28–29.
111. Ibid.
112. Ibid., 30.
113. Holtzman, *'El ha-Kera' she-ba-Lev*, 198.
114. Berdichevsky, *Mahbarot Hazon*, 29; Rubinstein, *Shivhei Ha-Besht*, 44.
115. Holtzman, *'El ha-kera' she-ba-Lev*, 194.
116. Elior, *Herut 'al ha-Luhot*, 93.
117. Berdichevsky, *Mahbarot Hazon*, 29.
118. Werses, *Sipur ve-Shorsho*, 25.
119. Shmuel Werses, "Ha-Hsidut be-Einei Sifrut ha-Haskalah: Min ha-Pulmus shel Hasidei Galitzyah," in *Ha-dat ve-ha-Hayim: Tenu'at ha-Haskalah ha-yehudit be-mizrah Eropah*, ed. Immanuel Etkes (Jerusalem: Zalman Shazar Center, 1993); David Assaf, "'Son'im—Sipur Ahavah'? Hitpathuyot mi-Mehkar Yahasei ha-Gomlin bein ha-Hasidut la-Haskalah," in *Ha-Haskalah le-Gevaneha: 'Iyunim hadashim be-Toldot ha-Haskalah u-ve-Sifrutehah*, ed. Shmuel Feiner and Israel Bartal (Jerusalem: Magnes, 2005), 184.
120. Etkes, *Ba'al ha-Shem*, 15, 277.
121. Rubinstein, *Shivhei Ha-Besht*, 59.
122. Joseph Perl, *Megaleh Temirin* (Vienna: A. Strauss, 1819), 2.
123. Etkes, *Ba'al ha-shem*, 276; Ross, "'Al Even ahat ve-'al ma-she-tahtehah," 37.
124. Berdichevsky, *Mahbarot Hazon*, 6.
125. Ibid., 27; Ross, "'Al Even ahat ve-'al ma-she-tahtehah," 48.
126. Berdichevsky, "'Al Derekh ha-Hasidut."
127. Micha Yosef Berdichevsky, "Mi-hHyei ha-Hasidim," *ha-Shiloah* 2, no. 7 (1897): 93.
128. Berdichevsky, *Mahbarot Hazon*, 30.
129. Carl Schmitt, *Political Theology: Four Chapters on the Concept of Sovereignty*, trans. George Schwab (Chicago: University of Chicago Press, 2005), 36.
130. Asad, *Formations of the Secular*, 189.
131. Homi Bhabha, *Nation and Narration* (London: Routledge, 1997), 297.
132. Sadan, *Avnei Bedek*, 38–39.
133. Homi Bhabha, "The Other Question," in *The Location of Culture* (London: Routledge, 1994), 38).
134. Naomi Seidman, *Faithful Renderings: Jewish-Christian Difference and the Politics of Translation* (Chicago: University of Chicago Press, 2006), 9, 30.
135. Scholem, *Ha-Shalav ha-'aharon*, 21.
136. Dan, *Ha-Sipur ha-hasidi*, 40–52.
137. Gershom Scholem, *Pirkei Yesod be-Havanat ha-Kabbalah u-Semalehah* (Jerusalem: Mosad Bialik, 1977), 40.
138. Quoted in Aharon Wertheim, *Halakhot ve-Halikhot ba-Hasidut* (Jerusalem: Mosad ha-Rav Kook, 1940), 44.
139. Green, "Hasidut," 211.
140. Etkes, *Ba'al ha-Shem*, 271.

141. Walter Benjamin, "The Task of the Translator," in *Walter Benjamin: Selected Writings*, vol. 1, *1913–1926*, ed. Marcus Bullock and Michael W. Jennings (Cambridge, MA: Harvard University Press, 1996), 262.

142. Ibid.; Derrida, "Des tours de Babel," 209–48.

143. Michal Ben-Naftali, explanation of "Naftulei Babel," in Jacques Derrida, *Naftulei Babel*, trans. Michal Ben-Naftali (Tel Aviv: Resling, 2002), 92.

144. Scholem, *Pirkei Yesod be-Havanat ha-Kabbalah u-Semalehah*, 46.

145. Berdichevsky, *Mahbarot Hazon*, 6.

146. Derrida, "Des tours de Babel," 209–48; see also Yair Adiel, "'Al Poetikah ve-Politikah shel Gishot la-Lashon: Keri'ah ba-Turim me'et Sayed Kashua," *Te'oryah u-Vikoret* 34 (2000): 11–41.

147. Luz, "'Al shtei Tfisot shel Kedushah be-Ma'amarav ha-mukdamim shel Micha Yosef Berdichevsky," 18; see also Nicham Ross, "Ha-ravi mi-Bi'ala' boreah min ha-Yeshivah—'Bein Shnei Harim' shel Peretz ve-Tadmitah ha-modernistit shel ha-Hasidut," in *Ma'aseh Sipur: Mehkarim ba-Siporet ha-yehudit*, vol. 2, ed. Avidov Lipsker and Rela Kushlovsky (Ramat Gan: Bar-Ilan University Press, 2009), 237.

148. Lachover, *Toldot ha-Sifrut ha-'ivrit ha-hadashah*, 81.

149. Elior, *Herut 'al ha-Luhot*, 269.

150. Berdichevsky, *Ketavim*, vol. 2, 318–34; Werses, *Sipur ve-Shorsho*, 107.

151. Elior, *Herut 'al ha-Luhot*, 203.

152. Schmitt, *Political Theology*, 5.

153. Ibid., 7.

154. Ibid., 17.

155. Ibid., 5–10.

156. Gershom Scholem, *'Od Davar: Pirkei Morasha u-Tehiyah* (Tel Aviv: Am Oved, 1989), 59.

157. Scholem, *Ha-Shalav ha-'aharon*, 333.

158. Ibid., 337.

159. Buber, *Be-Pardes ha-Hasidut*, 15, 39.

160. Scholem, *Ha-Shalav ha-'aharon*, 241–42; Shalom Ratzabi, "Mi-Bikoret le-Shlilah: Gershom Scholem 'al Tfisat ha-Hasidut shel Buber," in Gershom Scholem, *Ha-Shalav ha-'aharon: Mehkarei ha-Hasidut shel Gershom Scholem*, ed. David Assaf and Esther Liebes (Jerusalem: Am Oved, 2008), 361–62.

161. Yotan Hotam, *Gnosis moderni ve-Tsiyonut: Mashber ha-Tarbut, Filosofyat he-Hayim ve-Hagut le'umit yehudit* (Jerusalem: Magnes, 1997), 182; see also Ross, *Masoret ahuvah ve-Senu'ah*, 332.

162. Hotam, *Gnosis moderni ve-Tsiyonut*, 183.

163. Susan Bassnet and Harish Trivedi, "Introduction: Of Colonies, Cannibals, and Vernaculars," in *Post-Colonial Translation: Theory and Practice*, ed. Susan Bassnet and Harish Trivedi (London: Routledge, 1999), 5.

164. Berdichevsky, *Kitvei Micha Yosef Bin-Gurion (Berdichevsky): Ma'amarim*, 375–76.

165. Ibid., 62–63; first published in *ha-Me'orer*, 1907.

166. Ibid., 78.

167. Werses, *Sipur ve-Shorsho*, 114; Bacon, *Ha-Tsa'ir ha-boded ba-Siporet ha-'Ivrit, 1899–1908*, 33; Holtzman, *'El ha-Kera' she-ba-Lev*, 197.

168. Rubinstein, *Shivhei Ha-Besht*, 36.

169. Berdichevsky, *Mahbarot Hazon*, 24.
170. Ibid., 25.
171. Ibid.
172. Ibid., 23.
173. Rubinstein, *Shivhei Ha-Besht*, 38.
174. Berdichevsky, *Mahbarot Hazon*, 25.
175. Genesis 40:15.
176. Berdichevsky, *Kitvei Micha Yosef Bin-Gurion (Berdichevsky): Ma'amarim*, 29.
177. Rubinstein, *Shivhei Ha-Besht*, 36.
178. Elbaum, "Ha-Besht u-Veno shel R' Adam," 69.

# Index

Abraham of Kalisk, 38–40
absolutism; absolutist regime, 55, 80n147, 125, 144; enlightened, 74
Abu Lughod, Lila, 13n21, 150n56, 176n70
Acculturation, 82
Acre, 10–11, 16, 32, 36
act of telling stories, 174
aesthetics, 85, 117, 123, 127n95, 162, 171; aesthetic judgment, 115–16, 124; and depoliticization, 116, 117, 123; Kantian aesthetics, 115–16, 120–21, 124; romantic aesthetics, 121; universal aesthetics, 124, 172
Africa, 30; Jews, 35
Agnon, S. Y., 166,
agriculture, 75, 96, 158
Ahad Ha'am; and Berdichevsky, 167, 178; and Klausner, 120n81; "Resurrection of the Spirit" ("Tehiyat ha-Ruah"), 167
al-Jazzar, 11
Alexander I, 145n17
Alexander II, 144n9
Alexander III, 144n9
Algazi, Yom Tov ("the Great Sage from Jerusalem"), 40
allegory, 4–5, 7, 17, 24–26, 68, 87–92, 99, 101–2, 104–5, 107n31, 112–13, 116–18, 120, 127–132, 134, 138, 138n127; and satire, 79, 88, 90–92
America, 27, 30, 32–33
Anderson, Benedict, 13, 14, 42, 54, 84, 109, 150–51, 176
"angel in the house," 125
Angie, Antony, 25n24
anti-colonialism, 137
anti-maskilic tale, 45
antisemitism, 55, 88, 120n81, 157
anti-Zionism, 138
apostles, 45

Arabs, 40
Aramaic, 160, 168
Ararat, 76
Arendt, Hannah, 68, 77, 83
ars poetica, 17
Asad, Talal, 167, 183
Ashkenazi Jews, 40
Assaf, David, 181n119
assimilation, 27, 37, 77–78, 41, 144
Austria-Hungary, 1, 2, 66, 125, 127, 178
Austrian Empire, 75, 84, 125, 126
auto-emancipation, 57, 78, 95, 179. *See also* Pinsker, Leo
Avineri, Shlomo, 71n103
avodah be-vittul (worship in self-annihilation), 158
'Ayin, 157n94, 158. *See also* Yesh; Tzimtzum

Ba'al Shem Tov (Israel ben Eliezer Shem-Tov, Besht), 1, 9, 11, 14, 34, 41, 43, 47, 50, 87, 94, 111, 139, 149n45, 151, 153, 159, 162, 166, 169, 170, 176–81, 188–89; a letter that he sent to Gershon of Kitov, 176, 178; "Commentary on *Hodu*," 22; *Keter Shem Tov*, 109. *See also* In Praise of the Ba'al Shem Tov (Shivhei ha-Besht); Besht's circle; "my ḥavurah"
Babylonian exile, 5
Babylonian Talmud, 22n71, 46, 54n15, 65
Bachrach, Jacob. *See* Kaidaner (Bachrach), Jacob
Bacon, Yitzhak, 171n34, 179, 188n167
Bakhtin, Mikhail, 160–61
Balaban, Meir, 65n69, 66n75–76
balance of power, 129
Balibar, Étienne, 57
Bardach, Elijah, 65
Bartal, Israel, 144n7, 145n12, 165, 177
Basel Congress, 188

Bassnet, Susan, 187n163
Bauer, Bruno, 76, 95
*Bava Kamma*, 23, 65
Beiser, Fredrick C., 127n95
belles-lettres, 149–50
Ben Harosh, Yonatan, 30n112
Ben Ze'ev, Judah Leib, 61n45
Benbaji, Amir, 88n193, 235
Ben-Israel, Hedva, 63n65
Ben-Naftali, Michal, 184
Benjamin, Walter, 67, 168, 184
Bentham, Jeremy, 53
Berdichev, 29
Berdichevsky, Micha Yosef, 7, 56, 69–70, 135; "A Clarification," 188; and Ahad Ha'am, 167, 178; anthology of the works of the fathers of Hasidism, 176; autonomous subject, 173–74; *Ba-derekh* (On the Way), 173; creation of Jewish sovereignty by violent means, 188; "desire for life" in the center of his thought, 171; emphasizing "lyrical imagery," 172; "From the Lives of the Hasidim," 182; gnostic dimension of his thought, 186–87; hybridization of the hasidic text, 174–75, 183–85, 187; his relation to Hasidut, 166, 172, 174, 178, 181–82; individualism, 169–172, 188; "Land," 188; major-literature model, 168–170, 185; marriage of religion and secularism, 173–75; negation of the diaspora, 172; national subject, 169, 171–72, 190; national theology, 173, 185, 187; nationalized the hasidic text, 166, 168, 174, 179, 183; "On Hasidism," 166–67; "Old age and Adolescence," 167; "On the Question of the Past," 185; "Parah Adumah," 69; political theology, 187–90; preserving the religious content of the Hasidic texts, 167; "Redemption," 172; "The Exit," 172; the hasidic idea of minimalism, 171; "The World of Israel," 174, 185; "Two Camps," 172; universalism, 170–72, 174; "Witness to Hasidism," 182. *See also Sefer Hasidim*
Berger, Shlomo, 45–46
*beri'ah* (creation), 23
Berlin, 54, 61, 121
Berlin Haskalah, Berlin Maskilim, 61n45, 63n61, 65, 72, 80, 80n147, 82, 84, 86, 105–6, 112, 115–17, 120, 122–25, 133n113, 136–140

Berlin, Saul, 115
Besht's circle, 43, 151, 172n45, 176
*Be'ur* project, 138
Bhabha, Homi, 70n101, 72n110, 82n160, 83n162–63, 88n192, 183
Bialik, Hayim Nahman, 73, 120n81, 164, 171
Bible, 20, 27, 31, 58, 58n27, 60, 62, 84, 95n223, 109, 138n127, 150, 154, 156, 168, 180, 189
biblical language, language of the Bible, 31, 73, 73n114, 90, 106, 133n113, 138, 138n127, 160, 168, 169
Bick, Jacob Samuel, 53, 61, 80; "El Maskilei Benei 'Ami" (To the Maskilim Among My People), 96.
*Bikurei ha-Itim* (journal), 57–58, 61, 72, 75, 85–86, 92, 94
Bildung, 25, 28–29, 54, 121, 127n95
*binah* (discernment), 104, 105. *See also hokhmah*
Bishara, Azmi, 56n20
Bodin, Jean, 56
body, 4, 45, 53, 54, 117, 121, 124, 127–28, 138, 141–42
Bonteko, Willem Ijsbrantsz, 27
book of Exodus, 22n66, 23
book of Ezekiel, 5, 52, 54, 58, 60, 109, 154, 191
book of Genesis, 22n67, 189n175
book of Isaiah, 23, 135, 149
book of Jonah, 40
book of Kings, 59n34
book of Kohelet, 105, 115
book of Leviticus, 15n38, 47, 48
book of Numbers, 126n94, 129, 150–51, 155n88
book of Proverbs, 104, 140n137
Borges, Jorge Luis, 49
Boyarin, Daniel, 149n46, 149n49
Brainin, Reuben, 61n46, 66n77, 89
"breaking of the vessels," 50, 162, 186
Brenner, Joseph Hayim, 169, 188; "Mediations of an Author," 171; "The Image of the Zionist Immigrant in Our Literature," 172
Brinker, Menahem, 119n77, 126n94
British Mandatory government, 56n23
Brody, 7, 52, 60, 61n45, 66, 84, 125
Brown, Wendy, 57n24
Buber, Martin, 14, 109, 166, 174, 177, 186n159; *Gog and Magog*, 36

Budapest, 52
Burbank, Jane, 143n2, 143n5
Burke, Edmund, 124
Butler, Judith, 77n137, 78n142

calques. *See* loan translations
Campbell, Elena, 144n6
Campe, Joachim Heinrich, 29, 33; *Die Entdeckung von Amerika*, 27, 29–30; *Robinson der Jüngere* (adaption of *Robinson Crusoe*), 27
Canaan, 47–50
capitalism, 25, 27, 122, 128
Carey, Daniel, 126n93
Catholic Church, 61n45
Chakrabarty, Dipesh, 126
Chmielnicki persecutions (1648–49), 145
Chotzner, Joseph, 61n44, 63n60, 63n63, 69n90
Christianity, 29, 68, 89, 123, 129, 141, 145
citizenship, 4, 37, 55, 119, 122; individual, 37, 113; the politics of citizenship of Galician maskilim of Jewish in the empire, 125–27, 141, 144; universal, 73, 91, 113, 80n147
civil equality, 1–2, 114
Clermont-Tonnerre, 36, 144
Cohen, Margaret, 47n84
Cohen, Tova, 47n180, 58n31, 59n34, 125n90
Colebrook, Claire, 128n96, 131n110
collective rights for Jews, 37, 68, 148
colonialism; British colonialism, 188; colonial "other," 33; European colonial narrative, 32–34, 124, 144n9; Erter and the internal colonialism, 7, 53, 54, 63, 82, 83, 143; Jewish colonialism, 137; of the Empire, 76; "regime of truth," 145
Columbus, 30–31, 33
Communitas, 12
community; face-to-face community, 13, 43, 109, 176; hasidic community, 1, 12–14, 17–18, 19, 25, 38, 42–44, 65, 93, 99, 104, 109, 149n45, 150–52, 166, 174, 176–77, 183; imagined national community, 13–15, 42, 54, 58n27, 67, 83, 85, 86, 93, 109, 127, 132, 133n113, 150–51, 176, 177–78; Jewish community, 75, 78, 80n147, 82n158, 95, 100, 122, 144–46, 148, 153, 156, 187, 191; non-imagined communities, 109, 150; nonnational community, 150; protonational community, 28, 164

Congress of Vienna (1815), 61n45, 75, 79
consciousness, 101–2, 117, 128, 130, 133, 152
conservatism, 61, 116, 122, 125, 137, 140, 141, 144n9
Cover, Robert, 68n86
Crimea, 96, 137
Crimean War (1855), 144
Culler, Jonathan, 54n11
Cunz Martin, 23n74, 23n77

Damascus: Jews, 58n27, 137
Damascus Affair (1840), 63, 137
Dan, Joseph, 14n35, 24n78, 146n27, 146n29, 147, 151n62, 155n87, 157n95, 159n101, 169n22, 170n28, 176n75, 179n104, 184
Darnton, Robert, 61n52
Dauber, Jeremy, 115n60, 138n127
de Man, Paul, 92n224, 101, 130n107, 130n109, 133n111, 132; "Rhetoric and Temporality," 95
Defoe, Daniel: *Robinson Crusoe*, 27
Deleuze, Gilles, 67, 89, 92, 149n51, 162n123, 168, 169
*derashah* (homily), 13, 22–23, 24, 149
Derrida, Jacques, 73, 168, 184, 185
desire, 4, 5, 15, 21, 29, 88, 102, 108, 110, 115, 118, 124; homoerotic, 34; sexual, 112–13, 119, 121, 138, 140
deterritorialized language, 162, 164
*devequt* (communion with God), 12, 17, 43, 49, 151
dichotomy; between Hasidism and the Haskalah, 4, 5, 103, 147, 154; between universal reason and historical particularism, 4, 55; vitalistic, 187
*différance*, 73
diglossia, non-diglossia, 160, 163–65
*dina de-malkhuta dina*, 78
Dinur, Ben Zion (Dinburg), 41, 50, 153, 168n13, 177, 178
dissensus, 106, 117, 131, 141
Dnieper, 8, 32
Dov Ber of Mezhirech (the "Maggid" of Mezhirech), 14, 38, 50, 177–78
Dov Ber Melinitz, 169
Dovber Shneuri (the "Middle Rebbe"), 147
Dubnow, Simon, 41–42, 103, 145n17, 146, 147n37, 153, 159n103, 160n114, 171, 178
Dvir-Goldberg, Rivka, 14, 174n60, 177

Eade, John, 41n165, 45n188
Eastern Europe Hasidut, 2, 6, 36, 38–39, 86–87, 119, 126
Eastern European Haskalah, 2, 61, 68, 69, 86–87, 119, 147, 158
ecstasy, 81, 185
Edict of Toleration of Joseph II, 61n45, 74–75, 77, 80n147, 81
Egypt, 10, 23
Elazar of Disna, 38
Elbaum, Jacob, 14n26, 168, 177n83, 179, 189
Eliade, Mircea, 102
Eliav, Mordechai, 58n31, 74n123, 100n13
Eliaz, Yoad, 69n190
Elimelekh of Lizhensk, 50
Elior, Rachel, 14n30, 149n52, 157n93, 157n94, 158n97, 168n13, 171n30, 174n55, 174n58, 174n59, 177n86, 179n106, 181n116, 185n149, 185n151
Emancipation, 1, 6, 9, 37, 55, 57, 74–78, 82n158, 83, 89, 95, 96, 104, 120n81, 122, 126, 135, 141, 144, 146–48, 179
End of Days, 54n15, 93
England, 29, 37
Englander, Yakir, 117n72
Enlightenment, 27, 33, 36, 49, 53–56, 61n45, 66n77, 67n83, 75, 77, 81, 84, 90, 96, 99, 100, 108, 109, 111, 113–15, 119, 120, 123–27, 133, 140, 144, 148, 149, 153, 170, 172n42, 174, 181–82; blackmail of Enlightenment, 4; rationalistic Enlightenment, 3–4, 113; religious Enlightenment, 63n61, 119–20
equal rights for the Jews, 35, 79, 95n223
Erter, Issac, 52–97, 98–142, 147; "Alilyat Damesek," 137; *Ha-Tzofeh le-veit Yisra'el* (Watchman for the House of Israel), 4–7, 52–66, 87–88, 154, 159, 191; "Kol Kore li-Vney Yisra'el Toshvei Eretz Galitzyah," 96, 137; "Megilat Damesek," 58n27; "Tekhunat ha-Tzofeh," 4, 52, 74, 99, 106; "Telunot Sani ve-Sansani ve-Semangelof," 98n1; "The Watchman for the House of Israel—Gilgul Nefesh," 67n83, 90, 93, 98n1; "The Watchman for the House of Israel—Tashlikh," 66n77, 98n1. *See also*; "Hasidut ve-Hokhmah"; "Moznei Mishkal"; "The Watchman for the House of Israel"
Ethos, 125, 174, 179
Etkes, Immanuel, 14n29, 26n91, 38n151, 43, 149n45, 151n60, 153, 162n120, 169n22, 169n23, 176, 177n85, 181n120, 181n123, 184n140
Ettinger, Shmuel, 138n127
Euchel, Isaac, 115; "Iggerot Mešullam ben 'Uriyyah ha-'Eštamo'I," 27–28, 31, 116, 140
Eurocentrism, 126
Europe, 10, 42, 43, 76–82, 113–14, 118–20, 122, 124–26, 134, 136–37, 141, 145
European culture, 24, 29, 150, 152, 166, 181
Even-Zohar, Itamar, 163

Fahn, Re'uven, 55n18, 61n45, 85n170, 95n223, 169
faith, 29, 32, 44, 58, 63, 67, 82, 83, 119, 139, 155
Fanon, Frantz, 92, 124
Feiner, Shmuel, 27n99, 29n108, 30n109, 30n110, 61n48, 61n52, 80, 85n170, 86n181, 109n38, 114, 126n92, 133n113, 137n122, 147
Fernhof, Issac, 167, 169
Festa, Lynn, 126n93
fetish, 60, 66, 67, 69–71, 83, 88–90, 92
fiction, 54, 129, 152, 166, 168, 170, 176–77
fin-de-siècle, 166
folk story, folktale, 150, 152, 169, 176, 177
Foucault, Michel, 4, 8n3, 18, 53, 55–56, 79, 92, 96, 145n14
France, 12, 76, 92n223; Jews, 36, 144; National Assembly (1789), 36, 77
Francis II, 76
Frankists, 16
Frederick II (Frederick the Great), 61n45
Frederick William III, 75
French Revolution, 10, 36, 37, 54, 55, 78, 82n158
Frenk, Ezriel Nathan, 182
Freud, Sigmund, 71
Frieden, Ken, 20n59, 24n79, 25, 26, 27n102, 30n109, 30n113, 33n132
Friedlander, Yehuda, 60n43, 73n114, 76n134, 107n30, 128, 140n136, 191
Fuenn, Samuel Joseph, 147n35
Funkenstein, Amos, 67n83, 67n84, 78n139, 84n166

*gadlut* (greatness), 12–13, 49. *See also qaṭnut*
Galati, Galats, 8, 11–12, 32
Galicia Haskalah, Galicia maskilim, 7, 54–56, 58, 61, 65, 68, 73, 74, 75, 78, 80–82, 83–86, 91, 92, 95, 96–97, 100, 105, 106, 112, 114, 116, 120, 123–26, 136–38, 139, 140;

Hebrew literature, 57, 72, 73, 85, 96, 115, 117, 119, 121, 125, 137, 169; Jews, 65, 67, 69, 74, 75, 82–83, 86, 96–97, 98, 105, 113, 120, 132, 137, 138, 147
Gascoigne, John, 26n93
Gemorrah, 180
gender; gender blindness, 57, 108; gender identity, 3, 72, 113, 119, 124, 140, 163n127; gendered language, 161, 163; gender reversal, 26, 125; gender stereotypes, bias, 108, 112, 122
genealogy, 76
"German of the Mosaic faith," 62, 122, 139, 141
Germany Haskalah, Germany maskilim, 63n61, 115, 140, 166
Germany, 27, 30, 35, 99n7; Jews, 28, 68, 72, 74, 75, 80, 84, 119
Gershon of Kuty (Kitov), 9, 43, 153, 162, 176, 178
Gilboa, Menucha, 60n39, 86n176, 86n179, 86n180, 129
Gilon, Meir, 115n61, 140
Ginsburg, Shai, 133n111
the giving of the Torah, 16, 46–47
Glinert, Lewis, 159n109, 163
gnosticism, gnostic, 70, 186–87
God; and the prophet, 5, 52, 54, 59, 109, 189, 191; and the tzadik, 3, 12, 14, 17, 21, 24, 109, 149, 151, 152, 177; as sovereign, 14, 58, 186; as the source of the mankind intellectual scales, 60, 80, 110; as the source of the sovereign's authority, 100, 110–11, 119; transcendent God, 70, 186–87; wonder of God, 26, 31, 149
Goldenberg, Samuel Leib, 129, 133
Gonda, Moshe Eliyahu, 61n45, 61n53
good and evil, 22, 36, 60, 96, 111, 157, 186
Gordon, Judah Leib, 154; "Hakitzah Ami," 77n136, 122
Goshen-Gottstein, Alon, 51n215
Gramsci, Antonio, 174
Green, Arthur (Avraham), 8n2, 24, 32, 39n155, 43–44, 171n31, 184
Gries, Zeev, 14n24, 175n69
Griffin, Dustin, 92n228
Guattari, Félix, 67, 89, 92, 149n51, 162n123, 168, 169
Guttman, Yitzchack Julius, 58n31, 100n13

Habad, 7, 13, 146–47, 150, 157–58, 162, 165, 177n88

Habermas, Jürgen, 122, 123
Habsburg Empire, 55, 61, 63, 74, 76, 78, 80, 81, 83, 85, 91, 95
HaCohen Fishman, Y. L., 41n160
Ha-Cohen, Maymon, 40
HaCohen, Ran, 72
HaCohen, Shalom, 57, 61, 84, 133n113
Haifa, 8, 10, 33, 40
halakha, 7, 70, 174, 180, 184–85, 187
HaLevi, Aaron, 147
Halevi-Zwick, Judith, 133n113
Halkin, Simon, 53, 55, 62, 63n59, 63n61, 87, 90, 91, 117, 120, 171–72, 178n93
Halle-Wolfssohn, Aaron, 115; *Kalut Da'at u-Tzvi'ut*, 80
Halpern, Israel, 50
*ha-Magid* (journal), 166, 182
*ha-Me'asef* (journal), 30, 77, 80, 84, 85, 112, 115
*ha-Me'orer* (journal), 188
*ha-Melitz* (journal), 174
*ha-Shiloah* (Journal), 182
*ha-Tzfirah* (journal), 85–86, 96, 116
Haramati, Shlomo, 149n45, 168n17, 175n68
Harmony, 117
Hartman, Geoffrey H., 102, 114n56
hasidic court, 1, 2, 14, 80n147, 104, 109–10, 123, 125, 127, 141, 145
"hasidic edah," 14, 109. *See also* "kibbutz"
"Hasidic ethnicity," 177
hasidic hagiography, 3, 103, 108–9, 118, 125, 127, 128, 130, 132, 157, 160, 184. *See also* praise of the Tzadik
"Hasidut ve-Hokhmah" (Issac Erter), 4, 7; allegory, 99, 101–2, 104, 105, 112–13, 116, 117, 118, 120, 127–32, 134, 138; attack on the hasidic body, 121, 124, 127, 142; autobiographical aspect, 5–6, 107, 120–21, 129–30, 133; exposition, 111, 128–29, 138; fundamental dichotomy, 4, 104, 112; its composition, 102, 133; satirical elements, 53, 88, 104, 120; state of emergency, 99–101, 110; sexuality, 99, 112–13, 119, 138, 140, 142; the dream, 99, 101, 113, 117–20, 128, 138, 142; the satirical watchman, 4–5, 54, 92, 113
Hebrew (language), 3, 4, 27, 73–74, 86, 89, 94, 115, 119, 154, 160–65, 167, 169; "Yiddishized Hebrew," 31, 160–63; secularization, 186; territorialization, 94, 162, 168–69, 190

Hebrew literature, 86, 100, 115, 139, 142, 160, 166, 168–71, 183; Galician, 57, 72, 85, 96, 119, 125, 137; modern, 7, 52, 61, 154, 169; national, 91, 95, 120n81, 149, 170, 176, 183; nonnational, 7
Hebrew national revival, 56
Hegel, Friedrich, 58, 95, 102
Hegemony: hegemonic language of the new Hebrew literature, 169; hegemonic gaze, 53, 56, 99
Hess, Moses, 63
Heterotopia, 18, 25
Hevrat Dorshei Leshon Ever, 115
Hippocrates: *Aphorisms*, 67n83
*Hištalšelut*, 20
Hobbes, Thomas, 56
Hobsbawm, Eric, 72, 82n157
*hokhmah* (wisdom), 105; sefirah of *Hokhmah*, 23. *See also binah*
holiness, 15–16, 45, 49–50, 59–60, 71, 83, 87, 175, 179, 181, 183–85; sparks of holiness, 50, 155, 162, 184, 186
Holocaust, 56n23
Holquist, Michael, 160n115
Holtzman, Avner, 166n2, 166n4, 167, 170, 180n113, 181n115, 188n167
holy text, 48, 181, 184–85
Homberg, Herz, 75, 80n147, 84, 125–26; *Bne-Zion*, 75n124; *Imrei Shefer*, 125
Homiletic literature, 23, 29, 146
Horodezky, Samuel A., 14n32, 39n154, 170n27, 177n88
Horowitz, Shai Y., 170
Hotam, Yotam, 70, 186
Hovevei Tzion, 58n27
Howe, Stephen, 143
Hundert, Gershon David, 68n89
Hurwitz, Haim (Haikl), 29–30, 33; *Tsofnas Paneyekh*, 29
Hurwitz, Hirsch Baer, 29–30
Hybrid, 72, 77–78, 83, 143, 154, 173–75, 183–85, 187

Idel, Moshe, 50
identity; universal; ethical, 100; individual, 15, 28; Jewish, 4, 5, 77–78, 83, 89, 92, 94, 105, 120, 122, 127, 139; Jewish collective, 15, 114, 162; national, 13, 69, 71–73, 83, 95, 97, 105, 127–28, 154, 171; particular, 12–13, 73, 72, 22n19; universal, 127, 133, 120n81

immigration; hasidic immigration, 137, 177; immigration ('aliyah) to the Land of Israel, 42, 138
imperialism; European imperialism, 32–33, 75–76, 120, 122, 128; Napoleonic imperialism, 10, 35–37, 61–62
*In Praise of the Ba'al Shem Tov* (Shivhei ha-Besht), 94, 166, 169, 179–82, 188–90; "Death of the Son," 182; "The Besht's Prayer Produces Rain," 2–3; the story about the son of Rabbi Adam, 179–82. *See also Sefer Hasidim* (Berdichevsky) ("Ner le-ma'or")
individual, individualism, 170; individual author, 149, 169–70, 176; individual citizenship, 113; individual identity, 15, 29; individual rights, 148
infinite, 158
ingathering of the exiles, 42
integration, 57, 76, 78, 90, 104, 125, 127, 134–36, 141, 144, 145, 158, 164
"inter-hasidic literature," 147
irony, 89–90, 95–96, 115n61, 131, 133
irrationalism, 31–32, 87, 119–22; irrational particularism, 4, 77, 90; irrational rationality, 35
Israel ben Eliezer Shem-Tov. *See* Ba'al Shem-Tov (Besht)
Israel Jaffe, 179
Israel of Zamość (Israel ben Moses ha-Levi); "Nezed ha-Dema," 107n31, 108
Istanbul, 8–12, 15, 17–19, 35, 38, 40, 44, 49; the Jewish community, 10
Italy, 10, 119
itineraria, 8. *See also* travel narratives

Jacob Joseph of Poland, 178, 184
Jaffa, 8, 19, 40
Jameson, Fredric, 92, 124n89
Jassy, 12
Jay, Martin, 53n7, 56n21, 92n215, 96n226, 99n7
Jeitteles, Judah ben-Jonah, 76; "Al ha-Medabrim Alay Lemor Sone Hu et Hevrat ha-Adam," 85; *Benei ha-Ne'urim*, 85; "El ha-Mevakrim Bein Tov le-Ra Ohavey ha-Emet ve-ha-Tushiyah," 85
Jerusalem, 20, 42, 45, 49, 189
Jesus, 45
Jewish ethical (musar) literature, 107, 117

## Index

Jewish people (the), Chosen people, 5, 14, 16, 31, 36, 41, 43, 44, 48, 50, 53, 69, 82, 87, 92, 99, 101, 105, 108, 119, 133, 154, 157
Jewish Question (the), 1, 77–78, 84, 104, 106, 110, 113–14, 122, 126, 134, 141
Jewish state, 56, 67, 101, 137, 168
Jews of Eastern Europe, 2, 36, 38, 39, 55, 61, 86–87, 147
Jews of Europe, 35, 78
Joseph II. *See* Edict of Toleration of Joseph II
Judaism, Jewish religion, 16, 26, 58, 63, 67, 68, 72, 74, 76, 78, 81–82, 84, 87, 89, 90, 95, 100, 106, 117, 119, 136–37, 147, 148n42, 153, 154, 171, 174

Kabbalah, 17, 22, 25, 30, 38, 50, 59, 62, 63, 93, 96, 119, 180, 181, 184–86; anthropocentric kabbalistic dualism, 157–58
Kafka, Franz, 49
Kagan, Ziporah, 169
*Kahal*, 80n147, 122, 145–46, 148
Kaidaner (Bachrach), Jacob, 7, 146–47, 149–50, 152–53, 155–60, 162, 164; *Matzref ha-Avodah* (also known as *Vikuha Rabah*), 146n28; *Sipurim nora'im: Sipurim shel Ish Habad*, 146–47, 149–50
Kalir, Meir, 97
Kamenets-Podolsk, 9, 16, 18, 34–35, 47, 48, 49, 50
Kant, Immanuel, 4, 56, 66n77, 115–16, 120–21, 124
Kaps, Klement, 63n62
"Karaism," 27
Kaspe, Sviatoslav, 144n6, 144n9
Katz, Jacob, 63n64, 68, 91n158, 151n61
*Kerem Hemed* (journal), 98, 129, 133
*kibbutz*, 14, 177. *See also* "hasidic edah"
Klausner, Joseph, 58n33, 60n43, 61n45, 61n46, 61n47, 66n77, 74n121, 76n134, 85n171, 90–91, 97n231, 120, 163, 168
Klier, John D., 145n18, 145n20
knowledge, 19, 29–30, 60, 62, 80, 82, 101, 105–6, 152–53, 160, 175; scientific, 30, 108n36; render knowledge, 105
Kobler, Franz, 35n144
Koniuszek, 52
Krochmal, Nachman, 58, 69, 86n180, 133–35, 137n122, 147; *Moreh nevuchei ha-zman* (Guide for the Perplexed of the Time), 167
Kurzbeck, 203

Lacan, Jacques, 89, 130
Lachover, Fischel, 116n65, 170n25, 185
Land of Israel; a territory outside the land of Israel, 94, 96–97, 177; and the Napoleonic imperialism, 10–11, 35–37, 42; and political messianism, 41–42, 178; as text, 44–50; Jewish autonomy, 80–81, 157; Rabbi Nahman of Bratslav's journey to the Land of Israel, 6, 8–51; hasidic journeys to the Land of Israel, 9, 41, 170; in the hassidic theology, 6, 9, 20, 36, 50; its sanctity, 45, 48–49, 50; sacred geography, 28, 50; settlement, 16, 33, 36, 37, 43, 44, 75, 96, 137, 144; the British Mandatory, 56n23
language of the hasidic story, 3, 31, 181
language of the hasidim, 168
language of the maskilim, 168
Latour, Bruno, 175
Lavater, Johann Kaspar, 141
Lederhendler, Eli, 145n11, 145n13, 145n15, 153n81
Lefin, Mendel, 26, 27, 61n45, 80n147, 84, 123; *'Oniyyah so'arah*, 27
Leopold II, 75
Lerman, Eliyahu; *Letters of Eliyahu*, 173
Lessing, Gotthold Ephraim; *Nathan the Wise*, 77, 100, 113
letter of binding (mikhtav qišur), 14
Letteris, Meïr Halevi (Max), 5, 61, 85–86, 87n186, 96, 98n1, 116, 133n113, 137n122, 139–40; "Be'ur Kitvei Kodesh," 85; "Yonah Homiyah," 86, 137n122
Levi Isaac of Berditchev, 133n112
Levinsohn, Isaac Baer, 147n35, 147–48, 153–54, 158; *Te'udah be-Yisra'el*, 55, 148n42
Levison, Mordechai Schnaber, 26
Liberman, Haim, 27n98
Liebes, Yehuda, 32
Lilenblum, Moshe Lieb, 170
liminality, 12, 18; liminal place, 44; of European Jews, 28, 90, 114
Limor, Ora, 8n3, 18n49, 20n57, 20n63, 28n106, 44n82, 45
Linnaeus, Carl, 27
literature for a Jewish state, 168
Litvak, Olga, 66n77, 109, 119
Lloyd, David, 124, 135n118
loan translations, 31, 163
Loewenthal, Naftali, 160n113, 152n120
London, 84

Löwisohn, Salomon, 95n223
Lubavitch (Lyubavichi), 146n28, 147
Lucian; "Alexander the False Prophet," 85–86, 116, 139–40, 142
Lukács, Georg, 70n100
Luria, Ilya, 13n22, 145n13, 148n40, 177n88
Luria, Issac, 184
Luz, Ehud, 172n40, 172n45, 174n54, 185
Luzzatto, Moses Hayim (Ramhal), 3, 120n81
Luzzatto, Samuel David, 87
Lvov/Lemberg, 7, 61m45, 65–66, 67, 69n90, 92, 125

Magic, 3, 61, 67, 87, 155–56, 159, 181; and prayer, 3; black and white, 159
magic tales, 152
"Maggid" of Mezhirech. *See* Dov Ber of Mezhirech
Mahler, Raphael, 61n45, 62n54, 63n61, 67n82, 69n91, 75n126, 75n128, 75n129, 80n147, 80n150, 81n153, 84n167, 86n178, 109n37, 146n23, 153n73
Maimon, Salomon, 147
Maimonides (Moses ben Maimon), 63n61, 109
major language, 165
major literature, 162, 168–69, 170, 185
Margolin, Ron, 25n85, 25n89, 26n97, 27n99, 45n189
Maria Theresa, 61n45
Mark, Zvi, 41, 42
Markovits, Andrei S., 61n45, 76n133, 78n141
Marx, Karl, 70, 89; "On the Jewish Question," 77
Marxism, 67, 71, 83, 89, 91
maskilic criticism, 98, 158, 159
Mazower, Mark; *The Balkans*, 72
Mediterranean, Middle East, 10–11, 37, 58n27
Medvedevka, 8, 34, 43
Medzhybizh, 9, 34, 166, 170
Meir, Jonatan, 3, 42, 61n50, 65n69, 64n74, 65n75, 71n102, 86n175, 139n130
Menahem Mendel of Vitebsk, 38
Mendel Lefin, Menachem, 26, 27, 84, 61n45, 80n147
Mendele Moykher-Sforim (Shalom Jacob Abramovitsh), 73, 164; "Be-Seter Ra'am," 73n114
Mendelssohn, Moses, 27, 58, 60, 63n61, 65, 67–68, 74, 75n124, 76–77, 79, 80n147, 81, 82n158, 84–85, 93, 94, 100, 109, 115, 116, 119–20, 122–23, 136, 138, 141; *Jerusalem (Yerushalayim: Ktavim ktanim be-'Inyanei Yahdut ve-Yehudim)*, 77, 80n147, 113; *Kohelet Musar*, 61, 115n61
Mendelssohn-Frankfurt, Moses; *Meṣi'at ha-'areṣ ha-ḥadašah*, 27, 29, 30–31, 33
Mendieta, Eduardo, 122n83, 123n88
meni'ot (spiritual obstacles), 43–44
Menkin, Rachel, 61n45, 65n69, 65n70, 65n75, 66n76, 66n78, 80n147, 81n154, 82n159, 84n168
messiah, messianism, 16–17, 36, 41–45, 50–51, 54, 66–67, 69–71, 81, 87, 94, 120, 137, 142, 153, 168n13, 178; false, 67, 94; national, 43, 44, 66, 71, 83, 176; neutralized, 41, 153, 177–78; political, 41, 54n15; "weak Messianic power," 67, 69
Michael, Reuven, 80n149
Middle East, 11; Jews, 58n27, 175n64
Mieses, Judah Leib, 61, 65, 85, 147; *Kin'at ha-Emet*, 61, 109, 159
minor language, 169
minor literature, 89, 92, 149, 162, 168–70, 190
miracles, 56n23, 99, 110–12, 130, 139, 156, 159, 176, 181
Miron, Dan, 53n5, 58n28, 58n30, 80n148, 150n53, 154n85, 164, 171, 172
Mirsky, Nili, 117n66
*mitnagdim*, 17, 63, 147, 160
modern state, 36, 37, 76, 77, 89, 109, 114, 123
modernity, modernization, 25, 28, 29, 49, 61, 74, 75, 84, 144, 163–64, 175; hybridization and purification, 175
Mondschein, Yehoshua, 146n28
*Moniteur* (journal), 35
Moses, 24, 100, 109, 180, 191
Mosse, George L., 54n10
Mount Carmel, 40
"Moznei Mishkal" (Erter); attack on Orenstein, 7, 65–66, 66–67, 69, 74, 88, 92, 94; between satire and allegory, 79, 87–92; lampoon, 54, 66, 73n114, 92; the dream, 59–60, 62, 63, 66, 67, 71, 74, 79, 87–88, 91, 92; the material object of the book, 7, 61–62, 64–65, 66–71, 82–83, 87–88, 90, 92–94, 97; the satirical watchman, 54, 56, 60, 92; the weakness of the satire, 89
Mufti, Amir, 67n83, 77, 82n158, 84, 90n202, 114
"my ḥavurah," 14

mystic, mysticism, 14, 24, 26, 41, 61, 137, 151, 160, 174, 177, 180–81, 182, 184, 185, 189

"Nahal ha-Besor" (River of Good Tidings), 115, 123

Nahman of Bratslav; and Frankists, 16; and the European colonial project, 32–33; approach to the diaspora, 16; approach to the Haskalah, 32–33; hassidic and maskilic sea narrative in Nahman's journey to the Land of Israel, 25–26; Hassidic politics, 37, 38; *Ḥayyei Moharan*, 9, 44; his expression of opposition, 25, 33, 35, 37; *Liqquṭei Moharan*, 22–23, 46; *Megillat setarim* (Scroll of Secrets), 41, 42, 45, 51; Nahman's journey as a national and nonnational narrative, 24, 42–43, 44, 50; Nahman's journey to Land of Israel as a textual journey, 44–50; political messianism and the Land of Israel, 41–42, 44; repulsion and attraction for the Land of Israel, 15–16; sea obstacle in Nahman's journey, 19–22, 24–29, 31–32 *Sefer ha-Middot*, 21, 29; *Siḥot Ha-Ran* (Magid śiḥot), 9; *Sippurei ma'asiyot*, 9, 20; *Śivḥei ha-Ran*, 8, 9, 48;"supernal wisdom" (*ḥokhmah 'ila'ah*), 17; the imperial context of Nahman's journey, 10, 32–33, 35; "The King and the Emperor," 24, 25–26; "The King's Son and the Servant's Son Who Were Switched," 36; the story of his journey to the Land of Israel, 8–20, 25–29, 34–35, 47

Nahman of Horodenka, 17

Napoleon, 10–11, 12, 31n119, 35–37, 42, 61–62, 67, 76, 82n158, 127

narrative chain, 149

national narrative, 13, 24, 43, 69, 92, 94; pedagogy and performativity, 183

national will, 187

nationalism; auto-emancipatory, 37; European, 54, 55, 58, 93, 144n9, 183, 82n158; its theological tradition, 186; Jewish, 49, 57, 58n27, 63, 66, 67–69, 72–73, 77, 78, 82n158, 83–84, 91, 94–96, 121, 137, 148, 153, 154, 165, 167–68; modern, 49, 82; "pure," 175; territorial, 188; sovereign, 95, 186, 187

nation-state, 57–58, 78–79, 89, 95, 144n6

Natkes, Binyamin Zvi, 65

nature, 28–29, 31; force of nature, 20, 24–26

negation of the diaspora, 86, 172
neo-Hasidut, 170, 178
new Jew, 175, 189. *See also* negation of the diaspora
New York, 76
Nicholas I ("Iron Tsar"), 143, 145–46
Nietzsche, Friedrich, 167, 179, 188
Nigal, Gedalyah, 170n28, 171n30, 173n50, 174n54, 179n102, 179n105, 179n107
Niger, Shmuel, 160
Nikolayev, 8, 32, 48
Noah, Mordecai Manuel, 76
Novel, 14, 150, 151, 176

Odesa, 8, 32, 48
omniscient narrator, 4, 54, 152, 153
Onkelos, 23
Opalski, Magdalena, 156n89
opponents, 72, 89, 140, 147
oral culture, 13–14, 149, 175
Orenstein, Jacob Meshullam, 65–66; *Yeshu'ot Ya'akov*, 65–66, 94; Erter's satire against him, 7, 65–67, 69, 71, 74, 83, 84, 88, 92, 94. *See also Moznei Mishkal*
Oron, Michal, 149n46, 175n67
"other" and otherness, 83, 114, 160–61; the colonial "other," 33; the native "other," 33; the "other within," 7
Ottoman Empire, 10, 72

Padaya, Haviva, 177n85
pain of Jewish historicism, 171
Palestinians, 56n23
Pastor, Judah Leib, 65
plagiarism, 59, 62, 64, 66, 69, 70, 71
Plato, 79
Panopticon, 53, 95, 99
Pantheism, 172, 174, 184
parody, 3, 6, 62, 67n83, 111, 118, 161
particularism, 83, 124; historical, 4, 55; irrational, 4, 77, 90; particular identities, 12–13; particular Jewish identity, 73, 89, 137n122, 144n9; particular national identity of the concrete universal, 172
Passover, 24
Peled, Yoad, 76, 95n222
Pelli, Moshe, 58n32, 61n45, 76n132, 81n156, 84n169, 85n170, 86n183, 87n185, 90, 90n203, 92n214, 94n218, 100n12, 164n131, 164n132
Penance, 21
Peretz, Y. L., 166

Perl, Joseph, 6, 25, 53, 61, 62, 66n77, 70–71, 80n147, 87, 95, 133, 137, 147, 161, 181–82; *Boḥen Tzadik*, 6, 65n69, 96, 137; *Megaleh Temirin*, 6, 62, 85n171, 89, 102, 107n31, 164; *Revelation of the Hidden*, 181–82
personality crisis (narrative), 28
Piekarz, Mendel, 17n45, 17n46, 17n47, 17n48, 30n109, 30n111, 41, 47n196
pilgrimage, 12, 13, 15, 18, 20–21, 28, 37, 41, 42, 44–45, 49–50, 155n88. *See also* 'Aliyah la-Regel
Pinsker, Leo, 57. *See also* auto-emancipation
pneumatic leadership, 14, 177
poem, 57, 77n136, 85, 86, 112, 115, 122, 137n122, 150
poetic mechanism, 103
pogroms, 57
Poland, 37, 61n45, 68, 98, 99, 125, 129, 146, 178, 184; partition of Poland, 37, 61n45, 98, 143–44; Polish literature, 156
political theology, 56n23, 123; as foundation to Jewish polity, 36, 190; hasidic-kabbalistic, 25; Jewish, 189; of the Hasidism, 104, 110, 141; of the Haskalah, 104; of the Jewish sovereign, 104, 187–88; of Moses Mendelssohn, 94, 109; of the Watchman, 101, 110
politics of survival, 2, 125, 157
Portugal, 33
postcolonialism, 77, 83, 91, 114, 124, 126, 128, 187
praise of the tzadik, 125. *See also* hasidic hagiography
pray, 18, 21, 23, 26, 29, 36, 99, 155, 158; magical, 2–3
precepts (*miẓwot*), 17, j76, 87, 100, 119; associated with the Land of Israel, 46–47, 94; fulfill the precepts, 16, 46–47
Prophecy, 52, 54n15, 58, 131, 192
Protestants, 61n45, 68, 76, 122, 139, 141
proto-nationalism, 12, 13, 16, 24, 28, 36, 44, 57–58, 63, 66–69, 72–73, 82n158, 84–86, 88, 90–92, 148–49, 153, 154, 162, 164
proto-Zionism, 42, 137
Prussia, 61n45, 75, 116, 144
public sphere, public space, 2, 37, 65 72, 74–83, 86–87, 91, 94, 97, 99, 107, 113, 120, 122–25, 129, 134, 136–37, 139, 141–42

qaṭnut (smallness), 12–13, 17, 46–47, 49; *See also* gadlut
Qedošim, 15–16

rabbi, rabbinate, 12–14, 16, 40, 53, 58, 62, 65, 67n83, 82, 85, 86n180, 88, 89, 92, 94, 97, 115, 121, 135, 137–38, 145n17, 148n39, 177–78
rabbinic leadership, 14, 177
race, 13, 57, 144
Ramhal. *See* Luzzatto, Moses Hayim
Rancière, Jacques, 45, 47n192, 106, 117, 131
Rapoport, Solomon Judah Leib, 53, 61, 65, 68
Rapoport, Nahman-Nathan, 30
Rapoport-Albert, Ada, 9n4, 12n17, 13n20, 14, 21n62, 46–47, 49n205, 177
rationalistic denial, 33
rationality, rationalism, 3, 4–6, 25, 29, 30, 31–33, 47n196, 53, 56, 58, 60, 61, 62, 64, 67–68, 70–71, 77, 79, 87, 92, 100, 106–7, 108n36, 113, 118–22, 126, 133, 137n122, 138, 139, 142; critical rationalism, 4, 74, 107, 138; imagined, 2; irrational rationality, 32, 33, 35, 40
Ratzabi, Shalom, 186n160
Rav Safra, 22
Raz-Krakotzkin, Amnon, 56n23, 57n25
reason, 58, 60, 80, 112, 113, 115n61, 117, 126, 127, 138; ahistorical, 4, 55; natural, 26; universal, 56, 124, 138
Red Sea, 24
redemption, 36, 41, 43, 65, 66–67, 153, 157, 172; national, 41, 50, 153, 171, 178; personal, 171
reification, 70
Reiner, Elchanan, 45n188
religion; and secularism, 173, 175, 183, 185; natural, 58, 80n147, 87, 100; romantic, 109
Remov, Anatolyi, 143n2, 144n5
revival literature, 142
rhetoric of truth, 3
Ribal. *See* Levinsohn, Isaac Baer
rite of passage, 99
Robinson, William; *The History of America*, 27
Rodkinson (Frumkin), Michael Levi; *Kehal Hasidim* (Hasidic Congregation), 146, 148n39, 159n101
Romanelli, Samuel Aaron, 61n45; *Masaʿ ba-ʿArav*, 27
romanticism, 66n77, 82n158, 119, 120–21, 127n95, 137n122, 142, 150, 172
Rosenzweig, Franz, 186
Rosh Hashanah, 8, 14, 18, 40

## Index

Rosman, Moshe, 13n23, 148–49, 168n13, 169n22, 169, 175
Ross, Nicham, 166n3, 168n18, 170, 171n32, 171n37, 177n80, 179n103, 179n105, 179n107, 182n123, 182n125, 185n147, 187n161
Rubinstein, Avraham, 41n169, 43n177, 47n199, 153n77, 176n73, 178n97, 179n102, 180n109, 181n114, 181n121, 188n168, 189n173
Ruderman, David B., 26n94
Russian (language), 144–45, 162, 165
Russian Empire, 143–44; and the Jews, 143–46, 148, 153–54, 156–57, 178–79, 145n17; equal rights for the Jews, 35; ethnic diversity, 143n6; Pale of settlement, 37, 144; Russification, 144–46, 148, 154, 156, 160; "Statute Concerning the Organization of the Jews," 145n17; the hasidic politics of survival, 1–2, 7, 37, 146, 157, 159; the Polish uprising (1863), 144; the reforms of 1860s, 144; the Society for Promoting Enlightenment among Jews, 153

Sabbateanism, Sabbatai Zevi, 81, 171
Sachs, Shneur, 61
Sadan, Dov, 14n26, 73n114, 177n83, 183
sages of the Talmud and the Midrash, 29
Said, Edward, 144
Sallnow, Michael, 41n165, 45n188
Satan, 34, 173, 182
satire, 2, 3, 61, 95–96, 102–3, 108, 114–16, 121–24, 127, 131–32, 134–37, 140, 141, 150, 157. *See also* "Hasidut ve-Hokhmah" (Erter); "Moznei Mishkal" (Erter)
Schatz Uffenheimer, Rivka, 22n69, 22n70
Schiller, Friedrich, 30, 62, 66n77, 102–3, 116–17
Schmid, Anton, 85, 93n218, 95n223, 134n113
Schmitt, Carl, 54–56, 58, 99–100, 106n27, 110n41, 123, 136, 183, 186
Schneersohn, Menahem Mendel (*Tzemah Tzedek*), 146n28, 147
Scholem, Gershom, 14n25, 14n27, 41, 153, 171n37, 177n82, 177n83, 177, 178, 183–85, 186
Schwärmerei, 81
Schwarzfuchs, Simon, 36n145
Schweid, Eliezer, 42n171
science, 26, 29, 30
"script follows religion," 72–73
Scripture, 20, 32, 40, 85, 86, 109, 119, 138, 154, 158

Scroll of Esther, 58n27
sea, 10, 19–22, 24–32, 37, 40, 42, 43; sea travel narratives, 6, 22, 25, 27
secularism, 59, 184; and religion, 167, 173–75, 183, 185; Enlightenment secularism, 77; nationalist, 167
secularization, 154, 167
*Sefer Hasidim* (Micha Yosef Berdichevsky), 166–90; "A Candle of Light" (Ner lema'or), 179, 182; autobiographical author, 170; autonomous heteronomic structure of the subject, 175; "descent of tzadik," 30; establishment of an autonomous moral and individual subject, 172, 174; hybridity of religious motivation, 187; "I am Prayer," 185; its minor language, 162, 168–70; "Legends," 188; national teleology element, 178; nationalized the hasidic text, 166, 168, 174, 179, 183; "The Death of a Tzadik," 173; "The Soul of the Hasidim," 170, 185; theurgy, 182; "Two Worlds," 188; universalism, 172, 177
Sefirot, 23; *Hokhmah* ("wisdom"), 23; *Keter* ("crown"), 51; *Malkhut* ("kingdom"), 22, 50–51
Segalovich, Dov Ber, 144n28
Seidman, Naomi, 183n134
self, 17, 18, 44, 130–31; "self" and "other," 83, 161; self-constitution, 90, 99, 101, 106; self-determination, 57, 78–79
self-sacrifice (mesirut nefeš), 43, 152, 163
sensuality, 5, 71, 164
Sephardic Jews, 40
Shanes, Joshua, 63n64, 75n125, 80n147
Shavit, Zohar, 27n100
Shavuot, 155, 163
Shells, 184
Shenhav, Yehuda, 57n24, 78n143, 175
*Shibutz* ("inlay" or "mosaic"), 164
Shmeruk, Chone, 30n113, 160n111, 161, 162, 179n103
Shneur Zalman of Liadi, 36, 38–39, 146, 150–52, 155, 156, 158–60, 162; *Sefer ha-tanya'*, 38
Shochat, Azriel, 154n83, 164n133
Shoham, Uri, 54n12, 59n37, 62n57, 87n188, 101n15, 120, 129
Shteynberg, Yehuda, 166
*Shulhan Aruch*, 65, 67n83
*Sifrei sha'ashu'im*, 167

signifier and signified, 102, 181
Simeon (rabbi), 8, 10–11, 32
sin, sinners, 16, 19–22, 26, 33, 44, 48, 52, 56, 70, 121, 133, 192
Sinkoff, Nancy, 22n69, 25, 65n72, 69n91, 80n147
*Sipurei Kedoshim* (Tales of the Saints), 148n39
Slemon, Stephen, 128n97
Slutsky, Yehuda, 145n10
Smolenskin, Peretz, 58n27, 91
"Song of the Sea," 27
Sorkin, David, 63n61, 65n73, 74n122, 80m147, 119–120, 126
sovereign, sovereignty, 4, 12, 51, 78, 83, 99n7, 185–86; and a state of emergency, 54, 186; and the theological tradition of the nationality, 186; civil sovereignty, 89; European state sovereignty, 55, 119, 143; false sovereign, 111; God in a theocratic regime, 14; its source of authority, 109, 186; Jewish sovereignty, 54–58, 96, 104, 105, 119, 132, 140, 142, 146, 188, 210n147; nation-state sovereignty, 57, 58, 89, 132; national sovereignty, 53–54, 73, 80n15, 101, 109, 187, 189; of the European-Christian state, 92, 134, 140; of the empire, 2, 125, 146; of the enlightenment, 126; of the Hasidut, 109–110, 119, 123, 125; of the Haskalah, 56, 63, 104, 106, 109–11; of the tzadik, 3, 104, 106, 109–10, 133, 140; of the Watchman for the House of Israel, 7, 53–54, 58, 79, 92, 95, 99–101, 104, 108–10, 121, 130, 133, 138, 140; Westphalian sovereignty, 56, 95; Zionism, 56n23, 70
space; physical, 45; concrete of the Land of Israel, 45; "in between," 183; Jewish, 4, 86, 125, 141–42; linguistic, 6, 97; of the hasidic court, 2, 125; of political act, 178; Russian, 156; uninhabited, 34; the clash with time, 70; Zionist theology of space, 104n23
Spain, 33
Spivak, Gayatri Chakravorty, 77n137, 78
"Spring of Nations," 67
Stanislawski, Michael, 146n19, 146n21, 147n35
state of emergency, 54–55, 56, 99–101, 110, 186
Stern, Eliyahu, 614n51
Sternhartz, Nathan (R. Nathan of Nemirov), 6, 8, 9, 17, 18, 25, 26, 40, 41; *Ḥayyei Moharan*, 9, 44; *Liqquṭei Halakhot*, 25, 45, 48; *Magid śiḥot*, 9; "Nesi'ato le-'Ereṣ Yiśra'el," 9; "Seder ha-Nesi'ah šelo le-'Ereṣ Yiśra'el," 9, 19, 27, 33; *Šhvḥei ha-Ran*, 8, 9, 48; *Sippurei ma'asiyot*, 9, 20
Stoler, Ann Laura, 145n16, 146n22
structuralism, 161
subject; autonomous, 57, 106, 115n61, 124, 172–745; constitution, 29, 70, 115n61; historical, 71; hybrid, 83; national, 78, 83, 86, 90, 169, 171–72, 190; political, 125; proto-national, 12, 28, 90; rational, 4; universal, 124, 177
superstition, 17, 26, 87, 90
Surman, Jan, 63n62
Sussman, Henry, 67
Swift, Jonathan; *Gulliver's Travels*, 128
symptomatic reading, 103
synthetic language, 164, 169, 189
Syria, 11

Tarler, Joseph, 76, 129
Tarnopol, 61n45, 84, 125
Taub, Moshe, 162n124, 235
Taylor, Charls, 123
Teitelbaum, Mordechai, 147n33
Tel Aviv, 52
teleology, 3, 28, 41, 49, 50, 57, 63, 94, 153, 178, 189
Temple, 42, 58, 105, 106
territorialization of the language, 94, 97, 168–69, 190
"The Four Fathers of Damage," 65
"The Watchman for the House of Israel," 52
Theocentrism, 149
theology, 4, 57, 70, 79, 94, 101, 104, 109–10, 123, 141, 185–86, 190; hasidic, 6, 9, 25, 36, 67n83, 104, 110, 146, 149, 186; Jewish, 68, 117, 187–89; national, 173, 185; natural, 26, 29, 31; physico-theology, 26; Zionist theology, 56n23
theophany, 20
theosophy, 157
Tiberias, 18, 38, 43, 45
*tikun* (restoration), 16, 17, 30, 50, 155, 156, 157
time; imagined national, 14, 43, 150–51, 153, 176, 178; liturgical, 45; religious, 151
Tishbi, Isaiah, 178
tolerance, 58, 66, 77, 80, 100, 113–14, 158. *See also* Edict of Toleration of Joseph II

Torah, 15, 17, 23–25, 39, 46–48, 58, 65, 119, 123, 148n42, 151, 152, 155–56, 158, 179, 182, 184, 185
transcendence, 17, 55n19, 70, 73, 124, 127, 141, 186–87
translation, translating, 27, 29–31, 33, 84, 85, 116, 138, 139, 161, 162–63, 168, 169–170, 171, 174, 177, 179, 180, 182, 183–88
travel narratives, 8, 26, 30, 45
Trivedi, Harish, 187n163
Trumpener, Katie, 84n165
Turks, 10–11, 36, 37
Turner, Victor, 12, 18n49, 43
tzadik, 1–3, 12–14, 17, 18, 21–24, 28–30, 39, 44, 46, 49–51, 53, 86, 104, 106, 109–11, 117, 121, 123, 125, 131, 133, 140, 141, 145, 148–53, 156–57, 159, 163, 170, 175–77
tzadik of Komarno, 39
*tzimtzum*, 157n94. *See also ayin, yesh*

Uman, 27, 29–30, 47n196
universalism, universal, universality, 3, 4, 27, 31, 36, 55–56, 61, 62, 71, 77, 83, 86–89, 91–92, 96, 99, 100, 107–9, 112, 114, 116, 121, 123, 126, 138–40; concrete universal, 90, 171–72; in Berdichevsky, 168, 170–74, 177; the universality of aesthetic judgment, 124; the universality of the Panopticon, 99; universal citizenship, 73, 91, 105, 113, 120; universal identity, 127, 133; universal subject, 124, 172, 177
Urban, Martina, 166n1, 166n3, 167n7
Utopia, 18, 24, 78, 92, 96, 100, 102, 141; Jewish collective, 68; of the satire, 62, 63, 89; utopian-apocalyptic, 42

Vanantwerpen, Jonathan, 122n83, 123n88
Verman, Mark, 49n206
Vienna, 61, 75, 79, 84, 93, 95, 159
violations of the law, 81
violence, 4, 10, 26, 34, 37, 56, 70, 110, 113, 114, 124, 131, 132, 67n83, 120n81; and the national theology of Berdichevsky, 187–89; messianic, 45; of enlightenment and progress, 126; of a state of emergency, 55; of the sovereign, 7, 53, 55
Voltaire, 61n45
von Dohm, Wilhelm; *On the Civic Improvement of the Jews*, 77
von Hagen, Mark, 143n2, 144n5

wandering Jew, 114
war of Gog and Magog, 36, 42, 54n15
Weimar Republic, 99n7
Weiss, Haim, 59n38, 79n144
Weiss, Joseph, 30n110, 32n125, 33, 44n184, 44n186
Weisser, Meir Leib (Malbim), 104–5
Werses, Shmuel, 6, 61n151, 86n182, 90, 103, 107, 113n53, 118n74, 134, 137n122, 139n132, 157n34, 159n106, 160, 161, 162, 166n3, 167n5, 168n18, 173n47, 177n80, 177n81, 181, 185n150, 188n167
Werth, Paul, 144n4
Wertheim, Aharon, 184n138
Wessely, Naphtali Herz, 112, 115–18, 121, 123, 136; *Divrei Shalom ve-Emet*, 63n61, 74, 81, 115; *Shirei Tiferet*, 115, 117
Wieland, Christoph Martin, 116
wisdom literature, 105, 106, 169
wisdom novellas, 152
witness-narrator, 149, 152–53, 175
Wolff, Gershon, 61n147
Wolff, Larry, 80
Wolpe, Rebbeca, 25n86, 26n92, 27n102, 28n103, 28n104, 28n105, 30n114, 33n126, 33n131, 33n133, 50n208
World Zionist Organization, 58n27

Yassif, Eli, 146n25, 148n39, 152n65, 156n91, 159n101, 176n77
Yehoshua A. B.: "Facing the Forests," 142
*Yesh*, 157n94, 158. *See also ayin, tzimtzum*
Yiddish, 13, 27, 29, 31, 45, 62, 72, 159–65, 168–70, 189
Young, Robert, 83n162

Zamość, 108
Zeev, Mordecai, 65
*Zekhor berit*, 40
Zelkin, Mordechai, 144n4, 148n41, 148n42, 153n80, 158n100
Zhovkva (Zolkva), 9, 85, 109
Zitron, Shmuel Leib, 167
Žižek, Slavoj, 71, 88, 89
Zweifel, Eliezer, 91, 147n35, 147n38; *Hasidic Ethical Wills*, 166; *Shalom 'al Israel*, 166, 147n35

# Acknowledgments

I am grateful to Moshe Taube for his help in finding the Yiddish foundations of the Hebrew texts of the hasidic tale and to Kali Handelman for her meticulous editing of this book. Special thanks to Roni Masel and Guy Erlich for their efficient and intelligent help in completing this volume and to Vered Shimshi for her invaluable assistance in preparing the final version of the text, and for a meticulous and excellent index for the book. I would also like to thank Amir Benbaji for his insightful comments and Susannah Heschel and Shaul Magid for their encouragement and important contribution in clarifying a number of issues discussed in the book. I would like to give a special thank-you to Shmuel Seremoneta-Gertel and Eric Zakim for their work translating earlier versions of chapters of the book. My heartfelt thanks to the editors at the University of Pennsylvania Press, Jerome Singerman and Elisabeth Maselli, Noreen O'Connor-Abel, and Otto Bohlmann, who spared no effort in bringing the English-language edition to publication.

An abridged version of Chapter 4 was published in *Languages of Modern Jewish Cultures, Comparative Perspectives*, edited by Joshua L. Miller and Anita Norich (Ann Arbor: University of Michigan Press, 2016).

CPSIA information can be obtained
at www.ICGtesting.com
Printed in the USA
JSHW080327200723
44547JS00001B/1

9 781512 825077